Copyright © 2024

All rights reserved. No part of this publication may be reproduced, distributed, or transmitted in any form or by any means, including photocopying, recording, or other electronic or mechanical methods, without the prior written permission of the publisher, except in the case of brief quotations embodied in critical reviews and certain other noncommercial uses permitted by copyright law.

Disclosure: The information contained in this study guide is for general informational purposes only. The content is provided "as is" without any warranties, representations, or guarantees of any kind, whether express or implied, including but not limited to the implied warranties of merchantability, fitness for a particular purpose, and non-infringement.

The authors and publishers of this study guide have made every effort to ensure that the information presented is accurate, complete, and up-to-date. However, due to the constantly evolving nature of the project management field and the potential for human error, we cannot guarantee the absolute accuracy, reliability, or completeness of the content. The authors and publishers shall not be held liable for any errors, omissions, or inaccuracies in the information provided, or for any actions taken or not taken based on the content of this study guide.

The CAPM (Certified Associate in Project Management) is a registered trademark of the Project Management Institute (PMI). This study guide is an independent publication and is not affiliated with, endorsed, sponsored, or approved by PMI. PMI does not approve, endorse, or warrant the accuracy or quality of the content in this study guide.

The practice questions and mock exams provided in this study guide are for educational purposes only and may not reflect the actual content or format of the official CAPM exam. Success in these practice materials does not guarantee a passing score on the actual exam. It is the reader's responsibility to review the most current information directly from PMI regarding the CAPM exam requirements, format, and content.

The case studies, examples, and anecdotes presented in this study guide are fictional and are intended for illustrative purposes only. Any resemblance to actual persons, organizations, or events is purely coincidental.

The authors and publishers of this study guide are not engaged in rendering legal, accounting, or other professional services. If expert assistance is required, the services of a competent professional should be sought.

By using this study guide, you agree to release the authors and publishers from any liability arising from your use or reliance on the information provided. It is your responsibility to independently verify the accuracy and applicability of the content in relation to your specific circumstances and the current requirements of the CAPM exam.

All rights reserved. No part of this study guide may be reproduced, distributed, or transmitted in any form or by any means, including photocopying, recording, or other electronic or mechanical methods, without the prior written permission of the authors and publishers, except in the case of brief quotations embodied in critical reviews and certain other noncommercial uses permitted by copyright law.

By proceeding to use this study guide, you acknowledge that you have read, understood, and agreed to the terms and conditions outlined in this legal disclosure.

Table of Contents

INTRO..4

Project Management Fundamentals and Core Concepts................7

Predictive, Plan-Based Methodologies...30

Agile Frameworks/Methodologies..60

Business Analysis Frameworks..85

Practice Questions..113

INTRO:

Imagine stepping into the bustling world of project management, where every day presents new challenges and opportunities. Picture yourself at the helm of a complex project, tasked with turning a visionary idea into reality. The stakes are high, the timeline is tight, and resources are limited. Yet, you thrive in this fast-paced environment, expertly navigating obstacles and leading your team to success.

Take, for instance, the story of Maria, a budding project manager at a tech startup. Maria was handed a pivotal project: launching a new software product that promised to revolutionize the industry. With a clear vision and a dedicated team, Maria embarked on this journey, juggling client demands, tight deadlines, and unforeseen technical glitches. Despite these challenges, her meticulous planning and unyielding determination paid off. The product launch was a resounding success, catapulting the company to new heights and solidifying Maria's reputation as a stellar project manager.

This is the exhilarating world of project management, where the ability to lead projects from inception to completion can make a profound difference. As a project manager, you are the driving force behind organizational success, ensuring that goals are met, and objectives are achieved efficiently and effectively.

Now, imagine yourself in Maria's shoes, equipped with the skills and confidence to tackle any project head-on. This vision is within reach, and the CAPM certification is your gateway to making it a reality. The CAPM credential is not just a certification; it's a powerful tool that opens doors to new opportunities, higher salaries, and the chance to make a significant impact in your field.

Consider the transformative power of the CAPM certification. It's recognized globally, signaling to employers that you possess a solid foundation in project management. With this credential, you'll stand out in a competitive job market, poised for roles that demand exceptional project management skills. Companies across industries, from technology to healthcare to finance, seek professionals who can lead projects to success, and the CAPM certification positions you as a prime candidate for these opportunities.

Embark on this learning journey with determination and enthusiasm. The road to CAPM certification is rigorous, but with the right mindset, strategies, and support, you can conquer the exam and unlock a world of possibilities. Picture yourself as a confident, capable project manager, navigating complex projects with ease and delivering exceptional results.

Remember, every great achievement starts with a single step. By committing to this path, you're investing in your future and taking a significant step towards becoming a sought-after project management professional. Embrace the challenges, celebrate the victories, and know that you have the potential to make a tangible difference in your organization and career.

So, let's begin this journey together. With the knowledge and tools provided in this study guide, you'll be well-prepared to face the CAPM exam and excel in the dynamic world of project management. Your success story starts now.

Overview of the CAPM Exam
Purpose and Importance
The Certified Associate in Project Management (CAPM) is a globally recognized certification offered by the Project Management Institute (PMI). This certification is designed for individuals starting their careers in project management, as well as those who seek to formalize their knowledge and skills in this domain. The CAPM certification serves multiple critical purposes:

1. **Foundation of Knowledge**: It establishes a strong foundation in project management principles, practices, and methodologies. This foundation is rooted in the PMI's "A Guide to the Project Management Body of Knowledge" (PMBOK Guide), which is the cornerstone of the CAPM exam.

2. **Career Advancement**: The CAPM certification can significantly enhance your career prospects. It signals to employers that you possess a rigorous understanding of project management concepts, making you a valuable asset to any team or organization.
3. **Professional Credibility**: Earning the CAPM certification demonstrates your commitment to the project management profession and your dedication to continuous learning and professional development.
4. **Skill Enhancement**: It equips you with the skills necessary to effectively contribute to projects and manage them efficiently, even if you do not yet have extensive project management experience.
5. **Global Recognition**: PMI is a globally recognized institution, and the CAPM certification is respected worldwide. This global recognition can open doors to opportunities in various industries and geographical locations.

Exam Format and Structure

The CAPM exam is designed to assess your understanding of project management fundamentals and your ability to apply this knowledge in real-world scenarios. The exam format and structure are as follows:

1. **Number of Questions**: The exam consists of 150 multiple-choice questions. Of these, 15 are pretest questions that do not affect your score. These pretest questions are used by PMI to gather statistical information for future exams.
2. **Time Allotted**: You have three hours to complete the exam. It is essential to manage your time effectively to ensure you can answer all questions within the allotted time.
3. **Question Distribution**: The questions are distributed across various domains, reflecting the PMI's emphasis on different aspects of project management:
   - Project Management Fundamentals and Core Concepts: 36%
   - Predictive, Plan-Based Methodologies: 17%
   - Agile Frameworks/Methodologies: 20%
   - Business Analysis Frameworks: 27%
4. **Types of Questions**: The exam features various types of questions, including:
   - Scenario-based questions that test your ability to apply project management concepts to real-world situations.
   - Knowledge-based questions that assess your understanding of specific terms and concepts from the PMBOK Guide.
   - Analytical questions that require you to interpret data and make decisions based on project management principles.
5. **Exam Delivery**: The CAPM exam can be taken either online or at a PMI-authorized test center. The online proctored exam allows you to take the test from the comfort of your home or office, provided you meet the technical and environmental requirements set by PMI.

Qualification Requirements

To be eligible for the CAPM exam, you must meet certain educational and experiential prerequisites. PMI offers two pathways to eligibility:

1. **Educational Pathway**:
   - **Secondary Degree**: You must have a secondary degree (high school diploma, associate's degree, or the global equivalent).
   - **Project Management Education**: You need to have completed at least 23 contact hours of formal project management education. This education can be obtained through PMI's online courses, university programs, or training from PMI Registered Education Providers (R.E.P.s).
2. **Experience Pathway**:
   - **Project Experience**: If you do not have the required project management education, you can qualify by having at least 1,500 hours of project experience. This pathway is suitable for those who have gained practical experience in managing projects but may not have formal education in project management.

Application Process

1. **Application Submission**: The first step is to submit your application to PMI through their website. You will need to provide details about your educational background and, if applicable, your project management experience.

2. **Application Review**: PMI reviews your application to ensure you meet the eligibility criteria. This process typically takes a few days to a week.
3. **Payment**: Once your application is approved, you will need to pay the exam fee. PMI members receive a discount on the exam fee, so it may be beneficial to become a PMI member before applying.
4. **Scheduling the Exam**: After payment, you can schedule your exam. You have the option to choose between an online proctored exam or an exam at a PMI-authorized test center.
5. **Exam Preparation**: It is crucial to prepare thoroughly for the exam. Utilizing PMI's study materials, practice exams, and other resources will help you build the knowledge and confidence needed to pass the exam.

Exam Day Tips
1. **Familiarize Yourself with the Format**: Before the exam, make sure you are familiar with the format and the types of questions you will encounter.
2. **Time Management**: Allocate your time wisely during the exam. Aim to complete each question within a set time limit to ensure you have enough time to review your answers.
3. **Read Questions Carefully**: Pay close attention to the wording of each question. Look for keywords and eliminate obviously incorrect answers to improve your chances of selecting the correct one.
4. **Stay Calm and Focused**: It's natural to feel nervous on exam day, but staying calm and focused will help you perform your best. Take deep breaths and remind yourself that you are well-prepared.

By understanding the purpose and importance of the CAPM certification, the exam format and structure, and the qualification requirements, you are well on your way to becoming a certified project management professional. This certification not only enhances your knowledge and skills but also opens doors to new career opportunities and professional growth. Embrace the journey with determination and enthusiasm, knowing that you have the potential to make a significant impact in the field of project management.

Project Management Fundamentals and Core Concepts

Key Characteristics of a Project

Projects are unique endeavors with specific characteristics that set them apart from ongoing operations. Understanding these characteristics is crucial for effective project management. Let's explore the three key characteristics of a project: uniqueness, temporary nature, and progressive elaboration, and illustrate each with real-world examples.

1. Uniqueness

Definition: Every project is unique, meaning it creates a product, service, or result that is different from other products, services, or results. The uniqueness of a project stems from its specific goals, requirements, constraints, and deliverables.

Example: Building a Custom Home Imagine a construction company tasked with building a custom home for a client. Each home they build is unique because it is designed according to the client's specific preferences, such as layout, materials, and interior design. Unlike mass-produced homes, a custom home project requires tailored plans and specifications, making it a unique endeavor.

Differentiation from Ongoing Operations: Ongoing operations, such as manufacturing standard furniture, involve repetitive tasks that produce the same product repeatedly. In contrast, a project like building a custom home involves non-repetitive, unique tasks aimed at delivering a one-of-a-kind result.

2. Temporary Nature

Definition: A project is temporary, meaning it has a defined beginning and end. Projects are initiated to achieve specific objectives and are concluded when these objectives are met or when the project is terminated for other reasons.

Example: Organizing a Corporate Event Consider a company planning an annual corporate event. The project starts with the initiation phase, where goals are defined and a project plan is created. The event is executed on a specific date, and the project concludes once the event is successfully held and all post-event activities, such as feedback collection and vendor payments, are completed. The project team disbands, and the project officially ends.

Differentiation from Ongoing Operations: Ongoing operations, such as customer service support, are continuous activities without a defined end date. They aim to maintain and improve ongoing functions of the organization, unlike projects that have a temporary life span focused on achieving a singular goal.

3. Progressive Elaboration

Definition: Progressive elaboration refers to the iterative process of refining and detailing a project's plans and specifications as more information becomes available. It allows for incremental planning and adjustments to project scope and approach.

Example: Developing a New Software Application A tech company embarking on a project to develop a new software application often starts with a broad concept. As the project progresses, requirements become clearer through stakeholder feedback, market analysis, and prototyping. Initial plans are refined, and detailed specifications for features, user interface, and performance metrics are developed. This iterative process continues until the final product meets all requirements and is ready for release.

Differentiation from Ongoing Operations: Ongoing operations, such as routine maintenance of existing software, follow established procedures and guidelines. These activities do not typically involve the evolving and iterative planning that characterizes project work. Maintenance tasks are standardized and repetitive, focusing on sustaining the current system's functionality.

Projects stand out from ongoing operations due to their unique nature, defined life cycle, and progressive elaboration. Understanding these characteristics helps project managers effectively plan, execute, and close projects, ensuring they deliver valuable and distinctive outcomes. By recognizing and appreciating the differences between projects and operations, organizations can better allocate resources and manage both types of activities to achieve their strategic goals.

The Five Project Management Process Groups

The five project management process groups are the backbone of project management as outlined in the PMBOK® Guide. Each process group includes a set of activities that drive projects from inception to completion. Here's a detailed breakdown of each process group, including key activities and deliverables.

1. Initiation

Purpose: The Initiation process group defines and authorizes the project or a project phase. It sets the stage for planning and execution.

Key Activities:

- **Develop Project Charter**: Formally authorizes the existence of the project and provides the project manager with the authority to apply organizational resources.
  - *Deliverables*: Project Charter
- **Identify Stakeholders**: Identifies all people or organizations impacted by the project and documents relevant information regarding their interests, involvement, and impact on project success.
  - *Deliverables*: Stakeholder Register

Interactions: Initiation activities lead into planning, providing a foundation for scope, schedule, and budget development.

2. Planning

Purpose: The Planning process group establishes the total scope of the effort, defines and refines the objectives, and develops the course of action required to attain those objectives.

Key Activities:

- **Develop Project Management Plan**: Integrates all subsidiary plans and sets the baseline for project execution and control.
  - *Deliverables*: Project Management Plan
- **Plan Scope Management**: Defines how the project scope will be defined, validated, and controlled.
  - *Deliverables*: Scope Management Plan
- **Collect Requirements**: Determines, documents, and manages stakeholder needs and requirements.
  - *Deliverables*: Requirements Documentation, Requirements Traceability Matrix
- **Define Scope**: Develops a detailed project and product description.
  - *Deliverables*: Project Scope Statement
- **Create WBS**: Subdivides project deliverables and project work into smaller, more manageable components.
  - *Deliverables*: Work Breakdown Structure (WBS)
- **Plan Schedule Management**: Establishes policies, procedures, and documentation for planning, developing, managing, executing, and controlling the project schedule.
  - *Deliverables*: Schedule Management Plan
- **Define Activities**: Identifies and documents the specific actions to be performed.
  - *Deliverables*: Activity List, Activity Attributes
- **Sequence Activities**: Identifies and documents relationships among project activities.
  - *Deliverables*: Project Schedule Network Diagrams
- **Estimate Activity Durations**: Approximates the number of work periods needed to complete activities.
  - *Deliverables*: Duration Estimates
- **Develop Schedule**: Analyzes activity sequences, durations, resource requirements, and schedule constraints to create the project schedule.
  - *Deliverables*: Project Schedule, Schedule Baseline
- **Plan Cost Management**: Defines how project costs will be estimated, budgeted, managed, and controlled.
  - *Deliverables*: Cost Management Plan
- **Estimate Costs**: Develops an approximation of the monetary resources needed to complete project activities.
  - *Deliverables*: Cost Estimates
- **Determine Budget**: Aggregates estimated costs to establish a cost baseline.
  - *Deliverables*: Cost Baseline, Project Funding Requirements

- **Plan Quality Management**: Identifies quality requirements and standards for the project and its deliverables.
  - *Deliverables*: Quality Management Plan, Quality Metrics
- **Plan Resource Management**: Defines how to estimate, acquire, manage, and use team and physical resources.
  - *Deliverables*: Resource Management Plan, Resource Breakdown Structure (RBS)
- **Estimate Activity Resources**: Estimates team resources and the type and quantities of materials, equipment, and supplies.
  - *Deliverables*: Resource Requirements, Resource Breakdown Structure
- **Plan Communications Management**: Develops an approach to communicate project information effectively.
  - *Deliverables*: Communications Management Plan
- **Plan Risk Management**: Defines how to conduct risk management activities.
  - *Deliverables*: Risk Management Plan
- **Identify Risks**: Determines which risks might affect the project.
  - *Deliverables*: Risk Register
- **Perform Qualitative Risk Analysis**: Prioritizes risks for further analysis or action.
  - *Deliverables*: Risk Probability and Impact Assessment
- **Perform Quantitative Risk Analysis**: Numerically analyzes the effect of identified risks.
  - *Deliverables*: Quantitative Risk Analysis Report
- **Plan Risk Responses**: Develops options and actions to enhance opportunities and reduce threats.
  - *Deliverables*: Risk Response Plan
- **Plan Procurement Management**: Documents project procurement decisions and identifies potential sellers.
  - *Deliverables*: Procurement Management Plan, Procurement Strategy
- **Plan Stakeholder Engagement**: Develops approaches to involve project stakeholders based on their needs and expectations.
  - *Deliverables*: Stakeholder Engagement Plan

Interactions: The planning phase provides detailed roadmaps for execution and forms the basis for performance measurement and control.

3. Execution

Purpose: The Execution process group involves coordinating people and resources, as well as integrating and performing the activities of the project in accordance with the project management plan.

Key Activities:
- **Direct and Manage Project Work**: Leading and performing the work defined in the project management plan and implementing approved changes.
  - *Deliverables*: Deliverables, Work Performance Data, Issue Log
- **Manage Project Knowledge**: Using existing knowledge and creating new knowledge to achieve project objectives.
  - *Deliverables*: Lessons Learned Register
- **Manage Quality**: Translating the quality management plan into executable quality activities.
  - *Deliverables*: Quality Reports, Test and Evaluation Documents
- **Acquire Resources**: Obtaining team members, facilities, equipment, materials, and supplies.
  - *Deliverables*: Physical Resource Assignments, Project Team Assignments
- **Develop Team**: Improving competencies, team interaction, and the overall team environment.
  - *Deliverables*: Team Performance Assessments
- **Manage Team**: Tracking team performance, providing feedback, resolving issues, and managing changes to optimize project performance.
  - *Deliverables*: Change Requests, Project Management Plan Updates

- **Manage Communications**: Ensuring timely and appropriate collection, creation, distribution, storage, retrieval, and ultimate disposition of project information.
  - *Deliverables*: Project Communications
- **Implement Risk Responses**: Implementing agreed-upon risk response plans.
  - *Deliverables*: Change Requests, Project Documents Updates
- **Conduct Procurements**: Obtaining seller responses, selecting a seller, and awarding a contract.
  - *Deliverables*: Selected Sellers, Agreements
- **Manage Stakeholder Engagement**: Engaging stakeholders and managing their expectations.
  - *Deliverables*: Stakeholder Engagement Plan Updates, Change Requests

Interactions: Execution integrates and coordinates resources and activities to produce project deliverables and requires continuous interaction with planning and monitoring and controlling processes.

4. Monitoring and Controlling

Purpose: The Monitoring and Controlling process group tracks, reviews, and regulates the progress and performance of the project and identifies any areas where changes to the plan are required.

Key Activities:

- **Monitor and Control Project Work**: Tracking, reviewing, and reporting project progress against the objectives.
  - *Deliverables*: Work Performance Reports, Change Requests
- **Perform Integrated Change Control**: Reviewing all change requests, approving changes, and managing changes to deliverables and project documents.
  - *Deliverables*: Approved Change Requests, Change Log
- **Validate Scope**: Formalizing acceptance of the completed project deliverables.
  - *Deliverables*: Accepted Deliverables, Work Performance Information
- **Control Scope**: Monitoring the status of the project and product scope and managing changes to the scope baseline.
  - *Deliverables*: Scope Baseline Updates, Work Performance Information
- **Control Schedule**: Monitoring the status of project activities to update project progress and manage changes to the schedule baseline.
  - *Deliverables*: Schedule Forecasts, Schedule Baseline Updates
- **Control Costs**: Monitoring the status of the project to update the project budget and manage changes to the cost baseline.
  - *Deliverables*: Cost Forecasts, Cost Baseline Updates
- **Control Quality**: Monitoring and recording results of executing quality activities to assess performance and recommend necessary changes.
  - *Deliverables*: Quality Control Measurements, Verified Deliverables
- **Control Resources**: Ensuring that physical resources assigned and allocated to the project are available as planned.
  - *Deliverables*: Resource Utilization Reports, Resource Management Plan Updates
- **Monitor Communications**: Ensuring the information needs of the project and its stakeholders are met.
  - *Deliverables*: Work Performance Information, Communications Management Plan Updates
- **Monitor Risks**: Tracking identified risks, monitoring residual risks, identifying new risks, and evaluating risk process effectiveness.
  - *Deliverables*: Risk Register Updates, Risk Management Plan Updates
- **Control Procurements**: Managing procurement relationships, monitoring contract performance, and making necessary changes.
  - *Deliverables*: Procurement Documentation, Work Performance Information
- **Monitor Stakeholder Engagement**: Monitoring stakeholder relationships and adjusting engagement strategies.
  - *Deliverables*: Stakeholder Engagement Plan Updates, Work Performance Information

Interactions: Monitoring and controlling ensures that project objectives are met by measuring performance and making necessary adjustments. It interacts with all other process groups for effective project governance.

5. Closing
Purpose: The Closing process group finalizes all project activities to formally complete the project or phase.
Key Activities:
- **Close Project or Phase**: Finalizing all activities across all process groups to formally close the project or phase.
  - *Deliverables*: Final Product, Service, or Result Transition, Final Report
- **Close Procurements**: Completing and settling each contract, including resolving any open items.
  - *Deliverables*: Closed Procurements, Procurement File

Interactions: Closing formally concludes the project or phase, ensuring all work is completed and accepted. It provides lessons learned and documentation for future projects.

Understanding these process groups and their interactions helps ensure that project managers can effectively guide projects from start to finish, delivering successful outcomes and meeting stakeholder expectations.

Project management is organized around ten knowledge areas, each encompassing key processes, tools, and techniques essential for effective project management. To make these areas easier to remember, we'll use the mnemonic **"I Saw Six Cows Quietly Reading Comics, Really Peaceful Sight"** representing: Integration, Scope, Schedule, Cost, Quality, Resource, Communication, Risk, Procurement, and Stakeholder Management. Let's explore each knowledge area in detail.

1. Project Integration Management
Purpose: Ensures that project processes are coordinated and aligned with the overall objectives. **Key Processes:**
- **Develop Project Charter:** Authorizes the project.
- **Develop Project Management Plan:** Documents the approach.
- **Direct and Manage Project Work:** Leads project execution.
- **Manage Project Knowledge:** Handles project knowledge.
- **Monitor and Control Project Work:** Tracks progress.
- **Perform Integrated Change Control:** Manages changes.
- **Close Project or Phase:** Finalizes all activities.

Tools and Techniques:
- **Project Management Information System (PMIS):** Software tools for managing projects.
- **Expert Judgment:** Guidance from experienced professionals.
- **Meetings:** Facilitate communication and decision-making.

2. Project Scope Management
Purpose: Ensures that the project includes all the work required and only the work required. **Key Processes:**
- **Plan Scope Management:** Develops the scope management plan.
- **Collect Requirements:** Gathers stakeholder needs.
- **Define Scope:** Develops a detailed project scope statement.
- **Create WBS:** Breaks down the project into smaller components.
- **Validate Scope:** Ensures deliverables meet requirements.
- **Control Scope:** Monitors scope and manages changes.

Tools and Techniques:
- **Interviews:** Collect detailed information.
- **Focus Groups:** Gather insights from stakeholders.
- **Prototypes:** Create preliminary models for feedback.

3. Project Schedule Management
Purpose: Manages timely project completion. **Key Processes:**
- **Plan Schedule Management:** Develops the schedule management plan.
- **Define Activities:** Identifies specific project activities.

- **Sequence Activities:** Determines activity order.
- **Estimate Activity Durations:** Estimates time required.
- **Develop Schedule:** Creates the project schedule.
- **Control Schedule:** Monitors schedule and manages changes.

Tools and Techniques:
- **Gantt Charts:** Visualize project schedule.
- **Critical Path Method (CPM):** Identifies the longest path.
- **Schedule Compression:** Shortens the project duration.

4. Project Cost Management

Purpose: Ensures the project is completed within the approved budget. **Key Processes:**
- **Plan Cost Management:** Develops the cost management plan.
- **Estimate Costs:** Predicts project costs.
- **Determine Budget:** Aggregates costs to establish a budget.
- **Control Costs:** Monitors costs and manages changes.

Tools and Techniques:
- **Cost Estimating Software:** Provides cost estimates.
- **Earned Value Management (EVM):** Measures project performance.
- **Cost Aggregation:** Summarizes cost estimates.

5. Project Quality Management

Purpose: Ensures the project meets the required quality standards. **Key Processes:**
- **Plan Quality Management:** Develops the quality management plan.
- **Manage Quality:** Translates the quality plan into actionable quality activities.
- **Control Quality:** Monitors outcomes to ensure quality standards.

Tools and Techniques:
- **Quality Audits:** Review quality processes.
- **Control Charts:** Monitor process stability.
- **Inspection:** Examine deliverables for quality.

6. Project Resource Management

Purpose: Manages human and physical resources effectively. **Key Processes:**
- **Plan Resource Management:** Develops the resource management plan.
- **Estimate Activity Resources:** Estimates resources needed.
- **Acquire Resources:** Obtains necessary resources.
- **Develop Team:** Enhances team skills and cohesion.
- **Manage Team:** Tracks team performance.
- **Control Resources:** Ensures resources are used as planned.

Tools and Techniques:
- **Resource Calendars:** Identify resource availability.
- **Team Building Activities:** Improve team performance.
- **Performance Reviews:** Evaluate team members.

7. Project Communication Management

Purpose: Ensures timely and appropriate communication. **Key Processes:**
- **Plan Communications Management:** Develops the communications management plan.
- **Manage Communications:** Ensures effective information flow.
- **Monitor Communications:** Ensures communication needs are met.

Tools and Techniques:
- **Communication Technology:** Tools like email, instant messaging.
- **Communication Models:** Frameworks for communication flow.

- **Performance Reporting:** Status reports on project performance.

8. Project Risk Management
Purpose: Identifies, analyzes, and responds to project risks. **Key Processes:**
- **Plan Risk Management:** Develops the risk management plan.
- **Identify Risks:** Determines potential risks.
- **Perform Qualitative Risk Analysis:** Prioritizes risks based on impact.
- **Perform Quantitative Risk Analysis:** Numerically analyzes risk effects.
- **Plan Risk Responses:** Develops actions to address risks.
- **Implement Risk Responses:** Executes risk response plans.
- **Monitor Risks:** Tracks risk and response effectiveness.

Tools and Techniques:
- **Risk Register:** Records identified risks.
- **SWOT Analysis:** Analyzes strengths, weaknesses, opportunities, and threats.
- **Monte Carlo Simulation:** Predicts project outcomes based on risk.

9. Project Procurement Management
Purpose: Obtains necessary resources from external sources. **Key Processes:**
- **Plan Procurement Management:** Develops the procurement management plan.
- **Conduct Procurements:** Obtains seller responses and selects sellers.
- **Control Procurements:** Manages procurement relationships and performance.

Tools and Techniques:
- **Bidder Conferences:** Clarify procurement requirements.
- **Procurement Negotiations:** Finalize agreements.
- **Contract Management Software:** Manage procurement documents.

10. Project Stakeholder Management
Purpose: Identifies and engages stakeholders effectively. **Key Processes:**
- **Identify Stakeholders:** Determines stakeholders and their impact.
- **Plan Stakeholder Engagement:** Develops strategies to engage stakeholders.
- **Manage Stakeholder Engagement:** Communicates and works with stakeholders.
- **Monitor Stakeholder Engagement:** Tracks stakeholder engagement and adjusts strategies.

Tools and Techniques:
- **Stakeholder Analysis:** Identifies stakeholder interests and influences.
- **Engagement Strategies:** Develops tailored communication plans.
- **Feedback Surveys:** Gathers stakeholder feedback.

By understanding these ten knowledge areas and their associated processes, tools, and techniques, you can effectively manage projects and ensure successful outcomes. Remembering the mnemonic **"I Saw Six Cows Quietly Reading Comics, Really Peaceful Sight"** can help you recall the order and importance of these knowledge areas.

Critical Responsibilities and Competencies of a Project Manager

A project manager (PM) plays a pivotal role in the success of any project. They are responsible for planning, executing, and closing projects while managing teams, resources, and stakeholder expectations. Let's delve into the critical responsibilities and competencies of a project manager, categorized into technical, leadership, and strategic and business management skills.

Technical Skills
Technical skills are essential for managing the core aspects of project management. These skills ensure that the project manager can effectively apply project management methodologies, tools, and techniques to achieve project goals.

Key Technical Skills:
1. **Project Planning:** Developing detailed project plans that outline scope, schedule, cost, quality, and risk management strategies.

- *Example*: Creating a comprehensive project plan for a new product launch, including timelines, resource allocation, and risk mitigation strategies.
2. **Risk Management**: Identifying, analyzing, and responding to project risks to minimize their impact.
    - *Example*: In a software development project, identifying potential risks such as technical challenges, and then developing contingency plans to address these risks.
3. **Budgeting and Cost Management**: Estimating project costs, managing the budget, and controlling expenditures to keep the project within financial constraints.
    - *Example*: Managing the budget for a construction project by monitoring expenses and ensuring costs do not exceed the allocated budget.
4. **Scheduling**: Creating and managing project schedules to ensure timely completion of project activities.
    - *Example*: Developing a detailed Gantt chart to track the progress of tasks in a marketing campaign project.
5. **Quality Management**: Ensuring that project deliverables meet the required quality standards and stakeholder expectations.
    - *Example*: Implementing quality assurance processes in a manufacturing project to ensure products meet industry standards.

Application in Real-World Situations:
- **Case Study**: A project manager leading the development of a new mobile application must create a detailed project plan, allocate resources effectively, manage risks related to software bugs, and ensure that the project stays within budget and on schedule. They would also implement rigorous testing phases to maintain high-quality standards.

Leadership Skills

Leadership skills are crucial for motivating and guiding the project team, resolving conflicts, and ensuring effective communication among all stakeholders.

Key Leadership Skills:
1. **Team Building and Motivation**: Creating a cohesive team environment, fostering collaboration, and motivating team members to achieve project goals.
    - *Example*: Organizing team-building activities and recognizing individual contributions to maintain high morale in a challenging project.
2. **Communication**: Facilitating clear and open communication within the team and with stakeholders to ensure everyone is aligned with project objectives.
    - *Example*: Conducting regular status meetings and using collaboration tools to keep the project team informed and engaged.
3. **Conflict Resolution**: Identifying and resolving conflicts among team members or stakeholders to maintain a productive working environment.
    - *Example*: Mediating a disagreement between the marketing and sales teams about project priorities and finding a mutually acceptable solution.
4. **Decision-Making**: Making informed decisions quickly and effectively to keep the project on track.
    - *Example*: Deciding to reallocate resources to address an unexpected critical issue in a project to prevent delays.

Application in Real-World Situations:
- **Case Study**: In a healthcare project to implement a new patient management system, the project manager must lead a diverse team of IT professionals, healthcare staff, and external vendors. They must communicate effectively to ensure all parties understand the project's goals, resolve conflicts between stakeholders with differing priorities, and motivate the team through the project's challenges.

Strategic and Business Management Skills

Strategic and business management skills enable project managers to align projects with organizational goals, understand the broader business context, and make decisions that drive business success.

Key Strategic and Business Management Skills:
1. **Business Acumen**: Understanding the organization's strategy, goals, and competitive environment to ensure the project contributes to business objectives.

- *Example*: Aligning a new product development project with the company's strategic goal of expanding into new markets.
2. **Stakeholder Management**: Identifying and engaging stakeholders to ensure their needs and expectations are met throughout the project lifecycle.
    - *Example*: Conducting stakeholder analysis and developing a stakeholder engagement plan to maintain strong relationships with key stakeholders.
3. **Change Management**: Managing organizational change effectively to ensure smooth project implementation and adoption.
    - *Example*: Implementing a change management strategy to support the adoption of a new enterprise resource planning (ERP) system.
4. **Financial Management**: Understanding financial principles and practices to manage project finances effectively.
    - *Example*: Conducting cost-benefit analysis to evaluate the financial viability of a project before initiation.

Application in Real-World Situations:
- **Case Study**: In a project to expand a retail chain into a new region, the project manager must understand the market conditions, align the project with the company's growth strategy, manage relationships with local stakeholders, and implement change management practices to ensure a smooth transition for existing employees and processes.

Applying These Skills in Complex Projects

In a complex project, such as the construction of a new hospital, a project manager must integrate all these skills:
- **Technical Skills**: Develop a detailed project plan, manage the construction schedule, control costs, and ensure quality standards are met.
- **Leadership Skills**: Lead a diverse team of architects, engineers, contractors, and healthcare professionals, ensuring effective communication and resolving conflicts.
- **Strategic and Business Management Skills**: Align the project with the healthcare provider's strategic goals, manage stakeholder expectations, and navigate regulatory requirements.

By mastering these competencies, project managers can successfully navigate the complexities of their projects, deliver exceptional results, and contribute significantly to their organizations' success.

Organizational structures define how tasks are divided, coordinated, and supervised within a company. The three main types are **Functional**, **Matrix**, and **Projectized** structures. Each has unique characteristics, advantages, and disadvantages, and each influences project management processes and decision-making differently.

Functional Organizational Structure

Characteristics:
- Divides the organization into departments based on specialized functions (e.g., marketing, finance, HR).
- Each department is managed independently by a functional manager.
- Hierarchical structure with clear lines of authority.

Advantages:
- **Specialization:** Employees develop expertise in their functional areas, enhancing productivity and quality.
- **Efficiency:** Streamlined processes and clear responsibilities within departments.
- **Resource Utilization:** Optimal use of resources as they are grouped by function.

Disadvantages:
- **Silo Effect:** Departments may operate in isolation, hindering cross-functional communication and collaboration.
- **Slow Decision-Making:** Decisions can be slow due to the hierarchical nature.
- **Limited Career Growth:** Employees may have limited opportunities to gain experience outside their functional areas.

Influence on Project Management:

- **Project Manager's Authority:** Limited; functional managers have more control over resources and decisions.
- **Communication:** Predominantly vertical within departments, challenging cross-departmental collaboration.
- **Decision-Making:** Slow and bureaucratic, often requiring multiple levels of approval.

Example Industries/Companies:
- **Manufacturing:** Companies like Ford or General Motors, where specialization in production, finance, and marketing is critical.
- **Universities:** Academic institutions typically have departments like humanities, sciences, and administration, each managed independently.

Matrix Organizational Structure

Characteristics:
- Combines functional and projectized structures, creating a dual reporting system (functional and project managers).
- Employees work on projects while maintaining their functional roles.
- Can be weak, balanced, or strong depending on the power distribution between functional and project managers.

Advantages:
- **Flexibility:** Resources can be shared across projects, enhancing flexibility and efficiency.
- **Balanced Decision-Making:** Combines expertise from functional and project managers, leading to well-rounded decisions.
- **Skill Development:** Employees gain diverse experience by working on different projects.

Disadvantages:
- **Conflict of Authority:** Dual reporting can lead to confusion and conflicts between functional and project managers.
- **Complex Communication:** Requires robust communication channels to manage dual reporting and collaboration.
- **Resource Allocation Challenges:** Balancing resources between functional and project needs can be difficult.

Influence on Project Management:
- **Project Manager's Authority:** Varies; can be weak (functional manager dominates), balanced, or strong (project manager dominates).
- **Communication:** Requires extensive coordination and communication across functional and project teams.
- **Decision-Making:** Can be efficient but depends on the clarity of roles and communication effectiveness.

Example Industries/Companies:
- **Consulting Firms:** Companies like Deloitte or Accenture, where projects often span multiple functions and expertise areas.
- **Aerospace:** Companies like Boeing or Lockheed Martin, managing complex projects requiring diverse expertise.

Projectized Organizational Structure

Characteristics:
- Organizes activities around projects rather than functions.
- Project managers have full authority over resources and decision-making.
- Teams are often disbanded after project completion.

Advantages:
- **Project Focus:** Entire organization is oriented towards project goals, leading to high commitment and focus.
- **Clear Authority:** Project managers have clear authority, simplifying decision-making and resource allocation.
- **Flexibility:** High adaptability to changes and project-specific needs.

Disadvantages:

- **Resource Duplication:** Resources may be duplicated across projects, leading to inefficiency.
- **Job Security:** Employees may face uncertainty about their roles after project completion.
- **Isolation:** Teams may become isolated, losing touch with broader organizational goals and knowledge.

Influence on Project Management:
- **Project Manager's Authority:** High; project managers control resources and decision-making.
- **Communication:** Direct and efficient within project teams but may require coordination with other projects.
- **Decision-Making:** Fast and flexible, as project managers have autonomy.

Example Industries/Companies:
- **Construction:** Companies like Bechtel or Skanska, where projects (buildings, infrastructure) are central to operations.
- **Event Management:** Firms specializing in organizing events, where each event is managed as a separate project.

Comparison and Contrast

Aspect	Functional	Matrix	Projectized
Structure	Departments based on functions	Combination of functional and project	Organized around projects
Authority	Functional managers	Shared between functional and project	Project managers
Focus	Specialized functions	Balanced between projects and functions	Project goals
Flexibility	Low	Medium	High
Communication	Vertical within departments	Complex, requires robust systems	Direct within project teams
Decision-Making	Slow, hierarchical	Balanced but potentially conflicted	Fast, project-centric
Resource Utilization	Efficient within functions	Efficient but requires balancing	Potential duplication
Skill Development	Specialized within functions	Diverse experience	Project-focused skills
Examples	Manufacturing, Universities	Consulting, Aerospace	Construction, Event Management

Understanding these structures helps project managers navigate their roles and responsibilities effectively, ensuring successful project outcomes tailored to their organizational context.

Project Life Cycle and Its Phases

The project life cycle is a series of phases that a project goes through from its initiation to its closure. Understanding the project life cycle is crucial for effective project management, as it provides a structured approach to planning, executing, and completing projects. The project life cycle typically consists of the following phases: Initiation, Planning, Execution, Monitoring and Controlling, and Closing. Each phase has distinct characteristics and objectives, and they correspond closely with the project management process groups defined in the PMBOK® Guide.

1. Initiation Phase

Characteristics and Objectives:
- **Definition:** The initiation phase marks the beginning of the project, where the project's feasibility and value are evaluated.
- **Objectives:** To define the project at a high level and secure authorization to proceed.
- **Key Activities:**
    - Develop Project Charter: Formal authorization of the project.
    - Identify Stakeholders: Identify all parties affected by the project and their interests.

Related Process Group: Initiating

Real-World Example: In a software development project for a new mobile app, the initiation phase involves defining the app's purpose, identifying key stakeholders (e.g., target users, developers, investors), and obtaining approval from senior management to proceed.
Key Deliverables and Milestones:
- **Project Charter**: Document that formally authorizes the project.
- **Stakeholder Register**: List of identified stakeholders and their interests.

2. Planning Phase
Characteristics and Objectives:
- **Definition**: The planning phase involves developing a detailed project plan that outlines how the project will be executed, monitored, and controlled.
- **Objectives**: To establish the project's scope, objectives, and course of action.
- **Key Activities**:
    - Develop Project Management Plan: Integrate subsidiary plans for scope, schedule, cost, quality, resources, communication, risk, procurement, and stakeholder engagement.
    - Collect Requirements: Gather stakeholder requirements and document them.
    - Define Scope: Create a detailed description of the project and its deliverables.
    - Create Work Breakdown Structure (WBS): Break down project deliverables into smaller, manageable components.
    - Develop Schedule: Outline the project timeline.
    - Estimate Costs: Approximate the financial resources needed for the project.
    - Plan Risk Management: Identify potential risks and develop strategies to mitigate them.

Related Process Group: Planning
Real-World Example: In the mobile app development project, the planning phase includes creating a detailed project plan that outlines the features of the app, the project timeline, budget estimates, resource allocation, and risk management strategies.
Key Deliverables and Milestones:
- **Project Management Plan**: Comprehensive plan integrating all subsidiary plans.
- **Requirements Documentation**: Detailed list of stakeholder requirements.
- **Project Scope Statement**: Clear description of the project's scope.
- **Work Breakdown Structure (WBS)**: Hierarchical decomposition of project deliverables.
- **Project Schedule**: Timeline for project activities.
- **Cost Baseline**: Approved version of the project budget.
- **Risk Register**: Document listing identified risks and their responses.

3. Execution Phase
Characteristics and Objectives:
- **Definition**: The execution phase involves coordinating people and resources to carry out the project plan and produce the project deliverables.
- **Objectives**: To complete the project work as defined in the project management plan.
- **Key Activities**:
    - Direct and Manage Project Work: Perform the activities defined in the project plan.
    - Manage Project Knowledge: Use existing knowledge and create new knowledge.
    - Acquire Resources: Obtain the necessary team members, materials, and equipment.
    - Develop and Manage Team: Improve team performance and manage team dynamics.
    - Implement Risk Responses: Execute risk response plans.
    - Conduct Procurements: Obtain external resources and services.

Related Process Group: Executing
Real-World Example: For the mobile app project, the execution phase includes coding the app, creating the user interface, integrating backend services, and conducting initial testing.
Key Deliverables and Milestones:
- **Deliverables**: Completed project outputs (e.g., the working mobile app).

- **Work Performance Data**: Data on project progress and performance.
- **Change Requests**: Formal proposals for changes to the project plan.
- **Project Communications**: Updates and reports shared with stakeholders.

4. Monitoring and Controlling Phase
Characteristics and Objectives:
- **Definition**: The monitoring and controlling phase involves tracking, reviewing, and regulating project performance to ensure it stays on track.
- **Objectives**: To monitor project performance, manage changes, and ensure project objectives are met.
- **Key Activities**:
    - Monitor and Control Project Work: Track project performance and make necessary adjustments.
    - Perform Integrated Change Control: Review and approve changes to the project.
    - Validate and Control Scope: Ensure project deliverables meet requirements and manage scope changes.
    - Control Schedule and Costs: Monitor schedule and budget performance.
    - Perform Quality Control: Ensure deliverables meet quality standards.
    - Monitor Risks: Track identified risks and manage new risks.

Related Process Group: Monitoring and Controlling

Real-World Example: In the mobile app project, the monitoring and controlling phase involves tracking the project's progress against the plan, managing any changes to the app's features, and ensuring the project stays within budget and on schedule.

Key Deliverables and Milestones:
- **Performance Reports**: Regular updates on project status and performance metrics.
- **Approved Change Requests**: Documentation of approved changes.
- **Validated Deliverables**: Deliverables that meet acceptance criteria.
- **Updated Risk Register**: Document with the latest risk status and responses.

5. Closing Phase
Characteristics and Objectives:
- **Definition**: The closing phase marks the completion of the project or a project phase.
- **Objectives**: To finalize all activities, complete the project, and formally close it.
- **Key Activities**:
    - Close Project or Phase: Finalize all activities and obtain formal acceptance of the project deliverables.
    - Close Procurements: Complete and settle each contract and any remaining procurement activities.
    - Conduct Post-Project Review: Document lessons learned and ensure knowledge transfer.

Related Process Group: Closing

Real-World Example: In the mobile app project, the closing phase includes obtaining client approval for the app, conducting a final project review, documenting lessons learned, and releasing the project team.

Key Deliverables and Milestones:
- **Final Product, Service, or Result Transition**: Transfer of the app to the client or end users.
- **Final Report**: Comprehensive report summarizing project performance.
- **Lessons Learned Documentation**: Document capturing insights and lessons from the project.

Real-World Project Example: Mobile App Development
Let's illustrate the progression through the life cycle phases using a mobile app development project:
1. **Initiation**:
    - **Project Charter**: Defined the app's purpose and secured approval.
    - **Stakeholder Register**: Identified target users, developers, and investors.
2. **Planning**:
    - **Project Management Plan**: Developed a comprehensive plan covering scope, schedule, costs, quality, resources, communication, risks, and stakeholder engagement.

- - **Requirements Documentation**: Gathered and documented user requirements.
  - **WBS**: Created a hierarchical breakdown of all deliverables.
3. **Execution**:
   - **Direct and Manage Work**: Coordinated coding, UI design, and testing.
   - **Develop Team**: Conducted team-building activities and managed team performance.
   - **Acquire Resources**: Secured necessary tools and technologies.
4. **Monitoring and Controlling**:
   - **Monitor Work**: Tracked progress and performance metrics.
   - **Control Scope**: Managed changes to the app's features.
   - **Control Costs**: Ensured expenses stayed within budget.
   - **Quality Control**: Conducted testing to meet quality standards.
5. **Closing**:
   - **Project Closure**: Obtained client approval for the final app.
   - **Post-Project Review**: Documented lessons learned.
   - **Final Report**: Summarized project performance and outcomes.

By following the project life cycle phases, project managers can systematically guide their projects from inception to successful completion, ensuring all project objectives are met and stakeholder expectations are satisfied.

Project Management Offices (PMOs) come in three main types: Supportive, Controlling, and Directive. Each type serves distinct roles, offers specific levels of control and support, and provides different value to organizations. Let's delve into each type, examining their roles, responsibilities, and the value they offer, along with real-world examples.

1. Supportive PMO

Roles and Responsibilities:

- Provides a consultative role to projects by supplying templates, best practices, training, access to information, and lessons learned.
- Acts as a repository for project management information and standards.
- Facilitates knowledge sharing and supports project managers with tools and methodologies.

Value Provided:

- **Flexibility:** Offers support without imposing strict controls, allowing project managers the autonomy to manage their projects.
- **Knowledge Sharing:** Encourages a culture of continuous improvement through the dissemination of best practices and lessons learned.
- **Resource Optimization:** Helps project managers access the necessary resources and tools, improving efficiency.

Case Study/Example:

- **Tech Startups:** In many tech startups, where innovation and agility are key, a Supportive PMO can help standardize processes without stifling creativity. For instance, a Supportive PMO at a tech startup may provide agile methodologies, templates, and training sessions while allowing teams the freedom to adapt these tools to their specific needs.

2. Controlling PMO

Roles and Responsibilities:

- Provides support and requires compliance through various means.
- Implements project management frameworks, methodologies, templates, and governance processes.
- Monitors project compliance with established standards and procedures.
- Conducts regular project audits and reviews to ensure adherence to best practices and methodologies.

Value Provided:

- **Standardization:** Ensures consistency across projects, leading to improved predictability and control.
- **Risk Management:** Enhances risk management through regular monitoring and compliance checks.
- **Quality Assurance:** Maintains high standards of project delivery by enforcing compliance with methodologies and best practices.

Case Study/Example:
- **Financial Institutions:** A Controlling PMO is often found in financial institutions where regulatory compliance and risk management are crucial. For example, a Controlling PMO at a bank may enforce strict adherence to project management standards and conduct regular audits to ensure compliance with financial regulations and internal policies.

3. Directive PMO

Roles and Responsibilities:
- Directly manages and controls projects.
- Provides project managers for projects and has a high degree of control over projects.
- Ensures alignment with organizational goals and strategic objectives.
- Allocates resources, defines project priorities, and makes key decisions.

Value Provided:
- **High Control:** Offers a high degree of control over project outcomes, ensuring alignment with strategic goals.
- **Resource Allocation:** Optimizes resource allocation across projects, ensuring the most critical projects receive the necessary resources.
- **Strategic Alignment:** Ensures that all projects contribute to the organization's strategic objectives, improving overall organizational performance.

Case Study/Example:
- **Construction Companies:** In large construction firms, a Directive PMO can be critical to ensuring project success. For instance, a Directive PMO at a construction company like Bechtel or Skanska directly manages large-scale projects, allocating resources, setting priorities, and ensuring that projects align with the company's strategic goals and client requirements.

Comparison of PMO Types

Aspect	Supportive	Controlling	Directive
Control Level	Low	Moderate	High
Role	Advisory and consultative	Governance and compliance	Direct management and control
Flexibility	High	Medium	Low
Standardization	Low to medium	High	Very high
Implementation	Tech startups, R&D departments	Financial institutions, healthcare	Construction, aerospace, large corporations

Real-World Implementation Examples

1. **Supportive PMO in a Tech Startup:**
   - **Company:** XYZ Innovations, a tech startup focusing on developing cutting-edge software solutions.
   - **Implementation:** The Supportive PMO provides agile methodologies, templates, and training, helping project teams adopt best practices without imposing rigid controls. This approach fosters innovation while maintaining some level of process standardization.

2. **Controlling PMO in a Financial Institution:**
   - **Company:** Global Bank Inc.
   - **Implementation:** The Controlling PMO enforces compliance with project management standards and regulatory requirements. It conducts regular audits and reviews, ensuring that all projects adhere to the bank's stringent risk management and compliance policies, thereby reducing operational risks and improving project outcomes.

3. **Directive PMO in a Construction Firm:**
   - **Company:** Bechtel Corporation
   - **Implementation:** The Directive PMO directly manages major construction projects, allocating resources, setting project priorities, and ensuring alignment with strategic goals. This high level of control ensures that projects meet client specifications, are completed on time, and stay within budget.

Each type of PMO offers distinct advantages and fits different organizational needs. Understanding these differences helps organizations select and implement the most appropriate PMO structure to enhance project success and achieve strategic objectives.

Enterprise Environmental Factors (EEFs)

Enterprise Environmental Factors (EEFs) are conditions, not under the immediate control of the project team, that influence, constrain, or direct the project. These factors can affect the project positively or negatively and must be considered during project planning and execution. EEFs can be internal or external to the organization and have a significant impact on how projects are managed and executed.

Internal EEFs

Internal EEFs originate within the organization and can directly affect the project's processes and performance.

Examples of Internal EEFs:

1. **Organizational Culture and Structure:**
   - *Culture*: The shared values, norms, and beliefs within the organization can influence project management styles and team behavior.
   - *Structure*: Functional, matrix, or projectized structures determine the authority of the project manager and resource availability.
   - *Example*: A projectized organization may offer more autonomy to the project manager compared to a functional organization, where the project manager may have to negotiate for resources.

2. **Organizational Processes and Policies:**
   - Standardized guidelines, policies, and procedures that must be followed.
   - *Example*: An organization with strict quality assurance processes will require the project to include detailed quality management plans.

3. **Human Resources:**
   - Availability and competency of the organization's workforce.
   - *Example*: The skills and experience of team members can significantly impact project timelines and quality.

4. **Infrastructure:**
   - Facilities, equipment, and technology available to the project team.
   - *Example*: Adequate IT infrastructure can support the smooth execution of a software development project.

5. **Project Management Information Systems (PMIS):**
   - Tools and systems used for project management processes.
   - *Example*: Access to advanced PMIS can streamline project scheduling, tracking, and reporting.

6. **Stakeholder Risk Tolerance:**
   - Degree to which stakeholders are willing to accept risk.
   - *Example*: Conservative stakeholders may prefer low-risk, incremental project approaches.

External EEFs

External EEFs are factors outside the organization that can impact the project. These factors are often beyond the control of the project team.

Examples of External EEFs:

1. **Market Conditions:**
   - Economic conditions, market trends, and competition.
   - *Example*: A downturn in the economy might lead to budget cuts and resource constraints for a project.

2. **Social and Cultural Influences:**
   - Demographics, social trends, and cultural norms.
   - *Example*: A global project must consider cultural differences in communication styles and work ethics.

3. **Legal and Regulatory Environment:**
   - Laws, regulations, and standards that the project must comply with.
   - *Example*: A construction project must adhere to local building codes and safety regulations.

4. **Technological Advances**:
    - Innovations and technological changes that can impact project tools and processes.
    - *Example*: A project utilizing outdated technology might face challenges in integration with new systems.
5. **Environmental Factors**:
    - Environmental and ecological considerations that affect project planning and execution.
    - *Example*: Projects in regions prone to natural disasters must include robust risk management plans.
6. **Political Climate**:
    - Political stability, policies, and government actions.
    - *Example*: Political instability in a project location can pose significant risks to project timelines and security.

Identifying, Assessing, and Responding to EEFs
Identifying EEFs
1. **Stakeholder Analysis**:
    - Identify all stakeholders and their influence on the project. Engage them to gather insights on potential EEFs.
    - *Example*: Interviews and surveys with stakeholders can reveal internal processes or market conditions affecting the project.
2. **Environmental Scanning**:
    - Regularly monitor the external environment to identify potential factors.
    - *Example*: Analyzing industry reports, market trends, and legal updates to stay informed about external EEFs.
3. **SWOT Analysis**:
    - Assess strengths, weaknesses, opportunities, and threats related to the project environment.
    - *Example*: Conducting a SWOT analysis can help identify internal strengths like skilled resources and external threats like new regulations.

Assessing EEFs
1. **Impact Analysis**:
    - Determine the potential impact of each EEF on the project's objectives.
    - *Example*: Assessing how changes in market conditions might affect project funding or timelines.
2. **Risk Assessment**:
    - Evaluate the likelihood and severity of EEFs impacting the project. Use risk matrices or other tools.
    - *Example*: Identifying the probability of regulatory changes and their potential impact on project scope and cost.

Responding to EEFs
1. **Adaptation and Flexibility**:
    - Develop flexible plans that can accommodate changes in EEFs.
    - *Example*: Creating a flexible schedule that allows for adjustments based on market fluctuations or technological changes.
2. **Mitigation Strategies**:
    - Develop strategies to mitigate negative impacts of EEFs.
    - *Example*: Diversifying suppliers to mitigate risks related to supply chain disruptions.
3. **Contingency Planning**:
    - Establish contingency plans for high-impact EEFs.
    - *Example*: Having a backup plan for potential delays due to legal approvals.
4. **Stakeholder Engagement**:
    - Maintain open communication with stakeholders to manage expectations and gain support in addressing EEFs.
    - *Example*: Regular stakeholder meetings to discuss market trends and adapt project plans accordingly.
5. **Leveraging Positive EEFs**:

- o Identify and capitalize on EEFs that can positively influence the project.
- o *Example*: Utilizing advanced PMIS available within the organization to improve project management efficiency.

By effectively identifying, assessing, and responding to EEFs, project managers can navigate the complexities of the project environment and steer their projects towards success. This proactive approach helps in mitigating risks, leveraging opportunities, and ensuring that project objectives are met despite the external and internal influences.

Organizational Process Assets (OPAs) are critical components in project management. They include any assets—internal to an organization—that influence the success of a project. These assets can be policies, procedures, templates, historical information, and lessons learned. OPAs are essential as they provide a foundation of established practices and documented knowledge that can enhance project efficiency and effectiveness.

Importance of OPAs in Project Management

1. **Standardization:** OPAs provide standardized guidelines and procedures, ensuring consistency across projects. This standardization helps in maintaining quality and predictability.
2. **Efficiency:** By utilizing established templates, procedures, and tools, project teams can save time and effort, leading to more efficient project execution.
3. **Knowledge Management:** OPAs contain historical information and lessons learned from previous projects, which can help project managers avoid past mistakes and replicate successes.
4. **Compliance:** OPAs ensure that projects comply with organizational policies and regulatory requirements, minimizing risks and legal issues.
5. **Continuous Improvement:** By systematically documenting and updating OPAs, organizations can foster a culture of continuous improvement, adapting to changes and enhancing their project management capabilities over time.

Common Examples of OPAs

1. Policies

Definition: Formal guidelines that dictate the standards and rules within an organization. **Examples:**

- **Quality Policies:** Standards for maintaining quality across projects.
- **Risk Management Policies:** Guidelines for identifying and mitigating risks.
- **Human Resources Policies:** Procedures for hiring, training, and managing project teams. **Use in Projects:** Policies ensure that project teams adhere to organizational standards, reducing the likelihood of deviations and ensuring uniformity.

2. Procedures

Definition: Step-by-step instructions on how to perform specific tasks or processes. **Examples:**

- **Project Initiation Procedures:** Steps for defining project scope and objectives.
- **Change Management Procedures:** Process for handling project changes and approvals.
- **Communication Procedures:** Guidelines for internal and external communication. **Use in Projects:** Procedures provide clear instructions, reducing ambiguity and ensuring that tasks are performed consistently and correctly.

3. Templates

Definition: Pre-designed documents that provide a structured format for project-related documents. **Examples:**

- **Project Charter Template:** Standardized format for documenting project initiation.
- **Risk Register Template:** Format for recording and tracking project risks.
- **Status Report Template:** Standard format for reporting project progress. **Use in Projects:** Templates save time and ensure that all necessary information is included in project documents, enhancing consistency and completeness.

4. Historical Information and Lessons Learned

Definition: Documentation of past project experiences, including successes, failures, and insights. **Examples:**

- **Post-Project Reviews:** Reports analyzing the outcomes of completed projects.
- **Lessons Learned Database:** Repository of lessons from previous projects.

- **Historical Metrics:** Data on past project performance, such as timelines and budgets. **Use in Projects:** Historical information and lessons learned provide valuable insights that can guide decision-making, help avoid past mistakes, and leverage proven strategies.

Leveraging OPAs to Improve Project Efficiency and Effectiveness
1. **Using Templates and Procedures:**
    - **Example:** A project manager at a software development firm uses a standardized risk register template provided by the PMO. This template ensures that all potential risks are identified, assessed, and documented consistently. The accompanying risk management procedures guide the team on how to respond to identified risks, improving the overall risk management process.
2. **Implementing Policies:**
    - **Example:** In a construction company, strict quality policies are in place to ensure that all building projects meet regulatory standards. The project team follows these policies rigorously, using quality checklists and procedures to conduct regular inspections. This adherence to quality policies helps prevent defects and ensures the final deliverable meets client expectations.
3. **Applying Lessons Learned:**
    - **Example:** An IT services company maintains a lessons learned database that is reviewed at the start of every new project. By analyzing past projects, the project manager identifies common pitfalls, such as scope creep and communication breakdowns. The team then implements strategies to address these issues upfront, such as defining clearer scope statements and establishing robust communication plans, leading to smoother project execution.
4. **Referencing Historical Information:**
    - **Example:** A marketing agency uses historical metrics from previous campaigns to set realistic timelines and budgets for new projects. By comparing past performance data, the project manager can make informed decisions on resource allocation and scheduling, leading to more accurate planning and efficient project execution.

Organizational Process Assets are invaluable resources in project management. By leveraging policies, procedures, templates, historical information, and lessons learned, project managers can enhance consistency, efficiency, and effectiveness in their projects. These assets not only provide a foundation of best practices and knowledge but also enable continuous improvement and adaptation to changing project environments.

Identifying and Analyzing Project Stakeholders
The process of identifying and analyzing project stakeholders is crucial for the success of any project. Stakeholders can significantly impact the project, and understanding their needs, expectations, and influence helps in effective stakeholder management. Let's explore some key techniques for stakeholder identification and analysis: stakeholder mapping, power/interest grids, and salience models.

1. Identifying Stakeholders
Steps to Identify Stakeholders:
1. **Initiate the Process:** Start early in the project initiation phase. Gather a team that understands the project's scope and objectives.
2. **Review Project Documentation:** Examine project charters, contracts, and business cases to identify stakeholders already mentioned.
3. **Brainstorming Sessions:** Conduct sessions with the project team to list potential stakeholders.
4. **Interviews and Surveys:** Engage with key team members and stakeholders to uncover others who may be affected by the project.
5. **Stakeholder Registers and Organizational Charts:** Review existing registers and charts to identify stakeholders within and outside the organization.
6. **External Sources:** Consider regulatory bodies, suppliers, customers, and other external entities that might influence or be influenced by the project.

Deliverable:
- **Stakeholder Register:** A comprehensive document listing all identified stakeholders, their roles, interests, and contact information.

2. Analyzing Stakeholders

Once stakeholders are identified, the next step is to analyze their influence and interest in the project. This analysis helps prioritize stakeholders and develop appropriate engagement strategies.

Stakeholder Mapping

Definition: Stakeholder mapping visually represents the relationships between stakeholders and the project, highlighting their influence and interest levels.

Steps to Apply Stakeholder Mapping:
1. **List Stakeholders**: Use the stakeholder register to list all stakeholders.
2. **Determine Influence and Interest Levels**: Assess each stakeholder's power (influence) and interest in the project. This can be done through interviews, surveys, and team discussions.
3. **Create the Map**: Draw a matrix with influence on one axis and interest on the other. Place each stakeholder on the map based on their assessed levels.
   - High Influence/High Interest: Key players who need to be fully engaged.
   - High Influence/Low Interest: Keep satisfied with high-level updates.
   - Low Influence/High Interest: Keep informed with detailed updates.
   - Low Influence/Low Interest: Monitor with minimal engagement.

Real-World Scenario:
- **Example**: In a city infrastructure project, stakeholders such as city officials (high influence/high interest), local businesses (high influence/low interest), residents (low influence/high interest), and the general public (low influence/low interest) are mapped to develop targeted engagement strategies.

Power/Interest Grids

Definition: The power/interest grid categorizes stakeholders based on their level of power and interest in the project, helping prioritize stakeholder management efforts.

Steps to Apply Power/Interest Grids:
1. **List Stakeholders**: Start with the stakeholder register.
2. **Assess Power and Interest**: Evaluate each stakeholder's power to influence the project and their level of interest in project outcomes.
3. **Plot Stakeholders on the Grid**: Create a 2x2 grid with power on one axis and interest on the other. Place each stakeholder in one of the four quadrants.
   - High Power/High Interest: Manage closely and actively engage.
   - High Power/Low Interest: Keep satisfied with sufficient information.
   - Low Power/High Interest: Keep informed with regular updates.
   - Low Power/Low Interest: Monitor with less intensive communication.

Real-World Scenario:
- **Example**: For a new product launch, top executives (high power/high interest), regulatory bodies (high power/low interest), project team members (low power/high interest), and external contractors (low power/low interest) are plotted on the grid to guide engagement efforts.

Salience Model

Definition: The salience model classifies stakeholders based on their power, legitimacy, and urgency, helping identify who requires the most attention.

Steps to Apply the Salience Model:
1. **Identify Attributes**:
   - **Power**: The ability of the stakeholder to influence the project.
   - **Legitimacy**: The stakeholder's involvement and appropriateness in the project.
   - **Urgency**: The stakeholder's need for immediate attention.
2. **Classify Stakeholders**: Determine which stakeholders possess one, two, or all three attributes.
3. **Plot on Venn Diagram**: Use a Venn diagram to visualize stakeholders based on their attributes.
   - **Definitive Stakeholders**: Have all three attributes; these are the highest priority.
   - **Dominant Stakeholders**: Have power and legitimacy.
   - **Dangerous Stakeholders**: Have power and urgency.
   - **Dependent Stakeholders**: Have legitimacy and urgency.
   - **Dormant Stakeholders**: Have power but low legitimacy and urgency.
   - **Discretionary Stakeholders**: Have legitimacy but low power and urgency.

- **Demanding Stakeholders**: Have urgency but low power and legitimacy.

Real-World Scenario:
- **Example**: In an environmental project, the government regulatory agency (definitive stakeholder), local environmental groups (dependent stakeholders), powerful lobbyists (dangerous stakeholders), and the general public (discretionary stakeholders) are classified to prioritize stakeholder management.

Applying Stakeholder Analysis Techniques

Step-by-Step Instructions:

1. **Initiate Stakeholder Identification and Analysis**:
   - Form a project team and review project documents.
   - Conduct brainstorming sessions, interviews, and surveys to identify stakeholders.
   - Create a stakeholder register listing all identified stakeholders.
2. **Determine Stakeholder Attributes**:
   - Assess each stakeholder's influence, interest, power, legitimacy, and urgency through discussions and data gathering.
3. **Apply Analysis Techniques**:
   - **Stakeholder Mapping**: Create a visual map plotting stakeholders based on their influence and interest.
   - **Power/Interest Grid**: Plot stakeholders on a 2x2 grid to categorize them by power and interest levels.
   - **Salience Model**: Use a Venn diagram to classify stakeholders based on power, legitimacy, and urgency.
4. **Develop Engagement Strategies**:
   - Based on the analysis, create targeted communication and engagement plans for each stakeholder category.
   - For high influence/high interest stakeholders, ensure active and regular engagement.
   - For low influence/low interest stakeholders, maintain minimal engagement but keep them informed as needed.
5. **Implement and Monitor**:
   - Execute the stakeholder engagement plan and continuously monitor stakeholder needs and expectations.
   - Adjust strategies as necessary based on stakeholder feedback and changes in project dynamics.

By effectively identifying and analyzing stakeholders using these techniques, project managers can tailor their engagement strategies to address the needs and influence of each stakeholder, thereby enhancing project success and stakeholder satisfaction.

Effective stakeholder engagement is crucial for the success of any project. Different stakeholders have varying interests, influence, and needs, so it's important to tailor engagement strategies accordingly. Here's a detailed look at various stakeholder engagement strategies, their applications, and best practices for managing stakeholder expectations and resolving conflicts.

Stakeholder Engagement Strategies

1. Stakeholder Identification and Analysis
Strategy: Identify all stakeholders and analyze their interests, influence, and potential impact on the project.
Application: Use tools like the Stakeholder Register and Power/Interest Grid to categorize stakeholders based on their level of influence and interest. **Example:** A software development project may have stakeholders like users, sponsors, developers, and regulatory bodies. Identifying these groups helps in tailoring communication and engagement.

2. Communication Planning
Strategy: Develop a communication plan that outlines how, when, and what information will be shared with stakeholders. **Application:** Use a Communication Matrix to detail communication methods, frequency, and responsible parties. **Example:** For a construction project, regular updates might be needed for local authorities, while detailed technical reports are shared with engineers and architects.

3. Engagement Through Collaboration

Strategy: Involve stakeholders in project activities and decision-making processes. **Application:** Establish working groups or committees where key stakeholders can contribute to planning and execution. **Example:** In a community development project, forming advisory boards with community leaders ensures their input and buy-in.

4. Consultation
Strategy: Seek stakeholder input and feedback to incorporate their views and address concerns. **Application:** Conduct surveys, focus groups, or public consultations to gather insights. **Example:** An environmental impact assessment might involve public consultations to understand the concerns of residents and environmental groups.

5. Informing
Strategy: Keep stakeholders informed about project progress, changes, and decisions. **Application:** Use newsletters, emails, meetings, and dashboards to disseminate information. **Example:** A pharmaceutical company might send quarterly updates to regulatory agencies and shareholders about the progress of a new drug development.

6. Negotiation and Conflict Management
Strategy: Address and resolve conflicts through negotiation and mediation. **Application:** Use conflict resolution techniques to find mutually acceptable solutions. **Example:** In a large IT project, conflicts between departments over resource allocation can be resolved through facilitated negotiation sessions.

7. Empowerment
Strategy: Give stakeholders the authority to make decisions and take actions related to the project. **Application:** Delegate decision-making power to certain stakeholders, such as team leaders or user representatives. **Example:** In a healthcare project, empowering medical staff to make decisions about clinical protocols ensures that their expertise shapes the project outcomes.

Importance of Tailoring Communication and Engagement

Tailoring communication and engagement approaches to different stakeholder groups ensures that their specific needs and concerns are addressed, enhancing project buy-in and support. Here's why it's important:

- **Relevance:** Providing stakeholders with relevant information increases their understanding and interest in the project.
- **Clarity:** Clear and tailored communication helps avoid misunderstandings and misinterpretations.
- **Trust:** Personalized engagement builds trust and fosters stronger relationships with stakeholders.
- **Responsiveness:** Tailored approaches enable timely responses to stakeholder concerns and feedback, improving satisfaction.

Best Practices for Managing Stakeholder Expectations and Resolving Conflicts

1. Set Clear Expectations
- **Define Objectives:** Clearly outline project goals, scope, timelines, and deliverables from the start.
- **Document Agreements:** Use project charters, contracts, and memorandums of understanding (MOUs) to document stakeholder agreements and expectations.

2. Regular Updates and Transparency
- **Frequent Communication:** Maintain regular communication through status reports, meetings, and updates.
- **Transparency:** Be open about project progress, challenges, and changes to build trust and manage expectations.

3. Active Listening
- **Solicit Feedback:** Actively seek and consider stakeholder feedback through surveys, meetings, and feedback forms.
- **Respond to Concerns:** Address stakeholder concerns promptly and effectively to show that their input is valued.

4. Conflict Resolution Techniques
- **Identify Sources of Conflict:** Understand the root causes of conflicts, whether they are related to resources, priorities, or misunderstandings.
- **Use Mediation:** Engage neutral third parties to facilitate discussions and help find common ground.
- **Negotiation:** Employ negotiation techniques to reach agreements that satisfy all parties involved.

5. Flexibility and Adaptability

- **Adjust Plans:** Be willing to adjust project plans and strategies in response to stakeholder feedback and changing circumstances.
- **Manage Change:** Implement a structured change management process to handle changes smoothly and keep stakeholders informed.

6. Build Relationships
- **Personal Engagement:** Develop personal relationships with key stakeholders to better understand their perspectives and needs.
- **Trust and Respect:** Foster an environment of mutual trust and respect, which can help in resolving conflicts and managing expectations.

Examples of Successful Stakeholder Engagement
1. **Construction Industry:** In large infrastructure projects, companies like Skanska engage local communities through town hall meetings and public consultations to address concerns and incorporate community input, thereby gaining public support and minimizing opposition.
2. **Technology Sector:** Google often involves user groups in the beta testing of new products, gathering valuable feedback to refine their offerings and ensuring that the final product meets user needs.
3. **Healthcare:** In implementing electronic health records (EHR) systems, hospitals engage medical staff through training sessions, feedback loops, and pilot programs, ensuring that the systems meet clinical requirements and gain user acceptance.

Effective stakeholder engagement strategies, tailored communication, and proactive conflict resolution are essential for successful project management. By understanding and addressing the unique needs and concerns of different stakeholder groups, project managers can build strong relationships, enhance project support, and achieve better project outcomes.

Predictive, Plan-Based Methodologies

Key Activities in the Plan Scope Management Process

The Plan Scope Management process is critical for defining how the project scope will be defined, validated, and controlled. This process ensures that all stakeholders have a clear understanding of the project's scope and how it will be managed throughout the project life cycle. The key activities involved in this process include creating a Scope Management Plan and a Requirements Management Plan. These plans serve as essential guides for the project team in managing the project's scope.

1. Creating the Scope Management Plan

Purpose: The Scope Management Plan outlines how the project scope will be defined, developed, monitored, controlled, and verified. It provides a structured approach for managing scope throughout the project life cycle.

Key Activities:

1. **Define Scope Management Approach**:
    - Determine the processes and procedures for scope management.
    - Identify the tools and techniques to be used for defining, validating, and controlling the scope.
    - Example: Deciding to use a Work Breakdown Structure (WBS) for detailed scope definition.
2. **Document Scope Statement**:
    - Develop a high-level description of the project scope, including major deliverables, assumptions, and constraints.
    - Example: Outlining the key features of a new software application, such as user authentication, data storage, and user interface design.
3. **Establish Roles and Responsibilities**:
    - Define who will be responsible for scope management activities, including scope definition, validation, and control.
    - Example: Assigning a project manager to lead scope management efforts and a business analyst to gather and document requirements.
4. **Outline Scope Verification Process**:
    - Specify how the project deliverables will be verified and accepted.
    - Example: Establishing criteria for stakeholder approval and acceptance of deliverables, such as user acceptance testing (UAT) for software features.
5. **Develop Scope Control Mechanisms**:
    - Define how changes to the project scope will be identified, documented, and approved.
    - Example: Implementing a change control board (CCB) to review and approve scope changes.

Deliverable:

- **Scope Management Plan**: A document that outlines the approach, processes, roles, and tools for managing project scope.

2. Creating the Requirements Management Plan

Purpose: The Requirements Management Plan describes how project requirements will be identified, documented, managed, and tracked throughout the project life cycle. It ensures that the project deliverables meet stakeholder needs and expectations.

Key Activities:

1. **Define Requirements Collection Process**:
    - Specify the methods for gathering requirements from stakeholders.
    - Example: Using interviews, surveys, workshops, and focus groups to collect requirements.
2. **Document Requirements Prioritization Criteria**:
    - Establish criteria for prioritizing requirements based on factors such as stakeholder importance, feasibility, and impact.
    - Example: Prioritizing requirements based on their alignment with strategic goals and technical feasibility.
3. **Establish Requirements Traceability Matrix (RTM)**:
    - Develop a matrix to track requirements throughout the project life cycle, ensuring they are addressed in the final deliverables.

- Example: Creating an RTM that links each requirement to its corresponding design, development, and testing phases.
4. **Define Requirements Documentation Format**:
    - Specify the format and structure for documenting requirements, ensuring consistency and clarity.
    - Example: Using a standard template for requirements documentation that includes requirement ID, description, priority, and acceptance criteria.
5. **Outline Requirements Validation Process**:
    - Describe how requirements will be validated and verified with stakeholders.
    - Example: Conducting requirements validation sessions with stakeholders to ensure all requirements are accurately captured and agreed upon.

Deliverable:
- **Requirements Management Plan**: A document that details the approach, processes, and tools for managing project requirements.

How These Plans Guide the Project Team

1. Defining Project Scope:
- **Scope Management Plan**: Provides a clear framework for defining the project scope, including the use of tools like the WBS and techniques for scope definition. This ensures that the project scope is well-defined and understood by all stakeholders from the outset.
- **Requirements Management Plan**: Guides the team in gathering, documenting, and prioritizing requirements. This helps in creating a detailed project scope that aligns with stakeholder needs and expectations.

2. Controlling Project Scope:
- **Scope Management Plan**: Establishes processes for monitoring and controlling the project scope, including change control mechanisms. This helps the project team manage scope changes effectively and prevent scope creep.
- **Requirements Management Plan**: Provides a traceability matrix to track requirements throughout the project. This ensures that any changes to requirements are documented and managed, maintaining the integrity of the project scope.

3. Validating Project Scope:
- **Scope Management Plan**: Outlines the scope verification process, ensuring that deliverables are reviewed and accepted by stakeholders. This helps in achieving formal acceptance of project deliverables.
- **Requirements Management Plan**: Describes the requirements validation process, ensuring that the project deliverables meet the documented requirements and stakeholder expectations.

Real-World Example: Implementing a New Customer Relationship Management (CRM) System

1. **Scope Management Plan**:
    - **Scope Definition**: The project involves implementing a new CRM system with key features such as customer data management, sales tracking, and reporting.
    - **Roles and Responsibilities**: The project manager is responsible for scope management, while the IT team handles technical aspects and a business analyst gathers requirements.
    - **Scope Verification**: The CRM system will be tested and approved through UAT sessions with sales and customer service teams.
    - **Scope Control**: Any changes to the CRM system features will be reviewed by a CCB comprising project sponsors, IT leaders, and business stakeholders.
2. **Requirements Management Plan**:
    - **Requirements Collection**: Requirements are gathered through workshops with sales and customer service teams to understand their needs and challenges.
    - **Requirements Prioritization**: Features that directly impact customer interactions and sales efficiency are prioritized.
    - **Traceability Matrix**: An RTM is created to ensure all requirements are linked to design, development, and testing phases.

- **Requirements Documentation**: Requirements are documented in a standard format, including descriptions, priorities, and acceptance criteria.
- **Requirements Validation**: Validation sessions are held with stakeholders to confirm that all requirements are accurately captured and agreed upon.

By following the Scope Management Plan and Requirements Management Plan, the project team can effectively manage the CRM implementation project, ensuring that the scope is clearly defined, controlled, and validated, and that the final deliverables meet stakeholder needs and expectations.

Gathering requirements is a crucial step in project management, ensuring that stakeholders' needs are accurately captured and translated into project deliverables. Various techniques can be employed, each with its own set of procedures and best practices. Here, we'll discuss interviews, focus groups, workshops, and prototypes, providing step-by-step instructions on how to conduct each effectively. Additionally, we'll cover best practices for documenting and validating requirements using tools like a Requirements Traceability Matrix.

1. Interviews

Interviews involve direct conversations with stakeholders to gather detailed information about their needs and expectations.

Step-by-Step Instructions:
1. **Preparation:**
   - Identify stakeholders who will be interviewed.
   - Develop a list of open-ended questions to guide the conversation.
   - Schedule the interviews at convenient times for stakeholders.
2. **Conducting the Interview:**
   - Begin with introductions and explain the purpose of the interview.
   - Ask questions and allow stakeholders to elaborate on their answers.
   - Probe deeper into key areas to gain a comprehensive understanding.
   - Take detailed notes or record the conversation (with permission).
3. **Post-Interview:**
   - Summarize the key points and insights gathered.
   - Validate the summary with the interviewee to ensure accuracy.
   - Document the requirements in a structured format.

Best Practices:
- Build rapport with stakeholders to encourage open communication.
- Listen actively and avoid leading questions.
- Follow up with additional questions if needed to clarify requirements.

2. Focus Groups

Focus Groups involve gathering a small group of stakeholders to discuss their needs and expectations in a collaborative setting.

Step-by-Step Instructions:
1. **Preparation:**
   - Identify and invite a diverse group of stakeholders.
   - Prepare a set of topics and questions to guide the discussion.
   - Arrange a suitable venue and time for the session.
2. **Conducting the Focus Group:**
   - Start with introductions and an overview of the session's objectives.
   - Facilitate the discussion, ensuring all participants have the opportunity to speak.
   - Use prompts and follow-up questions to delve deeper into key topics.
   - Record the session or take detailed notes.
3. **Post-Session:**
   - Analyze the discussion to identify common themes and requirements.
   - Summarize the findings and validate them with the participants.
   - Document the requirements clearly and concisely.

Best Practices:

- Encourage participation from all group members.
- Manage dominant personalities to ensure balanced input.
- Use a neutral facilitator to guide the discussion and avoid bias.

3. Workshops

Workshops are intensive collaborative sessions where stakeholders work together to define requirements.

Step-by-Step Instructions:
1. **Preparation:**
    - Identify key stakeholders and invite them to the workshop.
    - Develop an agenda and set clear objectives for the session.
    - Prepare materials such as whiteboards, flip charts, and markers.
2. **Conducting the Workshop:**
    - Begin with a brief introduction and outline the session's goals.
    - Facilitate activities and discussions to gather requirements.
    - Use techniques like brainstorming, mind mapping, and role-playing to elicit ideas.
    - Document requirements in real-time using visual aids.
3. **Post-Workshop:**
    - Review the documented requirements with participants.
    - Refine and validate the requirements based on feedback.
    - Finalize and distribute the documented requirements to all stakeholders.

Best Practices:
- Set ground rules to ensure a productive and respectful environment.
- Keep the session focused and on track with a structured agenda.
- Use visual aids to enhance understanding and collaboration.

4. Prototypes

Prototypes are early models or simulations of the final product used to gather feedback on requirements.

Step-by-Step Instructions:
1. **Preparation:**
    - Develop an initial prototype based on preliminary requirements.
    - Identify stakeholders who will review and provide feedback.
2. **Conducting the Review:**
    - Present the prototype to stakeholders, explaining its features and functionality.
    - Gather feedback on what works well and what needs improvement.
    - Ask specific questions to clarify stakeholder preferences and expectations.
3. **Post-Review:**
    - Analyze the feedback and make necessary adjustments to the prototype.
    - Validate the updated prototype with stakeholders to ensure alignment with their needs.
    - Document the refined requirements based on the validated prototype.

Best Practices:
- Involve stakeholders early and often in the prototyping process.
- Iterate on the prototype based on continuous feedback.
- Use prototypes to uncover hidden requirements and clarify ambiguous ones.

Documenting and Validating Requirements

Requirements Traceability Matrix (RTM): The RTM is a tool used to ensure that all requirements are captured, tracked, and validated throughout the project lifecycle.

Creating an RTM:
1. **Identify Requirements:** List all requirements gathered from various techniques.
2. **Link Requirements to Objectives:** Map each requirement to specific project objectives or deliverables.
3. **Assign Unique IDs:** Give each requirement a unique identifier for easy tracking.
4. **Document Changes:** Record any changes to requirements and their impact on the project.
5. **Track Validation:** Ensure each requirement is validated through stakeholder reviews, testing, or prototypes.

Best Practices for RTM:

- Update the RTM regularly to reflect changes in requirements.
- Use the RTM to facilitate communication and transparency with stakeholders.
- Review the RTM during project milestones to ensure all requirements are being met.

Example of an RTM

Requirement ID	Requirement Description	Source	Objective Linked	Validation Method	Status
R001	User login functionality	Stakeholder A	User Authentication	Prototype review	Validated
R002	Data encryption	Compliance Team	Data Security	Testing	In Progress
R003	Multi-language support	Market Research	User Experience	Focus group feedback	Validated
R004	Reporting dashboard	Manager B	Data Analysis	Workshop review	Pending

Effective requirements gathering is fundamental to project success. By using interviews, focus groups, workshops, and prototypes, project managers can comprehensively capture stakeholder needs. Documenting and validating these requirements using tools like the Requirements Traceability Matrix ensures that all project goals are met and stakeholder expectations are managed.

Defining the Project Scope and Creating a Work Breakdown Structure (WBS)

The process of defining the project scope and creating a detailed Work Breakdown Structure (WBS) is essential for the successful planning and execution of a project. This process ensures that all project deliverables are clearly defined and broken down into manageable components, facilitating better control and oversight.

Defining the Project Scope

Steps to Define Project Scope:

1. **Develop a Project Scope Statement**:
   - **Purpose**: The project scope statement provides a detailed description of the project and its deliverables. It includes the project objectives, deliverables, boundaries, assumptions, and constraints.
   - **Example**: For a software development project, the scope statement might include objectives like "Develop a user-friendly mobile application," major deliverables such as "User interface design, back-end development, and testing," and boundaries like "The project will not include developing a desktop version."

2. **Identify Project Objectives**:
   - Define clear, measurable objectives that the project aims to achieve.
   - Example: "Increase user engagement by 20% within the first six months of app launch."

3. **Define Deliverables**:
   - Identify the tangible or intangible products or services that the project will produce.
   - Example: "A fully functional mobile app with user authentication, data storage, and reporting features."

4. **Set Project Boundaries**:
   - Clarify what is included and what is not included in the project scope to avoid scope creep.
   - Example: "The project will not cover marketing activities or user training."

5. **Document Assumptions and Constraints**:
   - Record any assumptions made during scope planning and any constraints that limit project options.
   - Example: "Assume availability of skilled developers; constrained by a budget of $200,000."

6. **Define Acceptance Criteria**:
   - Establish the conditions that must be met for project deliverables to be accepted by stakeholders.
   - Example: "The mobile app must pass user acceptance testing with no critical bugs."

Deliverable:
- **Project Scope Statement**: A comprehensive document outlining the project scope, deliverables, boundaries, assumptions, constraints, and acceptance criteria.

Creating a Work Breakdown Structure (WBS)

Steps to Create a WBS:

1. **Identify Major Deliverables**:
   - Break down the project scope into major deliverables or components.
   - Example: For a mobile app project, major deliverables might include "User Interface (UI) Design," "Backend Development," and "Testing."
2. **Decompose Deliverables into Smaller Components**:
   - Further break down each major deliverable into smaller, more manageable components called work packages.
   - Example: "User Interface Design" might be decomposed into "Wireframes," "Mockups," and "Prototype."
3. **Develop the WBS Structure**:
   - Create a hierarchical tree structure that visualizes the breakdown of deliverables.
   - Example: A hierarchical chart with levels showing the project, major deliverables, sub-deliverables, and work packages.
4. **Create the WBS Dictionary**:
   - Develop a detailed WBS Dictionary that provides descriptions of each work package, including scope, deliverables, responsible parties, and acceptance criteria.
   - Example: For the work package "Mockups," the WBS Dictionary entry might include:
     - *Description*: Create detailed visual representations of the app's UI.
     - *Deliverables*: High-fidelity mockups for all app screens.
     - *Responsible Party*: UI Designer.
     - *Acceptance Criteria*: Mockups reviewed and approved by the project manager and key stakeholders.

Example of Decomposing Project Deliverables:
- **Project**: Develop a Mobile Application
  - **1.0 User Interface Design**
    - 1.1 Wireframes
    - 1.2 Mockups
    - 1.3 Prototype
  - **2.0 Backend Development**
    - 2.1 Database Design
    - 2.2 API Development
    - 2.3 Integration
  - **3.0 Testing**
    - 3.1 Unit Testing
    - 3.2 Integration Testing
    - 3.3 User Acceptance Testing (UAT)

WBS Dictionary Entry Example:
- **Work Package**: 1.2 Mockups
  - *Description*: Create detailed visual representations of the app's user interface.
  - *Deliverables*: High-fidelity mockups for all app screens.
  - *Responsible Party*: UI Designer.
  - *Start Date*: [Insert Date]
  - *End Date*: [Insert Date]
  - *Acceptance Criteria*: Mockups reviewed and approved by the project manager and key stakeholders.

Importance of Establishing Clear Acceptance Criteria
Why Clear Acceptance Criteria Matter:
1. **Ensures Quality and Satisfaction**:
   - Clear acceptance criteria help ensure that deliverables meet the required quality standards and stakeholder expectations.

- Example: Acceptance criteria for the "Mockups" work package ensure that the visual design aligns with the project's branding guidelines and stakeholder preferences.
2. **Provides Clear Guidelines**:
    - They provide the project team with clear guidelines on what needs to be achieved for deliverables to be accepted.
    - Example: The criteria for "API Development" might include successful integration with the database and passing performance tests.
3. **Facilitates Validation and Verification**:
    - Acceptance criteria make it easier to validate and verify deliverables, ensuring they meet the project's requirements.
    - Example: UAT criteria ensure that the app's functionalities work as intended and provide a good user experience.
4. **Reduces Ambiguity**:
    - Clear criteria reduce ambiguity and misunderstandings about what constitutes a completed deliverable.
    - Example: For "User Interface Design," criteria might specify that mockups should be created using specific design software and include annotations for developer handoff.
5. **Streamlines Approval Processes**:
    - They streamline the approval process by providing a predefined set of conditions that must be met.
    - Example: Once the mockups meet the acceptance criteria, they can be quickly approved by the project manager and stakeholders without further debate.

By defining the project scope and creating a detailed WBS with clear acceptance criteria, project managers can ensure that all team members understand their responsibilities and deliverables. This structured approach helps in managing the project's scope effectively, preventing scope creep, and ensuring that the final deliverables meet stakeholder expectations.

Validating and controlling the project scope are critical processes in project management that ensure the project delivers what was agreed upon without unnecessary changes or additions. Proper scope validation and control help prevent scope creep, which can lead to project delays, cost overruns, and stakeholder dissatisfaction. Let's dive into these processes and the techniques used to manage them effectively.

Validating the Project Scope

Validating the project scope involves formalizing the acceptance of the completed project deliverables. This process ensures that the deliverables meet the agreed-upon requirements and that stakeholders formally accept them.

Steps in Validating Scope:
1. **Review Deliverables:** Assess the completed work against the project scope and requirements.
2. **Inspection:** Conduct a thorough examination of the deliverables to ensure they meet the criteria specified in the scope statement.
3. **Formal Acceptance:** Obtain formal sign-off from stakeholders or the project sponsor confirming that the deliverables meet their expectations and requirements.

Techniques for Validating Scope:
- **Inspection:** This technique involves a detailed review and examination of the project deliverables to ensure they meet the required standards and specifications. Inspections can include testing, measuring, and reviewing documentation.

Controlling the Project Scope

Controlling the project scope involves monitoring the status of the project and managing changes to the scope baseline. This process ensures that any changes are properly evaluated and approved before implementation, maintaining project integrity and alignment with objectives.

Steps in Controlling Scope:
1. **Measure Performance:** Compare the actual project performance against the scope baseline.
2. **Variance Analysis:** Identify any deviations from the scope baseline.

3. **Trend Analysis:** Examine project performance data over time to identify patterns or trends that may indicate potential issues.
4. **Implement Change Control:** Use a formal process to evaluate and approve or reject changes to the project scope.

Techniques for Controlling Scope:
- **Variance Analysis:** This technique involves comparing planned project outcomes with actual results to identify deviations. Variance analysis helps project managers understand the extent of deviations and their impact on project performance.

Example: If a construction project planned to complete a building foundation in 30 days but it took 40 days, variance analysis would help identify the causes and assess the impact on the overall project timeline and budget.

- **Trend Analysis:** This technique examines project performance data over time to identify trends that may indicate potential scope issues. Trend analysis helps in proactive scope management by identifying patterns early.

Example: In a software development project, trend analysis might reveal that the number of scope change requests is increasing steadily. This could indicate a need for better requirements gathering or stricter change control.

Managing Scope Changes

Effective management of scope changes is crucial to maintaining project control and delivering successful outcomes. The following tools and processes help manage scope changes effectively:

Change Control Processes:
1. **Change Request:** A formal request to alter the project scope, schedule, or budget. This document outlines the proposed change, its justification, and its potential impact.
2. **Impact Analysis:** Evaluating the potential effects of the proposed change on project objectives, deliverables, timeline, and budget.
3. **Change Control Board (CCB):** A group of stakeholders and project team members who review change requests and decide whether to approve or reject them.
4. **Documentation:** Keeping detailed records of all change requests, decisions, and actions taken to maintain an audit trail.

Tools for Managing Scope Changes:
- **Change Log:** A document that tracks all change requests, their status, and their outcomes. It helps in maintaining transparency and accountability.
- **Requirements Traceability Matrix (RTM):** A tool that helps track the relationship between requirements and deliverables, ensuring that all changes are properly evaluated and traced back to their source.

Real-World Examples

Example 1: Construction Project In a large infrastructure project, the client requested an additional feature—an underground parking lot—after the initial scope had been agreed upon. The project team used the change control process to:
- Submit a change request detailing the additional work, cost, and impact on the schedule.
- Conduct an impact analysis to assess how the change would affect the project's critical path and budget.
- Present the change request to the Change Control Board (CCB), which included senior management and client representatives.
- Upon approval, update the project plan, schedule, and budget to reflect the new scope.

Example 2: IT Project In a software development project, the marketing team requested a change in the user interface design after the initial design was completed. The project manager:
- Documented the change request and the reasons behind it.
- Conducted a variance analysis to compare the current scope with the proposed changes.
- Performed a trend analysis to assess the impact of similar changes on past projects.
- Presented the analysis to the CCB for review.
- The CCB approved the change, and the project plan was updated to include the new design requirements.

Best Practices for Documenting and Validating Requirements

1. **Detailed Documentation:** Clearly document all requirements, including their source, acceptance criteria, and any changes made.
2. **Regular Reviews:** Conduct regular reviews with stakeholders to validate requirements and ensure alignment with project objectives.
3. **Traceability:** Use a Requirements Traceability Matrix (RTM) to track requirements throughout the project lifecycle, ensuring all changes are accounted for and evaluated.
4. **Formal Sign-Off:** Obtain formal acceptance of requirements and changes from stakeholders to ensure agreement and commitment.

Example of a Change Log Entry

Change ID	Change Description	Requester	Impact Summary	Status	Decision Date	Approved By
001	Add underground parking lot	Client	Increased cost by $500,000; extends schedule by 2 months	Approved	2023-01-15	CCB
002	Update user interface design	Marketing	Requires 2 additional developers; impacts delivery date by 3 weeks	Approved	2023-02-20	CCB

By following these practices and utilizing the appropriate techniques and tools, project managers can effectively validate and control project scope, ensuring that projects stay on track and deliver the intended outcomes.

Key Activities in the Plan Schedule Management Process

The Plan Schedule Management process involves establishing the policies, procedures, and documentation for planning, developing, managing, executing, and controlling the project schedule. This process ensures that the project is completed within the defined time constraints. The main activities include defining activities, sequencing activities, estimating activity durations, and developing the project schedule. Let's delve into each of these key activities.

1. Defining Activities

Purpose: Defining activities involves identifying and documenting the specific actions required to produce the project deliverables.

Key Activities:
1. **Activity Identification**:
    - Break down work packages from the Work Breakdown Structure (WBS) into individual activities.
    - Example: In a software development project, activities might include coding, testing, and user training.
2. **Activity List**:
    - Create a comprehensive list of all project activities required to complete the project deliverables.
    - Example: An activity list for the "User Interface Design" work package might include creating wireframes, designing mockups, and conducting usability testing.
3. **Activity Attributes**:
    - Document additional details about each activity, such as duration, resource requirements, and assumptions.
    - Example: For the activity "Designing Mockups," attributes might include estimated duration of 5 days and the need for a graphic designer.
4. **Milestone List**:
    - Identify significant points or events in the project timeline that signify major progress or completion of phases.
    - Example: Milestones in a construction project might include "Foundation Completed" and "Building Structure Completed."

Deliverables:
- **Activity List**: A detailed list of all project activities.
- **Activity Attributes**: Documentation of activity details.
- **Milestone List**: A list of project milestones.

2. Sequencing Activities

Purpose: Sequencing activities involves identifying and documenting the logical relationships among project activities to determine the most efficient sequence of work.

Key Activities:
1. **Identify Dependencies**:
   - Determine the dependencies between activities, which can be finish-to-start, start-to-start, finish-to-finish, or start-to-finish.
   - Example: In a marketing campaign project, "Develop Content" must finish before "Review Content" can start (finish-to-start dependency).
2. **Create Network Diagrams**:
   - Use network diagrams to visually represent the sequence and dependencies of project activities.
   - Example: A precedence diagramming method (PDM) chart showing the sequence of activities in a software development project.
3. **Determine Leads and Lags**:
   - Identify opportunities to overlap activities (leads) or introduce delays (lags) between activities.
   - Example: In a construction project, installing windows (lag) can start 2 days after the exterior walls are completed.

Deliverables:
- **Project Schedule Network Diagrams**: Visual representation of activity sequences and dependencies.

3. Estimating Activity Durations

Purpose: Estimating activity durations involves approximating the number of work periods needed to complete individual activities, considering the resources required.

Key Activities:
1. **Expert Judgment**:
   - Leverage the expertise of team members and subject matter experts to estimate durations.
   - Example: Estimating the duration of software development tasks based on past experience.
2. **Analogous Estimating**:
   - Use historical data from similar projects to estimate activity durations.
   - Example: Estimating the duration of a marketing campaign based on a similar previous campaign.
3. **Parametric Estimating**:
   - Use statistical relationships between historical data and other variables to estimate durations.
   - Example: Estimating the time to code a software module based on the number of lines of code.
4. **Three-Point Estimating**:
   - Calculate average durations using optimistic, pessimistic, and most likely estimates.
   - Example: Estimating the duration of a task by considering best-case, worst-case, and most likely scenarios.
5. **Reserve Analysis**:
   - Determine contingency reserves to account for risks and uncertainties in duration estimates.
   - Example: Adding buffer time to account for potential delays in obtaining regulatory approvals.

Deliverables:
- **Activity Duration Estimates**: Estimated time required to complete each activity.
- **Basis of Estimates**: Documentation of the assumptions and methods used for estimating durations.

4. Developing the Project Schedule

Purpose: Developing the project schedule involves analyzing activity sequences, durations, resource requirements, and schedule constraints to create a detailed project timeline.

Key Activities:
1. **Schedule Network Analysis**:
   - Use techniques like the Critical Path Method (CPM) to identify the longest path of activities and determine the shortest project duration.
   - Example: Identifying critical tasks in a construction project that must be completed on time to avoid delays.
2. **Resource Leveling and Smoothing**:
   - Adjust the project schedule to address resource constraints and ensure resource availability.

- Example: Adjusting the schedule of a software development project to accommodate the availability of key developers.
3. **Schedule Compression**:
   - Apply techniques like crashing (adding resources) and fast-tracking (performing tasks in parallel) to shorten the project schedule without changing the project scope.
   - Example: Fast-tracking the design and development phases of a product launch project to meet a tight deadline.
4. **Develop Schedule Baseline**:
   - Establish the approved version of the project schedule that will be used to measure progress.
   - Example: Finalizing the project timeline for a construction project and getting stakeholder approval.
5. **Communication of Schedule**:
   - Share the final project schedule with stakeholders and the project team.
   - Example: Distributing the project schedule for a marketing campaign to all team members and stakeholders.

Deliverables:
- **Project Schedule**: A detailed timeline of all project activities.
- **Schedule Baseline**: The approved project schedule used for tracking progress.
- **Project Calendars**: Detailed work schedules for the project team.

Importance of Factors in Creating a Realistic and Achievable Schedule

1. Resource Availability:
- **Importance**: Ensuring that the necessary resources (personnel, equipment, materials) are available when needed is critical for maintaining the project schedule.
- **Impact**: Limited resource availability can cause delays and necessitate adjustments to the schedule.
- **Example**: In a construction project, delays in the delivery of materials can halt progress, requiring schedule adjustments.

2. Dependencies:
- **Importance**: Understanding the logical relationships between activities helps in sequencing them correctly and avoiding delays.
- **Impact**: Mismanaged dependencies can lead to bottlenecks and disruptions in the project flow.
- **Example**: In software development, coding must be completed before testing can begin. Incorrect sequencing can lead to idle times and delays.

3. Constraints:
- **Importance**: Identifying constraints such as deadlines, budget limits, and regulatory requirements helps in planning realistic schedules.
- **Impact**: Ignoring constraints can result in schedules that are unachievable, causing project overruns and stakeholder dissatisfaction.
- **Example**: A marketing campaign must be completed before a product launch event. Scheduling without considering this deadline can render the campaign ineffective.

4. Risk Factors:
- **Importance**: Anticipating potential risks and incorporating mitigation strategies into the schedule helps in maintaining project timelines.
- **Impact**: Unaddressed risks can cause unforeseen delays and require extensive rework.
- **Example**: Including contingency time for potential delays in regulatory approvals for a pharmaceutical project ensures the schedule remains realistic.

By considering these factors and following a structured approach to plan schedule management, project managers can develop realistic and achievable schedules that account for all necessary resources, dependencies, and constraints, thereby increasing the likelihood of project success.

The **Critical Path Method (CPM)** is a project management technique used for scheduling project activities. It identifies the sequence of crucial steps (critical path) that determine the minimum project duration. CPM helps project managers plan, schedule, and control project tasks, ensuring timely project completion.

Role of CPM in Project Scheduling
1. **Determining Project Duration:** CPM helps in identifying the longest path of dependent activities and thus the shortest possible project duration.
2. **Identifying Critical Activities:** It highlights tasks that cannot be delayed without affecting the overall project timeline.
3. **Resource Allocation:** Helps in efficient allocation of resources by identifying activities that need strict adherence to schedule.
4. **Project Monitoring:** Assists in tracking project progress and identifying potential delays early.
5. **Decision Making:** Facilitates informed decision-making by highlighting key project constraints and opportunities for schedule adjustments.

Step-by-Step Guide to Calculating the Critical Path

Step 1: List All Activities

Identify all activities required to complete the project. Each activity should have a unique identifier.

Step 2: Define Dependencies

Determine the dependencies between activities, indicating which activities must precede others.

Step 3: Estimate Activity Durations

Assign estimated durations to each activity.

Step 4: Draw the Network Diagram

Create a visual representation (network diagram) of the activities and their dependencies.

Step 5: Perform Forward Pass (Early Start and Finish)

Early Start (ES):
- For the starting activity, ES = 0.
- For subsequent activities, ES = Earliest possible time the activity can start (maximum EF of all predecessor activities).

Early Finish (EF):
- EF = ES + Duration.

Steps:
1. Begin with the initial activity. Set its ES to 0.
2. Calculate EF = ES + Duration.
3. Move to the next activities, setting their ES to the maximum EF of their predecessors.
4. Continue until all activities are processed.

Step 6: Perform Backward Pass (Late Start and Finish)

Late Finish (LF):
- For the final activity, LF = EF.
- For preceding activities, LF = Minimum LS of all successor activities.

Late Start (LS):
- LS = LF - Duration.

Steps:
1. Begin with the final activity. Set its LF to its EF.
2. Calculate LS = LF - Duration.
3. Move to the preceding activities, setting their LF to the minimum LS of their successors.
4. Continue until all activities are processed.

Step 7: Identify the Critical Path
- The critical path is the sequence of activities with zero float (the path where ES = LS and EF = LF).

Example

Consider a project with the following activities and durations:

Activity	Duration (days)	Predecessors
A	5	-
B	3	A
C	2	A
D	4	B, C
E	6	C

Step-by-Step Calculation:
Forward Pass:
1. Activity A: ES = 0, EF = 5 (0 + 5)
2. Activity B: ES = 5 (EF of A), EF = 8 (5 + 3)
3. Activity C: ES = 5 (EF of A), EF = 7 (5 + 2)
4. Activity D: ES = 8 (max EF of B and C), EF = 12 (8 + 4)
5. Activity E: ES = 7 (EF of C), EF = 13 (7 + 6)

Backward Pass:
1. Activity D: LF = 12, LS = 8 (12 - 4)
2. Activity E: LF = 13, LS = 7 (13 - 6)
3. Activity B: LF = 8 (min LS of D), LS = 5 (8 - 3)
4. Activity C: LF = 7 (min LS of D and E), LS = 5 (7 - 2)
5. Activity A: LF = 5 (min LS of B and C), LS = 0 (5 - 5)

Critical Path:
- Critical Path: A -> B -> D
- Duration: 12 days

Identifying and Managing Float
Float (Slack):
- **Total Float:** The amount of time an activity can be delayed without delaying the project end date.
    - Total Float = LS - ES or LF - EF
- **Free Float:** The amount of time an activity can be delayed without delaying the early start of any subsequent activity.
    - Free Float = ES (successor) - EF (current activity)

Managing Float:
- **Utilize Float for Flexibility:** Non-critical activities with float can be delayed or rescheduled without affecting the project deadline.
- **Allocate Resources Efficiently:** Float allows for the redistribution of resources from non-critical to critical activities when necessary.
- **Monitor and Control:** Regularly review float to ensure that it remains within acceptable limits and adjust schedules as required to manage project timelines effectively.

Real-World Examples of Scope Changes Managed with Change Control
Example 1: Construction Project
- **Scenario:** Midway through a building project, the client requested additional structural modifications.
- **Action:** The project manager raised a change request, detailing the impact on the project timeline and budget. The Change Control Board reviewed and approved the request. The project plan was updated, incorporating the new requirements while maintaining the overall project timeline by utilizing available float.

Example 2: IT Project
- **Scenario:** During the development of a new software application, stakeholders requested an additional feature.
- **Action:** The project manager conducted an impact analysis, demonstrating that the feature could be added without affecting the critical path. The change was approved, and the project team reallocated resources to accommodate the new feature, using float from non-critical activities to avoid delays.

The Critical Path Method is an essential tool for effective project scheduling, enabling project managers to identify critical activities, manage float, and ensure timely project completion. By following the forward and backward pass techniques, project managers can accurately calculate the critical path and make informed decisions to keep the project on track.

Schedule Compression Techniques: Crashing and Fast-Tracking
Schedule compression techniques are used to shorten the project schedule without altering the project scope. The two primary techniques are crashing and fast-tracking. These techniques help project managers meet tight deadlines, accommodate changes, or recover from delays. However, they come with potential risks and trade-offs that must be carefully considered.

1. Crashing
Definition: Crashing involves adding resources to critical path activities to reduce their duration. This typically increases project costs but shortens the project timeline.
When to Apply:
- When the project is behind schedule and needs to meet a fixed deadline.
- When additional budget is available to cover the increased costs of added resources.
- When tasks on the critical path can be shortened by adding resources without significantly impacting quality.

How to Apply:
1. **Identify Critical Path Activities**: Focus on activities that directly impact the project completion date.
2. **Assess Resource Availability**: Determine if additional resources (e.g., personnel, equipment) are available and can be effectively utilized.
3. **Calculate Cost and Time Trade-offs**: Evaluate the additional costs against the time saved. Use cost-time trade-off analysis to make informed decisions.
4. **Implement and Monitor**: Add resources to critical path activities, monitor their impact, and ensure that the project remains on track.

Real-World Example:
- **Construction Project**: In a building construction project, the contractor realizes that the project is behind schedule due to unforeseen delays. By adding additional labor and equipment to the critical tasks of framing and roofing, the contractor can accelerate these activities and recover lost time, ensuring the project meets the completion deadline.

Potential Risks and Trade-offs:
- **Increased Costs**: Adding resources usually increases project costs, which may not be feasible if the budget is tight.
- **Diminishing Returns**: Beyond a certain point, adding more resources may not proportionally reduce the activity duration due to inefficiencies (e.g., overcrowding at the worksite).
- **Quality Concerns**: Rapid acceleration might compromise the quality of work if not managed carefully.

2. Fast-Tracking
Definition: Fast-tracking involves performing activities in parallel that were initially planned to be done sequentially. This can shorten the project duration without increasing costs but may introduce additional risks.
When to Apply:
- When the project schedule is tight and cannot be extended.
- When activities can logically and safely overlap without significant rework or risk.
- When the risk of overlapping tasks is manageable and acceptable to stakeholders.

How to Apply:
1. **Identify Overlapping Opportunities**: Look for activities that can be started earlier while still being feasible and logical.
2. **Analyze Risks and Dependencies**: Assess the risks of overlapping activities, including potential rework and coordination issues.
3. **Plan and Implement Overlaps**: Adjust the schedule to reflect the new overlaps, ensuring that dependencies are managed.

4. **Monitor and Adjust**: Continuously monitor the impact of fast-tracking on the project schedule and quality, making adjustments as necessary.

Real-World Example:
- **Software Development Project**: In a software development project, the team decides to start the testing phase before the coding phase is entirely complete. By initiating testing on completed modules while development continues on others, the project can progress more quickly. This approach helps the team meet a tight release deadline.

Potential Risks and Trade-offs:
- **Increased Risk of Rework**: Overlapping tasks can lead to rework if earlier tasks influence the later ones negatively (e.g., defects found in testing requiring changes in the code).
- **Coordination Challenges**: Managing parallel tasks requires effective communication and coordination to avoid conflicts and ensure all team members are aligned.
- **Quality Concerns**: There may be a higher risk of errors and quality issues if the project team is not fully prepared to handle overlapping tasks.

Successful Implementation in Projects

Case Study: Crashing in a Manufacturing Project:
- **Project**: Manufacturing a new product line.
- **Challenge**: The project faced delays due to supplier issues, putting the launch date at risk.
- **Solution**: The project manager decided to crash the critical path activities by adding additional shifts and hiring temporary workers. This approach helped complete the manufacturing and assembly processes faster.
- **Outcome**: The project met its launch date, but with increased labor costs. The additional cost was justified by the successful market entry and revenue generated.

Case Study: Fast-Tracking in a Construction Project:
- **Project**: Construction of a commercial building.
- **Challenge**: Tight deadline to complete the building for a major tenant's move-in date.
- **Solution**: The project team fast-tracked the project by starting the interior design and finishing work while structural work was still ongoing. This involved careful coordination between teams to ensure safety and quality.
- **Outcome**: The building was completed on time, but the project required meticulous planning and communication to manage the overlapping activities and mitigate the risk of rework.

Crashing and fast-tracking are valuable schedule compression techniques that can help project managers meet deadlines and manage delays. However, they come with inherent risks and trade-offs, such as increased costs, risk of rework, and potential quality issues. Project managers must carefully assess these factors and plan accordingly to ensure the successful implementation of these techniques. By understanding when and how to apply crashing and fast-tracking, and by managing the associated risks, project managers can effectively shorten project schedules while maintaining project quality and stakeholder satisfaction.

Cost Management in project management involves planning, estimating, budgeting, and controlling costs to ensure that the project is completed within the approved budget. Effective cost management helps to avoid cost overruns, manage project financial resources efficiently, and ensure project success. Let's delve into the processes involved in cost management and explore commonly used cost estimation techniques.

Processes in Cost Management

1. Planning Cost Management

Purpose: Establishes the policies, procedures, and documentation for planning, managing, expending, and controlling project costs.

Key Activities:
- **Develop Cost Management Plan:** Define how project costs will be estimated, budgeted, managed, monitored, and controlled.
- **Identify Cost Control Measures:** Establish procedures for cost variance management and reporting.

Example: In a construction project, the cost management plan outlines how costs will be tracked, the frequency of cost reporting, and the process for managing cost changes.

2. Estimating Costs

Purpose: Develops an approximation of the monetary resources needed to complete project activities.

Key Activities:
- **Identify Cost Components:** Labor, materials, equipment, services, facilities, and inflation allowances.
- **Choose Estimation Techniques:** Select appropriate methods based on project scope, available data, and required accuracy.

Common Estimation Techniques:
- **Analogous Estimating:** Uses historical data from similar projects to estimate costs.
- **Parametric Estimating:** Uses statistical relationships between historical data and other variables to calculate an estimate.
- **Three-Point Estimating:** Uses optimistic, pessimistic, and most likely estimates to calculate an average cost.

Example: In software development, costs for a new project might be estimated using data from previous similar projects (analogous estimating) or by applying a cost per line of code (parametric estimating).

3. Determining the Budget

Purpose: Aggregates the estimated costs of individual activities or work packages to establish an authorized cost baseline.

Key Activities:
- **Compile Cost Estimates:** Combine costs from all project activities and add contingency reserves.
- **Establish Cost Baseline:** Set a time-phased budget that serves as a benchmark for measuring cost performance.

Example: In a marketing campaign, the budget might include costs for market research, creative development, media buys, and promotional events, with contingency funds for unexpected expenses.

4. Controlling Costs

Purpose: Monitors project costs to ensure that the project stays within the approved budget.

Key Activities:
- **Track Spending:** Monitor actual costs against the cost baseline.
- **Identify Variances:** Analyze deviations from the cost baseline.
- **Implement Corrective Actions:** Adjust project plans to address cost overruns or savings.

Example: In manufacturing, cost control might involve tracking labor and material costs daily, identifying cost variances, and implementing process improvements to reduce waste and save money.

Common Cost Estimation Techniques

1. Analogous Estimating

Definition: Uses historical data from similar projects to estimate costs. It's a top-down approach and is less time-consuming but can be less accurate if the past project isn't sufficiently similar.

Application:
- **Construction:** Estimating the cost of a new office building based on the cost per square foot from a previous similar project.
- **IT:** Estimating software development costs based on similar past projects in terms of complexity and size.

Example: A construction company might estimate the cost of a new commercial building by using the cost per square foot from a recently completed similar project, adjusting for inflation and site-specific factors.

2. Parametric Estimating

Definition: Uses statistical relationships between historical data and other variables (e.g., cost per unit) to calculate an estimate. This method is more accurate than analogous estimating if reliable data is available.

Application:
- **Manufacturing:** Estimating the cost of production based on the cost per unit multiplied by the number of units.
- **Software Development:** Estimating the cost based on the number of lines of code or function points.

Example: An aerospace company might estimate the cost of building a new aircraft using the cost per kilogram of the aircraft's weight, multiplied by the expected weight of the new model.

3. Three-Point Estimating

Definition: Uses three estimates to define an approximate range for an activity's cost: optimistic (O), pessimistic (P), and most likely (M). The formula for the estimate is:

$$E = \frac{O+4M+P}{6}$$

Application:

- **Engineering Projects:** Estimating the cost of designing a new product where there is uncertainty about the complexity.
- **Event Planning:** Estimating costs for an event with variable attendee numbers.

Example: In an engineering project, an estimator might predict the cost to be $80,000 in the best-case scenario (O), $120,000 in the worst-case scenario (P), and $100,000 in the most likely scenario (M). The estimate would be:

$$E = \frac{80,000+4(100,000)+120,000}{6} = 100,000$$

Best Practices for Cost Management
1. **Regular Monitoring and Reporting:** Track project costs regularly and compare them against the budget to identify variances early.
2. **Use of Contingency Reserves:** Allocate reserves for unexpected costs and manage them separately from the project budget.
3. **Stakeholder Involvement:** Keep stakeholders informed about cost performance and involve them in decision-making processes.
4. **Effective Change Control:** Implement a structured change control process to manage cost changes and ensure they are documented and approved.

Real-World Examples

Example 1: Construction Project
- **Scenario:** A construction company is building a new residential complex.
- **Application of Techniques:**
    - **Analogous Estimating:** The project manager uses the cost data from a similar completed project to estimate the new project's cost.
    - **Parametric Estimating:** The cost per square foot from previous projects is used to estimate the total cost based on the planned size of the new complex.
    - **Three-Point Estimating:** Considering the variability in material prices, the project manager calculates optimistic, pessimistic, and most likely cost estimates for materials.

Example 2: Software Development Project
- **Scenario:** A software company is developing a new application.
- **Application of Techniques:**
    - **Analogous Estimating:** The cost of developing a similar application in the past is used as a reference for the new project.
    - **Parametric Estimating:** The project manager estimates the cost based on the number of function points and the average cost per function point from historical data.

- **Three-Point Estimating:** Given the uncertainty in feature complexity, the project manager uses optimistic, pessimistic, and most likely estimates to determine the development cost.

By effectively planning, estimating, budgeting, and controlling costs, project managers can ensure that their projects are completed within budget, leading to successful project outcomes and satisfied stakeholders. Utilizing appropriate cost estimation techniques tailored to the project's context and industry can significantly enhance the accuracy and reliability of cost forecasts.

Earned Value Management (EVM) and Its Key Metrics

Earned Value Management (EVM) is a project management technique used to measure project performance and progress objectively. It integrates project scope, cost, and schedule measures to help project managers assess project performance and predict future performance trends. Key EVM metrics include Planned Value (PV), Earned Value (EV), Actual Cost (AC), Schedule Variance (SV), Cost Variance (CV), Schedule Performance Index (SPI), and Cost Performance Index (CPI).

Key Metrics and Their Definitions

1. **Planned Value (PV)**
   - **Definition**: The authorized budget assigned to scheduled work. It represents the value of the work planned to be completed by a specific time.
   - **Formula**: PV = (Planned % Complete) × (Total Budget)
   - **Example**: If the total budget is $100,000 and 50% of the work was planned to be completed by a certain date, then PV = 0.5 × 100,000 = 50,000.

2. **Earned Value (EV)**
   - **Definition**: The value of work actually performed. It represents the authorized budget for the work completed.
   - **Formula**: EV = (Actual % Complete) × (Total Budget)
   - **Example**: If the total budget is $100,000 and 40% of the work is actually completed, then EV = 0.4 × 100,000 = 40,000.

3. **Actual Cost (AC)**
   - **Definition**: The total cost incurred for the actual work completed by a specific time.
   - **Example**: If $45,000 has been spent on the project so far, then AC = 45,000.

4. **Schedule Variance (SV)**
   - **Definition**: A measure of schedule performance expressed as the difference between EV and PV.
   - **Formula**: SV = EV - PV
   - **Example**: If EV = 40,000 and PV = 50,000, then SV = 40,000 - 50,000 = -10,000.
   - **Interpretation**: A negative SV indicates the project is behind schedule.

5. **Cost Variance (CV)**
   - **Definition**: A measure of cost performance expressed as the difference between EV and AC.
   - **Formula**: CV = EV - AC
   - **Example**: If EV = 40,000 and AC = 45,000, then CV = 40,000 - 45,000 = -5,000.
   - **Interpretation**: A negative CV indicates the project is over budget.

6. **Schedule Performance Index (SPI)**
   - **Definition**: A measure of schedule efficiency expressed as the ratio of EV to PV.
   - **Formula**: SPI = EV / PV
   - **Example**: If EV = 40,000 and PV = 50,000, then SPI = 40,000 / 50,000 = 0.8.
   - **Interpretation**: An SPI less than 1 indicates the project is less efficient than planned and behind schedule.

7. **Cost Performance Index (CPI)**
   - **Definition**: A measure of cost efficiency expressed as the ratio of EV to AC.
   - **Formula**: CPI = EV / AC
   - **Example**: If EV = 40,000 and AC = 45,000, then CPI = 40,000 / 45,000 ≈ 0.89.
   - **Interpretation**: A CPI less than 1 indicates the project is over budget.

Tutorial on Calculating and Interpreting EVM Metrics

Let's consider a project with the following details:

- Total Budget: $200,000
- Planned % Complete: 60%
- Actual % Complete: 50%
- Actual Cost (AC): $130,000

Step-by-Step Calculation:
1. **Calculate Planned Value (PV)**
   - PV = (Planned % Complete) × (Total Budget)
   - PV = 0.60 × 200,000 = 120,000
2. **Calculate Earned Value (EV)**
   - EV = (Actual % Complete) × (Total Budget)
   - EV = 0.50 × 200,000 = 100,000
3. **Actual Cost (AC)**
   - AC = 130,000
4. **Calculate Schedule Variance (SV)**
   - SV = EV - PV
   - SV = 100,000 - 120,000 = -20,000
   - **Interpretation**: The project is behind schedule by $20,000 worth of work.
5. **Calculate Cost Variance (CV)**
   - CV = EV - AC
   - CV = 100,000 - 130,000 = -30,000
   - **Interpretation**: The project is over budget by $30,000.
6. **Calculate Schedule Performance Index (SPI)**
   - SPI = EV / PV
   - SPI = 100,000 / 120,000 = 0.83
   - **Interpretation**: The project is progressing at 83% of the planned rate.
7. **Calculate Cost Performance Index (CPI)**
   - CPI = EV / AC
   - CPI = 100,000 / 130,000 ≈ 0.77
   - **Interpretation**: For every dollar spent, the project is earning only $0.77 worth of work.

Significance in Monitoring and Controlling Project Performance
1. **Planned Value (PV)**: Helps in understanding the work that was supposed to be completed by a certain date according to the plan. It sets the baseline for comparison.
2. **Earned Value (EV)**: Shows the actual progress made in terms of budgeted cost. It's a measure of the project's true progress and performance.
3. **Actual Cost (AC)**: Tracks the actual expenditure incurred for the work performed. It's crucial for understanding cost performance.
4. **Schedule Variance (SV)**: Indicates whether the project is ahead or behind schedule. A negative SV shows delays, while a positive SV indicates ahead-of-schedule progress.
5. **Cost Variance (CV)**: Indicates whether the project is over or under budget. A negative CV signifies budget overruns, and a positive CV indicates cost savings.
6. **Schedule Performance Index (SPI)**: Provides a ratio that indicates the efficiency of time utilization. An SPI less than 1 shows inefficiency and schedule delays.
7. **Cost Performance Index (CPI)**: Provides a ratio that indicates cost efficiency. A CPI less than 1 shows that the project is over budget.

These EVM metrics offer valuable insights for project managers to monitor and control project performance effectively. They help in making informed decisions, identifying problem areas early, and taking corrective actions to keep the project on track.

Quality management in project management involves three primary processes: quality planning, quality assurance, and quality control. These processes ensure that the project meets the desired standards and satisfies stakeholder expectations.

Processes in Quality Management

1. Quality Planning
Purpose: Identifies the quality requirements and standards for the project and documents how the project will comply with these requirements.

Key Activities:
- **Define Quality Metrics:** Establish measurable criteria to gauge project quality.
- **Plan Quality Management:** Develop a quality management plan detailing how quality will be managed and measured.

Example: In a software development project, quality metrics might include the number of bugs found during testing, system uptime, and user satisfaction ratings.

2. Quality Assurance
Purpose: Ensures that the quality processes are being followed and that the project meets the quality requirements through planned and systematic activities.

Key Activities:
- **Process Audits:** Regular reviews of project activities to ensure compliance with quality standards.
- **Quality Audits:** Independent evaluations of project quality processes and outcomes.

Example: In manufacturing, quality assurance might involve regular audits of the production line to ensure that products meet specified standards and processes are followed correctly.

3. Quality Control
Purpose: Monitors specific project results to determine if they comply with relevant quality standards and identifies ways to eliminate causes of unsatisfactory performance.

Key Activities:
- **Inspection:** Examine products or deliverables to ensure they meet quality standards.
- **Testing:** Conduct tests to identify defects or issues.
- **Statistical Process Control (SPC):** Use statistical methods to monitor and control a process.

Example: In construction, quality control might involve inspecting materials for defects and testing the structural integrity of a building.

Tools and Techniques in Quality Management

1. Cost-Benefit Analysis
Definition: A method that compares the costs of implementing a quality measure against the benefits derived from it.

Application:
- **Software Development:** Evaluating the cost of additional testing tools versus the reduction in post-release bug fixes and customer support costs.
- **Construction:** Assessing the cost of higher-grade materials against the potential reduction in maintenance and repair costs over the building's lifespan.

Example: A pharmaceutical company might conduct a cost-benefit analysis to decide whether to invest in advanced quality control equipment. If the equipment reduces the number of defective products significantly, leading to higher customer satisfaction and reduced waste, the investment may be justified.

2. Benchmarking
Definition: Comparing project processes and performance metrics to industry best practices or standards.

Application:
- **Healthcare:** Comparing patient care procedures to those of leading hospitals to identify areas for improvement.
- **IT Services:** Comparing help desk response times and resolution rates to industry benchmarks to improve service quality.

Example: An automotive manufacturer might benchmark its production processes against those of a leading competitor to identify gaps in efficiency and quality. By adopting best practices from the benchmarked company, the manufacturer can enhance its own production processes.

3. Statistical Process Control (SPC)

Definition: A method of monitoring and controlling a process through statistical analysis to ensure it operates at its full potential.

Application:
- **Manufacturing:** Monitoring production lines for consistency and detecting variations that could indicate defects.
- **Software Development:** Using control charts to monitor the number of bugs reported during testing phases.

Example: In the food and beverage industry, SPC can be used to monitor the quality of products such as soda. By analyzing the consistency of carbonation levels or ingredient ratios, the company can maintain high quality and quickly address any deviations.

Examples of Quality Management Applications

1. **Construction Industry:**
   - **Quality Planning:** Establishing standards for materials, construction methods, and safety protocols.
   - **Quality Assurance:** Regular site inspections and audits to ensure adherence to standards.
   - **Quality Control:** Testing concrete strength and inspecting welds to ensure structural integrity.
2. **IT Industry:**
   - **Quality Planning:** Defining coding standards, testing protocols, and user experience criteria.
   - **Quality Assurance:** Conducting code reviews and process audits to ensure compliance with standards.
   - **Quality Control:** Performing automated tests to detect and fix software bugs before release.
3. **Healthcare Industry:**
   - **Quality Planning:** Setting standards for patient care, safety, and data handling.
   - **Quality Assurance:** Conducting audits of clinical procedures and patient records.
   - **Quality Control:** Monitoring patient outcomes and feedback to identify areas for improvement.

Quality management ensures that projects meet or exceed stakeholder expectations by systematically planning, assuring, and controlling quality. By utilizing tools and techniques like cost-benefit analysis, benchmarking, and statistical process control, organizations can continuously improve their processes and deliver high-quality outcomes.

Key Activities in Resource Management

Effective resource management is crucial for the successful completion of projects. It involves planning, estimating, acquiring, developing, managing, and optimizing the use of resources. Here are the key activities in resource management:

1. Estimating Resource Requirements

Purpose: Determine the type and quantity of resources (human, equipment, materials) needed to complete project activities.

Key Activities:
1. **Identify Resources:** List all the resources required for the project.
   - Example: In a construction project, resources might include workers, machinery, cement, and steel.
2. **Estimate Resource Quantities:** Calculate the amount of each resource needed.
   - Example: Determine the number of carpenters required and the amount of wood needed for building a house.
3. **Estimate Duration and Effort:** Assess how long each resource will be needed and the effort required.
   - Example: Estimating that four carpenters will need five days to complete the framing of a house.

Deliverables:
- Resource Requirements Document: A detailed list of required resources and their quantities.
- Resource Breakdown Structure (RBS): A hierarchical chart categorizing project resources.

2. Acquiring Resources

Purpose: Secure the necessary resources for the project.

Key Activities:

1. **Negotiate with Suppliers**: Arrange contracts and agreements with suppliers for materials and equipment.
    - Example: Negotiating with a supplier for a bulk discount on cement.
2. **Recruit Team Members**: Hire or allocate personnel required for the project.
    - Example: Hiring additional software developers for a new app development project.
3. **Procure Equipment**: Purchase or lease the necessary equipment.
    - Example: Leasing heavy machinery for a construction project.

Deliverables:
- Resource Assignments: Document specifying which resources are allocated to which tasks.
- Resource Contracts: Agreements with external suppliers and contractors.

3. Developing and Managing the Project Team
Purpose: Improve team competencies, interaction, and overall team environment to enhance project performance.
Key Activities:
1. **Team Building Activities**: Conduct activities to build trust and improve collaboration.
    - Example: Organizing team-building workshops or off-site retreats.
2. **Training and Development**: Provide training to enhance team members' skills.
    - Example: Offering courses on new software tools to developers.
3. **Performance Assessments**: Evaluate team members' performance and provide feedback.
    - Example: Conducting regular performance reviews and setting improvement goals.
4. **Conflict Resolution**: Address and resolve conflicts within the team.
    - Example: Mediating disputes between team members to maintain a harmonious work environment.

Deliverables:
- Team Performance Assessments: Documentation of team evaluations and feedback.
- Training Programs: Structured plans for team development activities.

4. Optimizing Resource Utilization
Purpose: Ensure that resources are used efficiently and effectively throughout the project.
Key Activities:
1. **Resource Allocation**: Assign resources to project tasks based on availability and project needs.
    - Example: Assigning specific developers to critical coding tasks based on their expertise.
2. **Resource Monitoring**: Track resource usage and ensure optimal utilization.
    - Example: Using software tools to monitor equipment usage and availability.
3. **Resource Adjustment**: Reallocate resources as needed to address changes or conflicts.
    - Example: Reassigning team members to different tasks to balance workloads.

Deliverables:
- Resource Utilization Reports: Regular reports on how resources are being used.
- Resource Reallocation Plans: Adjustments to resource assignments based on project needs.

Techniques for Optimizing Resource Utilization
Resource Leveling
Definition: Adjusting the start and finish dates of tasks to ensure that resource demand does not exceed resource availability.
When to Apply:
- When resources are over-allocated or there are conflicts in resource usage.
- When resource availability fluctuates, and a steady usage rate is desired.

How to Apply:
1. **Identify Over-Allocated Resources**: Use project management software to identify resources that are over-allocated.
    - Example: A project manager notices that a key engineer is scheduled for 150% of their available time.
2. **Adjust Task Schedules**: Shift the start and finish dates of tasks to resolve conflicts.
    - Example: Delaying non-critical tasks to balance the engineer's workload.
3. **Iterate and Optimize**: Continuously adjust schedules until resource demand is leveled.

Example:
- **Construction Project**: A construction manager identifies that both the plumbing and electrical tasks require the same skilled workers at the same time. By delaying the electrical work until after the plumbing work is completed, the manager can avoid over-allocation and ensure that workers are not overburdened.

Resource Smoothing
Definition: Adjusting the activities of the project to ensure that resource limits are not exceeded without affecting the critical path.

When to Apply:
- When minor adjustments can optimize resource usage without delaying the project.
- When specific resources are only available for limited periods.

How to Apply:
1. **Identify Resource Constraints**: Determine where resource usage peaks and exceeds availability.
    - Example: A project manager sees that a designer is scheduled for multiple tasks simultaneously.
2. **Adjust Non-Critical Activities**: Modify the schedules of non-critical activities to smooth out resource usage.
    - Example: Rescheduling non-critical design tasks to avoid overlap with critical tasks.
3. **Monitor Impact**: Ensure that these adjustments do not affect the project's critical path.

Example:
- **Software Development Project**: A project manager finds that a key developer is needed for two overlapping tasks. By rescheduling non-critical tasks to a later date, the manager ensures the developer's workload is balanced without impacting the project timeline.

Resolving Resource Conflicts and Improving Project Efficiency
Real-World Example: Resource Leveling in a Marketing Campaign

A marketing campaign involves creating content, designing graphics, and running ads. The project manager realizes that the same designer is needed for both content creation and ad design, causing a conflict.

1. **Identify Over-Allocation:** The designer is over-allocated, with 120% of their available time scheduled.
2. **Adjust Task Schedules:** The project manager shifts non-critical content creation tasks to after the ad design is completed.
3. **Monitor and Adjust:** By leveling the workload, the designer can focus on one task at a time, improving efficiency and reducing stress.

Real-World Example: Resource Smoothing in a Construction Project

A construction project requires a crane for both foundation work and later for roofing. The initial schedule overlaps these tasks, exceeding crane availability.

1. **Identify Resource Constraints:** The crane is overbooked, with conflicting tasks scheduled.
2. **Adjust Non-Critical Activities:** The project manager reschedules the roofing tasks to start immediately after the foundation work.
3. **Monitor Impact:** This adjustment ensures that the crane is used efficiently without affecting the project's critical path.

By effectively estimating resource requirements, acquiring necessary resources, developing and managing the project team, and optimizing resource utilization through techniques like resource leveling and resource smoothing, project managers can resolve conflicts and enhance project efficiency.

Communications Management is a crucial aspect of project management, ensuring that information is effectively generated, collected, distributed, stored, retrieved, and disposed of throughout the project. Effective communication keeps stakeholders informed and engaged, facilitating collaboration and decision-making. Communications Management involves three primary processes: planning, managing, and monitoring project communications.

Processes in Communications Management
1. Planning Communications Management

Purpose: Determines the communication needs of stakeholders, including what information is needed, who needs it, when it is needed, and how it will be delivered.

Key Activities:

- **Identify Stakeholder Communication Requirements:** Determine the information needs of project stakeholders.
- **Define Communication Methods:** Choose the appropriate methods for information distribution, such as meetings, reports, emails, and dashboards.
- **Establish Communication Frequency:** Set how often communications will occur (e.g., weekly status reports, monthly meetings).
- **Select Communication Channels:** Identify the best channels for communication (e.g., face-to-face meetings, video conferences, instant messaging).
- **Develop Communication Plan:** Document the communication requirements, methods, frequency, channels, and responsible parties.

Example: In a construction project, the communication plan might include weekly progress reports to the client, daily briefings with the project team, and monthly updates to regulatory authorities.

2. Managing Communications

Purpose: Ensures timely and appropriate collection, creation, distribution, storage, retrieval, management, monitoring, and the ultimate disposition of project information.

Key Activities:

- **Execute Communication Plan:** Implement the plan by generating and distributing the required information.
- **Facilitate Information Exchange:** Ensure that stakeholders can easily access and understand the information they need.
- **Manage Stakeholder Expectations:** Address any questions or concerns stakeholders may have about the project.
- **Update Communication Plan:** Make adjustments to the communication plan as necessary based on feedback and changes in the project.

Example: In a software development project, managing communications might involve holding daily stand-up meetings to discuss progress, sending out weekly status reports via email, and maintaining a project wiki for document storage and retrieval.

3. Monitoring Communications

Purpose: Ensures that the information needs of the project and its stakeholders are met.

Key Activities:

- **Evaluate Communication Effectiveness:** Assess whether the communications are reaching their intended audience and achieving their purpose.
- **Collect Feedback:** Gather feedback from stakeholders on the clarity, frequency, and usefulness of the communications.
- **Implement Improvements:** Make necessary adjustments to improve communication processes and address any identified issues.

Example: In an event planning project, monitoring communications might involve surveying stakeholders after key meetings to ensure they received and understood the necessary information, and making changes to communication methods if feedback indicates issues.

Importance of Communication Factors

1. Stakeholder Communication Requirements

Understanding and addressing stakeholder communication requirements is essential for project success. Different stakeholders have varying needs for information based on their role, interest, and influence on the project. Tailoring communication to meet these needs ensures stakeholders are informed, engaged, and supportive of the project.

Example: Senior executives might need high-level project status updates, while project team members require detailed technical information.

2. Communication Channels

Selecting appropriate communication channels is vital to ensure information is effectively transmitted and received. Channels can be formal (reports, presentations) or informal (chats, emails), synchronous (meetings, calls) or asynchronous (emails, documents).

Example: A combination of face-to-face meetings for detailed discussions and email for routine updates might be used in a project to ensure clear and efficient communication.

3. Communication Technologies

Utilizing the right communication technologies can enhance collaboration, improve information sharing, and streamline communication processes. Technologies include project management software, video conferencing tools, instant messaging apps, and collaborative platforms.

Example: Using project management software like Asana or Trello can help track tasks and deadlines, while Slack or Microsoft Teams facilitates real-time communication and collaboration.

Examples of Effective Communications Management

Example 1: Construction Project
- **Planning Communications Management:** The project manager develops a communication plan that includes weekly site meetings, daily progress reports via email, and monthly stakeholder review meetings.
- **Managing Communications:** The team uses video conferencing for remote stakeholder meetings and a shared online platform for document storage and retrieval.
- **Monitoring Communications:** Regular feedback is collected through surveys to ensure that the communication methods meet stakeholder needs, leading to adjustments in the frequency of updates.

Example 2: IT Project
- **Planning Communications Management:** The communication plan specifies daily stand-up meetings, bi-weekly sprint reviews, and a project dashboard accessible to all stakeholders.
- **Managing Communications:** The project manager ensures that meeting notes are documented and shared, and that the project dashboard is regularly updated.
- **Monitoring Communications:** Stakeholder feedback is reviewed, and changes are made to the meeting schedules and update formats to improve clarity and engagement.

Effective communication is the backbone of successful project management. By carefully planning, managing, and monitoring communications, project managers can ensure that information flows smoothly among stakeholders, facilitating collaboration, decision-making, and project success.

Risk Management Processes

Risk management is an essential aspect of project management that involves identifying, assessing, responding to, and monitoring risks to minimize their impact on project objectives. The main processes in risk management are risk identification, qualitative and quantitative risk analysis, risk response planning, and risk monitoring and control.

1. Risk Identification

Purpose: Identify potential risks that could affect the project and document their characteristics.

Key Activities:
1. **Brainstorming**:
    - Gather the project team and stakeholders to identify potential risks.
    - Use structured sessions to generate a list of risks.
    - Example: In a software development project, brainstorming sessions might reveal risks such as technical challenges, scope changes, or resource shortages.
2. **Checklists**:
    - Use pre-existing lists of common risks in similar projects to identify risks.
    - Example: A construction project might use a checklist to identify risks such as weather delays, equipment failure, and safety hazards.
3. **SWOT Analysis**:
    - Analyze the project's strengths, weaknesses, opportunities, and threats to identify internal and external risks.
    - Example: In a marketing campaign, a SWOT analysis might identify strengths like a strong brand, weaknesses like limited budget, opportunities like new market trends, and threats like competitor actions.
4. **Expert Interviews**:
    - Consult with subject matter experts to gain insights into potential risks.

- Example: Interviewing experienced engineers to identify risks in a new product design project.

Deliverables:
- **Risk Register**: A document listing identified risks, their descriptions, potential impacts, and initial responses.

2. Qualitative Risk Analysis

Purpose: Prioritize risks based on their probability of occurrence and impact on project objectives.

Key Activities:
1. **Probability and Impact Matrix**:
   - Assess the likelihood and impact of each identified risk using a qualitative scale (e.g., low, medium, high).
   - Plot risks on a matrix to visualize their significance.
   - Example: In a healthcare IT project, a risk with high impact and high probability, such as a data breach, would be prioritized for immediate action.
2. **Risk Categorization**:
   - Group risks by categories (e.g., technical, organizational, external) to identify common areas of concern.
   - Example: Categorizing risks in a construction project by source, such as environmental, legal, and technical.
3. **Risk Urgency Assessment**:
   - Determine the urgency of addressing each risk based on its potential impact and timing.
   - Example: In a product launch, a risk related to regulatory approval might be urgent due to impending deadlines.

Deliverables:
- **Updated Risk Register**: Includes prioritized risks with their probability, impact, and urgency ratings.

3. Quantitative Risk Analysis

Purpose: Numerically analyze the effect of identified risks on project objectives.

Key Activities:
1. **Monte Carlo Simulation**:
   - Use computer-based simulations to model the impact of risks on project outcomes.
   - Example: Simulating the schedule impact of multiple risks in a construction project to estimate completion dates.
2. **Decision Tree Analysis**:
   - Evaluate decisions under uncertainty by modeling potential outcomes and their probabilities.
   - Example: In an R&D project, a decision tree might be used to evaluate the financial impact of different research paths.
3. **Sensitivity Analysis**:
   - Determine how changes in risk variables affect project outcomes.
   - Example: Analyzing how variations in market demand impact revenue projections in a new product development project.

Deliverables:
- **Quantitative Risk Analysis Report**: Detailed analysis of the numerical impact of risks, including simulations and decision models.

4. Risk Response Planning

Purpose: Develop options and actions to enhance opportunities and reduce threats to project objectives.

Key Activities:
1. **Risk Mitigation**:
   - Develop actions to reduce the probability or impact of risks.
   - Example: In a software project, using automated testing tools to mitigate the risk of coding errors.
2. **Risk Avoidance**:
   - Modify project plans to eliminate risks or protect project objectives from their impact.
   - Example: Changing the project scope to exclude high-risk features in a construction project.
3. **Risk Transfer**:
   - Shift the impact of risks to a third party through contracts or insurance.

- Example: Purchasing insurance to transfer the risk of equipment damage in a manufacturing project.
4. **Risk Acceptance**:
    - Acknowledge the risk and choose to accept it without taking any action, usually due to cost-benefit considerations.
    - Example: Accepting the risk of minor schedule delays in a low-impact project phase.
5. **Risk Exploitation**:
    - Take actions to ensure that opportunities are realized.
    - Example: Investing in additional resources to accelerate project completion and take advantage of a market opportunity.
6. **Risk Enhancement**:
    - Increase the probability or positive impacts of opportunities.
    - Example: Enhancing a marketing campaign to maximize exposure and sales.
7. **Risk Sharing**:
    - Allocate ownership of an opportunity to a third party who is best able to capture the benefits.
    - Example: Forming a strategic partnership to jointly develop a new product.

Deliverables:
- **Risk Response Plan**: Document detailing the strategies for managing each identified risk, including actions, responsibilities, and timelines.

5. Risk Monitoring and Control

Purpose: Track identified risks, monitor residual risks, identify new risks, and evaluate the effectiveness of risk responses throughout the project lifecycle.

Key Activities:
1. **Risk Audits**:
    - Conduct regular audits to ensure risk management processes are effective and adhered to.
    - Example: A quarterly audit in a construction project to review and update the risk register.
2. **Risk Reviews**:
    - Periodically review and update the risk register and risk response plans.
    - Example: Monthly risk review meetings in a software development project to assess new and existing risks.
3. **Status Meetings**:
    - Include risk management as a topic in regular project status meetings.
    - Example: Discussing risk status and mitigation actions in weekly team meetings.
4. **Variance and Trend Analysis**:
    - Analyze project performance data to identify variances from the plan and emerging trends.
    - Example: Using trend analysis in a manufacturing project to detect potential delays in the supply chain.

Deliverables:
- **Updated Risk Register**: Reflects current risk status and any changes in risk responses.
- **Risk Reports**: Regular reports summarizing risk status, effectiveness of responses, and new risks.

Common Risk Identification Techniques

1. **Brainstorming**
    - Gather a diverse group of stakeholders to generate a comprehensive list of potential risks.
    - Example in IT Project: Brainstorming with developers, testers, and users to identify risks related to system performance, data security, and user acceptance.
2. **Checklists**
    - Use pre-defined lists of common risks to identify applicable risks in the current project.
    - Example in Construction Project: Using a checklist to identify risks such as regulatory compliance, site conditions, and equipment failure.
3. **SWOT Analysis**
    - Analyze internal strengths and weaknesses, and external opportunities and threats to identify risks.

- Example in Marketing Campaign: Conducting a SWOT analysis to identify strengths (brand reputation), weaknesses (limited budget), opportunities (emerging market trends), and threats (competitor actions).

By effectively applying these risk management processes and techniques, project managers can proactively manage risks, minimize their impact, and increase the likelihood of project success.

Procurement Management involves the processes necessary to purchase or acquire products, services, or results needed from outside the project team. It includes planning procurements, conducting procurements, and controlling procurements. Understanding different contract types and their implications is crucial for effective procurement management.

Key Concepts in Procurement Management

1. Procurement Planning

Purpose: Determines what to procure, when, and how. It involves identifying project needs that require external procurement and developing a procurement management plan.

Key Activities:
- **Identify Requirements:** Determine the goods and services needed for the project.
- **Conduct Market Research:** Analyze the market to identify potential suppliers and pricing.
- **Make or Buy Analysis:** Decide whether to produce in-house or procure externally.
- **Develop Procurement Plan:** Outline the procurement strategy, including selection criteria, contract types, and procurement timelines.

Example: In a software development project, the procurement planning might involve deciding to purchase certain software tools from a third party rather than developing them in-house.

2. Conducting Procurements

Purpose: Obtains seller responses, selects a seller, and awards a contract.

Key Activities:
- **Prepare Procurement Documents:** Create RFPs (Request for Proposals), RFQs (Request for Quotations), or IFBs (Invitations for Bid).
- **Advertise Procurement Opportunities:** Share the procurement requirements with potential suppliers.
- **Evaluate Proposals:** Assess supplier proposals based on pre-defined selection criteria.
- **Select Suppliers:** Choose the most suitable supplier(s) based on evaluations.
- **Negotiate Contracts:** Finalize the terms and conditions of the contract with the selected supplier.
- **Award Contracts:** Officially award the contract to the selected supplier.

Example: A construction project might involve sending out RFPs to several construction firms, evaluating their bids based on cost, experience, and proposed timelines, and then awarding the contract to the best-fit firm.

3. Controlling Procurements

Purpose: Manages procurement relationships, monitors contract performance, and makes necessary changes and corrections to ensure the procurement process aligns with project objectives.

Key Activities:
- **Monitor Contract Performance:** Ensure that the seller is meeting the contract terms and conditions.
- **Manage Procurement Relationships:** Maintain effective communication with suppliers to address issues and ensure smooth execution.
- **Make Contract Changes:** Implement any necessary changes to the contract through a formal change control process.
- **Close Procurements:** Complete and settle each contract, including resolving any open items.

Example: In a manufacturing project, controlling procurements might involve regularly reviewing supplier performance reports and conducting site visits to ensure that production quality and timelines are being met.

Various Contract Types

1. Fixed-Price Contracts

Definition: The price for the goods or services is set at the outset and is not subject to change unless the scope of work changes.

Types:
- **Firm Fixed Price (FFP):** The seller agrees to deliver the goods or services for a set price.
- **Fixed Price Incentive Fee (FPIF):** The seller receives an additional fee for meeting performance targets.
- **Fixed Price with Economic Price Adjustment (FP-EPA):** Adjustments are allowed for specific economic conditions, such as inflation.

Advantages:
- **Predictability:** Costs are known upfront, which simplifies budgeting.
- **Risk Transfer:** The seller assumes most of the risk for cost overruns.

Disadvantages:
- **Scope Rigidness:** Changes to scope can be costly and complicated.
- **Potential for Lower Quality:** Sellers might cut corners to stay within budget.

Example: An IT company might use a fixed-price contract for developing a specific software module, where the requirements are well-defined and unlikely to change.

2. Cost-Reimbursable Contracts

Definition: The seller is reimbursed for allowable costs incurred in performing the contract work, plus an additional amount representing seller profit.

Types:
- **Cost Plus Fixed Fee (CPFF):** The seller is reimbursed for costs and receives a fixed fee.
- **Cost Plus Incentive Fee (CPIF):** The seller is reimbursed for costs and earns an incentive fee for achieving performance targets.
- **Cost Plus Award Fee (CPAF):** The seller is reimbursed for costs and receives an award fee based on subjective evaluation.

Advantages:
- **Flexibility:** Better for projects where scope is not well-defined.
- **Quality Focus:** Encourages sellers to provide high-quality work since costs are reimbursed.

Disadvantages:
- **Cost Uncertainty:** Difficult to predict final project costs.
- **Administrative Burden:** Requires rigorous cost monitoring and auditing.

Example: A research and development project might use a cost-reimbursable contract to accommodate the uncertainty and complexity of developing new technologies.

3. Time and Materials (T&M) Contracts

Definition: The buyer pays the seller for the time spent and materials used in performing the work.

Advantages:
- **Flexibility:** Useful for projects with uncertain scope or duration.
- **Ease of Use:** Simple to implement and manage compared to other contract types.

Disadvantages:
- **Cost Risk:** Costs can escalate if the project duration or resource requirements increase.
- **Oversight Required:** Requires close monitoring to ensure efficiency.

Example: A consulting firm might use a T&M contract for providing expert advice on an ongoing basis, where the exact amount of work needed is not initially clear.

Application of Contract Types in Different Scenarios

1. **Construction Industry:**
   - **Fixed-Price:** Building a residential house where specifications are well-defined.
   - **Cost-Reimbursable:** Renovating a historic building where the extent of work is uncertain.
   - **T&M:** Ongoing maintenance services for a commercial property.
2. **IT Industry:**
   - **Fixed-Price:** Developing a specific software module with clear requirements.
   - **Cost-Reimbursable:** Research and development of new software technology.
   - **T&M:** Providing IT support and consulting services on an as-needed basis.

3. **Manufacturing Industry:**
    - **Fixed-Price:** Producing a standard product in large quantities.
    - **Cost-Reimbursable:** Custom manufacturing of a new product prototype.
    - **T&M:** Repair and upgrade services for manufacturing equipment.

Understanding these key concepts in procurement management, along with the advantages and disadvantages of different contract types, allows project managers to select the most appropriate procurement strategies for their projects. This ensures that goods and services are acquired efficiently, cost-effectively, and with the desired quality.

Agile Frameworks/Methodologies

The Four Core Values of the Agile Manifesto

The Agile Manifesto, created in 2001 by a group of software development experts, outlines a set of values and principles aimed at improving the process of software development. These values emphasize collaboration, flexibility, and delivering value to the customer.

Core Values

1. **Individuals and Interactions Over Processes and Tools**
   - **Explanation**: This value emphasizes the importance of people and their interactions over rigid processes and tools. Agile recognizes that even the best tools and processes cannot replace the value of a motivated and communicative team.
   - **Example**: In an Agile software development team, daily stand-up meetings (scrum meetings) are held to discuss progress and challenges, ensuring effective communication and collaboration among team members.

2. **Working Software Over Comprehensive Documentation**
   - **Explanation**: Agile values functional software over extensive documentation. While documentation is important, the primary measure of progress is working software that delivers value to the customer.
   - **Example**: Instead of spending months writing detailed specifications, an Agile team focuses on developing small, functional increments of the software that can be demonstrated to stakeholders for feedback.

3. **Customer Collaboration Over Contract Negotiation**
   - **Explanation**: Agile promotes active collaboration with customers throughout the project to ensure their needs and feedback are continuously integrated, rather than relying solely on contract terms.
   - **Example**: An Agile team holds regular sprint reviews and demo sessions where customers can see the progress and provide feedback, allowing the team to make necessary adjustments quickly.

4. **Responding to Change Over Following a Plan**
   - **Explanation**: Agile values flexibility and responsiveness to change over rigidly adhering to a predefined plan. Agile teams are prepared to adapt their approach based on new information and changing requirements.
   - **Example**: During a sprint, if a customer identifies a new important feature or change, the Agile team is able to re-prioritize the backlog and incorporate the change in the upcoming iterations.

The Twelve Principles of the Agile Manifesto

The Agile Manifesto is supported by twelve principles that provide a detailed guide for implementing Agile practices.

1. **Our highest priority is to satisfy the customer through early and continuous delivery of valuable software.**
   - **Example**: An e-commerce development team delivers a basic online shopping feature early in the project and continues to add enhancements and new features in subsequent sprints, ensuring continuous value delivery.

2. **Welcome changing requirements, even late in development. Agile processes harness change for the customer's competitive advantage.**
   - **Example**: A mobile app development team welcomes customer feedback at any stage and makes iterative adjustments to the app, even if it means altering completed features.

3. **Deliver working software frequently, from a couple of weeks to a couple of months, with a preference to the shorter timescale.**
   - **Example**: A financial software team releases new software updates every two weeks, allowing customers to start using new features and providing feedback rapidly.

4. **Business people and developers must work together daily throughout the project.**
   - **Example**: In a startup, the product owner (a business stakeholder) and developers have daily stand-up meetings to ensure alignment and immediate resolution of any issues.

5. **Build projects around motivated individuals. Give them the environment and support they need, and trust them to get the job done.**

- **Example**: An Agile team at a tech company is given autonomy and resources to innovate, and management trusts the team to deliver quality work without micromanagement.
6. **The most efficient and effective method of conveying information to and within a development team is face-to-face conversation.**
    - **Example**: Despite being a remote team, an Agile software development team uses video calls for daily stand-ups to maintain personal interaction and effective communication.
7. **Working software is the primary measure of progress.**
    - **Example**: A project manager in an Agile marketing software project tracks progress based on the functionality delivered and ready to use, rather than on milestones or documentation completed.
8. **Agile processes promote sustainable development. The sponsors, developers, and users should be able to maintain a constant pace indefinitely.**
    - **Example**: An Agile team ensures they follow a sustainable work pace by avoiding overtime and burnout, allowing the team to maintain productivity over the long term.
9. **Continuous attention to technical excellence and good design enhances agility.**
    - **Example**: A software development team uses code reviews and refactoring practices to maintain high-quality code, making it easier to adapt and change the software as needed.
10. **Simplicity—the art of maximizing the amount of work not done—is essential.**
- **Example**: An Agile team regularly reviews their backlog to remove unnecessary features and focus on delivering the most critical functionalities.
11. **The best architectures, requirements, and designs emerge from self-organizing teams.**
- **Example**: A software development team collaborates to define the best approach to the architecture and design, leveraging the collective expertise and creativity of all team members.
12. **At regular intervals, the team reflects on how to become more effective, then tunes and adjusts its behavior accordingly.**
- **Example**: After each sprint, an Agile team holds a retrospective meeting to discuss what went well, what could be improved, and actions to take for the next sprint.

Real-World Applications and Significance
Fostering Collaboration
- **Example**: In a healthcare IT project, Agile principles promote collaboration between developers and healthcare professionals. Daily interactions and regular reviews ensure that the software meets the real needs of doctors and nurses, leading to higher quality solutions.

Enhancing Adaptability
- **Example**: An Agile team developing a retail application quickly adapts to changing customer preferences by continuously integrating feedback. When a new market trend emerges, the team can pivot and add relevant features without significant delays or disruptions.

Improving Customer Satisfaction
- **Example**: A startup building a new product uses Agile to involve early adopters in the development process. By delivering working software frequently and incorporating user feedback, the startup ensures that the final product closely aligns with customer needs and expectations.

By adhering to the Agile values and principles, teams can create a flexible, collaborative, and customer-focused approach to project management, leading to more successful outcomes and higher satisfaction for all stakeholders involved.

Agile and predictive methodologies, such as Waterfall, represent two fundamentally different approaches to project management. Each has its strengths and weaknesses, and the choice between them depends on various factors including project scope, complexity, stakeholder requirements, and industry practices. Let's compare and contrast these methodologies in terms of project planning, execution, and delivery, and explore their respective benefits and challenges with industry-specific examples.

Key Differences Between Agile and Predictive Methodologies
1. Project Planning
Agile Methodology:

- **Incremental Planning:** Agile involves iterative planning, where the project is broken down into small, manageable increments called sprints (typically 1-4 weeks long).
- **Flexibility:** Agile allows for changes in requirements throughout the project lifecycle. Plans are continuously refined based on stakeholder feedback and evolving project needs.
- **Collaborative Approach:** Planning involves continuous collaboration with stakeholders, ensuring that their needs are regularly reviewed and addressed.

Predictive (Waterfall) Methodology:
- **Comprehensive Upfront Planning:** Waterfall requires detailed planning at the beginning of the project. All requirements are gathered, and a comprehensive project plan is created before execution begins.
- **Fixed Scope:** Changes to the project scope are difficult to accommodate once the planning phase is complete. The plan serves as a blueprint for the entire project.
- **Sequential Approach:** Each phase of the project (e.g., requirements, design, implementation, testing, and maintenance) is completed before moving on to the next.

2. Project Execution

Agile Methodology:
- **Iterative Development:** Agile involves iterative cycles of development and testing. Each sprint delivers a potentially shippable product increment.
- **Frequent Releases:** Agile teams aim for continuous delivery of features, allowing for early and regular releases of the product.
- **Cross-Functional Teams:** Teams are typically cross-functional, with members possessing diverse skills to complete each increment independently.

Predictive (Waterfall) Methodology:
- **Linear Execution:** The project follows a linear sequence of phases. Execution starts only after comprehensive planning and design are completed.
- **Single Release:** The product is delivered in a single release after all phases are completed, making it difficult to address issues or changes mid-project.
- **Specialized Teams:** Teams are often specialized, working on their respective phases (e.g., designers, developers, testers) sequentially.

3. Project Delivery

Agile Methodology:
- **Continuous Delivery:** Agile emphasizes delivering value to customers as early and frequently as possible. Each sprint aims to produce a working product increment.
- **Customer Feedback:** Continuous stakeholder and customer feedback are integral, allowing for adjustments based on real-time input.
- **Flexibility in Scope:** The project scope can evolve based on feedback, making Agile suitable for projects with high uncertainty and changing requirements.

Predictive (Waterfall) Methodology:
- **Single Delivery Point:** Delivery occurs at the end of the project lifecycle, making it crucial to get all requirements right from the start.
- **Minimal Changes:** Changes are typically minimized and controlled through formal change management processes, making it less flexible to adapt to new information or stakeholder feedback.
- **Scope Fixed:** The project scope is defined early and remains mostly unchanged throughout the project lifecycle.

Factors Influencing the Choice of Methodology

1. **Project Scope and Requirements:**
   - **Agile:** Suitable for projects with evolving or unclear requirements, such as software development projects where user needs may change.
   - **Waterfall:** Ideal for projects with well-defined, stable requirements, such as construction projects where changes can be costly and time-consuming.

2. **Stakeholder Involvement:**
    - **Agile:** Requires high stakeholder engagement and frequent feedback. It is beneficial for projects where stakeholders can provide ongoing input.
    - **Waterfall:** Suitable for projects where stakeholders define requirements upfront and have limited involvement during execution.
3. **Project Complexity and Uncertainty:**
    - **Agile:** Effective for complex projects with high uncertainty, allowing teams to adapt to changes and new discoveries.
    - **Waterfall:** Best for projects with low uncertainty and a clear, linear progression of tasks.
4. **Industry Practices:**
    - **Agile:** Common in software development, IT, and creative industries where flexibility and rapid iteration are crucial.
    - **Waterfall:** Frequently used in construction, manufacturing, and defense industries where structure and predictability are paramount.

Industry-Specific Examples
Agile Methodology
Example 1: Software Development
- **Scenario:** A tech company is developing a new mobile application. The requirements are expected to evolve based on user feedback.
- **Approach:** The project team adopts Agile, using two-week sprints to develop features incrementally. Regular user testing sessions are held to gather feedback and make necessary adjustments.
- **Benefits:** The company can quickly adapt to user needs, improving the app based on real-time feedback, leading to higher user satisfaction and a better final product.
- **Challenges:** Requires continuous stakeholder engagement and effective communication within cross-functional teams.

Example 2: Marketing Campaigns
- **Scenario:** A marketing agency is running a digital marketing campaign for a new product launch.
- **Approach:** The agency uses Agile to iterate on ad creatives, targeting strategies, and social media content based on performance metrics and customer feedback.
- **Benefits:** The campaign can be adjusted quickly based on what resonates with the audience, optimizing engagement and conversion rates.
- **Challenges:** Needs close monitoring of performance data and swift decision-making to implement changes.

Predictive (Waterfall) Methodology
Example 1: Construction Projects
- **Scenario:** A construction firm is building a new office complex.
- **Approach:** The firm uses Waterfall to plan the project in detail, including architectural designs, material specifications, and timelines. Execution follows a strict sequence: foundation, structure, finishing, and inspection.
- **Benefits:** Clear milestones and deliverables ensure all aspects of construction are carefully coordinated, reducing the risk of delays and cost overruns.
- **Challenges:** Any changes to the project scope can be costly and disruptive, requiring extensive re-planning.

Example 2: Manufacturing
- **Scenario:** A manufacturing company is producing a new product line.
- **Approach:** The company adopts Waterfall to design the product, set up production processes, and ensure quality control measures are in place before mass production.
- **Benefits:** The structured approach ensures consistent product quality and efficient use of resources.
- **Challenges:** Limited flexibility to accommodate changes once production starts, making it essential to get the design and processes right from the beginning.

Both Agile and Waterfall methodologies have their place in project management. The choice between them should be based on project-specific factors, including the nature of the requirements, stakeholder involvement, and industry practices. By understanding the strengths and challenges of each approach, project managers can select the methodology that best fits their project needs, ensuring successful outcomes.

Overview of Popular Agile Frameworks

Agile frameworks provide structured methods for implementing Agile principles and practices in project management. Among the most popular Agile frameworks are Scrum, Kanban, and Lean. Each framework has its unique principles, practices, and ceremonies, making them suitable for different types of projects and organizational contexts.

Scrum

Core Principles and Practices

Scrum is an iterative and incremental Agile framework primarily used for managing software development projects. It emphasizes collaboration, accountability, and iterative progress toward a well-defined goal.

Key Elements:

1. **Roles**:
   - **Product Owner**: Responsible for maximizing the value of the product and managing the product backlog.
   - **Scrum Master**: Facilitates Scrum processes and removes impediments for the team.
   - **Development Team**: Cross-functional group responsible for delivering potentially shippable increments of the product.

2. **Artifacts**:
   - **Product Backlog**: An ordered list of all desired work on the project, managed by the Product Owner.
   - **Sprint Backlog**: A list of tasks to be completed during the sprint, selected from the product backlog.
   - **Increment**: The sum of all completed product backlog items at the end of a sprint.

3. **Ceremonies**:
   - **Sprint Planning**: A meeting where the team plans the work to be completed in the upcoming sprint.
   - **Daily Scrum**: A short daily meeting where team members synchronize activities and plan for the next 24 hours.
   - **Sprint Review**: A meeting at the end of the sprint to inspect the increment and adapt the product backlog.
   - **Sprint Retrospective**: A meeting for the team to reflect on the sprint and plan improvements for the next sprint.

Suitability:
- Scrum is ideal for projects with complex requirements and the need for frequent feedback and iteration. It is commonly used in software development but can be applied to various fields requiring iterative progress.

Case Study:
- **Example**: A software development company used Scrum to manage the development of a new e-commerce platform. By holding regular sprint reviews and retrospectives, the team was able to incorporate customer feedback quickly and make continuous improvements, leading to a successful and timely product launch.

Kanban

Core Principles and Practices

Kanban is an Agile framework that emphasizes visualizing work, limiting work in progress, and improving flow. It is flexible and focuses on continuous delivery without the need for time-boxed iterations.

Key Elements:

1. **Principles**:
   - **Visualize the Workflow**: Use a Kanban board to visualize the flow of work items through various stages.
   - **Limit Work in Progress (WIP)**: Set limits on the number of work items in each stage to ensure a smooth workflow.
   - **Manage Flow**: Monitor and optimize the flow of work items to identify and eliminate bottlenecks.

- **Make Process Policies Explicit**: Clearly define and communicate the rules and policies governing the workflow.
- **Improve Collaboratively**: Use data and team insights to make continuous, incremental improvements.
2. **Kanban Board**:
    - A visual tool that displays work items and their progress through different stages, typically columns labeled "To Do," "In Progress," and "Done."

Suitability:
- Kanban is suitable for projects requiring a continuous delivery model and where the focus is on improving process efficiency and flow. It is often used in operational environments, support teams, and maintenance projects.

Case Study:
- **Example**: A customer support team implemented Kanban to manage incoming support tickets. By visualizing the workflow on a Kanban board and limiting WIP, the team reduced response times and improved customer satisfaction.

Lean
Core Principles and Practices
Lean is an Agile framework focused on delivering maximum value to the customer by eliminating waste and optimizing processes. It originated in manufacturing but has been adapted to various industries, including software development.

Key Elements:
1. **Principles**:
    - **Value**: Define value from the customer's perspective.
    - **Value Stream**: Map the value stream to identify and eliminate waste.
    - **Flow**: Create a smooth flow of work to ensure value delivery.
    - **Pull**: Implement a pull system to produce work based on customer demand.
    - **Perfection**: Continuously improve processes to achieve perfection.
2. **Practices**:
    - **Kaizen**: A practice of continuous improvement through small, incremental changes.
    - **5S**: A workplace organization method (Sort, Set in Order, Shine, Standardize, Sustain) to improve efficiency.
    - **Just-In-Time (JIT)**: Producing only what is needed, when it is needed, to reduce inventory and waste.

Suitability:
- Lean is suitable for projects aiming to maximize efficiency and minimize waste. It is widely used in manufacturing, product development, and any industry where process optimization is crucial.

Case Study:
- **Example**: An automotive company implemented Lean principles in their production line. By mapping the value stream and applying JIT practices, they reduced waste, improved production times, and increased overall efficiency.

Real-World Application and Significance
Fostering Collaboration
- **Scrum Example**: A cross-functional team in a tech startup uses Scrum to enhance collaboration. Regular sprint planning and daily stand-ups ensure everyone is aligned and working towards the same goal, leading to a cohesive team effort.

Enhancing Adaptability
- **Kanban Example**: A marketing team adopts Kanban to manage campaign tasks. By visualizing work on a Kanban board and adjusting WIP limits, they quickly adapt to changing priorities and market conditions without the rigidity of fixed iterations.

Improving Customer Satisfaction

- **Lean Example**: A healthcare provider uses Lean principles to streamline patient intake processes. By mapping the value stream and eliminating waste, they reduce wait times and improve patient satisfaction.

Each Agile framework—Scrum, Kanban, and Lean—offers unique benefits and is suitable for different project types and organizational contexts. Scrum is ideal for iterative development with a focus on team collaboration and feedback. Kanban emphasizes continuous flow and process improvement, making it suitable for operational environments. Lean focuses on maximizing value and eliminating waste, making it ideal for efficiency-driven projects. Understanding these frameworks allows organizations to choose the best approach for their specific needs and enhance project success through collaboration, adaptability, and customer satisfaction.

Agile projects rely on clearly defined roles to ensure effective collaboration and successful delivery of the project. The key roles in Agile, particularly in Scrum (one of the most popular Agile frameworks), include the Scrum Master, Product Owner, and Development Team. Each role has specific responsibilities and competencies, and they must work closely together to ensure project success.

Key Roles and Responsibilities

1. Scrum Master

Duties:
- **Facilitate Scrum Events:** Organize and facilitate daily stand-ups, sprint planning, sprint reviews, and retrospectives.
- **Remove Impediments:** Identify and eliminate obstacles that prevent the team from achieving their goals.
- **Coach the Team:** Educate the team on Agile principles and Scrum practices, fostering a culture of continuous improvement.
- **Ensure Process Adherence:** Ensure that the Scrum process is followed and that the team understands and adheres to Scrum practices.

Competencies:
- **Facilitation Skills:** Ability to guide team discussions and foster a collaborative environment.
- **Problem-Solving Skills:** Proactively identify and resolve issues that hinder team progress.
- **Knowledge of Agile and Scrum:** Deep understanding of Agile principles and the Scrum framework.
- **Communication Skills:** Excellent verbal and written communication skills to interact effectively with the team and stakeholders.

Challenges and Strategies:
- **Challenge:** Team Resistance to Change.
    - **Strategy:** Provide training and coaching to help the team understand the benefits of Agile and how it improves their work.
- **Challenge:** Managing Conflicts within the Team.
    - **Strategy:** Facilitate open and honest communication, encouraging the team to address conflicts constructively during retrospectives.

2. Product Owner

Duties:
- **Define Product Vision:** Clearly articulate the product vision and ensure it aligns with the stakeholders' needs and business goals.
- **Manage the Product Backlog:** Create, prioritize, and refine the product backlog items to ensure the team works on the most valuable features.
- **Stakeholder Communication:** Act as the primary liaison between the team and stakeholders, ensuring that stakeholder expectations are managed and met.
- **Approve Deliverables:** Review and accept or reject the completed work at the end of each sprint.

Competencies:
- **Visionary Thinking:** Ability to create a compelling product vision and align it with business objectives.
- **Decision-Making:** Make informed decisions quickly to prioritize work and manage the backlog effectively.
- **Negotiation Skills:** Negotiate with stakeholders to balance their needs and manage expectations.

- **Domain Knowledge:** Deep understanding of the business domain and the needs of the customers and users.

Challenges and Strategies:
- **Challenge:** Conflicting Stakeholder Interests.
  - **Strategy:** Facilitate workshops to gather input and build consensus, and prioritize backlog items based on value and strategic alignment.
- **Challenge:** Insufficient Backlog Refinement.
  - **Strategy:** Schedule regular backlog refinement sessions and collaborate closely with the development team to ensure clear and detailed user stories.

3. Development Team

Duties:
- **Deliver Increments:** Develop and deliver potentially shippable product increments at the end of each sprint.
- **Self-Organize:** Manage their own work and collaborate to achieve sprint goals without direct supervision.
- **Continuous Improvement:** Participate in retrospectives to identify areas for improvement and implement changes.
- **Maintain Quality:** Ensure that the work meets the agreed-upon quality standards and technical requirements.

Competencies:
- **Technical Skills:** Proficiency in the relevant technologies and tools required to build the product.
- **Collaboration:** Ability to work effectively as a team, sharing knowledge and supporting each other.
- **Adaptability:** Willingness to adapt to changing requirements and improve processes continuously.
- **Problem-Solving:** Ability to address technical challenges and find effective solutions.

Challenges and Strategies:
- **Challenge:** Scope Creep.
  - **Strategy:** Work closely with the Product Owner to manage and prioritize the backlog, and maintain a focus on the sprint goal.
- **Challenge:** Technical Debt.
  - **Strategy:** Allocate time for refactoring and maintenance, and follow best practices to ensure code quality.

Collaboration for Successful Project Delivery

Scrum Master and Product Owner:
- **Collaboration:** The Scrum Master supports the Product Owner by facilitating communication with the team and stakeholders. They help ensure that the Product Owner's priorities are clear and that the team understands the product vision.
- **Example:** The Scrum Master might help organize a backlog refinement session, where the Product Owner explains the highest-priority items, and the team asks questions to clarify requirements.

Scrum Master and Development Team:
- **Collaboration:** The Scrum Master works with the Development Team to remove impediments and ensure that they have the resources and support needed to complete their work.
- **Example:** If the team faces a technical roadblock, the Scrum Master intervenes to find a solution, such as securing additional resources or expertise.

Product Owner and Development Team:
- **Collaboration:** The Product Owner communicates the product vision and prioritizes backlog items, while the Development Team provides feedback on feasibility and effort estimates.
- **Example:** During sprint planning, the Product Owner presents the prioritized backlog items, and the team discusses each item, providing estimates and identifying any potential challenges.

Common Challenges and Strategies

Scrum Master
- **Challenge:** Facilitating Effective Retrospectives.

- **Strategy:** Use varied retrospective techniques to keep the sessions engaging and productive, ensuring actionable outcomes.

Product Owner
- **Challenge:** Overcommitment of Features.
  - **Strategy:** Prioritize backlog items based on value and capacity, ensuring that the team commits to a realistic amount of work each sprint.

Development Team
- **Challenge:** Integrating New Team Members.
  - **Strategy:** Foster a welcoming environment, provide onboarding and mentoring, and ensure that new members understand the Agile principles and team processes.

Effective collaboration among the Scrum Master, Product Owner, and Development Team is crucial for Agile project success. By understanding their roles and responsibilities, fostering open communication, and addressing challenges proactively, Agile teams can deliver high-quality products that meet stakeholder needs and adapt to changing requirements.

The Concept of User Stories in Agile Planning and Estimation

User stories are a fundamental component of Agile methodologies, particularly in frameworks like Scrum and Kanban. They are short, simple descriptions of a feature or functionality from the perspective of the end user. User stories help the team understand the value and purpose of the work, ensuring that development focuses on delivering user-centric outcomes.

Role of User Stories in Agile Planning and Estimation

User stories play a crucial role in Agile planning and estimation by:
1. **Facilitating Communication**: They serve as a medium for conversations between stakeholders and the development team, ensuring a shared understanding of requirements.
2. **Prioritization**: User stories are used to prioritize work based on business value, user needs, and strategic goals.
3. **Estimation**: They provide a unit for estimating effort, which helps in planning sprints and releases.
4. **Tracking Progress**: User stories help track progress by breaking down features into manageable pieces that can be completed within a sprint.

Writing Effective User Stories Using INVEST Criteria

The INVEST criteria ensure that user stories are well-formed and effective. Each letter in the acronym stands for a key characteristic of a good user story:
1. **Independent**: The user story should be self-contained, with no dependencies on other stories.
   - **Example**: "As a user, I want to reset my password so that I can regain access to my account without contacting support."
2. **Negotiable**: The details of the user story can be changed and negotiated without altering its intent.
   - **Example**: "As an admin, I want to generate user activity reports so that I can monitor system usage trends."
3. **Valuable**: The story must deliver value to the end user or the customer.
   - **Example**: "As a shopper, I want to see customer reviews on product pages so that I can make informed purchasing decisions."
4. **Estimable**: The team should be able to estimate the effort required to complete the story.
   - **Example**: "As a developer, I want to integrate a third-party payment gateway so that we can accept online payments."
5. **Small**: The story should be small enough to be completed within a single sprint.
   - **Example**: "As a user, I want to receive email notifications for new messages in my inbox."
6. **Testable**: There must be clear criteria to test and verify the completion of the story.
   - **Example**: "As a project manager, I want to set deadlines for tasks so that I can track project timelines."

Examples of Well-Crafted User Stories from Various Domains

1. **E-commerce**:
   - "As a shopper, I want to filter products by price range so that I can find items within my budget."

2. **Healthcare**:
    - "As a doctor, I want to access patient history quickly so that I can provide accurate diagnoses and treatment plans."
3. **Finance**:
    - "As a bank customer, I want to transfer funds between my accounts so that I can manage my finances efficiently."
4. **Education**:
    - "As a student, I want to view my assignment grades online so that I can track my academic progress."

Estimating User Stories Using Story Points and Planning Poker
Story Points
Concept: Story points are a unit of measure for expressing the overall effort required to implement a user story. This includes factors such as complexity, risk, and time.
Process:
1. **Relative Estimation**: Story points are assigned based on the relative effort compared to other stories.
    - **Example**: If a simple task like logging in is assigned 2 points, a more complex task like implementing a payment gateway might be assigned 8 points.
2. **Fibonacci Sequence**: Many teams use the Fibonacci sequence (1, 2, 3, 5, 8, 13, etc.) for estimating story points to reflect the increasing uncertainty with larger stories.

Planning Poker
Concept: Planning poker is a collaborative estimation technique that helps teams reach consensus on the effort required for user stories.
Process:
1. **Preparation**: Each team member is given a set of cards with numbers (representing story points).
2. **Discussion**: The Product Owner presents a user story, and the team discusses its details.
3. **Individual Estimation**: Each team member selects a card that represents their estimate and places it face down.
4. **Reveal and Discuss**: All cards are revealed simultaneously. If there is a significant difference in estimates, the team discusses the reasons and tries to reach a consensus.
5. **Re-estimate if Necessary**: The process is repeated until a consensus is reached.

Example:
- The team is estimating the story "As a user, I want to reset my password." After discussion, estimates range from 2 to 8 points. The team discusses the differences, considering aspects like user interface changes and backend validation, and agrees on 5 points after further discussion.

Significance of Accurate and Reliable Estimates
Accurate and reliable estimates are crucial for:
1. **Sprint Planning**: Helps determine how much work can be committed to in a sprint.
2. **Release Planning**: Provides a basis for forecasting release dates and milestones.
3. **Resource Allocation**: Ensures the team is appropriately resourced to meet project timelines.
4. **Stakeholder Communication**: Sets realistic expectations with stakeholders regarding delivery timelines and scope.

By using user stories effectively and employing techniques like story points and planning poker, Agile teams can create accurate and reliable estimates, leading to better planning, resource management, and successful project outcomes.

Concept of Velocity in Agile Projects
Velocity in Agile projects measures the amount of work a team can complete during a single sprint. It's a key metric for sprint planning and forecasting future work.

Significance of Velocity in Sprint Planning and Forecasting
1. **Sprint Planning:**
    - **Commitment:** Velocity helps the team understand how much work they can realistically commit to in the next sprint based on past performance.

- o **Workload Distribution:** Knowing their velocity, teams can distribute tasks more evenly and avoid over-committing.
2. **Forecasting:**
    - o **Release Planning:** Velocity is used to predict how many sprints are needed to complete the remaining work in the product backlog.
    - o **Predictability:** Provides a data-driven basis for setting expectations with stakeholders about delivery timelines and project progress.

Calculating Velocity
Velocity Calculation:
- Velocity is calculated by summing the story points (or other units of measure) for all the user stories or tasks completed in a sprint.
- **Historical Data:** To get a reliable measure of velocity, average the completed story points over several past sprints.

Steps:
1. **Collect Data:** Gather the story points for all user stories completed in each sprint.
2. **Sum Story Points:** Add up the story points for each completed story within a sprint.
3. **Average Over Sprints:** Calculate the average story points completed per sprint over several sprints.

Example Calculation:
- **Sprint 1:** 30 story points completed.
- **Sprint 2:** 25 story points completed.
- **Sprint 3:** 35 story points completed.
- **Sprint 4:** 40 story points completed.

Average Velocity: Average Velocity = (30 + 25 + 35 + 40) / 4 = 130 / 4 = 32.5

Factors Influencing Velocity
1. **Team Size:**
    - o Larger teams may complete more work, but coordination and communication overhead can reduce efficiency.
    - o Smaller teams may have higher efficiency but can complete fewer story points due to limited capacity.
2. **Experience:**
    - o Experienced teams tend to have higher velocity due to better understanding of the domain, tools, and processes.
    - o Newer or less experienced teams may take longer to complete tasks, resulting in lower velocity.
3. **Project Complexity:**
    - o Projects with higher complexity or more unknowns can lead to lower velocity as the team spends more time in discovery and problem-solving.
    - o Simpler projects or well-understood domains can boost velocity as tasks are more straightforward.
4. **Team Stability:**
    - o Stable teams with consistent members tend to develop a rhythm, leading to more predictable velocity.
    - o Teams with frequent changes in membership can experience fluctuations in velocity.
5. **Technical Debt and Defects:**
    - o Accumulation of technical debt and addressing defects can reduce the available capacity for new feature development, impacting velocity.

Using Velocity in Sprint Planning
Example 1: Committing to User Stories
- **Average Velocity:** 32.5 story points per sprint.
- **Product Backlog User Stories:**
    - o Story A: 8 points
    - o Story B: 5 points

- Story C: 13 points
- Story D: 3 points
- Story E: 8 points

Planning:
- The team can start by selecting stories that add up to their average velocity.
- Possible combination: Story A (8) + Story B (5) + Story C (13) + Story D (3) + Story E (8) = 37 points.
- Since 37 points exceed the average velocity of 32.5, the team might drop Story E or replace it with a smaller story.

Example 2: Release Planning
- **Remaining Backlog:** 200 story points.
- **Average Velocity:** 32.5 story points per sprint.

Forecasting: Number of Sprints Needed = 200 story points / 32.5 story points per sprint ≈ 6.15
- The team would need approximately 7 sprints to complete the remaining work, considering some variability and uncertainty.

Managing Velocity in Agile Teams
1. **Regular Review:** Continuously monitor and review velocity to ensure it reflects the team's true capacity and identify any trends or issues.
2. **Retrospectives:** Use sprint retrospectives to discuss factors affecting velocity and implement improvements.
3. **Adjust for Changes:** Recalculate velocity if there are significant changes in team composition, scope, or working conditions.
4. **Buffer for Uncertainty:** Avoid committing 100% of the velocity to planned work; leave some buffer for unforeseen tasks and changes.

Common Challenges and Strategies

Challenge: Variability in Velocity
- **Strategy:** Use a rolling average over multiple sprints to smooth out fluctuations and provide a more stable estimate.

Challenge: Over-commitment
- **Strategy:** Base sprint commitments on historical velocity data and adjust for any known upcoming challenges or holidays.

Challenge: New or Changing Team Members
- **Strategy:** Factor in a temporary dip in velocity as new team members get up to speed, and reassess velocity after stabilization.

By understanding and effectively utilizing velocity, Agile teams can plan more accurately, manage stakeholder expectations, and continuously improve their processes.

Sprint Planning and Backlog Grooming in Agile Projects

Sprint planning and backlog grooming are essential ceremonies in Agile project management that ensure the team is focused on delivering the most valuable features and that upcoming work is well-defined and achievable. Here's an overview of each process and best practices for facilitating them effectively.

Sprint Planning

Sprint Planning is the ceremony that kicks off a sprint. It involves defining the sprint goal, selecting user stories from the product backlog, and breaking them down into actionable tasks. The key activities in sprint planning ensure that the team understands what needs to be done and how they will accomplish it.

Key Activities in Sprint Planning
1. **Define the Sprint Goal**
    - **Purpose:** The sprint goal provides a clear and concise statement of what the team aims to achieve during the sprint. It aligns the team and stakeholders on the sprint's primary objective.
    - **Activity:** The Product Owner proposes a goal based on the product backlog and business priorities. The team discusses and agrees on a goal that is achievable and valuable.
2. **Select User Stories**

- **Purpose**: Choosing the most valuable user stories ensures that the team is working on features that deliver the highest value to the customer.
- **Activity**: The Product Owner presents the top-priority user stories from the product backlog. The team discusses each story, clarifies any questions, and agrees on which stories to include in the sprint based on their capacity.

3. **Estimate and Break Down User Stories into Tasks**
    - **Purpose**: Breaking down user stories into smaller, manageable tasks helps the team understand the work required and facilitates better tracking of progress.
    - **Activity**: The team collaborates to break each selected user story into tasks, estimates the effort required for each task, and assigns tasks to team members.

Example: In a two-week sprint for an e-commerce platform, the sprint goal might be to improve the checkout process. Selected user stories could include "As a user, I want to save my payment details for future purchases" and "As a user, I want to receive an email confirmation after placing an order." These stories are broken down into tasks such as designing the user interface, implementing the backend logic, and writing test cases.

Best Practices for Sprint Planning
1. **Prepare in Advance**: The Product Owner should have a prioritized and well-refined backlog ready before the meeting.
2. **Collaborative Discussion**: Encourage open dialogue among team members to clarify requirements and ensure a shared understanding.
3. **Realistic Commitment**: Base commitments on the team's past velocity and current capacity to avoid overcommitting.
4. **Focus on the Sprint Goal**: Keep discussions aligned with achieving the sprint goal.

Backlog Grooming (Refinement)

Backlog Grooming (or refinement) is an ongoing process that involves reviewing and updating the product backlog to ensure that it is current, prioritized, and ready for future sprints. Regular backlog grooming helps keep the backlog manageable and ensures the team is always working on the most valuable tasks.

Key Activities in Backlog Grooming
1. **Review and Prioritize User Stories**
    - **Purpose**: Ensure that the most valuable and relevant user stories are prioritized and ready for upcoming sprints.
    - **Activity**: The Product Owner reviews the backlog with the team, discusses priorities, and reorders items based on business value and dependencies.
2. **Refine and Clarify User Stories**
    - **Purpose**: Provide clear, detailed, and actionable user stories to avoid confusion during sprint planning.
    - **Activity**: The team discusses each user story, adds details, clarifies requirements, and splits large stories into smaller, more manageable ones if necessary.
3. **Estimate User Stories**
    - **Purpose**: Assign effort estimates to user stories to help in sprint planning and capacity management.
    - **Activity**: The team uses techniques like planning poker to estimate the effort required for each user story, ensuring that all stories in the backlog have an initial estimate.
4. **Identify and Manage Dependencies**
    - **Purpose**: Recognize any dependencies between user stories to ensure they are addressed in the right order.
    - **Activity**: The team identifies dependencies, discusses how to manage them, and adjusts the backlog accordingly.

Example: In an ongoing project for a mobile banking app, backlog grooming might involve prioritizing new user stories such as "As a user, I want to view my transaction history" and refining stories like "As a user, I want to set up recurring payments" by adding acceptance criteria and splitting them into smaller tasks.

Best Practices for Backlog Grooming
1. **Regular Sessions**: Schedule regular grooming sessions, ideally once a week, to keep the backlog up to date.

2. **Involve the Team**: Ensure that the entire team participates in grooming sessions to leverage their insights and foster a shared understanding.
3. **Focus on High-Priority Items**: Spend more time refining high-priority items that are likely to be included in the next sprint.
4. **Keep it Manageable**: Aim to have a refined backlog that covers at least the next two to three sprints to avoid last-minute rushes.

Importance of Regularly Refining and Prioritizing the Product Backlog

Regular refinement and prioritization of the product backlog are crucial for ensuring that the team is always working on the most valuable features. This process helps:

1. **Align Work with Business Goals**: By continuously prioritizing user stories, the team ensures that their efforts align with the overall business objectives.
2. **Improve Efficiency**: Clear, well-defined user stories reduce the time spent during sprint planning and help the team start work more quickly.
3. **Enhance Adaptability**: Regular grooming allows the team to respond to changing requirements and priorities effectively.
4. **Reduce Risks**: Identifying and managing dependencies early reduces the risk of delays and bottlenecks.

Facilitating Effective Sprint Planning and Backlog Grooming Sessions

Sprint Planning Best Practices:
- **Set a Time Box**: Limit the duration of the sprint planning meeting to avoid prolonged discussions.
- **Define Clear Objectives**: Start with a clear sprint goal and ensure all discussions are focused on achieving it.
- **Visualize Work**: Use tools like digital boards or physical task boards to visualize selected user stories and tasks.
- **Engage the Whole Team**: Ensure that all team members are actively involved in discussions and decisions.

Backlog Grooming Best Practices:
- **Prepare Ahead**: The Product Owner should review and prioritize the backlog before the grooming session.
- **Use Consistent Criteria**: Apply consistent criteria for prioritizing and refining user stories to maintain quality.
- **Document Discussions**: Keep detailed notes on decisions made during grooming to ensure clarity and continuity.
- **Foster Collaboration**: Encourage collaboration and input from all team members to leverage diverse perspectives.

By following these practices and ensuring regular, effective sprint planning and backlog grooming sessions, Agile teams can maintain a focused, adaptable, and high-performing workflow that consistently delivers value to stakeholders.

Purpose and Structure of Daily Standups in Agile Projects

Daily standups are short, time-boxed meetings held every day in Agile projects, typically lasting 15 minutes. The primary purpose is to foster team coordination, identify impediments, and ensure continuous progress toward the sprint goal.

Purpose of Daily Standups

1. **Fostering Team Coordination:** Standups provide a regular platform for team members to communicate about their work, ensuring everyone is aligned and aware of each other's tasks.
2. **Identifying Impediments:** Team members can quickly highlight any obstacles they are facing, enabling the team or the Scrum Master to address them promptly.
3. **Ensuring Progress:** Regular updates help ensure the team is progressing toward the sprint goal, allowing for real-time adjustments and continuous improvement.

Structure of Daily Standups

The structure of a daily standup typically involves each team member answering three key questions:

1. **What did I do yesterday?**
   - Team members share what they accomplished since the last standup, providing visibility into their progress.

2. **What will I do today?**
    - Team members outline their plan for the day, setting clear expectations and keeping the team informed.
3. **What impediments are in my way?**
    - Team members identify any blockers or challenges, enabling the team to support each other and resolve issues quickly.

Benefits of Daily Standups
1. **Transparency:** Promotes open communication and transparency about progress and challenges.
2. **Accountability:** Encourages team members to commit to daily goals and hold themselves accountable.
3. **Collaboration:** Enhances collaboration and teamwork, as members stay informed about each other's tasks and can offer help.
4. **Agility:** Allows for quick adjustments and course corrections, maintaining the project's agility.

Examples of Effective Standup Formats
1. **Classic Round-Robin:**
    - Each team member speaks in turn, addressing the three key questions.
    - Works well for small to medium-sized teams.
    - Ensures every team member has an opportunity to contribute.
2. **Walk the Board:**
    - Focuses on the team's task board (e.g., Kanban or Scrum board).
    - Team members discuss the status of tasks directly from the board.
    - Helps visualize progress and identify bottlenecks.
    - Particularly effective for larger teams or those using visual task management tools.
3. **Themed Standups:**
    - Each standup has a specific focus, such as "Technical Tuesdays" or "Feedback Fridays."
    - Can help address recurring issues or themes more deeply while still keeping the meeting short.

Techniques for Keeping Standups Focused and Productive
1. **Time-Boxing:**
    - Strictly enforce the 15-minute time limit to keep the meeting concise and focused.
    - Use a timer if necessary to ensure the meeting doesn't overrun.
2. **Stand Up:**
    - Physically standing up helps keep the meeting brief and energetic.
    - Encourages quick updates and reduces the likelihood of long discussions.
3. **Parking Lot:**
    - Use a "parking lot" for off-topic or in-depth discussions that arise during the standup.
    - Address these topics after the standup or in a separate meeting to keep the daily standup focused.
4. **Facilitator Role:**
    - The Scrum Master or a designated facilitator can guide the standup, ensuring it stays on track.
    - Helps manage the flow of the meeting and ensures everyone gets a chance to speak.
5. **Use Visual Aids:**
    - Utilize task boards, burndown charts, or other visual aids to quickly convey progress and issues.
    - Visual tools can make it easier to identify where the team stands and what needs attention.

Examples of Daily Standups in Action

Example 1: Software Development Team
- **Classic Round-Robin Format:**
    - **Yesterday:** "I completed the login feature and started working on the user profile page."
    - **Today:** "I will continue with the user profile page and begin integration testing."
    - **Impediments:** "I am facing issues with the API response time, which is delaying my testing."

Example 2: Marketing Team
- **Walk the Board Format:**
    - Team members gather around the Kanban board.
    - Discuss each task in the "In Progress" and "Done" columns.

- o Identify any tasks stuck in the "Blocked" column and address issues.

Example 3: Cross-Functional Team
- **Themed Standup Format:**
  - o **Technical Tuesdays:** Focus on technical challenges and solutions.
  - o **What did I do yesterday:** "I resolved the database performance issue."
  - o **What will I do today:** "I will optimize the query for faster data retrieval."
  - o **Impediments:** "I need access to the staging environment for further testing."

By maintaining a structured and disciplined approach to daily standups, Agile teams can enhance communication, quickly identify and resolve impediments, and ensure consistent progress towards their sprint goals. Effective standups contribute significantly to the overall success and agility of the project.

Continuous Integration and Continuous Delivery (CI/CD) in Agile Projects

Continuous Integration (CI) and Continuous Delivery (CD) are essential practices in Agile software development that focus on automating and streamlining the software release process. These practices help ensure code quality, reduce integration issues, and enable frequent releases to customers, aligning perfectly with Agile principles of rapid and incremental delivery.

Continuous Integration (CI)

Concept: Continuous Integration is the practice of frequently merging all developer working copies to a shared mainline. The main goal is to detect and fix integration issues early by integrating work continuously and automatically testing it.

Key Activities:
1. **Frequent Code Integration**: Developers commit code changes frequently, at least once a day, to the main repository.
2. **Automated Builds**: Each commit triggers an automated build process that compiles the code and runs tests.
3. **Automated Testing**: Automated tests are executed to validate that the new code does not break existing functionality.

Benefits:
- **Early Detection of Issues**: Integration issues are detected early, reducing the complexity of fixing them.
- **Improved Code Quality**: Frequent integration and testing ensure that code quality is maintained throughout the development process.
- **Reduced Integration Problems**: By integrating code continuously, the risk of significant integration problems at the end of the project is minimized.

Continuous Delivery (CD)

Concept: Continuous Delivery extends Continuous Integration by ensuring that the software can be released to production at any time. It focuses on automating the release process so that new changes can be deployed quickly and reliably.

Key Activities:
1. **Automated Deployment**: The deployment process is automated to ensure consistency and reliability.
2. **Release Readiness**: Every code change is always in a deployable state, passing all necessary tests and checks.
3. **Frequent Releases**: Software is released frequently, often multiple times a day, based on business needs and user feedback.

Benefits:
- **Faster Time to Market**: Features and bug fixes are delivered to customers more quickly.
- **Reduced Deployment Risk**: Smaller, incremental releases reduce the risk associated with big-bang deployments.
- **Increased Customer Feedback**: Frequent releases allow for quicker user feedback, which can be incorporated into subsequent iterations.

Role of Automation Tools and Pipelines in Implementing CI/CD

Automation tools and pipelines play a crucial role in implementing CI/CD practices. They help streamline the process of integrating, testing, and deploying code, making it possible to achieve the goals of CI/CD.

Key Components of CI/CD Pipelines:
1. **Source Control**: Version control systems (e.g., Git) to manage code changes and enable collaboration.
2. **Build Automation**: Tools to automate the compilation of code and the creation of executable artifacts.
3. **Automated Testing**: Frameworks to run unit tests, integration tests, and other automated tests.
4. **Deployment Automation**: Tools to automate the deployment of applications to various environments (e.g., staging, production).
5. **Monitoring and Feedback**: Systems to monitor the deployed applications and gather feedback for continuous improvement.

Popular CI/CD Tools and Platforms:
1. **Jenkins**:
    - **Description**: An open-source automation server used for building, testing, and deploying code.
    - **Features**: Extensible with a vast library of plugins, supports various version control systems and integrates with many other tools.
    - **Example**: A software company uses Jenkins to automate the build and test process for their web application, ensuring that every commit is validated before deployment.
2. **GitLab CI/CD**:
    - **Description**: A built-in continuous integration and delivery tool in GitLab, a web-based DevOps lifecycle tool.
    - **Features**: Seamlessly integrates with GitLab repositories, provides powerful pipeline configuration through .gitlab-ci.yml files.
    - **Example**: A development team uses GitLab CI/CD to manage their entire DevOps lifecycle, from code commits to deployment, within a single platform.
3. **Travis CI**:
    - **Description**: A hosted continuous integration service used to build and test software projects hosted on GitHub.
    - **Features**: Easy integration with GitHub, supports multiple programming languages, and provides a straightforward configuration using .travis.yml files.
    - **Example**: An open-source project uses Travis CI to automatically run tests on each pull request, ensuring that contributions do not introduce new bugs.
4. **CircleCI**:
    - **Description**: A cloud-based continuous integration and delivery platform that automates the build, test, and deployment process.
    - **Features**: Fast build processing, easy configuration with YAML files, and robust support for parallel testing.
    - **Example**: A mobile app development team uses CircleCI to automate the testing and deployment of their application to both Android and iOS platforms.
5. **Azure DevOps**:
    - **Description**: A set of development tools provided by Microsoft, which includes Azure Pipelines for CI/CD.
    - **Features**: Integration with Azure services, support for multiple languages and platforms, and scalability for large teams.
    - **Example**: A large enterprise uses Azure DevOps to manage their CI/CD pipelines, ensuring seamless integration with their existing Azure infrastructure.

Implementing CI/CD: A Real-World Example
Scenario: A fintech startup developing a new online banking platform.
Implementation:
1. **Setup Source Control**: The team uses GitHub to manage their code repositories.
2. **Automate Builds with Jenkins**: Jenkins is configured to trigger builds for every commit made to the main branch. The build process includes compiling the code and running unit tests.
3. **Automate Testing with Selenium**: Automated UI tests are run using Selenium to ensure that the user interface works as expected.

4. **Deployment Automation with Docker and Kubernetes**: The application is containerized using Docker and deployed to a Kubernetes cluster. Jenkins pipelines handle the deployment process, ensuring that new versions of the application are deployed seamlessly.
   5. **Monitoring with Prometheus and Grafana**: The deployed application is monitored using Prometheus, and Grafana dashboards provide real-time insights into the application's performance and health.

Benefits:
- **Reduced Integration Issues**: Frequent integration and automated testing catch issues early, reducing the complexity of fixes.
- **Improved Code Quality**: Continuous feedback from automated tests ensures that code quality is maintained.
- **Faster Releases**: Automated deployments and frequent releases enable the team to deliver new features to customers quickly and reliably.

By leveraging CI/CD practices and tools, Agile teams can ensure high code quality, minimize integration issues, and deliver value to customers more frequently and reliably. This approach aligns with Agile principles of continuous improvement, customer satisfaction, and adaptability.

Purpose and Format of Agile Retrospectives

Agile retrospectives are meetings held at the end of each sprint or iteration to reflect on the team's performance and identify opportunities for improvement. The primary purpose is to promote continuous improvement by allowing the team to discuss what worked well, what didn't, and how processes can be enhanced.

Purpose of Agile Retrospectives
1. **Continuous Improvement**: Enable the team to make incremental improvements to their processes and practices.
2. **Team Collaboration**: Foster open communication and teamwork by discussing successes and challenges.
3. **Problem Solving**: Identify and address issues that hinder the team's performance.
4. **Accountability**: Encourage team members to take ownership of their actions and commitments.

Format of Agile Retrospectives
A typical retrospective involves several key steps:
1. **Set the Stage**: Create a conducive environment for open discussion. The facilitator might start with an icebreaker or a brief recap of the sprint.
2. **Gather Data**: Collect feedback on what went well, what didn't go well, and areas for improvement.
3. **Generate Insights**: Analyze the feedback to identify patterns and root causes.
4. **Decide What to Do**: Agree on actionable steps to address the identified issues and enhance positive practices.
5. **Close the Retrospective**: Summarize the discussion, outline the action items, and end on a positive note.

Common Retrospective Techniques

1. "What Went Well, What Didn't Go Well, What Can Be Improved"
Purpose: This simple format helps the team focus on different aspects of their work and identify clear areas for improvement.

Steps:
1. **What Went Well**: Team members share positive aspects of the sprint.
2. **What Didn't Go Well**: Discuss challenges and problems faced during the sprint.
3. **What Can Be Improved**: Suggest actionable improvements for the next sprint.

Example:
- **What Went Well**: "Our daily standups were concise and effective."
- **What Didn't Go Well**: "We faced delays due to unclear requirements."
- **What Can Be Improved**: "We need more detailed requirements from the Product Owner before starting the sprint."

2. "Sailboat" Metaphor
Purpose: This creative format uses a visual metaphor to help the team think about various aspects of their project in a new way.

Steps:
1. **Sailboat:** The team represents the project.
2. **Wind:** Positive forces that are driving the team forward.
3. **Anchors:** Negative forces that are slowing the team down.
4. **Rocks:** Risks or obstacles that could hinder progress.
5. **Island:** The goal or sprint objective the team is aiming to reach.

Example:
- **Wind:** "Collaboration was excellent, and we completed tasks ahead of time."
- **Anchors:** "Technical debt slowed us down significantly."
- **Rocks:** "We foresee potential integration issues with the new API."
- **Island:** "Our goal is to deliver the new feature set by the next release."

Creating a Safe and Collaborative Environment
1. **Psychological Safety:** Ensure team members feel safe to share their thoughts without fear of blame or retaliation.
   - **Strategy:** Emphasize that retrospectives are a blameless space focused on learning and improvement.
2. **Inclusivity:** Encourage participation from all team members to get diverse perspectives.
   - **Strategy:** Use techniques like round-robin sharing or silent brainstorming to ensure everyone has a voice.
3. **Respect:** Foster an atmosphere of respect where all opinions are valued.
   - **Strategy:** Establish ground rules for discussions, such as listening without interrupting and providing constructive feedback.

Examples of Action Items from Effective Retrospectives
1. **Improve Communication:**
   - **Action Item:** Schedule more frequent check-ins with the Product Owner to clarify requirements early in the sprint.
2. **Enhance Collaboration:**
   - **Action Item:** Implement pair programming sessions to enhance knowledge sharing and code quality.
3. **Address Technical Debt:**
   - **Action Item:** Allocate 10% of each sprint's capacity to refactoring and reducing technical debt.
4. **Optimize Processes:**
   - **Action Item:** Streamline the code review process by using automated tools to handle routine checks.
5. **Increase Transparency:**
   - **Action Item:** Create a shared dashboard to track sprint progress and impediments in real-time.

Effective Retrospective Practices
1. **Rotate Facilitators:** To keep retrospectives fresh and engaging, rotate the facilitator role among team members.
2. **Vary Techniques:** Use different retrospective formats and techniques to keep discussions interesting and productive.
3. **Follow-Up:** Ensure that action items are tracked and reviewed in subsequent retrospectives to measure progress and accountability.

Agile retrospectives are vital for fostering a culture of continuous improvement. By using structured formats, creating a safe environment, and following through on action items, teams can enhance their processes, address challenges, and achieve better outcomes with each iteration.

Burn-Down and Burn-Up Charts in Agile Projects

Burn-down and burn-up charts are visual tools used in Agile project management to track progress, identify deviations from the plan, and forecast the likelihood of achieving the sprint or project goals. They provide a clear and straightforward way to monitor the team's progress and ensure that the project remains on track.

Burn-Down Charts
Purpose and Benefits
- **Tracking Progress**: Burn-down charts show the amount of work remaining over time.
- **Identifying Deviations**: They help identify if the team is ahead or behind schedule.
- **Forecasting Completion**: They allow teams to predict if they will complete the work by the end of the sprint or project.

Creating a Burn-Down Chart
Step-by-Step Guide:
1. **Define the Y-Axis and X-Axis**:
    - **Y-Axis**: Represents the total amount of work (e.g., story points, tasks, or hours).
    - **X-Axis**: Represents time (e.g., days in the sprint).
2. **Plot the Total Work**:
    - At the start of the sprint, plot the total amount of work to be done at the top of the Y-axis.
3. **Draw the Ideal Trend Line**:
    - Draw a straight line from the top of the Y-axis (total work) to the end of the X-axis (end of the sprint). This line represents the ideal pace at which work should be completed.
4. **Track Daily Progress**:
    - Each day, update the chart by plotting the remaining work. Connect these points to form the actual progress line.

Example:
- A sprint starts with 100 story points to complete over 10 days.
- Each day, the team updates the chart with the remaining story points.

Interpreting a Burn-Down Chart
- **On Track**: If the actual progress line is close to the ideal trend line, the team is on track.
- **Ahead of Schedule**: If the actual progress line is below the ideal trend line, the team is ahead of schedule.
- **Behind Schedule**: If the actual progress line is above the ideal trend line, the team is behind schedule.

Limitations and Pitfalls
- **Focus on Work Remaining**: Burn-down charts only show work remaining, not work completed.
- **Daily Updates**: They require daily updates to be effective, which can be time-consuming.
- **Misleading Trends**: They can be misleading if the scope of work changes frequently during the sprint.

Burn-Up Charts
Purpose and Benefits
- **Tracking Progress**: Burn-up charts show both the amount of work completed and the total amount of work.
- **Identifying Scope Changes**: They clearly indicate any changes in the scope of work.
- **Forecasting Completion**: They help predict the likelihood of completing the work by the end of the sprint or project.

Creating a Burn-Up Chart
Step-by-Step Guide:
1. **Define the Y-Axis and X-Axis**:
    - **Y-Axis**: Represents the total amount of work (e.g., story points, tasks, or hours).
    - **X-Axis**: Represents time (e.g., days in the sprint).
2. **Plot the Total Work**:
    - At the start of the sprint, plot the total amount of work at the top of the Y-axis.
3. **Track Daily Progress**:
    - Each day, update the chart by plotting the cumulative work completed. Connect these points to form the actual progress line.
4. **Add Scope Line**:
    - If the scope changes, update the total work line to reflect the new scope.

Example:
- A sprint starts with 100 story points to complete over 10 days.

- Each day, the team updates the chart with the cumulative story points completed.

Interpreting a Burn-Up Chart
- **On Track**: If the actual progress line approaches the total work line, the team is on track.
- **Scope Changes**: If the total work line increases or decreases, it indicates a change in the scope of work.
- **Completion Forecast**: By projecting the trend of the actual progress line, the team can forecast the completion date.

Limitations and Pitfalls
- **Complexity**: Burn-up charts can be more complex to create and interpret compared to burn-down charts.
- **Scope Management**: Frequent changes in scope can make the chart difficult to manage and interpret accurately.
- **Visual Clarity**: With multiple lines, the chart can become cluttered and harder to read.

Comparison and Use Cases
Burn-Down Chart Use Cases:
- Ideal for teams that need a simple, straightforward way to track work remaining and monitor daily progress.
- Suitable for sprints with stable scope and minimal changes.

Burn-Up Chart Use Cases:
- Better for projects with frequent scope changes, as they clearly show the impact of these changes.
- Useful for long-term projects where tracking cumulative progress and scope adjustments are crucial.

Best Practices for Using Burn-Down and Burn-Up Charts
1. **Update Regularly**: Ensure the charts are updated daily to reflect the most accurate status.
2. **Review in Stand-Ups**: Discuss the charts during daily stand-up meetings to keep the team informed.
3. **Use in Retrospectives**: Analyze the charts in sprint retrospectives to identify areas for improvement.
4. **Communicate Clearly**: Use the charts to communicate progress and potential issues to stakeholders.

By effectively using burn-down and burn-up charts, Agile teams can gain valuable insights into their progress, identify potential deviations from the plan, and make informed decisions to ensure they meet their sprint and project goals.

Principles and Practices of Kanban
Kanban is an Agile methodology that focuses on visualizing work, limiting work in progress (WIP), and managing the flow of tasks. It aims to improve efficiency and continuously deliver value to customers.

Key Principles of Kanban
1. **Visualize the Workflow:** Making the work visible to everyone involved helps in understanding the progress and identifying bottlenecks.
2. **Limit Work in Progress (WIP):** By limiting the amount of work in progress, teams can reduce multitasking and focus on completing tasks.
3. **Manage Flow:** Monitoring and managing the flow of work through the system to ensure smooth progress and continuous delivery.

Practices of Kanban
1. Visualizing the Workflow
Purpose: Visualization helps teams see the progress of tasks and identify bottlenecks quickly.
Kanban Boards:
- **Structure:** A Kanban board typically consists of columns representing different stages of the workflow (e.g., To Do, In Progress, Done).
- **Cards:** Each task or user story is represented by a card that moves across the board as it progresses through the stages.
- **Customization:** Boards can be customized to fit the specific workflow of a team or project.

Example:
- **Columns:** To Do, In Progress, Review, Done.
- **Cards:** Each card represents a user story or task, such as "Develop login feature," "Design homepage," etc.

2. Limiting Work in Progress (WIP)

Purpose: Limiting WIP helps teams focus on completing tasks before starting new ones, reducing context switching and improving flow.
Setting WIP Limits:
- **Column WIP Limits:** Set maximum limits for each column to control the number of tasks in each stage of the workflow.
- **Adjusting Limits:** Regularly review and adjust WIP limits based on team capacity and workflow efficiency.

Example:
- **Column Limits:** To Do (5), In Progress (3), Review (2).
- **Effect:** If the "In Progress" column has a limit of 3, no more than 3 tasks can be in progress at any time. This ensures that team members complete existing tasks before starting new ones.

3. Managing Flow
Purpose: Ensuring a smooth flow of tasks through the workflow helps in delivering value continuously and predictably.
Flow Management Practices:
- **Daily Standups:** Discuss the progress of tasks and address any blockers.
- **Queue Management:** Prioritize tasks in the backlog and ensure the most important tasks are ready to be worked on next.
- **Review and Adjust:** Continuously review the workflow and make adjustments to improve flow.

Example:
- **Daily Standup:** Team members discuss tasks in progress, identify blockers, and plan for the day.
- **Flow Review:** Regularly analyze the workflow to identify bottlenecks and make necessary adjustments.

Common Kanban Metrics
1. Cycle Time
Definition: The time it takes for a task to move from the start of the workflow to completion.
Importance:
- **Predictability:** Shorter and consistent cycle times improve predictability.
- **Efficiency:** Reducing cycle time helps in delivering value faster.

Example:
- **Calculation:** If a task enters the "In Progress" column on Monday and is completed on Wednesday, the cycle time is 3 days.

2. Throughput
Definition: The number of tasks completed in a given time period.
Importance:
- **Capacity Measurement:** Throughput helps in understanding the team's capacity to deliver work.
- **Performance Tracking:** Monitoring throughput over time helps in assessing and improving team performance.

Example:
- **Calculation:** If the team completes 20 tasks in a two-week sprint, the throughput is 20 tasks per sprint.

Using Kanban Boards and WIP Limits
Kanban Boards:
- **Visual Representation:** A Kanban board provides a clear visual representation of the workflow, making it easy to track progress and identify bottlenecks.
- **Card Movement:** Tasks are represented by cards that move across the board from left to right as they progress through the stages.

WIP Limits:
- **Focus:** WIP limits ensure that team members focus on completing tasks before starting new ones.
- **Bottleneck Identification:** When a column reaches its WIP limit, it indicates a potential bottleneck that needs to be addressed.

Example:

- **Board Setup:** A software development team uses a Kanban board with columns for Backlog, Development, Testing, and Done.
- **WIP Limits:** The Development column has a WIP limit of 4, and the Testing column has a limit of 3.
- **Impact:** If Testing is full, the team must address the bottleneck before pulling more tasks into Development.

Improving Performance with Kanban Metrics
Cycle Time:
- **Measure and Analyze:** Regularly measure cycle time for tasks and analyze trends.
- **Identify Improvements:** Shorten cycle time by addressing delays and optimizing workflow stages.

Throughput:
- **Track Over Time:** Monitor throughput to understand the team's delivery capacity.
- **Set Goals:** Use throughput data to set realistic goals and improve team performance.

Example:
- **Cycle Time Analysis:** If cycle time is increasing, the team might identify that tasks are getting stuck in the Review stage and take action to streamline the review process.
- **Throughput Improvement:** If throughput is low, the team might analyze their WIP limits and workflow efficiency, adjusting WIP limits or reassigning tasks to improve productivity.

Creating a Safe and Collaborative Environment
1. **Psychological Safety:** Ensure that team members feel safe to share their thoughts without fear of blame or retaliation.
    - **Strategy:** Emphasize that retrospectives are a blameless space focused on learning and improvement.
2. **Inclusivity:** Encourage participation from all team members to get diverse perspectives.
    - **Strategy:** Use techniques like round-robin sharing or silent brainstorming to ensure everyone has a voice.
3. **Respect:** Foster an atmosphere of respect where all opinions are valued.
    - **Strategy:** Establish ground rules for discussions, such as listening without interrupting and providing constructive feedback.

Kanban's principles and practices help teams visualize their work, limit WIP, and manage flow, leading to continuous improvement and more predictable delivery. By using Kanban boards, setting WIP limits, and tracking key metrics like cycle time and throughput, teams can optimize their processes, identify bottlenecks, and enhance overall performance.

Overview of Popular Agile Project Management Tools
Agile project management tools are designed to facilitate Agile planning, tracking, and collaboration. Three popular tools are JIRA, Trello, and Asana. Each tool offers unique features and benefits that support Agile methodologies, helping teams manage their projects more effectively.

JIRA
Key Features and Benefits:
- **Issue and Project Tracking**: JIRA is known for its robust issue and project tracking capabilities, allowing teams to track tasks, bugs, and user stories.
- **Custom Workflows**: Teams can create custom workflows to match their specific processes.
- **Agile Boards**: Supports Scrum and Kanban boards, providing visualizations of work in progress.
- **Backlog Management**: Features for managing and prioritizing product backlogs.
- **Reporting and Analytics**: Offers detailed reports and analytics, including burndown charts, velocity charts, and sprint reports.
- **Integration**: Integrates with many other tools, such as Confluence, Bitbucket, and Slack.

Example Use Case:
- **Software Development Team:** A software development team uses JIRA to manage their sprint planning and tracking. They create a Scrum board to visualize their backlog, plan sprints, and monitor progress. Each user

story and task is tracked as an issue in JIRA, and the team uses the built-in reporting tools to analyze their performance and identify areas for improvement.

Best Practices for Using JIRA:
1. **Customize Workflows**: Tailor workflows to fit the team's specific processes.
2. **Regular Backlog Grooming**: Keep the backlog updated and prioritized.
3. **Use Automation**: Leverage JIRA's automation rules to streamline repetitive tasks.
4. **Monitor Progress**: Regularly review dashboards and reports to track progress and adjust plans as needed.

Trello

Key Features and Benefits:
- **Kanban Boards**: Trello uses a card-based system to represent tasks, which can be moved across lists that represent different stages of the workflow.
- **Simple and Intuitive Interface**: Known for its user-friendly and intuitive interface, making it easy for teams to get started.
- **Customizable Lists and Cards**: Users can create custom lists and cards, adding due dates, attachments, labels, and checklists.
- **Power-Ups**: Offers integrations and additional features through Power-Ups, such as calendar views, time tracking, and integrations with other tools.
- **Collaboration**: Real-time collaboration features, including comments, mentions, and notifications.

Example Use Case:
- **Marketing Team**: A marketing team uses Trello to manage their campaign planning. They create a board with lists for ideas, in progress, under review, and completed. Each card represents a campaign task, and team members can add comments, attach files, and move cards across lists as work progresses. Power-Ups like the calendar view help them track deadlines.

Best Practices for Using Trello:
1. **Define Clear Lists**: Create lists that represent distinct stages of your workflow.
2. **Use Labels and Checklists**: Organize tasks using labels and break down tasks into smaller steps with checklists.
3. **Leverage Power-Ups**: Enhance Trello's functionality with Power-Ups that add necessary features.
4. **Maintain Board Hygiene**: Regularly archive completed tasks and clean up the board to keep it manageable.

Asana

Key Features and Benefits:
- **Task and Project Management**: Asana allows teams to manage tasks and projects with lists, boards, and timelines.
- **Custom Fields**: Users can add custom fields to tasks for additional information tracking.
- **Task Dependencies**: Supports setting dependencies between tasks to visualize and manage workflow.
- **Timeline View**: Offers a Gantt-chart-like view for project planning and scheduling.
- **Workload Management**: Provides insights into team workloads to balance assignments.
- **Integration**: Integrates with numerous tools like Slack, Google Drive, and Microsoft Teams.

Example Use Case:
- **Product Development Team**: A product development team uses Asana to plan and track their product roadmap. They create projects for each product release, using task dependencies to manage the sequence of tasks. The timeline view helps them visualize the project schedule and ensure tasks are completed on time. Custom fields are used to track additional task information, such as priority and estimated effort.

Best Practices for Using Asana:
1. **Define Projects and Tasks Clearly**: Ensure that each project and task is well-defined with clear descriptions and due dates.
2. **Utilize Views**: Make use of list, board, and timeline views to manage different aspects of the project.
3. **Set Task Dependencies**: Use dependencies to clarify task order and manage workflow.
4. **Monitor Workload**: Regularly check the workload view to ensure balanced task distribution among team members.

Comparison and Suitability
- **JIRA**: Best suited for software development teams that need detailed issue tracking, custom workflows, and robust reporting. It's ideal for Agile teams using Scrum or Kanban.
- **Trello**: Great for teams looking for a simple, visual task management tool. It's especially useful for non-technical teams or projects that benefit from a flexible Kanban-style board.
- **Asana**: Suitable for a wide range of teams, including marketing, product development, and operations, that need versatile task and project management capabilities. It's ideal for teams that benefit from timeline views and workload management.

Real-World Agile Project Examples
1. **JIRA in Software Development**:
   - A large e-commerce company uses JIRA to manage its development projects. Each sprint starts with a sprint planning session where user stories from the product backlog are selected. Developers track their tasks using a Scrum board, and the team monitors progress with burndown charts. The integration with Bitbucket allows developers to link their code commits directly to JIRA issues.
2. **Trello in Marketing**:
   - A digital marketing agency uses Trello to manage client campaigns. They create boards for each client with lists representing campaign stages (e.g., planning, execution, review, and completed). Cards are used for individual tasks, and team members collaborate by adding comments, attachments, and due dates. Power-Ups like calendar and time tracking help the team stay on schedule and measure effort.
3. **Asana in Product Development**:
   - A tech startup uses Asana to manage its product development lifecycle. The team creates projects for each product feature, using tasks and subtasks to break down work. Dependencies are set to manage task sequences, and the timeline view helps the team visualize the project schedule. Custom fields are used to track priority, status, and effort, while the workload view ensures that team members are not overloaded.

Best Practices for Configuring and Using Agile Tools
1. **JIRA**:
   - **Customize Workflows**: Tailor workflows to fit the team's processes.
   - **Use Automation**: Set up automation rules to handle repetitive tasks.
   - **Regular Backlog Grooming**: Keep the backlog updated and prioritized.
   - **Leverage Integrations**: Integrate with other tools like Confluence and Bitbucket for a seamless workflow.
2. **Trello**:
   - **Define Clear Lists**: Create lists that represent distinct stages of your workflow.
   - **Use Labels and Checklists**: Organize tasks using labels and break down tasks into smaller steps with checklists.
   - **Leverage Power-Ups**: Enhance Trello's functionality with Power-Ups that add necessary features.
   - **Maintain Board Hygiene**: Regularly archive completed tasks and clean up the board to keep it manageable.
3. **Asana**:
   - **Define Projects and Tasks Clearly**: Ensure that each project and task is well-defined with clear descriptions and due dates.
   - **Utilize Views**: Make use of list, board, and timeline views to manage different aspects of the project.
   - **Set Task Dependencies**: Use dependencies to clarify task order and manage workflow.
   - **Monitor Workload**: Regularly check the workload view to ensure balanced task distribution among team members.

By using these Agile project management tools effectively, teams can improve their planning, tracking, and collaboration, leading to more efficient and successful project outcomes.

Business Analysis Frameworks

Role and Responsibilities of a Business Analyst in Project Management

A Business Analyst (BA) plays a crucial role in bridging the gap between business needs and technological solutions. They work closely with stakeholders to understand their requirements and translate these into detailed specifications for the project team. The BA ensures that the final deliverables align with the business objectives and meet stakeholder expectations.

Key Responsibilities of a Business Analyst

1. **Identify Business Needs**:
   - **Stakeholder Engagement**: Work with stakeholders to understand their needs, challenges, and objectives.
   - **Problem Identification**: Analyze current processes and systems to identify areas for improvement.
2. **Define Requirements**:
   - **Requirements Gathering**: Collect detailed business and technical requirements from stakeholders through interviews, surveys, workshops, and observation.
   - **Documentation**: Document the requirements clearly and concisely in formats such as Business Requirements Documents (BRDs), Functional Requirements Documents (FRDs), and User Stories.
3. **Analyze and Validate Requirements**:
   - **Requirements Analysis**: Evaluate the gathered requirements to ensure they are clear, complete, and aligned with business goals.
   - **Validation**: Work with stakeholders to validate the requirements and obtain their approval.
4. **Ensure Solution Alignment**:
   - **Solution Design**: Collaborate with the project team to ensure the proposed solutions meet the documented requirements.
   - **Traceability**: Maintain traceability of requirements throughout the project lifecycle to ensure they are addressed in the final deliverables.
5. **Facilitate Communication**:
   - **Bridge the Gap**: Act as a liaison between business stakeholders and the project team to ensure clear and consistent communication.
   - **Manage Expectations**: Ensure stakeholders have realistic expectations about what the project will deliver and by when.
6. **Support Testing and Implementation**:
   - **Test Planning**: Assist in the development of test plans and test cases based on the requirements.
   - **User Acceptance Testing (UAT)**: Facilitate UAT by coordinating with stakeholders and the project team.
   - **Implementation Support**: Provide support during the implementation phase to address any issues that arise.

Contributions to Project Success

Business Analysts contribute to the success of projects in several ways:

1. **Clear Requirements Definition**: By gathering and documenting detailed requirements, BAs ensure that the project team understands what needs to be delivered.
2. **Stakeholder Alignment**: Through regular communication and validation, BAs ensure that stakeholder expectations are managed and aligned with the project scope.
3. **Risk Mitigation**: By identifying potential issues early in the project, BAs help mitigate risks and avoid costly rework.
4. **Quality Assurance**: By facilitating UAT and ensuring requirements traceability, BAs help ensure that the final deliverables meet the specified requirements and quality standards.

Key Deliverables Produced by Business Analysts

1. **Business Requirements Document (BRD)**:
   - **Purpose**: To capture high-level business requirements and objectives.
   - **Content**: Includes business goals, stakeholder needs, scope, and high-level requirements.

- **Example**: A BRD for a new customer relationship management (CRM) system might outline the need to improve customer data management, track interactions, and generate sales reports.
2. **Functional Requirements Document (FRD)**:
    - **Purpose**: To detail the functional requirements of the system, describing how it should behave.
    - **Content**: Includes detailed descriptions of system functionalities, use cases, and user interactions.
    - **Example**: An FRD for an e-commerce website might detail requirements for the shopping cart, payment processing, and order tracking functionalities.
3. **Use Cases**:
    - **Purpose**: To describe specific scenarios of how users will interact with the system.
    - **Content**: Includes a description of the interaction between the user and the system, preconditions, main flow, alternative flows, and postconditions.
    - **Example**: A use case for an online banking application might describe the steps a user takes to transfer funds between accounts.
4. **Process Maps**:
    - **Purpose**: To visually represent the workflow and processes within the organization or system.
    - **Content**: Includes flowcharts or diagrams that illustrate the sequence of activities, decision points, and interactions.
    - **Example**: A process map for a loan approval process might show the steps from loan application submission to approval, including all review and decision points.

Real-World Example of Business Analyst Deliverables

Scenario: Implementing a new Human Resources Information System (HRIS).

1. **Business Requirements Document (BRD)**:
    - Captures the need for a centralized system to manage employee data, track performance reviews, and handle payroll.
    - Outlines the business objectives, such as improving data accuracy, enhancing reporting capabilities, and reducing administrative workload.
2. **Functional Requirements Document (FRD)**:
    - Details the specific functionalities required, such as employee self-service portals, performance management modules, and payroll processing.
    - Describes how each functionality should work, including user interactions and system responses.
3. **Use Cases**:
    - Describes scenarios like "Employee Submits Leave Request" and "Manager Approves Performance Review."
    - Provides step-by-step descriptions of each interaction, including alternative flows for different conditions (e.g., request approval or denial).
4. **Process Maps**:
    - Visualizes the end-to-end process of managing employee records, from hiring to termination.
    - Illustrates the flow of data and interactions between different departments and the HRIS.

By delivering these key documents and maintaining effective communication with stakeholders, Business Analysts ensure that the project remains aligned with business needs, and that the solutions developed meet stakeholder expectations. This comprehensive approach helps drive the success of the project, resulting in solutions that deliver real value to the organization.

Key Concepts and Principles of Business Analysis

Business analysis is a disciplined approach for introducing and managing change to organizations, whether they are for-profit businesses, governments, or non-profits. It involves understanding business needs, assessing the impact of changes, capturing, analyzing, and documenting requirements, and supporting the communication and delivery of solutions.

Core Concepts and Principles

1. Requirements Elicitation

Purpose: Gather requirements from stakeholders through various techniques to understand their needs and constraints.

Techniques:
- **Interviews:** Direct conversations with stakeholders to uncover requirements.
- **Workshops:** Collaborative sessions to gather requirements and build consensus.
- **Surveys/Questionnaires:** Structured forms for stakeholders to provide input.
- **Observations:** Watching how users interact with current systems to identify needs.
- **Document Analysis:** Reviewing existing documentation to understand current processes and systems.

Example: Conducting a workshop with end-users to gather requirements for a new customer relationship management (CRM) system.

2. Requirements Analysis
Purpose: Analyze, prioritize, and validate requirements to ensure they are complete, consistent, and aligned with business objectives.

Activities:
- **Modeling:** Use diagrams like use cases, process flows, and data models to represent requirements visually.
- **Prioritization:** Determine the importance of each requirement to address the most critical needs first.
- **Validation:** Ensure requirements are feasible, clear, and aligned with business goals.

Example: Creating a data flow diagram to visualize the interactions between different parts of a new software system.

3. Requirements Documentation
Purpose: Create clear and detailed documentation of the requirements for stakeholders and project teams.

Types of Documentation:
- **Business Requirements Document (BRD):** High-level business objectives and stakeholder needs.
- **Functional Requirements Document (FRD):** Detailed specifications of what the system should do.
- **User Stories:** Short descriptions of functionality from the user's perspective, often used in Agile projects.

Example: Writing user stories for an e-commerce website's checkout process, including "As a customer, I want to be able to save my payment information for future purchases."

4. Requirements Management
Purpose: Continuously manage and track requirements throughout the project lifecycle to ensure they are met.

Activities:
- **Traceability:** Track requirements from inception through to delivery and ensure they are fulfilled by the solution.
- **Change Management:** Handle changes to requirements systematically to minimize disruption and ensure stakeholder agreement.
- **Version Control:** Maintain versions of requirements documents to track changes over time.

Example: Using a Requirements Traceability Matrix (RTM) to link user stories to test cases and ensure all requirements are tested.

Importance of a Structured Approach to Business Analysis
Applying a structured approach to business analysis ensures that the project outcomes align with organizational goals and stakeholder needs. It helps in:
- **Clarity:** Clear and unambiguous requirements reduce misunderstandings and rework.
- **Consistency:** A structured approach ensures that all aspects of requirements are covered and documented consistently.
- **Alignment:** Ensures that the project goals are aligned with business objectives, leading to better outcomes and higher stakeholder satisfaction.
- **Risk Management:** Identifies and mitigates risks associated with changes in requirements early in the project lifecycle.

Best Practices and Industry Standards
International Institute of Business Analysis (IIBA) Business Analysis Body of Knowledge (BABOK)

BABOK Overview:
- **BABOK** provides a globally recognized standard for business analysis practices and principles.

- It outlines six core knowledge areas: Business Analysis Planning and Monitoring, Elicitation and Collaboration, Requirements Life Cycle Management, Strategy Analysis, Requirements Analysis and Design Definition, and Solution Evaluation.

Relevance:
- **Guidance:** Offers best practices and methodologies for effective business analysis.
- **Consistency:** Ensures a consistent approach to business analysis across projects and organizations.
- **Certification:** Provides a basis for professional certification (e.g., CBAP - Certified Business Analysis Professional), which can enhance the credibility and skills of business analysts.

Best Practices in Business Analysis

1. **Engage Stakeholders Early and Often:**
    - **Practice:** Regularly involve stakeholders in the requirements gathering and validation process.
    - **Benefit:** Ensures that requirements are aligned with stakeholder needs and expectations.
2. **Use Visual Models:**
    - **Practice:** Create visual models (e.g., process flows, use case diagrams) to represent requirements.
    - **Benefit:** Enhances understanding and communication among stakeholders.
3. **Prioritize Requirements:**
    - **Practice:** Use techniques like MoSCoW (Must have, Should have, Could have, Won't have) to prioritize requirements.
    - **Benefit:** Focuses on delivering the most critical features first, ensuring value is delivered early.
4. **Maintain Traceability:**
    - **Practice:** Use a Requirements Traceability Matrix (RTM) to track requirements through to delivery.
    - **Benefit:** Ensures all requirements are addressed and helps manage changes effectively.
5. **Iterative Review and Validation:**
    - **Practice:** Regularly review and validate requirements with stakeholders.
    - **Benefit:** Identifies issues early, reducing the risk of rework and ensuring the solution meets business needs.

Examples of Applying Best Practices

Example 1: Healthcare System Implementation
- **Elicitation:** Conducted workshops with doctors, nurses, and administrative staff to gather requirements for a new patient management system.
- **Analysis:** Created process flow diagrams to map out current and future state workflows.
- **Documentation:** Developed user stories and a detailed Functional Requirements Document (FRD).
- **Management:** Used an RTM to ensure all requirements were tested and met before deployment.

Example 2: Financial Services CRM Upgrade
- **Elicitation:** Used surveys and interviews with sales and customer service teams to gather requirements for a CRM upgrade.
- **Analysis:** Prioritized requirements using the MoSCoW method.
- **Documentation:** Created a Business Requirements Document (BRD) and user stories.
- **Management:** Implemented change management processes to handle requirement changes due to regulatory updates.

By applying these principles and practices, business analysts can effectively capture, analyze, document, and manage requirements, ensuring that project outcomes align with organizational goals and deliver value to stakeholders.

Conducting a Needs Assessment to Identify and Prioritize Business Problems or Opportunities

A needs assessment is a systematic process used to identify and prioritize business problems or opportunities. It involves understanding the current state, defining the desired future state, and identifying the gaps that need to be addressed to achieve business goals. This process is critical for defining the scope and objectives of projects, ensuring they address the most critical business issues.

Common Techniques Used in Needs Assessments

1. Gap Analysis

Purpose: To identify the differences between the current state and the desired future state and determine what needs to be done to bridge the gaps.
Steps:
1. **Define the Current State**: Document the existing processes, performance levels, and resources.
2. **Define the Desired Future State**: Specify the desired outcomes, goals, and performance levels.
3. **Identify Gaps**: Compare the current state to the future state to identify the gaps.
4. **Prioritize Gaps**: Assess the importance and urgency of each gap to prioritize actions.

Example:
- **Scenario**: A retail company wants to improve its customer service.
- **Current State**: Average customer satisfaction score is 70%.
- **Desired Future State**: Target customer satisfaction score is 90%.
- **Gap**: A 20% improvement in customer satisfaction.
- **Action Plan**: Implement training programs for customer service representatives, update customer service protocols, and invest in customer feedback systems.

2. Root Cause Analysis
Purpose: To identify the underlying causes of a problem rather than just addressing the symptoms.
Steps:
1. **Define the Problem**: Clearly state the problem to be analyzed.
2. **Collect Data**: Gather data related to the problem.
3. **Identify Possible Causes**: Brainstorm possible causes of the problem.
4. **Analyze Causes**: Use tools like the 5 Whys or Fishbone Diagram to drill down to the root causes.
5. **Verify Root Causes**: Validate the identified root causes with data.

Example:
- **Scenario**: A manufacturing company faces frequent production delays.
- **Problem**: Production delays leading to missed delivery deadlines.
- **Possible Causes**: Equipment failures, supply chain issues, inadequate staffing.
- **Root Cause Analysis**: Using the 5 Whys, the team discovers that equipment maintenance is often neglected due to lack of a preventive maintenance schedule.
- **Action Plan**: Implement a preventive maintenance program to reduce equipment failures.

3. SWOT Analysis
Purpose: To evaluate the internal and external factors that impact an organization's ability to achieve its objectives.
Steps:
1. **Identify Strengths**: Assess internal strengths that can be leveraged.
2. **Identify Weaknesses**: Identify internal weaknesses that need to be addressed.
3. **Identify Opportunities**: Recognize external opportunities that can be capitalized on.
4. **Identify Threats**: Identify external threats that could hinder progress.

Example:
- **Scenario**: A tech startup is planning to launch a new software product.
- **Strengths**: Innovative technology, skilled development team.
- **Weaknesses**: Limited marketing budget, lack of brand recognition.
- **Opportunities**: Growing demand for the software, potential partnerships.
- **Threats**: Competitors with larger budgets, rapid technological changes.
- **Action Plan**: Focus on leveraging technological strengths and development skills while addressing weaknesses through strategic partnerships and targeted marketing efforts.

Step-by-Step Instructions for Applying Needs Assessment Techniques
Applying Gap Analysis
1. **Assemble the Team**: Gather stakeholders and team members with relevant knowledge.
2. **Document Current State**: Collect data and document the current state of processes, performance, and resources.
3. **Define Desired State**: Establish clear, measurable goals for the future state.

4. **Identify Gaps**: Compare current state data to desired state goals to identify gaps.
5. **Develop Action Plan**: Prioritize gaps based on their impact and urgency, and create an action plan to address them.

Applying Root Cause Analysis
1. **Define the Problem**: Clearly articulate the problem to be analyzed.
2. **Gather Data**: Collect relevant data and evidence related to the problem.
3. **Identify Causes**: Brainstorm possible causes of the problem.
4. **Analyze with 5 Whys or Fishbone Diagram**:
    - **5 Whys**: Ask "Why?" repeatedly to drill down to the root cause.
    - **Fishbone Diagram**: Categorize potential causes and analyze each category.
5. **Validate Causes**: Verify the identified root causes with additional data or testing.
6. **Implement Solutions**: Develop and implement solutions to address the root causes.

Applying SWOT Analysis
1. **Assemble the Team**: Include stakeholders and team members from different functions.
2. **Conduct Brainstorming Session**: Facilitate a session to identify strengths, weaknesses, opportunities, and threats.
3. **Document Findings**: Create a SWOT matrix to document the findings.
4. **Analyze and Prioritize**: Evaluate the identified factors and prioritize actions to leverage strengths and opportunities while addressing weaknesses and threats.
5. **Develop Strategies**: Create strategies to maximize strengths and opportunities and mitigate weaknesses and threats.

Real-World Examples of Needs Assessments

Example 1: Healthcare Provider Enhancing Patient Experience

Scenario: A hospital aims to improve patient satisfaction scores.

- **Gap Analysis**:
    - **Current State**: Patient satisfaction score is 75%.
    - **Desired State**: Target score is 90%.
    - **Gap**: A 15% improvement is needed.
    - **Action Plan**: Implement new patient care protocols, enhance staff training, and upgrade facilities.
- **Root Cause Analysis**:
    - **Problem**: Long waiting times in the emergency department.
    - **Root Cause**: Insufficient staffing during peak hours.
    - **Action Plan**: Adjust staffing schedules to ensure adequate coverage during peak times.
- **SWOT Analysis**:
    - **Strengths**: High-quality medical staff, state-of-the-art equipment.
    - **Weaknesses**: Inconsistent patient care processes.
    - **Opportunities**: Expanding community healthcare programs.
    - **Threats**: Increased competition from nearby hospitals.
    - **Action Plan**: Standardize patient care processes and promote community healthcare initiatives.

Example 2: Retail Chain Expanding E-commerce Capabilities

Scenario: A retail chain wants to expand its online presence.

- **Gap Analysis**:
    - **Current State**: Limited online sales capabilities.
    - **Desired State**: Full-featured e-commerce platform.
    - **Gap**: Need to develop and implement new online sales infrastructure.
    - **Action Plan**: Invest in e-commerce technology, hire skilled developers, and train staff.
- **Root Cause Analysis**:
    - **Problem**: Low online sales.
    - **Root Cause**: Outdated website and poor user experience.
    - **Action Plan**: Redesign the website to be more user-friendly and implement modern e-commerce features.

- **SWOT Analysis**:
  - **Strengths**: Strong brand reputation, large customer base.
  - **Weaknesses**: Lack of online marketing expertise.
  - **Opportunities**: Growing trend of online shopping.
  - **Threats**: Competitors with advanced e-commerce platforms.
  - **Action Plan**: Leverage brand reputation and customer base while investing in online marketing and technology upgrades.

By conducting thorough needs assessments using techniques like gap analysis, root cause analysis, and SWOT analysis, organizations can identify and prioritize their most critical business problems or opportunities. This process ensures that projects are scoped and planned effectively, addressing the issues that will deliver the most significant business value.

Purpose and Structure of a Business Case

A business case is a document that justifies the initiation of a project or investment. It provides a comprehensive analysis of the problem or opportunity, the proposed solution, and the expected benefits, costs, and risks. The primary purpose is to convince stakeholders and decision-makers that the project is worth investing in and aligns with organizational goals.

Role of a Business Case

1. **Justification:** Demonstrates the need for the project and why it is worth pursuing.
2. **Alignment:** Ensures the project aligns with strategic objectives and organizational goals.
3. **Decision-Making:** Provides decision-makers with the necessary information to approve, reject, or request modifications to the project proposal.
4. **Planning:** Serves as a foundation for detailed project planning and management.

Key Components of a Business Case

1. **Problem Statement:**
   - **Purpose:** Clearly define the problem or opportunity the project aims to address.
   - **Example:** "The current customer relationship management system is outdated, leading to inefficiencies and customer dissatisfaction."
2. **Objectives:**
   - **Purpose:** Outline the specific goals the project aims to achieve.
   - **Example:** "Enhance customer satisfaction by 20% within one year by implementing a new CRM system."
3. **Options Analysis:**
   - **Purpose:** Present and evaluate different options for addressing the problem or opportunity.
   - **Example:** "Option 1: Upgrade the existing CRM system. Option 2: Implement a new off-the-shelf CRM solution. Option 3: Develop a custom CRM system."
4. **Cost-Benefit Analysis:**
   - **Purpose:** Compare the costs and benefits of each option to determine the most cost-effective solution.
   - **Example:** "Option 2 has a total cost of $500,000 and is expected to generate $1,000,000 in benefits over five years."
5. **Risk Assessment:**
   - **Purpose:** Identify and evaluate potential risks associated with the project and propose mitigation strategies.
   - **Example:** "Risk: Data migration issues. Mitigation: Develop a detailed data migration plan and conduct thorough testing."

Template/Outline for Developing a Compelling Business Case

1. Executive Summary
- Brief overview of the problem, proposed solution, and key benefits.
- Highlight the importance and urgency of the project.

2. Problem Statement

- Detailed description of the problem or opportunity.
- Evidence or data supporting the existence and impact of the problem.

3. Objectives
- Specific, measurable, achievable, relevant, and time-bound (SMART) objectives.
- Alignment with organizational goals and strategies.

4. Options Analysis
- Description of each option considered.
- Evaluation criteria and analysis of each option's pros and cons.

5. Cost-Benefit Analysis
- Detailed breakdown of costs for each option.
- Quantitative and qualitative benefits.
- Comparison of net benefits for each option.

6. Risk Assessment
- Identification of potential risks.
- Probability and impact assessment.
- Mitigation strategies for each risk.

7. Implementation Plan
- High-level timeline and key milestones.
- Resources and skills required.
- Dependencies and constraints.

8. Conclusion and Recommendations
- Summary of the analysis.
- Recommended option with justification.
- Call to action for decision-makers.

Best Practices for Presenting a Business Case to Stakeholders and Decision-Makers

1. **Know Your Audience:**
   - Tailor the presentation to the interests and concerns of your audience.
   - Use language and examples that resonate with them.
2. **Be Clear and Concise:**
   - Focus on the key points and avoid unnecessary details.
   - Use bullet points, charts, and graphs to make the information easily digestible.
3. **Highlight Benefits:**
   - Emphasize the benefits and value the project will bring to the organization.
   - Use data and evidence to support your claims.
4. **Address Risks:**
   - Be transparent about potential risks and your strategies for mitigating them.
   - Demonstrate that you have thoroughly considered and planned for these risks.
5. **Engage Your Audience:**
   - Encourage questions and feedback.
   - Be prepared to discuss and defend your analysis and recommendations.
6. **Use Visual Aids:**
   - Incorporate visual aids like slides, charts, and diagrams to enhance understanding and retention.
   - Ensure visuals are clear, professional, and relevant.

Example Business Case Outline

1. Executive Summary
- Project Title: CRM System Upgrade
- Summary: Upgrade the existing CRM system to improve customer satisfaction and operational efficiency.

2. Problem Statement

- The current CRM system is outdated, leading to inefficiencies, data inaccuracies, and customer dissatisfaction.

3. Objectives
- Increase customer satisfaction by 20% within one year.
- Reduce operational costs by 15% through improved efficiencies.

4. Options Analysis
- **Option 1:** Upgrade existing CRM system.
- **Option 2:** Implement a new off-the-shelf CRM solution.
- **Option 3:** Develop a custom CRM system.
- Analysis: Option 2 offers the best balance of cost, time, and functionality.

5. Cost-Benefit Analysis
- **Option 1:** Cost: $300,000, Benefits: $600,000.
- **Option 2:** Cost: $500,000, Benefits: $1,000,000.
- **Option 3:** Cost: $800,000, Benefits: $1,200,000.
- Recommendation: Option 2 provides the highest net benefit.

6. Risk Assessment
- **Risk:** Data migration issues.
- **Mitigation:** Detailed migration plan and thorough testing.
- **Risk:** User adoption resistance.
- **Mitigation:** Comprehensive training and support program.

7. Implementation Plan
- Timeline: 12 months.
- Key Milestones: Requirement gathering, vendor selection, implementation, testing, go-live.
- Resources: Project team, external consultants, training programs.

8. Conclusion and Recommendations
- Summary: Implementing a new off-the-shelf CRM solution (Option 2) offers the best balance of benefits and risks.
- Recommendation: Proceed with Option 2.
- Call to Action: Approve the project and allocate the necessary budget and resources.

By following these guidelines and best practices, you can develop a compelling business case that effectively justifies project investments and secures stakeholder buy-in.

Techniques for Gathering and Eliciting Requirements

Gathering and eliciting requirements is a crucial step in the project management process, ensuring that the project's objectives are clearly defined and understood. Various techniques can be used, each with its strengths and limitations. Here, we'll explore interviews, workshops, focus groups, surveys, and observation, and provide guidelines for selecting the most appropriate techniques based on project factors.

1. Interviews

Description: One-on-one or small group discussions with stakeholders to gather detailed information.

Strengths:
- **In-Depth Information:** Allows for deep exploration of requirements and underlying needs.
- **Personal Interaction:** Builds relationships and trust with stakeholders.
- **Flexibility:** Can adapt questions based on responses and explore new areas as they arise.

Limitations:
- **Time-Consuming:** Can be time-intensive, especially with a large number of stakeholders.
- **Bias:** Interviewer's or interviewee's biases can affect the outcomes.
- **Resource-Intensive:** Requires significant preparation and follow-up.

Guidelines:

- Use for complex projects requiring detailed understanding.
- Ideal when stakeholders have unique perspectives or critical knowledge.
- Schedule interviews when stakeholders have sufficient availability.

Example Questions:
- "Can you describe the current process for handling customer inquiries?"
- "What are the biggest challenges you face with the existing system?"
- "What features would you find most valuable in a new solution?"

2. Workshops

Description: Collaborative sessions where stakeholders and team members work together to identify requirements.

Strengths:
- **Collaboration**: Encourages active participation and consensus-building.
- **Efficiency**: Can gather input from multiple stakeholders simultaneously.
- **Creativity**: Facilitates brainstorming and innovative solutions.

Limitations:
- **Group Dynamics**: Dominant personalities can influence the outcomes.
- **Scheduling**: Difficult to align schedules for all participants.
- **Preparation**: Requires significant planning and facilitation skills.

Guidelines:
- Use for projects needing broad input and stakeholder alignment.
- Best when stakeholders can dedicate focused time to the workshop.
- Prepare a clear agenda and skilled facilitator to manage the session.

Example Activities:
- **Brainstorming**: Generate a wide range of ideas and solutions.
- **Prioritization**: Rank requirements based on importance and feasibility.
- **Process Mapping**: Visualize current and desired workflows.

3. Focus Groups

Description: Structured group discussions led by a moderator to gather diverse perspectives on requirements.

Strengths:
- **Diverse Insights**: Brings together stakeholders with different viewpoints.
- **Interactive**: Participants can build on each other's ideas.
- **Cost-Effective**: Gathers a lot of information in a relatively short time.

Limitations:
- **Groupthink**: Risk of consensus overshadowing individual input.
- **Moderator Bias**: The moderator's influence can shape the discussion.
- **Limited Depth**: May not explore topics as deeply as individual interviews.

Guidelines:
- Use for exploratory phases to gather a broad range of ideas.
- Best when the project needs diverse input and perspectives.
- Ensure the moderator is skilled in managing group dynamics and eliciting input.

Example Questions:
- "What are your initial thoughts on the proposed project?"
- "How do you currently solve this problem, and what improvements would you suggest?"
- "What potential challenges do you foresee with this initiative?"

4. Surveys

Description: Questionnaires distributed to stakeholders to collect quantitative and qualitative data.

Strengths:
- **Wide Reach**: Can gather input from a large number of stakeholders.
- **Anonymity**: Encourages honest and unbiased feedback.

- **Quantifiable**: Provides data that can be easily analyzed.

Limitations:
- **Limited Interaction**: No opportunity for follow-up questions or clarification.
- **Response Rates**: May be low, impacting the representativeness of the data.
- **Design Challenges**: Poorly designed surveys can lead to ambiguous or unusable data.

Guidelines:
- Use for large projects where stakeholder input is widespread.
- Best when quantifiable data is needed for analysis.
- Design clear, concise questions and pilot the survey to ensure effectiveness.

Example Questions:
- "How satisfied are you with the current system? (Rate from 1 to 5)"
- "What features do you think are missing from the current solution?"
- "Please describe any challenges you face with the current process."

5. Observation

Description: Directly observing stakeholders as they perform their tasks to understand their workflows and challenges.

Strengths:
- **Real-World Insights**: Provides a true picture of how tasks are performed.
- **Unobtrusive**: Can reveal issues stakeholders may not mention.
- **Contextual Understanding**: Helps understand the context in which processes occur.

Limitations:
- **Time-Consuming**: Requires significant time to observe and document processes.
- **Limited Scope**: May not capture all variations in tasks.
- **Observer Bias**: Presence of the observer may influence behavior.

Guidelines:
- Use for understanding workflows and identifying process inefficiencies.
- Best for projects involving complex or manual processes.
- Ensure minimal disruption to the observed processes.

Example Scenarios:
- Observing customer service representatives to identify bottlenecks in handling inquiries.
- Watching warehouse staff to understand the logistics and challenges of inventory management.

Guidelines for Selecting Techniques

1. **Project Complexity**:
   - **High Complexity**: Use in-depth techniques like interviews and workshops.
   - **Low Complexity**: Surveys and focus groups may be sufficient.
2. **Stakeholder Availability**:
   - **Limited Availability**: Surveys and observation can be less intrusive.
   - **High Availability**: Workshops and interviews provide deeper insights.
3. **Organizational Culture**:
   - **Collaborative Culture**: Workshops and focus groups can harness team dynamics.
   - **Hierarchical Culture**: Interviews and surveys may be more appropriate.

Effective Questions and Prompts

Open-Ended Questions:
- "Can you walk me through your daily tasks?"
- "What challenges do you encounter in your role?"
- "How would you improve the current system?"

Specific Probes:
- "What steps do you take to complete this task?"

- "What information do you need to perform this process?"
- "Can you describe a recent instance where you faced a problem?"

Clarifying Questions:
- "Can you explain what you mean by that?"
- "Why do you think this issue occurs?"
- "How do you currently resolve this issue?"

Real-World Examples

Example 1: Improving a Customer Support System
- **Technique Used**: Interviews and observation.
- **Process**: Conducted interviews with customer support agents to understand their challenges and observed them during live calls to identify inefficiencies.
- **Outcome**: Identified that the agents lacked quick access to knowledge base articles, leading to long call times. Recommended integrating a searchable knowledge base into their CRM system.

Example 2: Developing a New Software Feature
- **Technique Used**: Workshops and surveys.
- **Process**: Held workshops with end-users to brainstorm feature ideas and used surveys to prioritize these features based on user preferences.
- **Outcome**: Prioritized features that addressed the most common user pain points and delivered a software update that significantly improved user satisfaction.

By understanding and selecting the appropriate requirements gathering techniques based on project needs and context, Business Analysts can effectively capture and document requirements, ensuring that projects are well-defined and aligned with stakeholder expectations.

Analyzing and Documenting Requirements

Effective requirements analysis and documentation are crucial to the success of any project. This process involves capturing, organizing, and specifying what the project must deliver. Various tools like use cases, user stories, and requirements traceability matrices (RTMs) help in achieving this.

Tools for Analyzing and Documenting Requirements

1. Use Cases

Purpose: Use cases describe how users will interact with the system to achieve specific goals. They provide a detailed narrative of all possible interactions between the user and the system.

Components:
- **Actor:** The user or external system that interacts with the system.
- **Use Case Name:** A brief and descriptive title.
- **Preconditions:** Conditions that must be true before the use case starts.
- **Main Flow:** The primary sequence of steps taken to achieve the goal.
- **Alternative Flows:** Possible variations in the main flow.
- **Postconditions:** Conditions that must be true after the use case completes.

Example:
- **Use Case Name:** User Login
- **Actor:** User
- **Preconditions:** User is registered and has a valid username and password.
- **Main Flow:**
    1. User enters username and password.
    2. System validates credentials.
    3. System grants access to the user.
- **Alternative Flows:** 1a. User enters incorrect password. 2a. System displays an error message.
- **Postconditions:** User is logged into the system.

2. User Stories

Purpose: User stories are short, simple descriptions of a feature told from the perspective of the user. They are commonly used in Agile methodologies to capture requirements.

Format:
- **Template:** As a [type of user], I want [some goal] so that [some reason].
- **Acceptance Criteria:** Conditions that define when the story is complete.

Example:
- **User Story:** As a customer, I want to be able to save my payment information so that I can make future purchases more quickly.
- **Acceptance Criteria:**
    - Payment information is saved securely.
    - Users can edit or delete saved payment information.
    - Saved information is auto-filled during the checkout process.

3. Requirements Traceability Matrix (RTM)

Purpose: RTMs track requirements throughout the project lifecycle, ensuring each requirement is addressed by the project deliverables and verifying that all requirements are tested.

Components:
- **Requirement ID:** Unique identifier for each requirement.
- **Requirement Description:** Detailed description of the requirement.
- **Source:** Origin of the requirement (e.g., stakeholder name).
- **Priority:** Importance of the requirement.
- **Status:** Current status (e.g., drafted, approved, implemented).
- **Test Cases:** References to test cases that verify the requirement.

Example:

Requirement ID	Description	Source	Priority	Status	Test Cases
R001	User must be able to login	Stakeholder A	High	Approved	TC001, TC002
R002	Payment information saved	Stakeholder B	Medium	In Progress	TC003, TC004

Importance of Clear, Concise, Complete, Consistent, and Testable Requirements

Clear: Requirements should be unambiguous and easily understood.
- **Example:** "The system shall display the user's account balance" is clear compared to "The system shall show the balance."

Concise: Requirements should be brief but comprehensive.
- **Example:** "The system shall send a confirmation email upon order completion" is concise.

Complete: Requirements should cover all aspects of the need.
- **Example:** "The system shall support English, Spanish, and French languages" is complete for language requirements.

Consistent: Requirements should not contradict each other.
- **Example:** Ensure that "The system shall allow users to reset their password" does not conflict with "The system shall not store user passwords."

Testable: Requirements should be verifiable through testing.
- **Example:** "The system shall process 100 transactions per second" is testable.

Examples of Well-Written Requirements Statements

- **Functional Requirement:** "The system shall allow users to reset their password using their registered email address."
- **Non-Functional Requirement:** "The system shall respond to user inputs within 2 seconds under normal operating conditions."
- **Business Requirement:** "The system shall increase customer satisfaction by providing a 24/7 support chat feature."

Common Challenges in Requirements Analysis

1. Conflicting Requirements

Challenge: Different stakeholders may have requirements that conflict with each other.
- **Example:** Marketing wants a feature that IT deems too risky to implement.

Strategies for Resolution:
- **Negotiation:** Facilitate discussions between stakeholders to reach a compromise.
- **Prioritization:** Use prioritization techniques like MoSCoW (Must have, Should have, Could have, Won't have) to resolve conflicts based on the project's goals and constraints.

2. **Ambiguous Requirements**

Challenge: Requirements that are unclear or open to interpretation can lead to misunderstandings and incorrect implementations.
- **Example:** "The system should be user-friendly" is ambiguous.

Strategies for Resolution:
- **Clarification:** Engage with stakeholders to clarify ambiguous requirements.
- **Detailing:** Break down high-level requirements into more detailed and specific sub-requirements.

3. **Incomplete Requirements**

Challenge: Missing or incomplete requirements can result in overlooked functionality or rework.
- **Example:** Not specifying all user roles in a system can lead to missing permissions features.

Strategies for Resolution:
- **Comprehensive Elicitation:** Use multiple elicitation techniques to gather all necessary information.
- **Review and Validation:** Regularly review requirements with stakeholders to ensure completeness.

Best Practices for Requirements Analysis
1. **Engage Stakeholders Early and Often:** Continuous stakeholder involvement ensures that requirements are accurate and aligned with business needs.
2. **Use Visual Models:** Diagrams and visual aids help in understanding and validating requirements.
3. **Prioritize Requirements:** Focus on high-priority requirements that deliver the most value.
4. **Iterate and Refine:** Requirements should be revisited and refined throughout the project lifecycle.
5. **Maintain Traceability:** Use RTMs to track requirements from inception to implementation and testing.

By employing these tools and adhering to best practices, business analysts can ensure that requirements are well-documented, clear, concise, complete, consistent, and testable, ultimately leading to successful project outcomes.

Requirements Life Cycle Management

Concept: Requirements Life Cycle Management is the continuous process of managing requirements from their initial identification through their fulfillment and beyond. It ensures that requirements remain relevant, are accurately documented, and are aligned with the project objectives throughout the project life cycle.

Significance: Effective requirements life cycle management is crucial for maintaining alignment between stakeholders' needs and project deliverables. It helps in tracking changes, managing dependencies, and ensuring that all requirements are met, thereby reducing the risk of project failure and enhancing stakeholder satisfaction.

Key Activities in Requirements Management
1. **Establishing a Requirements Baseline**
    - **Purpose:** To create an agreed-upon set of requirements that serves as a foundation for further development and changes.
    - **Activities:**
        - Document and validate requirements with stakeholders.
        - Secure formal approval from all key stakeholders.
        - Baseline the approved requirements to create a reference point.
    - **Example:** In a software development project, the initial set of functional and non-functional requirements is documented, reviewed, and signed off by stakeholders to form the baseline.
2. **Tracking Requirements Changes**
    - **Purpose:** To monitor and control changes to requirements, ensuring that all modifications are evaluated and approved.
    - **Activities:**
        - Implement a change control process to handle change requests.

- Evaluate the impact of proposed changes on the project scope, schedule, and budget.
- Document and track all changes and their approvals.
    - **Example**: A change request to add a new feature in an e-commerce platform is submitted. The impact on the project timeline and resources is analyzed before approval.
3. **Communicating Updates to Stakeholders**
    - **Purpose**: To ensure all stakeholders are informed of the current requirements and any changes, maintaining transparency and alignment.
    - **Activities**:
        - Regularly update stakeholders on the status of requirements.
        - Use communication tools and techniques to share changes and their implications.
        - Maintain clear documentation and accessible records of requirements updates.
    - **Example**: Weekly project meetings are held where the Business Analyst presents any changes to the requirements and discusses the impacts with the team and stakeholders.

Tools and Techniques for Effective Requirements Management

1. **Version Control Systems**
    - **Purpose**: To manage changes to requirements documents and maintain a history of revisions.
    - **Tools**: Git, Subversion (SVN), Microsoft Team Foundation Server (TFS).
    - **Example**: Using Git, a Business Analyst tracks changes to the requirements document, ensuring that previous versions can be retrieved if needed.
2. **Change Request Forms**
    - **Purpose**: To formally document proposed changes to requirements, including their rationale and impact.
    - **Elements**: Description of the change, reason for the change, impact analysis, approvals.
    - **Example**: A change request form is submitted to add a mobile payment feature. The form includes the expected benefits, technical implications, and estimated effort.
3. **Impact Analysis Matrices**
    - **Purpose**: To assess the effects of changes on existing requirements, project scope, and other project elements.
    - **Components**: Matrix showing relationships between requirements and project elements.
    - **Example**: An impact analysis matrix is used to evaluate how adding a new report generation feature affects the current data processing and user interface requirements.

Examples of Effective Requirements Management

Example 1: Establishing a Requirements Baseline in Healthcare IT Project
- **Scenario**: Developing a new electronic health record (EHR) system.
- **Activity**: Initial requirements for patient data management, user access control, and compliance with healthcare regulations are documented and reviewed by stakeholders. Formal approval is obtained to baseline these requirements.
- **Outcome**: The baseline serves as a reference, ensuring that all subsequent changes are controlled and aligned with the initial scope.

Example 2: Tracking Requirements Changes in a Financial Software Project
- **Scenario**: Enhancing a financial reporting system.
- **Activity**: A change request is submitted to include a new tax reporting feature. The impact on existing reports, system performance, and development timeline is analyzed. Approval is granted, and the changes are documented and tracked using a version control system.
- **Outcome**: The project team can efficiently manage and implement the change without disrupting the overall project timeline and objectives.

Example 3: Communicating Updates in an E-Commerce Platform Development
- **Scenario**: Developing a new online shopping platform.
- **Activity**: Regular sprint reviews are held where the Business Analyst updates stakeholders on the status of requirements, discusses any changes, and ensures all feedback is incorporated.

- **Outcome**: Stakeholders remain informed and engaged, and the project continues to meet their evolving needs and expectations.

Best Practices for Requirements Management
1. **Consistent Documentation**: Maintain clear and consistent documentation for all requirements and changes.
2. **Stakeholder Involvement**: Involve stakeholders throughout the project to ensure their needs are understood and met.
3. **Regular Reviews**: Conduct regular reviews of requirements and their alignment with project objectives.
4. **Change Control Process**: Implement a robust change control process to manage and track changes.
5. **Effective Communication**: Ensure transparent and continuous communication with all stakeholders regarding requirements status and updates.

By employing these tools, techniques, and best practices, project teams can effectively manage requirements throughout the project life cycle, ensuring that they remain relevant, aligned with project objectives, and capable of delivering the intended business value.

Evaluating Proposed Solutions Against Business Requirements and Objectives

Evaluating proposed solutions involves assessing how well different options meet the defined business requirements and objectives. This process ensures that the chosen solution provides the best value and aligns with organizational goals.

Common Evaluation Criteria
1. **Feasibility:**
   - **Purpose:** Assess whether the solution can be implemented given the current constraints, such as technical capabilities, resources, and time.
   - **Example:** Evaluating if the IT infrastructure can support a new software application.
2. **Cost-Effectiveness:**
   - **Purpose:** Determine the financial viability of the solution by comparing costs against the expected benefits.
   - **Example:** Analyzing the total cost of ownership (TCO) of a cloud-based service versus an on-premises solution.
3. **Scalability:**
   - **Purpose:** Ensure that the solution can grow with the organization's future needs.
   - **Example:** Assessing whether a customer relationship management (CRM) system can handle an increasing number of users and data as the company expands.
4. **Alignment with Organizational Standards:**
   - **Purpose:** Verify that the solution adheres to the organization's policies, standards, and regulatory requirements.
   - **Example:** Ensuring that a new data processing system complies with data protection regulations like GDPR.
5. **Functionality:**
   - **Purpose:** Check if the solution meets all the functional requirements defined by the stakeholders.
   - **Example:** Confirming that an e-commerce platform includes essential features like payment processing and inventory management.
6. **Usability:**
   - **Purpose:** Evaluate how easy and intuitive the solution is for end-users.
   - **Example:** Conducting usability testing on a new user interface to ensure it is user-friendly.
7. **Support and Maintenance:**
   - **Purpose:** Consider the vendor's ability to provide ongoing support and maintenance.
   - **Example:** Reviewing the service level agreements (SLAs) of a software vendor.

Techniques for Conducting Solution Evaluations
1. **Proof-of-Concept (PoC) Studies:**
   - **Purpose:** Test the feasibility and functionality of a solution in a small-scale, controlled environment.
   - **Process:**

- Define objectives and success criteria.
- Set up the PoC environment.
- Execute tests and document results.
    - **Example:** A PoC study to assess the performance of a new database technology.
2. **Vendor Demonstrations:**
    - **Purpose:** Allow vendors to showcase their solutions, focusing on how they meet the organization's requirements.
    - **Process:**
        - Provide vendors with a list of requirements and scenarios to demonstrate.
        - Schedule and conduct demonstrations.
        - Evaluate the demonstrations based on predefined criteria.
    - **Example:** Vendor demo sessions for selecting an enterprise resource planning (ERP) system.
3. **User Acceptance Testing (UAT):**
    - **Purpose:** Validate that the solution meets user requirements and is ready for deployment.
    - **Process:**
        - Develop UAT test cases based on user requirements.
        - Conduct testing with actual users.
        - Document issues and feedback.
    - **Example:** UAT for a new human resources management system (HRMS) involving HR staff.

Best Practices for Documenting and Presenting Evaluation Results

1. **Create a Structured Evaluation Report:**
    - **Include:** Executive summary, evaluation criteria, methodology, detailed findings, and recommendations.
    - **Benefit:** Provides a clear and comprehensive overview of the evaluation process and results.
2. **Use Visual Aids:**
    - **Include:** Charts, graphs, and tables to summarize key findings.
    - **Benefit:** Enhances understanding and makes complex data more accessible.
3. **Compare Alternatives Side-by-Side:**
    - **Include:** A comparison matrix that highlights the strengths and weaknesses of each solution against the evaluation criteria.
    - **Benefit:** Helps stakeholders easily see how each solution measures up.
4. **Provide a Clear Recommendation:**
    - **Include:** A concise recommendation supported by the evaluation findings.
    - **Benefit:** Guides stakeholders toward making an informed decision.
5. **Engage Stakeholders Early and Often:**
    - **Include:** Regular updates and opportunities for stakeholders to provide input throughout the evaluation process.
    - **Benefit:** Ensures alignment and buy-in from all relevant parties.
6. **Ensure Transparency and Objectivity:**
    - **Include:** Document the evaluation process and criteria clearly and avoid biases.
    - **Benefit:** Builds trust in the evaluation results and recommendations.

Example of a Structured Evaluation Report

1. Executive Summary
- Brief overview of the evaluation objectives, methodology, and key findings.

2. Evaluation Criteria
- List of criteria used to evaluate the solutions (e.g., feasibility, cost-effectiveness, scalability).

3. Methodology
- Description of the evaluation process, including PoC studies, vendor demonstrations, and UAT.

4. Detailed Findings
- In-depth analysis of each solution against the evaluation criteria.
- Use tables and charts to summarize key points.

5. Comparison Matrix
- Side-by-side comparison of solutions based on the evaluation criteria.

6. Recommendations
- Clear and concise recommendation supported by the findings.
- Include next steps for implementation.

7. Appendices
- Additional data, test results, and supporting documents.

Evaluating proposed solutions against business requirements and objectives is essential for selecting the most appropriate solution. By using common evaluation criteria such as feasibility, cost-effectiveness, scalability, and alignment with organizational standards, and employing techniques like PoC studies, vendor demonstrations, and UAT, organizations can make informed decisions. Best practices for documenting and presenting evaluation results ensure that stakeholders have a clear understanding of the evaluation process and outcomes, facilitating successful project investments.

Measuring Solution Performance and Benefits Realization in Business Analysis

Importance: Measuring solution performance and benefits realization is critical in business analysis as it ensures that the implemented solution meets the defined objectives and delivers the expected value. By tracking performance metrics and key performance indicators (KPIs), organizations can assess whether the solution is effective, identify areas for improvement, and make informed decisions for future investments.

Common Performance Metrics and Key Performance Indicators (KPIs)

User Adoption Rates:
- **Definition**: The percentage of users who adopt and regularly use the new solution compared to the total potential user base.
- **Importance**: High user adoption rates indicate that the solution is meeting user needs and adding value to their work processes.
- **Example**: For a new CRM system, the user adoption rate could be measured by the number of sales representatives actively using the system within the first three months after implementation.

Process Cycle Times:
- **Definition**: The time taken to complete a specific business process from start to finish.
- **Importance**: Reduced process cycle times can indicate improved efficiency and productivity.
- **Example**: In a manufacturing setting, the process cycle time could be measured by the time taken to complete the assembly of a product from the moment an order is received to the shipment of the finished product.

Cost Savings:
- **Definition**: The reduction in costs achieved through the implementation of the solution compared to previous costs.
- **Importance**: Cost savings directly impact the bottom line and demonstrate the financial benefits of the solution.
- **Example**: For an IT service management tool, cost savings could be measured by the reduction in overtime pay for IT support staff due to more efficient incident resolution processes.

Defining, Collecting, and Reporting Metrics

Defining Metrics:
1. **Align with Objectives**: Ensure that metrics align with the business objectives and expected benefits of the solution.
2. **Specific and Measurable**: Define metrics in specific and measurable terms to enable accurate tracking and assessment.
3. **Relevant and Realistic**: Select metrics that are relevant to the solution's impact and realistic given the available data and resources.

Collecting Metrics:

1. **Data Sources**: Identify reliable data sources for each metric, such as system logs, user surveys, or financial records.
2. **Data Collection Methods**: Use appropriate methods for data collection, such as automated tools, manual tracking, or third-party analytics.
3. **Frequency of Collection**: Determine the frequency of data collection based on the nature of the metric and the project timeline (e.g., daily, weekly, monthly).

Reporting Metrics:
1. **Regular Reporting**: Establish a regular reporting schedule to keep stakeholders informed about performance.
2. **Visualizations**: Use charts, graphs, and dashboards to present data in a clear and understandable format.
3. **Context and Analysis**: Provide context and analysis alongside the metrics to explain trends, variances, and implications for the business.

Role of Business Analysts in Establishing Performance Baselines and Targets

Establishing Baselines:
- **Baseline Definition**: A performance baseline represents the initial state of a metric before the implementation of the solution.
- **Activities**:
    - Collect historical data to understand current performance levels.
    - Analyze data to establish a clear and accurate baseline.
- **Example**: For a customer support system, the baseline for average response time to support tickets could be established by analyzing historical data over the past six months.

Setting Targets:
- **Target Definition**: Performance targets represent the desired state or goal for a metric after the solution is implemented.
- **Activities**:
    - Collaborate with stakeholders to set realistic and achievable targets.
    - Ensure targets align with strategic business goals and expected benefits.
- **Example**: For a supply chain optimization project, a target could be set to reduce inventory holding costs by 20% within the first year of implementation.

Examples of Metrics in Practice

User Adoption Rates:
- **Definition**: Percentage of users logging into a new enterprise resource planning (ERP) system at least once a week.
- **Data Collection**: Automated tracking of user login data through the ERP system.
- **Reporting**: Monthly dashboard showing user adoption trends, segmented by department.

Process Cycle Times:
- **Definition**: Average time taken to process customer orders from receipt to delivery.
- **Data Collection**: System-generated timestamps for each stage of the order process.
- **Reporting**: Weekly report highlighting average cycle times, with comparisons to the baseline and target.

Cost Savings:
- **Definition**: Reduction in operational costs achieved by automating manual invoice processing.
- **Data Collection**: Financial records comparing pre- and post-implementation costs.
- **Reporting**: Quarterly financial summary showing cost savings, with detailed breakdowns of specific savings areas.

Business Analysts' Contribution to Performance and Benefits Realization

1. **Requirements Definition**: Ensure performance metrics and benefits are clearly defined in the project requirements.
2. **Data Analysis**: Analyze collected data to identify trends, deviations, and areas for improvement.
3. **Stakeholder Communication**: Regularly communicate performance results and insights to stakeholders, facilitating data-driven decision-making.

4. **Continuous Improvement**: Use performance data to recommend process improvements, additional features, or corrective actions to enhance solution effectiveness.

By effectively measuring solution performance and benefits realization, Business Analysts help ensure that projects deliver their intended value, support strategic business goals, and provide actionable insights for continuous improvement.

Purpose and Application of Strategic Analysis Techniques

Strategic analysis techniques like SWOT and PEST analysis are essential tools in business analysis. They help organizations understand internal and external factors that influence their strategy, identify opportunities and threats, and make informed decisions to achieve their goals.

SWOT Analysis

Purpose:
- SWOT analysis assesses an organization's internal strengths and weaknesses, and external opportunities and threats.
- It provides a holistic view of the organization's strategic position and helps in decision-making.

Application:
- Used in strategic planning to align projects with business goals.
- Helps identify areas for improvement and potential risks.

Step-by-Step Guide to Conducting a SWOT Analysis:
1. **Define the Objective:**
    - Determine the purpose of the analysis (e.g., launching a new product, entering a new market).
2. **Gather Data:**
    - Collect relevant information from internal and external sources (e.g., financial reports, market research, employee feedback).
3. **Identify Strengths:**
    - List internal attributes that give the organization a competitive advantage.
    - Example: Strong brand reputation, skilled workforce, robust financial position.
4. **Identify Weaknesses:**
    - List internal attributes that place the organization at a disadvantage.
    - Example: Outdated technology, high employee turnover, limited market reach.
5. **Identify Opportunities:**
    - List external factors that the organization can exploit to its advantage.
    - Example: Emerging markets, technological advancements, favorable regulatory changes.
6. **Identify Threats:**
    - List external factors that could harm the organization.
    - Example: Economic downturns, increased competition, changing consumer preferences.
7. **Analyze and Prioritize:**
    - Evaluate the importance of each factor and prioritize them based on their impact on the organization.
8. **Develop Strategies:**
    - Create strategies to leverage strengths, address weaknesses, capitalize on opportunities, and mitigate threats.

Example of SWOT Analysis Insights:
- **Strength:** Strong brand reputation -> **Strategy:** Leverage brand strength in marketing campaigns to enter new markets.
- **Weakness:** Outdated technology -> **Strategy:** Invest in upgrading technology to improve operational efficiency.
- **Opportunity:** Growing demand for sustainable products -> **Strategy:** Develop and market eco-friendly product lines.
- **Threat:** Increasing competition -> **Strategy:** Differentiate through superior customer service and innovative features.

PEST Analysis

Purpose:
- PEST analysis examines external macro-environmental factors: Political, Economic, Social, and Technological.
- It helps organizations understand the broader context in which they operate and identify external influences on strategy.

Application:
- Used to assess the external environment and inform strategic decisions.
- Helps in identifying potential opportunities and threats from external factors.

Step-by-Step Guide to Conducting a PEST Analysis:
1. **Define the Objective:**
   - Determine the purpose of the analysis (e.g., market entry strategy, product development).
2. **Identify Political Factors:**
   - Examine government policies, regulations, and political stability.
   - Example: Trade regulations, tax policies, political stability.
3. **Identify Economic Factors:**
   - Assess economic conditions and trends that impact the organization.
   - Example: Inflation rates, economic growth, exchange rates.
4. **Identify Social Factors:**
   - Analyze demographic and cultural trends that influence the market.
   - Example: Population growth, lifestyle changes, consumer attitudes.
5. **Identify Technological Factors:**
   - Evaluate technological advancements and innovations that could affect the organization.
   - Example: Emerging technologies, research and development activity, automation.
6. **Analyze and Prioritize:**
   - Evaluate the significance of each factor and prioritize them based on their potential impact on the organization.
7. **Develop Strategies:**
   - Formulate strategies to respond to the identified factors.

Example of PEST Analysis Insights:
- **Political:** New trade regulations -> **Strategy:** Adjust supply chain strategies to comply with new regulations.
- **Economic:** Economic downturn -> **Strategy:** Implement cost-saving measures and focus on essential products.
- **Social:** Increasing health consciousness -> **Strategy:** Introduce health-oriented products and services.
- **Technological:** Rapid tech advancements -> **Strategy:** Invest in R&D to stay ahead in technology adoption.

Using SWOT and PEST Analyses to Inform Project Scope and Objectives

Example: New Product Launch
1. **Conduct SWOT Analysis:**
   - Identify internal strengths (e.g., strong R&D capabilities) and weaknesses (e.g., limited marketing budget).
   - Identify external opportunities (e.g., growing demand for eco-friendly products) and threats (e.g., new competitors).
2. **Conduct PEST Analysis:**
   - Identify political factors (e.g., favorable government policies for green products).
   - Assess economic factors (e.g., rising consumer spending power).
   - Analyze social factors (e.g., increasing environmental awareness).
   - Evaluate technological factors (e.g., advancements in sustainable materials).
3. **Define Project Scope and Objectives:**
   - Based on the SWOT analysis, decide to leverage R&D strengths to develop eco-friendly products.
   - Address the weakness of limited marketing budget by prioritizing cost-effective digital marketing strategies.

- Capitalize on the opportunity of growing demand by setting an objective to capture a 10% market share within the first year.
- Mitigate the threat of new competitors by emphasizing unique product features and superior customer service.

4. **Develop Project Plan:**
   - Outline key activities, resources, and timelines required to achieve the objectives.
   - Use insights from PEST analysis to inform risk management and contingency planning.

Best Practices for Conducting Strategic Analyses:
1. **Engage Stakeholders:** Involve key stakeholders to gather diverse perspectives and ensure buy-in.
2. **Regular Updates:** Periodically review and update analyses to reflect changes in the internal and external environment.
3. **Data-Driven:** Use reliable data sources to inform analyses and avoid subjective judgments.
4. **Document and Communicate:** Clearly document findings and communicate them effectively to stakeholders.
5. **Actionable Insights:** Focus on generating actionable insights that can directly inform strategic decisions and project planning.

By conducting thorough SWOT and PEST analyses, organizations can gain a deep understanding of their strategic environment and make informed decisions that align with their business goals. These analyses help in defining project scope and objectives, identifying risks and opportunities, and developing strategies to achieve desired outcomes.

Business Process Improvement Techniques

Business process improvement (BPI) techniques are essential tools for identifying inefficiencies, bottlenecks, and waste within business processes. These techniques provide a structured approach for optimizing processes to enhance efficiency, reduce costs, and improve overall performance. Here, we will explore three common BPI techniques: process mapping, value stream mapping, and Lean Six Sigma.

1. Process Mapping

Description: Process mapping involves creating a visual representation of the steps involved in a business process. It helps in understanding the flow of activities, identifying inefficiencies, and designing improvements.

Steps:
1. **Identify the Process:** Define the scope and boundaries of the process to be mapped.
2. **Gather Information:** Collect detailed information about each step in the process through observations, interviews, and documentation reviews.
3. **Create the Map:** Use flowcharts or diagrams to represent the sequence of activities, decision points, inputs, and outputs.
4. **Analyze the Process:** Identify bottlenecks, redundancies, and non-value-added activities.
5. **Design Improvements:** Propose changes to optimize the process and eliminate inefficiencies.

Example:
- **As-Is Process:** A process map for the customer onboarding process in a bank shows steps including document submission, verification, account creation, and customer notification. The map highlights delays in document verification.
- **To-Be Process:** The redesigned process eliminates manual verification by implementing an automated document verification system, reducing the onboarding time by 50%.

2. Value Stream Mapping (VSM)

Description: Value stream mapping is a Lean management technique that visualizes the flow of materials and information through a process. It focuses on identifying value-added and non-value-added activities to improve efficiency.

Steps:
1. **Define the Value Stream:** Select a specific product or service to analyze.
2. **Map the Current State:** Create a visual map of the current process, showing every step from start to finish, including value-added and non-value-added activities.
3. **Analyze the Current State:** Identify sources of waste, such as delays, excess inventory, and rework.

4. **Design the Future State**: Develop a new value stream map that eliminates waste and optimizes the flow of value-added activities.
5. **Implement and Monitor**: Execute the changes and continuously monitor the process for further improvements.

Example:
- **As-Is Value Stream Map**: A VSM for a manufacturing process shows steps including material receipt, assembly, quality inspection, and shipping. The map reveals long wait times between assembly and inspection.
- **To-Be Value Stream Map**: The future state map integrates quality checks into the assembly process, reducing wait times and improving throughput.

3. Lean Six Sigma
Description: Lean Six Sigma combines Lean principles, which focus on eliminating waste, with Six Sigma methodologies, which aim to reduce variation and improve quality. It uses a data-driven approach to process improvement.

Steps:
1. **Define**: Identify the problem, set improvement goals, and define the scope.
2. **Measure**: Collect data to understand current performance and establish baselines.
3. **Analyze**: Analyze data to identify root causes of inefficiencies and defects.
4. **Improve**: Develop and implement solutions to address root causes and improve the process.
5. **Control**: Monitor the process to ensure sustained improvements and make necessary adjustments.

Example:
- **As-Is Analysis**: A Lean Six Sigma project in a call center identifies high call handling times and customer dissatisfaction. Data analysis reveals that a significant portion of call time is spent on redundant verification steps.
- **To-Be Process**: Implementing a streamlined verification process and training agents on efficient call handling techniques reduces call handling time by 30% and improves customer satisfaction scores.

Application of Techniques by Business Analysts

1. Documenting As-Is Processes
- **Process Mapping**: Business Analysts create detailed process maps to capture the current state of operations. For instance, mapping the procurement process in a manufacturing company might reveal steps such as requisition approval, vendor selection, purchase order creation, and goods receipt.
- **Value Stream Mapping**: Analysts use VSM to document the current flow of materials and information, identifying areas of waste. For example, mapping the value stream for product development can highlight excessive handoffs and approval delays.
- **Lean Six Sigma**: Analysts gather data on key performance metrics, such as cycle time and defect rates, to establish a baseline for improvement. In a software development project, this might involve measuring the average time from code commit to deployment and identifying defect patterns.

2. Designing To-Be Processes
- **Process Mapping**: Using insights from the as-is process map, analysts design a streamlined to-be process that removes unnecessary steps and optimizes workflow. For instance, redesigning the claims processing workflow in an insurance company to incorporate automated data entry and validation.
- **Value Stream Mapping**: Analysts create a future state value stream map that outlines a more efficient process flow with reduced waste. In a healthcare setting, this could involve redesigning the patient admission process to minimize wait times and paperwork.
- **Lean Six Sigma**: Analysts apply Lean Six Sigma methodologies to design solutions that address root causes of inefficiencies. For example, implementing standardized work procedures and quality control measures in a manufacturing line to reduce defects and rework.

3. Measuring Improvement Outcomes
- **Process Mapping**: Analysts use before-and-after process maps to compare performance metrics, such as cycle time and throughput, demonstrating the impact of process improvements.

- **Value Stream Mapping**: By comparing current and future state value stream maps, analysts quantify improvements in lead time, inventory levels, and production efficiency.
- **Lean Six Sigma**: Analysts use control charts and other statistical tools to monitor process performance and ensure that improvements are sustained over time. They might track metrics like defect rates, process capability (Cpk), and overall equipment effectiveness (OEE) to measure success.

Examples of Effective Questions and Prompts in Requirements Elicitation Sessions

1. Open-Ended Questions
- "Can you walk me through your daily tasks?"
- "What challenges do you encounter in your role?"
- "How would you improve the current system?"

2. Specific Probes
- "What steps do you take to complete this task?"
- "What information do you need to perform this process?"
- "Can you describe a recent instance where you faced a problem?"

3. Clarifying Questions
- "Can you explain what you mean by that?"
- "Why do you think this issue occurs?"
- "How do you currently resolve this issue?"

By applying these business process improvement techniques, Business Analysts can systematically identify inefficiencies, optimize processes, and measure the outcomes of their improvements, ensuring that the organization achieves its operational and strategic goals.

Identifying and Analyzing Project Stakeholders

Stakeholders are individuals, groups, or organizations that have an interest in or can influence the outcome of a project. Identifying and analyzing stakeholders is crucial for project success, as it helps in understanding their needs, expectations, and influence, and in planning how to engage and manage them effectively.

Process of Identifying and Analyzing Stakeholders

1. **Identify Stakeholders:**
    - **Purpose:** Determine all potential stakeholders who are affected by the project or can affect the project.
    - **Techniques:** Brainstorming sessions, stakeholder registers, interviews, organizational charts.
2. **Analyze Stakeholders:**
    - **Purpose:** Understand stakeholders' interests, influence, expectations, and potential impact on the project.
    - **Techniques:** Stakeholder analysis matrices, power/interest grids, stakeholder mapping.
3. **Prioritize Stakeholders:**
    - **Purpose:** Focus efforts on managing key stakeholders who have the most influence or interest.
    - **Techniques:** Power/interest grid, influence/impact matrix.

Common Stakeholder Analysis Techniques

1. Power/Interest Grid

Purpose: Categorizes stakeholders based on their level of power (influence) and interest in the project. Helps prioritize engagement efforts.

Quadrants:
1. **High Power, High Interest:** Manage closely.
2. **High Power, Low Interest:** Keep satisfied.
3. **Low Power, High Interest:** Keep informed.
4. **Low Power, Low Interest:** Monitor (minimal effort).

Example:
- **High Power, High Interest:** Project sponsor, key client.
- **High Power, Low Interest:** Senior management not directly involved in the project.

- **Low Power, High Interest:** End-users of the project deliverables.
- **Low Power, Low Interest:** Peripheral stakeholders with minimal impact.

2. Stakeholder Mapping

Purpose: Visual representation of stakeholders, showing their relationships, influence, and communication needs.

Components:
- **Stakeholder Influence Diagrams:** Show connections and influence among stakeholders.
- **Stakeholder Maps:** Visual maps categorizing stakeholders by their attributes (e.g., power, interest, impact).

Example:
- **Mapping Process:**
    1. Identify all stakeholders.
    2. Determine attributes (power, interest, influence).
    3. Place stakeholders on the map accordingly.

Developing and Maintaining Positive Relationships with Key Stakeholders

Importance:
- **Project Success:** Key stakeholders can significantly influence project outcomes.
- **Support and Buy-in:** Positive relationships ensure support, reduce resistance, and foster collaboration.
- **Resource Access:** Engaged stakeholders provide necessary resources and information.

Key Stakeholders:
1. **Sponsors:** Provide funding, resources, and support.
2. **Users:** Utilize the project deliverables and provide valuable feedback.
3. **Subject Matter Experts (SMEs):** Offer expertise and technical knowledge crucial for project success.

Best Practices for Effective Stakeholder Communication and Collaboration

1. **Understand Stakeholder Needs:**
    - Regularly gather and understand the needs, expectations, and concerns of stakeholders.
    - **Techniques:** Surveys, interviews, feedback sessions.
2. **Develop a Communication Plan:**
    - Tailor communication strategies to different stakeholder groups based on their needs and influence.
    - Include frequency, methods, and types of communication.
3. **Engage Early and Often:**
    - Involve stakeholders from the beginning and maintain regular interaction throughout the project.
    - **Example:** Hold kickoff meetings, regular status updates, and review sessions.
4. **Use Appropriate Communication Channels:**
    - Select communication methods that suit the preferences and accessibility of stakeholders.
    - **Example:** Email for detailed updates, meetings for discussions, and dashboards for real-time information.
5. **Foster Transparency:**
    - Be open and honest about project progress, challenges, and decisions.
    - **Example:** Share project dashboards, regular reports, and meeting minutes.
6. **Build Trust and Rapport:**
    - Establish trust through consistent and reliable communication.
    - **Example:** Acknowledge stakeholder contributions, address concerns promptly, and deliver on promises.
7. **Seek Feedback and Act on It:**
    - Regularly solicit feedback and show that it is valued by making necessary adjustments.
    - **Example:** Implement a feedback loop in project meetings to review and incorporate stakeholder input.
8. **Conflict Resolution:**
    - Address conflicts promptly and fairly to maintain positive relationships.
    - **Example:** Use negotiation and mediation techniques to resolve disagreements.

Examples of Stakeholder Engagement

Example 1: IT System Implementation Project
- **Stakeholder Identification:** Includes IT staff, end-users, department heads, and external vendors.
- **Power/Interest Grid:** IT staff (High Power, High Interest), End-users (Low Power, High Interest), Department heads (High Power, Low Interest), Vendors (Low Power, Low Interest).
- **Communication Plan:**
    - Weekly status meetings with IT staff.
    - Monthly updates to department heads.
    - Training sessions for end-users.
    - Regular email updates to vendors.

Example 2: New Product Development
- **Stakeholder Identification:** Marketing team, product users, suppliers, senior management.
- **Stakeholder Mapping:** Identifies the marketing team as key influencers with high interest, senior management as decision-makers with high power but varying interest, and users with high interest but low direct influence.
- **Engagement Strategy:**
    - Regular brainstorming and feedback sessions with the marketing team.
    - Bi-monthly executive briefings for senior management.
    - Surveys and beta testing with users.
    - Performance reviews and regular meetings with suppliers.

By systematically identifying and analyzing stakeholders, prioritizing engagement efforts, and fostering positive relationships, project managers can ensure that stakeholder needs are addressed and that they have the support necessary for project success. Using techniques like power/interest grids and stakeholder mapping, along with best practices in communication and collaboration, facilitates effective stakeholder management and contributes to achieving project goals.

The Role of Effective Communication in Business Analysis

Effective communication is critical in business analysis as it facilitates clear understanding, ensures stakeholder engagement, and drives successful project outcomes. Business Analysts (BAs) need to effectively convey ideas, requirements, and project updates to various stakeholders, ensuring that everyone is aligned and informed throughout the project lifecycle.

Impact on Stakeholder Engagement and Project Outcomes

1. **Stakeholder Engagement:** Effective communication fosters trust and collaboration, making stakeholders feel valued and heard. This engagement is crucial for gathering accurate requirements and gaining stakeholder buy-in.
2. **Clarity and Understanding:** Clear communication ensures that all parties have a shared understanding of project objectives, requirements, and deliverables, reducing the risk of misunderstandings and errors.
3. **Project Outcomes:** By maintaining open lines of communication, BAs can identify issues early, manage expectations, and ensure that the project stays on track, ultimately leading to successful project outcomes.

Common Communication Challenges and Strategies for Overcoming Them

1. Technical Jargon

Challenge: Stakeholders may not understand technical terms, leading to confusion and miscommunication.

Strategy:
- **Simplify Language:** Use plain language and avoid technical jargon when communicating with non-technical stakeholders.
- **Define Terms:** When technical terms are necessary, provide clear definitions and examples.
- **Visual Aids:** Use diagrams and visuals to explain complex concepts.

Example:
- **Scenario:** Explaining the architecture of a new IT system to a business stakeholder.
- **Solution:** Use a high-level diagram to illustrate system components and their interactions, and provide simple explanations for technical terms.

2. Conflicting Priorities
Challenge: Different stakeholders may have conflicting priorities, leading to disagreements and delays.
Strategy:
- **Prioritize Requirements**: Facilitate discussions to prioritize requirements based on business value and impact.
- **Find Common Ground**: Identify areas of agreement and build consensus around shared goals.
- **Escalate When Necessary**: Escalate conflicts to higher management for resolution if they cannot be resolved at the team level.

Example:
- **Scenario**: Conflicting priorities between the marketing and sales departments regarding feature development.
- **Solution**: Organize a prioritization workshop to discuss the business value of each feature and reach a consensus on the most critical features.

3. Resistance to Change
Challenge: Stakeholders may resist changes due to fear of the unknown or perceived negative impacts on their work.
Strategy:
- **Communicate Benefits**: Clearly articulate the benefits of the change and how it will positively impact stakeholders.
- **Involve Stakeholders**: Involve stakeholders early in the process and seek their input to foster a sense of ownership.
- **Provide Training**: Offer training sessions to help stakeholders adapt to the new processes or systems.

Example:
- **Scenario**: Resistance from employees to a new software implementation.
- **Solution**: Conduct user training sessions and create materials highlighting the benefits of the new software, such as increased efficiency and ease of use.

Effective Communication Techniques

1. Active Listening
Description: Actively listening involves fully concentrating, understanding, responding, and remembering what is being said.
Application:
- **Requirements Workshops**: Listen attentively to stakeholder needs and concerns, paraphrase their statements to ensure understanding, and ask clarifying questions.
- **Project Status Meetings**: Show engagement by nodding, making eye contact, and summarizing key points discussed.

Example:
- **Scenario**: A stakeholder expresses concerns about a project's timeline.
- **Technique**: The BA listens attentively, paraphrases the concern ("So, you're worried about meeting the deadline, is that correct?"), and addresses it by discussing potential solutions.

2. Questioning
Description: Asking the right questions to elicit detailed information, clarify understanding, and explore deeper insights.
Application:
- **Requirements Gathering**: Use open-ended questions to explore needs and closed-ended questions to confirm specifics.
- **User Training Sessions**: Encourage questions from participants to ensure they understand the new system or process.

Example:
- **Scenario**: Gathering requirements for a new feature.

- **Technique**: The BA asks, "Can you describe how this feature will help you in your daily tasks?" followed by, "What specific functionalities do you need this feature to include?"

3. Visual Aids

Description: Using diagrams, charts, and other visuals to convey complex information clearly and effectively.

Application:
- **Requirements Workshops**: Use process flow diagrams and wireframes to illustrate workflows and interface designs.
- **Project Status Meetings**: Present progress through Gantt charts, burn-down charts, and dashboards.

Example:
- **Scenario**: Explaining a new process flow to a team.
- **Technique**: The BA creates a process flow diagram showing each step and decision point, making it easier for the team to visualize and understand the new process.

Examples of Communication Techniques in Various Contexts

Requirements Workshops
- **Active Listening**: Ensures all stakeholder voices are heard and understood, fostering a collaborative environment.
- **Questioning**: Helps uncover detailed requirements and potential issues.
- **Visual Aids**: Process maps and wireframes aid in visualizing requirements and gaining consensus.

Project Status Meetings
- **Active Listening**: Demonstrates respect for stakeholder input and concerns, leading to better stakeholder relationships.
- **Questioning**: Clarifies status updates and identifies potential risks or roadblocks.
- **Visual Aids**: Dashboards and charts effectively communicate progress and performance metrics.

User Training Sessions
- **Active Listening**: Encourages feedback and questions from participants, ensuring they understand the training material.
- **Questioning**: Helps assess participant understanding and address any gaps in knowledge.
- **Visual Aids**: Step-by-step guides, screenshots, and videos make the training content more accessible and easier to follow.

Effective communication is vital for Business Analysts to engage stakeholders, ensure clarity, and drive successful project outcomes. By understanding and overcoming common communication challenges, and utilizing techniques like active listening, questioning, and visual aids, BAs can facilitate better collaboration, clearer requirements, and smoother project execution. These skills are essential in various business analysis contexts, from requirements workshops and project status meetings to user training sessions, ensuring that all stakeholders are aligned and informed throughout the project lifecycle.

Practice Questions

Practice Exam Introduction
Welcome to the practice exam section of your CAPM Exam Prep Study Guide. This section is designed to help you assess your knowledge and understanding of the material covered in the CAPM certification exam. By working through these questions, you'll gain valuable practice and insight into the types of questions you may encounter on the actual exam.

Instant Feedback: By having the answer and explanation readily available right after each question, you can quickly assess your understanding of each concept. If you answered correctly, the explanation will reinforce your knowledge. If you answered incorrectly, you can immediately learn from your mistake and clarify any misunderstandings.

Efficient Learning: Providing answers and explanations directly after each question eliminates the need to flip back and forth between the questions and an answer key. This streamlined approach allows you to focus on the content and maintain your momentum as you progress through the practice test.

Enhanced Retention: Research has shown that receiving immediate feedback on your responses can significantly improve learning and retention. By reviewing the answer and explanation right after answering a question, you'll be more likely to remember the information and apply it effectively in the future.

How to Use This Section:
- We encourage you to take a piece of paper or something similar to cover the answers as you work through each question. This will help simulate an exam environment and ensure that you are testing your knowledge without immediate reliance on the answer.
- Note that some important topics might be covered several times to reinforce key concepts and ensure a thorough understanding.

Dive into the questions, test your knowledge, and use the explanations to enhance your understanding. This practice will not only prepare you for the exam but also help solidify the essential project management principles and practices. Good luck!

1. A project manager is developing a project charter for a new product development initiative. Which of the following components should be included in the project charter to clearly define the project's objectives and stakeholders' expectations?
a. Work breakdown structure (WBS) and activity list
b. Detailed project schedule and budget
c. High-level project description, objectives, and success criteria
d. Quality management plan and quality metrics

Answer: c. High-level project description, objectives, and success criteria. Explanation: The project charter is a high-level document that authorizes the project and provides a summary of the project's objectives, scope, and key stakeholders. It should include a high-level project description, objectives, and success criteria to align stakeholders' expectations and set the project's direction. The WBS, activity list, detailed schedule, budget, and quality management plan are developed later in the project planning process.

2. During the execution phase of a project, the project manager notices that the actual cost (AC) is higher than the earned value (EV), and the cost performance index (CPI) is less than 1. Which of the following statements best describes the project's cost performance?
a. The project is experiencing a cost underrun and is under budget.
b. The project is experiencing a cost overrun and is over budget.
c. The project's cost performance is on track and within budget.
d. The project's schedule is ahead of the planned timeline.

Answer: b. The project is experiencing a cost overrun and is over budget. Explanation: When the actual cost (AC) is higher than the earned value (EV), it indicates that the project has spent more money than planned for the work completed. A cost performance index (CPI) less than 1 further confirms that the project is over budget, as CPI = EV / AC. A CPI < 1 means that the project is getting less value for each unit of cost spent than planned.

3. A project stakeholder approaches the project manager with a request to add new features to the project scope. The project is already in the execution phase, and the proposed changes are not part of the original scope baseline. How should the project manager handle this situation?
a. Immediately incorporate the requested changes into the project scope
b. Reject the requested changes outright to avoid scope creep
c. Initiate the change control process and assess the impact of the changes
d. Escalate the decision to the project sponsor without further analysis

Answer: c. Initiate the change control process and assess the impact of the changes. Explanation: When faced with a change request during project execution, the project manager should follow the established change control process. This involves documenting the requested changes, assessing their impact on the project's scope, schedule, cost, and resources, and presenting the analysis to the change control board (CCB) for a decision. Immediately incorporating or rejecting changes without proper analysis can lead to scope creep, delays, or stakeholder dissatisfaction.

4. A project manager is overseeing a large construction project using the Waterfall methodology. During the execution phase, it becomes clear that a key deliverable will not meet the agreed-upon standards. What is the most appropriate action to take during the phase-gate review?
a. Move on to the next phase and address the issue later
b. Revise the project scope to exclude the problematic deliverable
c. Implement corrective actions to bring the deliverable up to standard before proceeding
d. Request additional budget to hire more resources

Answer: c. Implement corrective actions to bring the deliverable up to standard before proceeding. Explanation: In the Waterfall methodology, phase-gate reviews are used to ensure that each phase is completed satisfactorily before moving on to the next. If a deliverable does not meet standards, corrective actions must be taken to resolve the issue before proceeding to ensure project success.

5. During the planning phase of a project, the project manager creates a Requirements Traceability Matrix (RTM). What is the primary purpose of this document?
a. To outline the project's scope and objectives
b. To track the status of project deliverables
c. To link requirements to their origins and trace them throughout the project lifecycle
d. To manage changes to project requirements

Answer: c. To link requirements to their origins and trace them throughout the project lifecycle. Explanation: The Requirements Traceability Matrix (RTM) is a tool used to ensure that all project requirements are accounted for and tracked throughout the project lifecycle. It helps in linking requirements to their origins, making sure that each requirement is fulfilled.

6. A project manager is validating the scope of a project. Which of the following activities is involved in scope validation?
a. Developing a detailed project schedule
b. Reviewing project deliverables with the customer for acceptance
c. Performing quality audits
d. Conducting team-building activities

Answer: b. Reviewing project deliverables with the customer for acceptance. Explanation: Scope validation involves obtaining formal acceptance of the completed project deliverables from the customer or sponsor. This ensures that the deliverables meet the agreed-upon requirements and criteria.

7. A project is behind schedule, and the project manager decides to use schedule compression techniques. Which of the following is an example of fast-tracking?
a. Adding more resources to critical path activities
b. Performing activities in parallel that were originally planned in sequence
c. Increasing the working hours for the project team
d. Reducing the scope of the project

Answer: b. Performing activities in parallel that were originally planned in sequence. Explanation: Fast-tracking is a schedule compression technique that involves performing activities in parallel that were initially planned to be done sequentially. This can help shorten the project schedule but may increase risks.

8. In the context of cost of quality (COQ), which of the following is an example of appraisal cost?
a. Training team members on quality standards
b. Conducting inspections and testing of deliverables
c. Reworking defective products
d. Implementing preventive measures

Answer: b. Conducting inspections and testing of deliverables. Explanation: Appraisal costs are associated with measuring and monitoring activities to ensure that the project deliverables meet quality standards. This includes inspections, testing, and other forms of quality control.

9. A project manager is conducting a quality audit. What is the primary purpose of this audit?
a. To identify areas where project performance can be improved
b. To adjust the project schedule based on current progress
c. To validate the project's scope with stakeholders
d. To manage changes to the project budget

Answer: a. To identify areas where project performance can be improved. Explanation: Quality audits are conducted to ensure that project activities comply with organizational and project policies, processes, and procedures. The primary purpose is to identify inefficiencies and areas for improvement to enhance project performance.

10. In the forming stage of team development, what is the primary focus of the project manager?
a. Resolving conflicts and issues among team members
b. Building trust and establishing clear roles and responsibilities
c. Fostering a high level of productivity and performance
d. Implementing a rewards and recognition system

Answer: b. Building trust and establishing clear roles and responsibilities. Explanation: During the forming stage of team development, the project manager's primary focus is on building trust among team members, establishing clear roles, and setting expectations. This stage is crucial for setting a strong foundation for team collaboration.

11. Which communication method is most appropriate for sharing complex information that requires immediate feedback and discussion?
a. Push communication
b. Pull communication
c. Interactive communication
d. Passive communication

Answer: c. Interactive communication. Explanation: Interactive communication involves real-time exchange of information, such as meetings or phone calls, allowing for immediate feedback and discussion. This method is ideal for complex information that requires clarification and collaborative decision-making.

12. A project manager is assessing project risks and categorizing them. Which of the following risks would be considered an organizational risk?
a. Changes in regulatory requirements
b. Natural disasters
c. Lack of stakeholder support
d. Technical failures

Answer: c. Lack of stakeholder support. Explanation: Organizational risks are related to the project's environment within the organization, such as lack of stakeholder support, changes in organizational priorities, or resource constraints. These risks can significantly impact the project's success.

13. During a procurement process, the project manager is involved in vendor negotiations. What is the primary objective of these negotiations?
a. To establish a fixed price for all deliverables

b. To ensure the vendor meets all project requirements at the lowest possible cost
c. To build a collaborative relationship with the vendor for future projects
d. To finalize the project schedule and milestones

Answer: b. To ensure the vendor meets all project requirements at the lowest possible cost. Explanation: The primary objective of procurement negotiations is to ensure that the vendor can meet the project's requirements at a cost that is favorable to the project while maintaining quality and adherence to the project schedule.

14. A team is using the Agile framework for a software development project. During the Sprint Review, the product owner provides feedback on the increment and suggests several changes. What should the team do next to incorporate these changes?
a. Immediately implement the changes in the current sprint.
b. Create new user stories for the changes and add them to the product backlog.
c. Delay the changes until the next release cycle.
d. Discuss the changes in the next Sprint Retrospective.

Answer: b. Create new user stories for the changes and add them to the product backlog. Explanation: In Agile, any feedback or changes suggested during the Sprint Review are added to the product backlog as new user stories. These will be prioritized by the product owner and implemented in future sprints.

15. A project manager is working with a team that follows Scrum. They notice that the team often struggles to complete their tasks by the end of the sprint. Which technique can be used during Sprint Planning to improve task estimation accuracy?
a. Critical path method
b. Planning poker
c. Earned value management
d. Delphi technique

Answer: b. Planning poker. Explanation: Planning poker is an Agile estimation technique used during Sprint Planning to estimate the effort required for user stories. It encourages discussion and consensus among the team, leading to more accurate estimates.

16. In a Scrum team, who is responsible for maximizing the value of the product and managing the product backlog?
a. Scrum Master
b. Development Team
c. Product Owner
d. Project Manager

Answer: c. Product Owner. Explanation: The Product Owner is responsible for maximizing the value of the product by managing the product backlog. This includes prioritizing user stories and ensuring the team focuses on delivering the highest value features.

17. A team using Kanban wants to improve their workflow by limiting work-in-progress (WIP). What is the primary benefit of implementing WIP limits?
a. Increased team workload
b. Faster delivery of individual tasks
c. Reduced multitasking and increased focus
d. Longer cycle times

Answer: c. Reduced multitasking and increased focus. Explanation: WIP limits help reduce multitasking by limiting the number of tasks a team works on simultaneously. This increases focus and efficiency, leading to improved workflow and faster overall delivery.

18. A Scrum team is holding a Sprint Retrospective. What is the main purpose of this event?
a. To review the product increment and get feedback from stakeholders.
b. To refine and prioritize the product backlog.
c. To plan the work for the next sprint.
d. To reflect on the past sprint and identify improvements for the next sprint.

Answer: d. To reflect on the past sprint and identify improvements for the next sprint. Explanation: The Sprint Retrospective is a meeting where the Scrum team reflects on the past sprint to identify what went well, what didn't, and how they can improve in the next sprint.

19. In Extreme Programming (XP), which practice involves writing tests before writing the corresponding code to ensure functionality?
a. Pair programming
b. Test-driven development
c. Continuous integration
d. Refactoring

Answer: b. Test-driven development. Explanation: Test-driven development (TDD) is an XP practice where developers write automated tests before writing the code that implements the functionality. This ensures the code meets the specified requirements and reduces defects.

20. A project team is using the Lean principle of eliminating waste. Which of the following is considered waste in Lean methodology?
a. Overproduction
b. High-quality product
c. Customer feedback
d. Team collaboration

Answer: a. Overproduction. Explanation: In Lean methodology, overproduction is considered waste because it leads to excess inventory, increased storage costs, and potential obsolescence. Lean aims to eliminate waste to improve efficiency and deliver value.

21. During an Agile project, the team uses story points to estimate the effort required for user stories. What is the main advantage of using story points over traditional time-based estimates?
a. Story points are easier to calculate.
b. Story points are based on objective criteria.
c. Story points help measure team velocity and compare relative effort.
d. Story points are more precise than time estimates.

Answer: c. Story points help measure team velocity and compare relative effort. Explanation: Story points allow teams to estimate the relative effort of user stories, helping measure team velocity and track progress. This method is less prone to inaccuracies compared to time-based estimates, as it abstracts effort into relative terms.

22. A project team is using a Cumulative Flow Diagram (CFD) to visualize their workflow. What key metric can be derived from the CFD?
a. Velocity
b. Lead time
c. Burn rate
d. Schedule variance

Answer: b. Lead time. Explanation: A Cumulative Flow Diagram (CFD) shows the status of work items over time, helping to visualize flow efficiency and identify bottlenecks. Lead time, the time taken from work item initiation to completion, can be derived from the CFD.

23. During an Agile project, the team identifies a high-priority risk that could significantly impact the project's success. Which Agile technique can they use to manage this risk proactively?
a. Risk-adjusted backlog
b. Monte Carlo simulation
c. Critical path analysis
d. Earned value management

Answer: a. Risk-adjusted backlog. Explanation: A risk-adjusted backlog incorporates risk management into the prioritization process by adjusting the priority of backlog items based on their risk impact. This allows the team to address high-priority risks proactively during the project.

24. A project manager is using the critical path method (CPM) to analyze the project schedule. The project network diagram shows that Activity A (duration: 3 days) and Activity B (duration: 5 days) are parallel activities, both preceding Activity C (duration: 4 days). What is the total float for Activity B?
a. 0 days
b. 2 days

c. 3 days
d. 5 days

Answer: b. 2 days. Explanation: The total float for an activity is the amount of time it can be delayed without delaying the project completion date. In this case, the critical path is determined by the longest path: A (3 days) + C (4 days) = 7 days. Activity B (5 days) has a total float of 2 days because it can be delayed by up to 2 days without extending the project duration beyond 7 days.

25. A project has a budget at completion (BAC) of $500,000 and is 60% complete. The actual cost (AC) is $350,000, and the earned value (EV) is $325,000. What is the project's schedule variance (SV)?
a. -$25,000
b. $25,000
c. -$50,000
d. $50,000

Answer: a. -$25,000. Explanation: The schedule variance (SV) is calculated as SV = EV - PV, where PV (planned value) is the budgeted cost of work scheduled. In this case, PV = 60% × $500,000 = $300,000. Therefore, SV = $325,000 - $300,000 = -$25,000. A negative SV indicates that the project is behind schedule, as the earned value is less than the planned value.

26. A project manager is conducting a qualitative risk analysis. Which of the following tools is most appropriate for prioritizing identified risks based on their probability and impact?
a. Ishikawa diagram
b. Pareto chart
c. Risk register
d. Probability and impact matrix

Answer: d. Probability and impact matrix. Explanation: The probability and impact matrix is a tool used in qualitative risk analysis to prioritize risks based on their likelihood of occurrence (probability) and potential effect on project objectives (impact). Risks are plotted on the matrix and assigned ratings such as low, medium, or high. The Ishikawa diagram is used to identify the root causes of a problem, the Pareto chart is used to prioritize issues based on frequency or impact, and the risk register is a comprehensive document that captures all identified risks and their attributes.

27. During the closing phase of a project, the project manager is conducting a lessons learned review. Which of the following is the primary benefit of documenting and sharing lessons learned?
a. To assign blame for project failures
b. To celebrate individual team members' successes
c. To improve future project performance
d. To justify the project manager's decisions

Answer: c. To improve future project performance. Explanation: The primary purpose of conducting a lessons learned review and documenting the findings is to identify what worked well, what didn't work well, and what can be improved in future projects. By capturing and sharing these insights, the organization can enhance its project management practices, avoid repeating past mistakes, and leverage successful strategies. Lessons learned should focus on constructive feedback and continuous improvement rather than assigning blame or highlighting individual achievements.

28. A project manager is developing a communication management plan. Which of the following factors should be considered when determining the appropriate communication methods and frequencies for each stakeholder group?
a. Stakeholders' communication preferences and information needs
b. Project team members' years of experience
c. Availability of communication technology and tools
d. Project manager's personal communication style

Answer: a. Stakeholders' communication preferences and information needs. Explanation: When creating a communication management plan, the project manager should tailor the communication approach to each stakeholder group based on their specific preferences, requirements, and expectations. This involves understanding how stakeholders wish to receive information (e.g., email, meetings, reports) and how often they need updates. While the availability of technology and the project manager's style may influence the communication methods, the primary focus should be on meeting the stakeholders' needs to keep them informed and engaged throughout the project.

29. A project team is using a Pareto chart to analyze the causes of customer complaints. The chart reveals that 80% of the complaints are related to two main issues: product defects and late deliveries. What should the project team do next?
a. Focus on resolving the remaining 20% of the complaints
b. Investigate and address the root causes of product defects and late deliveries
c. Redistribute the workload evenly among team members
d. Close the project and initiate a new one to address the issues

Answer: b. Investigate and address the root causes of product defects and late deliveries. Explanation: The Pareto principle, also known as the 80/20 rule, states that approximately 80% of effects come from 20% of causes. In this scenario, the Pareto chart has identified that product defects and late deliveries are the vital few causes responsible for the majority of customer complaints. The project team should prioritize investigating and addressing the root causes of these issues using problem-solving techniques like root cause analysis or Ishikawa diagrams. By tackling the most significant sources of complaints, the team can efficiently improve customer satisfaction and project outcomes.

30. A project manager is reviewing the resource breakdown structure (RBS) and notices that a key team member is overallocated. Which of the following resource leveling techniques is most appropriate to resolve this issue?
a. Resource smoothing
b. Crashing
c. Fast tracking
d. Critical chain method

Answer: a. Resource smoothing. Explanation: Resource leveling is a technique used to adjust the project schedule to address overallocation or underallocation of resources. Resource smoothing is a specific resource leveling technique that involves delaying non-critical activities within their available float to reduce the peak demand for a specific resource, without extending the project duration. In this case, resource smoothing can help redistribute the overallocated team member's workload by rescheduling non-critical tasks. Crashing and fast tracking are schedule compression techniques, while the critical chain method focuses on managing resource constraints in the project schedule.

31. During a project's execution phase, the project manager calculates the following earned value management (EVM) metrics: - Schedule Variance (SV) = -$10,000 - Cost Variance (CV) = $5,000 - Budget at Completion (BAC) = $500,000 - Actual Cost (AC) = $300,000. What is the project's To-Complete Performance Index (TCPI)?
a. 0.95
b. 1.05
c. 1.10
d. 1.15

Answer: a. 0.95. Explanation: The To-Complete Performance Index (TCPI) is an earned value management metric that measures the cost efficiency needed to complete the remaining work within the budget. It is calculated as (BAC - EV) / (BAC - AC), where EV is the earned value. In this case, EV = AC + CV = $300,000 + $5,000 = $305,000. Therefore, TCPI = ($500,000 - $305,000) / ($500,000 - $300,000) = $195,000 / $200,000 = 0.95. A TCPI less than 1 indicates that the project must operate more efficiently than it has so far to complete the remaining work within the budget.

32. A project manager is conducting a make-or-buy analysis for a critical component of the project deliverable. Which of the following factors should be given the highest priority in the decision-making process?
a. Short-term cost savings
b. Supplier reputation and reliability
c. Opportunity for team members to learn new skills
d. Potential for future business opportunities with the supplier

Answer: b. Supplier reputation and reliability. Explanation: In a make-or-buy decision, the project manager must carefully consider various factors to determine whether it is more beneficial to produce the component internally or procure it from an external supplier. While cost, learning opportunities, and future business prospects are important considerations, the highest priority should be given to the supplier's reputation and reliability. A reliable supplier with a proven track record of delivering high-quality products or services on time is essential to mitigate risks and ensure the project's success. Choosing an unreliable supplier to save costs in the short term can lead to delays, quality issues, and ultimately, project failure.

33. A project team is using a fishbone diagram (Ishikawa diagram) to identify the potential causes of a quality issue. Which of the following is not one of the typical main categories used in a fishbone diagram?
a. People
b. Materials
c. Budget
d. Environment

Answer: c. Budget. Explanation: A fishbone diagram, also known as an Ishikawa diagram or cause-and-effect diagram, is a visual tool used to identify and categorize the potential causes of a problem or effect. The diagram resembles a fish skeleton, with the problem statement placed at the "head" and the main categories of causes branching out as "bones." The typical main categories used in a fishbone diagram are often referred to as the 6 Ms: Machine (equipment), Method (process), Material, Man (people), Measurement, and Mother Nature (environment). While budget is an essential aspect of project management, it is not one of the standard categories used in a fishbone diagram when analyzing quality issues.

34. A project manager is tasked with managing a new project that aims to develop a mobile application. Which of the following best defines the project?
a. A temporary endeavor undertaken to create a unique product, service, or result
b. A series of ongoing, repetitive activities to maintain current operations
c. A permanent endeavor to enhance the company's technological infrastructure
d. A routine task performed to support the company's daily functions

Answer: a. A temporary endeavor undertaken to create a unique product, service, or result. Explanation: A project is defined as a temporary endeavor with a definite beginning and end, undertaken to create a unique product, service, or result. This distinguishes it from operations, which are ongoing and repetitive activities.

35. Which of the following distinguishes project management from operations management?
a. Project management focuses on ongoing activities, while operations management focuses on temporary endeavors
b. Project management deals with routine tasks, whereas operations management addresses unique and new initiatives
c. Project management is concerned with temporary, unique efforts, while operations management involves ongoing, repetitive tasks
d. Project management is primarily concerned with maintaining stability, whereas operations management seeks to drive change

Answer: c. Project management is concerned with temporary, unique efforts, while operations management involves ongoing, repetitive tasks. Explanation: Project management deals with temporary efforts to create unique outputs, while operations management focuses on continuous, repetitive activities that maintain the ongoing efficiency of an organization.

36. A company decides to establish a PMO to improve project performance. Which type of PMO provides direct management of projects?
a. Supportive PMO
b. Controlling PMO
c. Directive PMO
d. Consultative PMO

Answer: c. Directive PMO. Explanation: A Directive PMO directly manages and controls projects, providing high control and governance. This type of PMO assigns project managers and takes a hands-on approach to project execution.

37. In which phase of the project life cycle are project requirements defined and project objectives established?
a. Initiating
b. Planning
c. Executing
d. Closing

Answer: b. Planning. Explanation: The Planning phase involves defining project requirements, establishing clear objectives, and developing the project management plan. This phase is crucial for setting the foundation and direction for the project's execution.

38. A project manager is identifying stakeholders for a new marketing campaign. Which of the following groups should be considered stakeholders?
a. Only internal team members involved in the project
b. Only the project's executive sponsor
c. Internal team members, executive sponsors, and external parties affected by the project
d. Only external parties affected by the project

Answer: c. Internal team members, executive sponsors, and external parties affected by the project. Explanation: Stakeholders include anyone who can impact or be impacted by the project, including internal team members, executive sponsors, and external parties such as customers or suppliers.

39. Which of the following best describes project governance?
a. The process of managing changes to the project scope, schedule, and cost
b. The framework within which project decisions are made
c. The set of processes used to monitor and control project performance
d. The method of assigning tasks to project team members

Answer: b. The framework within which project decisions are made. Explanation: Project governance is the framework that provides structure, processes, and guidelines for making decisions related to the project. It ensures alignment with organizational objectives and standards.

40. During the initiating phase of a project, a project manager is responsible for creating which key document?
a. Project management plan
b. Project charter
c. Risk management plan
d. Stakeholder engagement plan

Answer: b. Project charter. Explanation: The project charter is created during the initiating phase and formally authorizes the project. It outlines the project's objectives, identifies stakeholders, and grants the project manager the authority to apply organizational resources to the project.

41. A project manager is reviewing the project life cycle phases. In which phase is the primary focus on delivering the project's outputs and meeting project objectives?
a. Initiating
b. Planning
c. Executing
d. Closing

Answer: c. Executing. Explanation: The Executing phase involves coordinating people and resources to carry out the project management plan and deliver the project's outputs. The focus is on meeting the project's objectives and ensuring the project deliverables are completed.

42. Which stakeholder management process involves prioritizing stakeholders based on their power, influence, and interest?
a. Identify Stakeholders
b. Plan Stakeholder Engagement
c. Manage Stakeholder Engagement
d. Monitor Stakeholder Engagement

Answer: b. Plan Stakeholder Engagement. Explanation: The Plan Stakeholder Engagement process involves analyzing stakeholders and prioritizing them based on their power, influence, and interest in the project. This helps in developing appropriate strategies to engage and communicate with them effectively.

43. A project manager must ensure that all decisions are aligned with the organization's overall strategic objectives. Which component of project governance addresses this requirement?
a. Project management methodologies
b. Organizational process assets
c. Governance framework
d. Project team structure

Answer: c. Governance framework. Explanation: The governance framework establishes the rules, policies, and procedures that ensure project decisions align with the organization's strategic objectives. It provides the necessary oversight and direction to achieve project and organizational goals.

44. During the project execution phase, a project manager notices that actual costs have significantly exceeded the planned budget. Which process should the project manager initiate to bring the project back on track?
a. Perform integrated change control
b. Control costs

c. Control schedule
d. Direct and manage project work

Answer: b. Control costs. Explanation: The Control Costs process involves monitoring the project's financial performance and managing changes to the cost baseline. This includes analyzing cost variances and taking corrective actions to align actual costs with the budget.

45. A project manager is defining the project scope and needs to ensure that all deliverables are included. Which document should the project manager use as a primary reference?
a. Project charter
b. Requirements traceability matrix
c. Work breakdown structure (WBS)
d. Project management plan

Answer: c. Work breakdown structure (WBS). Explanation: The WBS is a hierarchical decomposition of the total scope of work to be carried out by the project team to accomplish the project objectives and create the deliverables. It ensures that all deliverables are included in the project scope.

46. A project team is developing the project schedule and needs to estimate the duration of each activity. Which technique is most suitable when there is a lack of detailed information about each activity?
a. Analogous estimating
b. Parametric estimating
c. Three-point estimating
d. Bottom-up estimating

Answer: a. Analogous estimating. Explanation: Analogous estimating uses historical data from similar projects to estimate the duration of activities when detailed information is lacking. It is less time-consuming and provides a quick estimate compared to other techniques.

47. A project manager is using earned value management (EVM) to assess project performance. The project has an earned value (EV) of $150,000, a planned value (PV) of $175,000, and an actual cost (AC) of $160,000. What is the schedule variance (SV) and what does it indicate?
a. SV = -$25,000, indicating the project is behind schedule
b. SV = $25,000, indicating the project is ahead of schedule
c. SV = -$10,000, indicating the project is behind schedule
d. SV = $15,000, indicating the project is ahead of schedule

Answer: a. SV = -$25,000, indicating the project is behind schedule. Explanation: Schedule Variance (SV) is calculated as SV = EV - PV. In this case, SV = $150,000 - $175,000 = -$25,000. A negative SV indicates that the project is behind schedule.

48. The project sponsor requests a detailed report on project performance, including forecasts of future performance based on current trends. Which report should the project manager provide?
a. Status report
b. Variance report
c. Progress report
d. Performance report

Answer: d. Performance report. Explanation: A performance report provides detailed information on project performance, including past performance data, current performance metrics, and forecasts for future performance. It helps stakeholders understand the project's progress and future outlook.

49. During the Define Scope process, the project manager needs to document the project and product deliverables in detail. Which document will serve this purpose?
a. Project charter
b. Scope statement
c. WBS dictionary
d. Requirements traceability matrix

Answer: b. Scope statement. Explanation: The scope statement details the project and product deliverables, including project objectives, deliverables, boundaries, and acceptance criteria. It serves as a reference for project planning and execution.

50. A project manager is conducting a qualitative risk analysis. Which tool or technique is most appropriate for prioritizing identified risks based on their probability and impact?
a. Monte Carlo simulation
b. Probability and impact matrix
c. Sensitivity analysis
d. Expected monetary value analysis

Answer: b. Probability and impact matrix. Explanation: The probability and impact matrix is used in qualitative risk analysis to prioritize risks by assessing their likelihood of occurrence and potential impact on project objectives. This helps in identifying the most significant risks.

51. The project team is in the Control Schedule process and needs to manage changes to the project schedule. Which technique involves compressing the schedule by performing activities in parallel that were originally planned in sequence?
a. Crashing
b. Fast tracking
c. Resource leveling
d. Rolling wave planning

Answer: b. Fast tracking. Explanation: Fast tracking is a schedule compression technique that involves performing activities in parallel that were originally planned to be done sequentially. This can reduce the project duration but may increase risk.

52. A project manager is planning resource management for a large project. Which document will provide detailed information on when and how project team members will be acquired and released?
a. Resource management plan
b. Staffing management plan
c. Team charter
d. RACI matrix

Answer: a. Resource management plan. Explanation: The resource management plan provides detailed information on how project resources will be acquired, allocated, managed, and released. It includes the roles and responsibilities, project organization charts, and the resource acquisition strategy.

53. The project sponsor is concerned about potential risks that could impact the project's success. Which document should the project manager refer to in order to address these concerns and outline risk responses?
a. Risk register
b. Risk management plan
c. Issue log
d. Stakeholder register

Answer: b. Risk management plan. Explanation: The risk management plan outlines how risks will be identified, analyzed, responded to, and monitored throughout the project. It provides the framework for managing project risks and includes the risk register, which details specific risks and their responses.

54. A project manager is conducting a quality audit to assess the project's adherence to quality standards. Which of the following is the primary objective of a quality audit?
a. To identify the root causes of quality issues
b. To recommend improvements in project processes
c. To evaluate the project's overall performance
d. To verify the quality of the final deliverables

Answer: b. To recommend improvements in project processes. Explanation: A quality audit is a structured, independent process to determine if project activities comply with organizational and project policies, processes, and procedures. The primary objective is to recommend improvements to enhance the project's quality management processes.

55. During a team meeting, a conflict arises between two key team members. According to Tuckman's stages of team development, in which stage is the team most likely operating?
a. Forming

b. Storming
c. Norming
d. Performing

Answer: b. Storming. Explanation: The storming stage is characterized by conflicts and challenges as team members assert their opinions and roles within the team. This stage is essential for growth and development, leading to better understanding and cohesion in later stages.

56. A project manager needs to communicate a significant change in the project scope to all stakeholders. Which communication method is most appropriate for ensuring the message is understood and feedback is received?
a. Push communication
b. Pull communication
c. Interactive communication
d. One-way communication

Answer: c. Interactive communication. Explanation: Interactive communication involves a two-way exchange, such as meetings or video conferences, allowing for immediate feedback and ensuring that all stakeholders understand the change and can discuss its implications.

57. A project team has identified several risks and needs to prioritize them based on their potential impact on project objectives. Which tool or technique should they use?
a. Monte Carlo simulation
b. Risk probability and impact matrix
c. SWOT analysis
d. Decision tree analysis

Answer: b. Risk probability and impact matrix. Explanation: The risk probability and impact matrix is used to prioritize risks based on their likelihood of occurring and their potential impact on project objectives. This helps in focusing on the most significant risks.

58. In a project where multiple vendors are involved, the project manager must ensure that vendor performance meets contractual obligations. Which process is primarily concerned with this activity?
a. Plan Procurement Management
b. Conduct Procurements
c. Control Procurements
d. Close Procurements

Answer: c. Control Procurements. Explanation: The Control Procurements process involves managing procurement relationships, monitoring contract performance, and making necessary changes to ensure vendors meet their contractual obligations.

59. A stakeholder expresses dissatisfaction with the current project progress. What is the most appropriate initial action for the project manager to take?
a. Update the stakeholder management plan
b. Conduct a stakeholder analysis
c. Schedule a meeting with the stakeholder to understand their concerns
d. Implement changes to the project plan

Answer: c. Schedule a meeting with the stakeholder to understand their concerns. Explanation: The project manager should first understand the stakeholder's concerns by scheduling a meeting. This allows for open communication and helps in identifying the root cause of dissatisfaction and finding appropriate solutions.

60. Which of the following best describes the purpose of a resource histogram?
a. To depict project milestones and deadlines
b. To track the quality of project deliverables
c. To display resource usage over time
d. To identify project risks and issues

Answer: c. To display resource usage over time. Explanation: A resource histogram is a bar chart that shows the allocation and usage of resources over time. It helps in identifying periods of over or underutilization and aids in effective resource management.

61. A project manager is using control charts to monitor the quality of project deliverables. Which aspect of quality management is primarily being addressed with this tool?
a. Quality assurance
b. Quality planning
c. Quality control
d. Quality improvement

Answer: c. Quality control. Explanation: Control charts are used in quality control to monitor processes and ensure that project deliverables meet the specified quality standards. They help in identifying variations and taking corrective actions when necessary.

62. During the risk management process, a project manager decides to allocate additional resources to a task that is likely to cause delays. Which risk response strategy is being employed?
a. Avoidance
b. Mitigation
c. Transfer
d. Acceptance

Answer: b. Mitigation. Explanation: Mitigation involves taking actions to reduce the likelihood or impact of a risk. By allocating additional resources to a task, the project manager is attempting to minimize the potential delay.

63. A project is nearing completion, and the project manager needs to ensure all stakeholders formally accept the final deliverables. Which process should the project manager use to achieve this?
a. Perform Quality Assurance
b. Control Quality
c. Validate Scope
d. Monitor and Control Project Work

Answer: c. Validate Scope. Explanation: The Validate Scope process involves reviewing deliverables with the customer or sponsor to ensure they meet the project requirements and obtaining formal acceptance. This process is crucial for project closure and stakeholder satisfaction.

64. A project manager is tasked with creating a project charter for a new initiative. Which of the following is not typically included in the project charter?
a. Project purpose and justification
b. Detailed project schedule
c. High-level project requirements
d. Project approval requirements

Answer: b. Detailed project schedule. Explanation: The project charter includes high-level project information such as purpose, justification, high-level requirements, and approval requirements. A detailed project schedule is developed later during the project planning phase.

65. During the initiation phase, the project sponsor asks the project manager to identify all stakeholders. Which tool or technique is most appropriate for this task?
a. Stakeholder analysis
b. SWOT analysis
c. Monte Carlo simulation
d. Root cause analysis

Answer: a. Stakeholder analysis. Explanation: Stakeholder analysis involves identifying all stakeholders, analyzing their needs and expectations, and assessing their potential impact on the project. This helps in developing appropriate engagement strategies.

66. A project manager is developing a project charter and needs to include information on the project's high-level risks. Why is it important to identify high-level risks at this stage?
a. To perform a detailed risk analysis
b. To define the project scope
c. To allocate budget for risk management
d. To gain initial approval from stakeholders

Answer: d. To gain initial approval from stakeholders. Explanation: Identifying high-level risks in the project charter helps stakeholders understand potential challenges and uncertainties, which is crucial for gaining their initial approval and support.

67. The project sponsor wants to ensure that the project aligns with the organization's strategic objectives. Which section of the project charter should address this concern?
a. Project purpose and justification
b. Project scope statement
c. High-level project requirements
d. Summary milestone schedule

Answer: a. Project purpose and justification. Explanation: The project purpose and justification section explains how the project aligns with the organization's strategic objectives and the business need it addresses.

68. A key stakeholder has requested additional features that are not included in the project charter. How should the project manager handle this request?
a. Add the features to the project scope immediately
b. Document the request and perform integrated change control
c. Reject the request as it is not in the charter
d. Escalate the request to the project sponsor

Answer: b. Document the request and perform integrated change control. Explanation: The project manager should document the request and follow the integrated change control process to evaluate its impact on the project and make informed decisions.

69. In developing the project charter, the project manager must define the project boundaries. Which document will help in identifying what is included and excluded from the project scope?
a. Project scope statement
b. Requirements traceability matrix
c. Work breakdown structure (WBS)
d. Project management plan

Answer: a. Project scope statement. Explanation: The project scope statement defines the project boundaries by specifying what is included and excluded from the project scope, ensuring clarity and alignment among stakeholders.

70. During the stakeholder identification process, the project manager discovers conflicting interests among stakeholders. What should be the next step to manage these conflicts?
a. Ignore the conflicts and proceed with the project plan
b. Use stakeholder engagement strategies to address the conflicts

c. Escalate the conflicts to the project sponsor
d. Remove the conflicting stakeholders from the project

Answer: b. Use stakeholder engagement strategies to address the conflicts. Explanation: The project manager should use stakeholder engagement strategies to address and manage conflicts by understanding stakeholder needs and expectations, and finding a balanced approach to satisfy key stakeholders.

71. A project manager is creating a stakeholder register. Which information is not typically included in the stakeholder register?
a. Stakeholder identification information
b. Stakeholder impact and influence
c. Stakeholder engagement strategy
d. Stakeholder performance metrics

Answer: d. Stakeholder performance metrics. Explanation: The stakeholder register includes identification information, impact and influence, and engagement strategies. Performance metrics are not typically part of the stakeholder register.

72. The project manager needs to gain formal authorization to start the project. Which document is required to achieve this?
a. Project charter
b. Statement of work (SOW)
c. Project management plan
d. Risk management plan

Answer: a. Project charter. Explanation: The project charter formally authorizes the project and grants the project manager the authority to apply organizational resources to project activities.

73. During a project initiation meeting, a stakeholder expresses concerns about potential regulatory compliance issues. How should the project manager address these concerns in the project charter?
a. Exclude compliance issues from the charter to avoid complexity
b. Include a high-level assessment of regulatory compliance risks
c. Delay addressing compliance issues until the planning phase
d. Escalate the concerns to the project sponsor

Answer: b. Include a high-level assessment of regulatory compliance risks. Explanation: The project charter should include a high-level assessment of regulatory compliance risks to ensure that all potential issues are identified and addressed early in the project lifecycle.

74. A business analyst is conducting a feasibility study for a proposed project. Which of the following is not typically included in a feasibility study?
a. Technical feasibility
b. Economic feasibility
c. Operational feasibility
d. Legal feasibility

Answer: d. Legal feasibility. Explanation: A feasibility study is an assessment of the practicality of a proposed project or system. It typically evaluates the project from several perspectives, including technical feasibility (can it be built?), economic feasibility (is it financially viable?), and operational feasibility (can the organization effectively use and maintain it?). Legal feasibility, which assesses whether the project complies with relevant laws and regulations, is usually considered as part of the broader project planning process but is not a core component of a traditional feasibility study.

75. During a requirements gathering workshop, a stakeholder suggests a new feature that would significantly enhance the user experience. However, the business analyst realizes that implementing this feature would require doubling the project's budget. What should the business analyst do next?
a. Implement the feature without further analysis to satisfy the stakeholder
b. Reject the feature outright due to budget constraints
c. Conduct a cost-benefit analysis and present the findings to the project sponsor
d. Escalate the decision to the development team

Answer: c. Conduct a cost-benefit analysis and present the findings to the project sponsor. Explanation: When faced with a request for a new feature or requirement that has a significant impact on the project's budget, the business analyst should perform a cost-benefit analysis. This involves estimating the costs of implementing the feature (including development, testing, and maintenance) and comparing them against the expected benefits (such as increased user satisfaction, revenue, or efficiency gains). The business analyst should then present the findings to the project sponsor, who can make an informed decision on whether to approve the feature based on its value to the organization and the available budget.

76. A business analyst is using the MoSCoW method to prioritize requirements. Which of the following best describes the "Should Have" category?
a. Non-negotiable requirements that must be delivered for the project to be considered a success
b. Important requirements that add significant value but are not essential for the initial release
c. Nice-to-have requirements that can be included if time and resources permit
d. Requirements that are not relevant to the current project scope

Answer: b. Important requirements that add significant value but are not essential for the initial release. Explanation: The MoSCoW method is a prioritization technique used in requirements management. It categorizes requirements into four groups: Must Have (non-negotiable), Should Have (important but not critical), Could Have (desirable but not necessary), and Won't Have (out of scope for the current project). The "Should Have" category represents requirements that are important and add significant value to the product or system but are not essential for the initial release. These requirements can be deferred to a later release if necessary, based on time, resource, or budget constraints.

77. A business analyst is creating a RACI matrix for a project. What does the "C" in RACI stand for?
a. Consulted
b. Coordinated
c. Controlled
d. Communicated

Answer: a. Consulted. Explanation: A RACI matrix is a responsibility assignment chart that maps out the roles and responsibilities of stakeholders in a project. RACI is an acronym that stands for Responsible (those who do the work), Accountable (the one ultimately answerable for the completion of the task), Consulted (those whose input is sought), and Informed (those who are kept up-to-date on progress). The "C" in RACI represents "Consulted," which refers to the stakeholders who provide input, feedback, or expertise for a particular task or decision but are not directly involved in the execution of the work.

78. A company is considering two mutually exclusive projects: Project A and Project B. Project A has an initial investment of $100,000 and an expected net present value (NPV) of $50,000. Project B has an initial investment of $150,000 and an expected NPV of $75,000. The company's cost of capital is 10%. Which project should the company choose based on the profitability index (PI)?
a. Project A
b. Project B
c. Both projects, as they have positive NPV
d. Neither project, as they do not meet the required rate of return

Answer: b. Project B. Explanation: The profitability index (PI) is a financial metric used to evaluate the attractiveness of investment opportunities. It is calculated by dividing the present value of future cash flows by the initial investment. In this case, Project A has a PI of 1.5 ($150,000 / $100,000), while Project B has a PI of 1.5 ($225,000 / $150,000). When comparing mutually exclusive projects, the one with the higher PI is considered more attractive. Therefore, the company should choose Project B based on the profitability index. Both projects have a positive NPV, indicating that they are expected to add value to the company, but Project B offers a higher return per dollar invested.

79. A business analyst is conducting a root cause analysis using the 5 Whys technique. What is the primary goal of this technique?
a. To identify the most superficial cause of a problem
b. To assign blame for the problem to a specific individual or team
c. To develop a comprehensive list of all possible causes
d. To drill down to the underlying reason for a problem

Answer: d. To drill down to the underlying reason for a problem. Explanation: The 5 Whys is a simple yet powerful technique used in root cause analysis to identify the fundamental reason behind a problem or issue. The technique involves repeatedly asking "Why?" (usually five times) to peel away the layers of symptoms and uncover the root cause. By asking "Why?" at each level, the analyst moves beyond the superficial causes and gets to the heart of the problem. The goal is not to assign blame or create an exhaustive list of causes but to focus on identifying the underlying issue that, if addressed, will prevent the problem from recurring in the future.

80. A business analyst is using a decision tree to evaluate the expected monetary value (EMV) of a project. The project has two possible outcomes: success (probability 70%, payoff $100,000) and failure (probability 30%, loss $50,000). What is the project's EMV?
a. $35,000
b. $55,000
c. $70,000
d. $85,000

Answer: b. $55,000. Explanation: The expected monetary value (EMV) is a decision-making tool that calculates the average outcome of a decision based on the probability and value of each possible outcome. In a decision tree, each branch represents a possible outcome, with its associated probability and payoff or loss. To calculate the EMV, multiply the probability of each outcome by its respective value and sum the results. In this case, the EMV = (0.7 × $100,000) + (0.3 × -$50,000) = $70,000 - $15,000 = $55,000. A positive EMV indicates that the project is expected to be profitable on average, considering the given probabilities and outcomes.

81. A company wants to improve its customer satisfaction scores. A business analyst is tasked with identifying the key drivers of customer satisfaction and recommending improvement initiatives. Which of the following tools would be most appropriate for this analysis?
a. SWOT analysis
b. PESTEL analysis
c. Kano model
d. MoSCoW method

Answer: c. Kano model. Explanation: The Kano model is a customer satisfaction framework that categorizes product or service attributes based on their impact on customer satisfaction. The model distinguishes between three types of attributes: basic (must-have), performance (more is better), and excitement (unexpected delighters). By using the Kano model, the business analyst can identify which attributes are most critical for driving customer satisfaction and prioritize improvement efforts accordingly. SWOT and PESTEL analyses focus on assessing the internal and external factors influencing an organization, while the MoSCoW method is used for prioritizing requirements based on their importance and urgency.

82. A business analyst is mapping the current state of a business process using Business Process Model and Notation (BPMN). Which of the following symbols represents a decision point in the process flow?
a. Rectangle
b. Circle
c. Diamond
d. Triangle

Answer: c. Diamond. Explanation: Business Process Model and Notation (BPMN) is a graphical representation for specifying business processes in a workflow. It uses a standardized set of symbols to depict the various elements of a process, such as activities, events, gateways, and sequence flows. In BPMN, a diamond shape represents a gateway, which is used to control the divergence and convergence of sequence flows in a process. Specifically, a gateway with an "X" inside the diamond indicates an exclusive (XOR) gateway, which represents a decision point where the process flow follows one path or another based on a condition. Rectangles represent activities, circles represent events, and triangles are not part of the BPMN symbol set.

83. A business analyst is eliciting requirements for a new software system. During interviews with stakeholders, the analyst discovers conflicting requirements between two departments. What is the best approach for the analyst to resolve this conflict?
a. Choose the requirement that aligns with the analyst's personal preference
b. Ignore the conflicting requirements and focus on other areas of the project
c. Escalate the conflict to the project sponsor for resolution
d. Facilitate a requirements workshop to reach a consensus among stakeholders

Answer: d. Facilitate a requirements workshop to reach a consensus among stakeholders. Explanation: Conflicting requirements are a common challenge in requirements elicitation, especially when dealing with multiple stakeholders or departments with different needs and priorities. To resolve conflicts, the business analyst should take an impartial, collaborative approach and facilitate a requirements workshop with the relevant stakeholders. During the workshop, the analyst should encourage open communication, actively listen to each stakeholder's concerns, and help the group find common ground. Techniques such as brainstorming, prioritization exercises, and trade-off analysis can be used to identify win-win solutions and reach a consensus on the requirements. Choosing requirements based on personal preference or ignoring the conflict altogether can lead to stakeholder dissatisfaction and project failure, while escalating every conflict to the sponsor can delay decision-making and undermine the analyst's credibility as a facilitator.

84. A project manager is developing the project management plan and needs to integrate all subsidiary plans. Which of the following is NOT typically considered a subsidiary plan?
a. Scope Management Plan
b. Risk Management Plan
c. Project Charter
d. Quality Management Plan

Answer: c. Project Charter. Explanation: The Project Charter is not a subsidiary plan; it is a document that formally authorizes the project and provides the project manager with the authority to apply organizational resources to project activities. Subsidiary plans are detailed plans that are part of the overall project management plan.

85. During the creation of the Scope Management Plan, which tool or technique is primarily used to ensure all work required, and only the work required, is included in the project?
a. Work Breakdown Structure (WBS)
b. SWOT Analysis
c. Monte Carlo Simulation
d. Pareto Chart

Answer: a. Work Breakdown Structure (WBS). Explanation: The WBS is a hierarchical decomposition of the total scope of work to be carried out by the project team. It ensures that all work required is included and helps prevent scope creep by detailing every component of the project.

86. A project manager is in the process of developing the Requirements Management Plan. Which key activity is included in this process?
a. Defining the project schedule
b. Documenting how requirements will be analyzed, documented, and managed
c. Performing risk assessment
d. Developing the project budget

Answer: b. Documenting how requirements will be analyzed, documented, and managed. Explanation: The Requirements Management Plan describes how requirements will be identified, analyzed, documented, and managed throughout the project. This ensures that project requirements are properly tracked and met.

87. To create a realistic project schedule, the project manager uses a technique to estimate the duration of activities by considering the optimistic, pessimistic, and most likely durations. Which technique is being used?
a. Critical Path Method (CPM)
b. Fast Tracking
c. Three-Point Estimating
d. Bottom-Up Estimating

Answer: c. Three-Point Estimating. Explanation: Three-Point Estimating uses the optimistic (O), pessimistic (P), and most likely (M) estimates to calculate an expected duration. This technique helps in providing a more accurate estimate by considering uncertainty and risks.

88. In the Cost Management Plan, the project manager outlines how project costs will be planned, structured, and controlled. Which of the following is a key input for developing this plan?
a. Project Scope Statement
b. Risk Register
c. Resource Calendars
d. Cost Baseline

Answer: a. Project Scope Statement. Explanation: The Project Scope Statement is a key input for developing the Cost Management Plan as it provides detailed information on the project's deliverables and work required, which directly impacts cost estimation and budgeting.

89. A project manager is conducting a scope validation process. What is the main objective of this process?
a. To ensure the project deliverables meet quality standards
b. To gain formal acceptance of the completed deliverables
c. To document lessons learned from the project
d. To create the project scope statement

Answer: b. To gain formal acceptance of the completed deliverables. Explanation: Scope validation is the process of obtaining formal acceptance from the customer or sponsor for the completed project deliverables. This ensures that the deliverables meet the requirements and are approved.

90. During the development of the Schedule Management Plan, a project manager decides to use a Gantt chart. What is the primary purpose of this tool?
a. To identify potential project risks
b. To visually represent the project schedule and track progress
c. To perform a cost-benefit analysis
d. To determine the project's critical path

Answer: b. To visually represent the project schedule and track progress. Explanation: A Gantt chart is a visual tool used to display the project schedule, showing the start and finish dates of project activities. It helps in tracking progress and managing the project timeline.

91. A project manager is using bottom-up estimating to determine the project costs. What is the main advantage of this technique?
a. It provides a quick and high-level cost estimate
b. It allows for a detailed and accurate cost estimation
c. It uses historical data from similar projects
d. It is less time-consuming than other estimation methods

Answer: b. It allows for a detailed and accurate cost estimation. Explanation: Bottom-up estimating involves estimating the costs of individual work packages or activities and then aggregating them to get the total project cost. This method is detailed and accurate but can be time-consuming.

92. In the Requirements Management Plan, how are requirements typically categorized?
a. Based on their impact on the project schedule
b. By stakeholder group
c. By priority and type
d. Based on the project's budget

Answer: c. By priority and type. Explanation: Requirements are typically categorized by priority (e.g., high, medium, low) and type (e.g., functional, non-functional, regulatory) to help in managing and tracking them effectively throughout the project.

93. A project manager is developing the Cost Management Plan and needs to account for potential cost changes during the project. Which process should be included to handle these changes?
a. Cost Estimating

b. Cost Budgeting
c. Cost Control
d. Cost Analysis

Answer: c. Cost Control. Explanation: Cost Control is the process of monitoring project costs and managing changes to the cost baseline. It involves tracking cost performance, identifying variances, and implementing corrective actions to keep the project within budget.

94. A project manager is developing a Quality Management Plan. Which tool or technique should be used to identify and prioritize potential quality issues?
a. Pareto chart
b. Monte Carlo simulation
c. Gantt chart
d. Critical path method

Answer: a. Pareto chart. Explanation: A Pareto chart helps identify and prioritize potential quality issues by showing the frequency of problems. It follows the Pareto principle, suggesting that 80% of problems come from 20% of causes, allowing focus on the most significant issues.

95. A project manager needs to determine the resources required for project activities. Which document will provide the most detailed information on resource requirements?
a. Resource management plan
b. Work breakdown structure (WBS)
c. Project charter
d. Stakeholder register

Answer: a. Resource management plan. Explanation: The resource management plan details the types and quantities of resources required, their availability, and how they will be acquired and managed throughout the project, ensuring efficient resource allocation.

96. A project team is experiencing communication breakdowns leading to misunderstandings and delays. Which component of the Communications Management Plan is critical to address this issue?
a. Communication matrix
b. Work performance reports
c. Stakeholder engagement strategy
d. Issue log

Answer: a. Communication matrix. Explanation: The communication matrix outlines the communication requirements, methods, and frequency for each stakeholder. It ensures that the right information is delivered to the right people at the right time, reducing misunderstandings and delays.

97. During a project risk assessment, the project manager identifies a risk that could severely impact the project schedule. Which process involves developing options and actions to enhance opportunities and reduce threats to project objectives?
a. Perform qualitative risk analysis
b. Plan risk responses
c. Identify risks
d. Control risks

Answer: b. Plan risk responses. Explanation: Plan risk responses involves developing strategies and actions to enhance opportunities and reduce threats to project objectives. It includes identifying risk owners and developing contingency plans to address identified risks.

98. A project manager is procuring specialized equipment for a project. To ensure that the procurement process is managed effectively, which document should outline the types of contracts to be used and the procurement activities required?
a. Procurement management plan
b. Statement of work (SOW)
c. Project charter
d. Resource management plan

Answer: a. Procurement management plan. Explanation: The procurement management plan outlines how procurements will be planned, conducted, and managed. It includes information on contract types, procurement processes, and how vendors will be selected and managed.

99. A project stakeholder has a significant influence on the project but has shown little interest in project outcomes. Which strategy should the project manager employ according to the Stakeholder Engagement Plan?
a. Keep satisfied
b. Manage closely
c. Monitor
d. Keep informed

Answer: a. Keep satisfied. Explanation: For stakeholders with high influence but low interest, the "Keep satisfied" strategy ensures that their needs and concerns are addressed, preventing them from becoming a risk to the project. This involves providing regular updates and involving them in key decisions.

100. During the execution phase, the project team realizes that several activities require quality inspections. Which component of the Quality Management Plan will guide how these inspections are to be conducted?
a. Quality metrics
b. Quality checklist
c. Quality audit
d. Quality assurance

Answer: b. Quality checklist. Explanation: Quality checklists are part of the Quality Management Plan and provide a structured approach to ensure that specific quality standards are met during inspections. They list the criteria and steps for inspections, ensuring consistency and thoroughness.

101. The project manager needs to ensure that all project risks are continually monitored and controlled throughout the project lifecycle. Which document is essential for this ongoing process?
a. Risk register
b. Project scope statement
c. Work breakdown structure (WBS)
d. Communications management plan

Answer: a. Risk register. Explanation: The risk register is a dynamic document used to record all identified risks, their analysis, and risk responses. It is continuously updated and reviewed to monitor risk status and effectiveness of risk responses throughout the project lifecycle.

102. A project manager is preparing a stakeholder engagement plan and needs to categorize stakeholders based on their level of interest and power. Which tool should be used for this purpose?
a. Stakeholder power/interest grid
b. RACI matrix
c. Fishbone diagram
d. Decision tree analysis

Answer: a. Stakeholder power/interest grid. Explanation: The stakeholder power/interest grid categorizes stakeholders based on their level of interest and power in the project. It helps the project manager develop appropriate engagement strategies for each stakeholder group, ensuring effective stakeholder management.

103. During project planning, the project manager identifies the need for frequent, detailed communication with the project team and less frequent, high-level updates for the project sponsor. Which component of the Communications Management Plan will address these differing needs?
a. Communication requirements analysis
b. Communication technology
c. Performance reporting
d. Communication models

Answer: a. Communication requirements analysis. Explanation: Communication requirements analysis determines the information needs of the project stakeholders and defines the type and frequency of communications required. It ensures that each stakeholder receives the appropriate level of detail and frequency of updates.

104. A project manager notices that the project's cost performance index (CPI) is consistently below 1.0. What does this indicate about the project's budget performance?

a. The project is under budget
b. The project is over budget
c. The project is ahead of schedule
d. The project is behind schedule

Answer: b. The project is over budget. Explanation: A CPI below 1.0 indicates that the project is over budget, meaning the project is spending more money than planned for the work performed.

105. During a project review, a key stakeholder requests a significant change to the project scope. Which process should the project manager follow to handle this request?
a. Perform Integrated Change Control
b. Validate Scope
c. Control Quality
d. Control Costs

Answer: a. Perform Integrated Change Control. Explanation: The Perform Integrated Change Control process involves evaluating and deciding on change requests, ensuring that changes are appropriately reviewed, approved, and documented.

106. A project manager is validating the scope of the project deliverables with the customer. Which of the following activities is NOT part of the Validate Scope process?
a. Inspecting deliverables
b. Obtaining formal acceptance of deliverables
c. Documenting any necessary changes
d. Performing quality audits

Answer: d. Performing quality audits. Explanation: Quality audits are part of the Manage Quality process, not Validate Scope. Validate Scope focuses on inspecting deliverables, obtaining formal acceptance, and documenting any necessary changes.

107. A project is experiencing delays, and the project manager decides to use schedule compression techniques. Which of the following is an example of crashing?
a. Adding more resources to critical path activities
b. Performing activities in parallel that were originally planned in sequence
c. Reducing project scope to shorten the schedule
d. Extending the project timeline

Answer: a. Adding more resources to critical path activities. Explanation: Crashing involves adding more resources to critical path activities to complete them faster, even though it may increase project costs.

108. A project manager is monitoring project costs and notices a variance from the cost baseline. Which document should be updated to reflect the cost variance and corrective actions?
a. Project Charter
b. Risk Management Plan
c. Cost Management Plan
d. Cost Baseline

Answer: d. Cost Baseline. Explanation: The Cost Baseline should be updated to reflect any variances and corrective actions taken. This ensures that the project budget is accurately tracked and managed.

109. During a quality control review, a project manager uses control charts to monitor project performance. What is the primary purpose of using control charts in this context?
a. To identify potential project risks
b. To assess project team performance
c. To determine if a process is stable and in control
d. To prioritize project tasks

Answer: c. To determine if a process is stable and in control. Explanation: Control charts help determine if a process is stable and in control by tracking performance data over time and identifying any deviations from the expected range.

110. A project manager receives a change request that could impact the project schedule. Before approving the change, which document should be reviewed to understand its potential impact on the project timeline?
a. Project Charter
b. Schedule Management Plan
c. Communications Management Plan
d. Stakeholder Register

Answer: b. Schedule Management Plan. Explanation: The Schedule Management Plan should be reviewed to understand how the change request could impact the project timeline. This plan outlines how the schedule will be managed and controlled throughout the project.

111. Which of the following tools or techniques is used to control the project schedule by comparing actual performance to the planned schedule?
a. Earned Value Management (EVM)
b. SWOT Analysis
c. Monte Carlo Simulation
d. Pareto Chart

Answer: a. Earned Value Management (EVM). Explanation: EVM is used to compare actual performance to the planned schedule and cost, providing a clear picture of project performance and helping identify variances.

112. During the Control Scope process, a project manager finds that several deliverables do not meet the agreed-upon specifications. What is the best course of action?
a. Update the project management plan to reflect the new specifications
b. Reject the deliverables and request rework
c. Approve the deliverables and proceed with the project
d. Escalate the issue to the project sponsor

Answer: b. Reject the deliverables and request rework. Explanation: If deliverables do not meet the agreed-upon specifications, the project manager should reject them and request rework to ensure that they meet the project requirements before moving forward.

113. A project manager is using variance analysis to monitor project performance. Which of the following variances indicates that the project is performing better than planned in terms of cost?
a. Positive cost variance
b. Negative cost variance
c. Zero cost variance
d. Neutral cost variance

Answer: a. Positive cost variance. Explanation: A positive cost variance indicates that the project is performing better than planned in terms of cost, meaning that it is under budget.

114. During a project, the project manager notices that some resources are being underutilized while others are overloaded. Which process should the project manager use to address this issue?
a. Develop team
b. Control resources
c. Estimate activity resources
d. Acquire resources

Answer: b. Control resources. Explanation: The Control Resources process ensures that the physical resources assigned and allocated to the project are available as planned. It involves monitoring resource utilization, identifying variances, and taking corrective actions to optimize resource allocation.

115. A project manager is reviewing the effectiveness of the communication methods used in the project. Which technique is most appropriate for this assessment?
a. Variance analysis
b. Communication models
c. Performance reporting
d. Communication requirements analysis

Answer: d. Communication requirements analysis. Explanation: Communication requirements analysis involves determining the information needs of the project stakeholders and evaluating the effectiveness of the communication methods used. This helps ensure that information is distributed appropriately and effectively.

116. During the Monitor Risks process, the project manager identifies a new risk that could impact the project schedule. What should be the next step?
a. Update the risk register
b. Perform quantitative risk analysis
c. Revise the project schedule
d. Implement a risk response

Answer: a. Update the risk register. Explanation: When a new risk is identified, the first step is to update the risk register with the details of the new risk. This ensures that the risk is documented and can be analyzed and managed appropriately.

117. A project manager is overseeing a contract with a vendor and needs to ensure that the vendor is meeting their contractual obligations. Which process should the project manager focus on?
a. Plan procurement management
b. Control procurements
c. Conduct procurements
d. Close procurements

Answer: b. Control procurements. Explanation: The Control Procurements process involves managing procurement relationships, monitoring contract performance, making changes and corrections as needed, and ensuring that the vendor meets their contractual obligations.

118. The project manager is reviewing the stakeholder engagement activities and realizes that some stakeholders are not as engaged as planned. What action should the project manager take?
a. Update the stakeholder engagement plan
b. Conduct a stakeholder analysis
c. Escalate the issue to the project sponsor
d. Revise the project charter

Answer: a. Update the stakeholder engagement plan. Explanation: If stakeholders are not as engaged as planned, the project manager should update the stakeholder engagement plan to include new strategies and actions to increase their engagement. This helps ensure that stakeholder expectations and involvement are managed effectively.

119. A project team has identified a risk response that requires additional resources. How should the project manager proceed?
a. Implement the risk response immediately
b. Update the resource management plan
c. Perform a cost-benefit analysis

d. Request approval for additional resources

Answer: d. Request approval for additional resources. Explanation: Before implementing a risk response that requires additional resources, the project manager should request approval for the needed resources. This ensures that the response is feasible and that necessary resources are secured.

120. While monitoring project communications, the project manager discovers that important project updates are not reaching all stakeholders. What should be done to resolve this issue?
a. Perform a root cause analysis
b. Update the communications management plan
c. Reassign the communication responsibilities
d. Increase the frequency of communications

Answer: b. Update the communications management plan. Explanation: Updating the communications management plan ensures that communication requirements, methods, and responsibilities are adjusted to address gaps and ensure that important updates reach all stakeholders.

121. During a project, a key stakeholder's influence on the project increases significantly. What should the project manager do to manage this change?
a. Update the stakeholder register
b. Increase the frequency of status reports
c. Perform a stakeholder analysis
d. Escalate the change to the project sponsor

Answer: a. Update the stakeholder register. Explanation: When a stakeholder's influence changes, the project manager should update the stakeholder register to reflect the new level of influence and adjust the stakeholder engagement plan accordingly.

122. A vendor has delivered a component that does not meet the project requirements. What should the project manager do first?
a. Issue a change request
b. Initiate a procurement audit
c. Review the contract
d. Terminate the contract

Answer: c. Review the contract. Explanation: The first step is to review the contract to understand the terms and conditions related to quality and delivery requirements. This helps determine the appropriate actions and remedies available to address the issue.

123. The project team is monitoring risks and identifies that a previously low-priority risk has become more likely. What should the project manager do?
a. Reassess the risk
b. Implement the risk response plan
c. Update the risk management plan
d. Inform the project sponsor

Answer: a. Reassess the risk. Explanation: When the likelihood of a risk changes, the project manager should reassess the risk to determine its new impact and probability. This ensures that appropriate risk responses are planned and implemented based on the updated risk assessment.

124. A project manager is closing out a project and needs to ensure that all project deliverables have been accepted. Which document is most critical for verifying that deliverables meet the acceptance criteria?
a. Project Charter
b. Scope Management Plan
c. Requirements Traceability Matrix
d. Work Breakdown Structure (WBS)

Answer: c. Requirements Traceability Matrix. Explanation: The Requirements Traceability Matrix links project requirements to their origins and tracks them throughout the project lifecycle. It is critical for verifying that all deliverables meet the acceptance criteria established by stakeholders.

125. During the closure of a project phase, the project manager needs to ensure all documentation is complete and archived. What is the primary purpose of archiving project documentation?
a. To ensure compliance with project management standards
b. To support future project audits
c. To facilitate knowledge transfer and organizational learning
d. To provide a basis for stakeholder communication

Answer: c. To facilitate knowledge transfer and organizational learning. Explanation: Archiving project documentation helps preserve project knowledge and lessons learned, which can be used to improve future projects and support organizational learning.

126. A project manager is preparing a final project report. Which of the following should be included in this report?
a. Detailed descriptions of all project tasks
b. Performance metrics comparing planned vs. actual results
c. List of all project team members
d. Copies of all project contracts

Answer: b. Performance metrics comparing planned vs. actual results. Explanation: The final project report should include performance metrics comparing planned vs. actual results to provide a summary of the project's success and identify areas for improvement.

127. During the final project meeting, stakeholders provide feedback on what went well and what could be improved. What is the best way for the project manager to document this feedback?
a. Update the risk register
b. Create a change request
c. Document lessons learned
d. Revise the project charter

Answer: c. Document lessons learned. Explanation: Documenting lessons learned involves capturing what went well and what could be improved, providing valuable insights for future projects and ensuring continuous improvement.

128. After project completion, the project manager conducts a formal review to evaluate project performance. Which document is typically produced as a result of this review?
a. Project Scope Statement
b. Post-Project Evaluation Report
c. Stakeholder Register
d. Project Management Plan

Answer: b. Post-Project Evaluation Report. Explanation: A Post-Project Evaluation Report summarizes the project's performance, including successes, challenges, and lessons learned. It provides a comprehensive review of the project's outcomes and areas for improvement.

129. A project is completed, and the project manager needs to release the project team. What is the first step in this process?
a. Conduct a team performance review
b. Update the project schedule
c. Verify the completion of all project deliverables
d. Prepare a final project budget

Answer: a. Conduct a team performance review. Explanation: Conducting a team performance review is the first step in releasing the project team. It provides feedback on their performance, recognizes their contributions, and identifies areas for professional development.

130. During project closure, the project manager needs to ensure all procurement contracts are formally closed. Which process should be followed?
a. Perform Integrated Change Control
b. Close Procurements
c. Control Procurements
d. Validate Scope

Answer: b. Close Procurements. Explanation: Close Procurements is the process of completing and settling each contract, including resolving any open items. This ensures all contractual obligations are met and formally closes the procurement contracts.

131. A project manager is documenting lessons learned and realizes that some critical risks were not identified during the project. What should be included in the lessons learned documentation regarding this issue?
a. A list of the unidentified risks
b. A detailed explanation of the impact of unidentified risks and recommendations for improving risk identification in future projects
c. An updated risk register
d. A revised project schedule

Answer: b. A detailed explanation of the impact of unidentified risks and recommendations for improving risk identification in future projects. Explanation: Lessons learned documentation should include a detailed explanation of the impact of unidentified risks and provide recommendations for improving the risk identification process in future projects to enhance overall project management practices.

132. As part of the project closure process, the project manager needs to obtain formal acceptance of the project deliverables from the client. Which document is typically used to record this acceptance?
a. Project Charter
b. Work Breakdown Structure (WBS)
c. Acceptance Letter or Form
d. Project Management Plan

Answer: c. Acceptance Letter or Form. Explanation: An Acceptance Letter or Form is used to record the formal acceptance of the project deliverables from the client. This document signifies that the deliverables meet the agreed-upon criteria and the project is considered complete.

133. A project manager is preparing for the final project handover to the operations team. What is a critical activity to ensure a smooth transition?
a. Conducting a final project budget review
b. Providing comprehensive training and documentation to the operations team
c. Updating the project schedule with actual completion dates
d. Creating a new project charter for the operations team

Answer: b. Providing comprehensive training and documentation to the operations team. Explanation: Providing comprehensive training and documentation is critical to ensuring a smooth transition to the operations team. It helps them understand the project deliverables and how to maintain and operate them effectively.

134. A project manager is working in an organization with a strong functional structure. Which characteristic is most likely to be observed in this environment?
a. Project managers have high authority over resources
b. Functional managers control project budgets
c. Project teams are co-located
d. Projects have dedicated resources

Answer: b. Functional managers control project budgets. Explanation: In a strong functional structure, functional managers have significant authority over resources and budgets, while project managers have limited authority and rely on functional managers to allocate resources for project activities.

135. A project team is gathering work performance data to track project progress. Which of the following is an example of work performance data?
a. Status of deliverables
b. Earned value analysis results
c. Updated risk register
d. Approved change requests

Answer: a. Status of deliverables. Explanation: Work performance data consists of raw observations and measurements about project activities, such as the status of deliverables, work completed, and start/finish dates of activities. Earned value analysis results, updated risk registers, and approved change requests are examples of work performance information and reports.

136. The project manager is utilizing organizational process assets (OPAs) to assist in planning the project. Which of the following is considered an OPA?
a. Industry standards
b. Historical project information
c. Government regulations
d. Market conditions

Answer: b. Historical project information. Explanation: Organizational process assets include any artifacts, processes, or knowledge bases that the organization has developed over time. Historical project information, such as lessons learned and past project files, is an example of an OPA. Industry standards, government regulations, and market conditions are considered enterprise environmental factors (EEFs).

137. A project manager is assessing enterprise environmental factors (EEFs) that could impact the project. Which of the following is an EEF?
a. Templates for project documents
b. Configuration management knowledge bases
c. Organizational culture and structure
d. Project management methodology

Answer: c. Organizational culture and structure. Explanation: Enterprise environmental factors are external and internal conditions that influence the project. Organizational culture and structure, which affect how projects are managed and executed, are examples of EEFs. Templates, configuration management knowledge bases, and project management methodology are organizational process assets.

138. During project execution, the project manager is required to provide regular performance updates to stakeholders. Which document should be used to compile and present this information?
a. Project charter
b. Work performance reports
c. Risk register
d. Scope statement

Answer: b. Work performance reports. Explanation: Work performance reports are compiled from work performance data and information, and they provide stakeholders with status updates, performance metrics, and forecasts. These reports help stakeholders understand project progress and make informed decisions.

139. A project manager needs to access specific organizational policies and procedures for managing risks. Where should the project manager look for this information?
a. Enterprise environmental factors
b. Organizational process assets
c. Project charter
d. Stakeholder register

Answer: b. Organizational process assets. Explanation: Organizational process assets include the organization's policies, procedures, and guidelines for various project management activities, including risk management. These assets provide the project manager with the necessary information to manage risks according to organizational standards.

140. The project manager is analyzing work performance data to identify trends and variances. Which tool or technique is most appropriate for this analysis?
a. Monte Carlo simulation
b. Fishbone diagram
c. Earned value management
d. Stakeholder analysis

Answer: c. Earned value management. Explanation: Earned value management (EVM) is a technique used to analyze work performance data by comparing planned progress with actual progress. It helps identify trends and variances in project performance, providing valuable insights for decision-making.

141. A project team is utilizing historical information from previous projects to improve planning accuracy. Which type of organizational process asset is being used?

a. Project management information systems
b. Organizational culture
c. Historical databases
d. Governance framework

Answer: c. Historical databases. Explanation: Historical databases are organizational process assets that contain information from past projects, such as lessons learned, performance metrics, and project documentation. These databases help the project team improve planning accuracy by leveraging past experiences.

142. During a project review, the project manager needs to provide a detailed analysis of project performance and future projections. Which document should be used for this purpose?
a. Work performance reports
b. Project scope statement
c. Issue log
d. Risk management plan

Answer: a. Work performance reports. Explanation: Work performance reports provide a detailed analysis of project performance, including progress metrics, variances, and forecasts. They compile data from various sources to give stakeholders a comprehensive view of the project's status and future projections.

143. A project manager needs to account for external regulations that could impact project execution. Where should this information be documented?
a. Organizational process assets
b. Enterprise environmental factors
c. Project charter
d. Work breakdown structure

Answer: b. Enterprise environmental factors. Explanation: Enterprise environmental factors include external regulations and standards that can impact project execution. These factors must be considered and documented during project planning to ensure compliance and mitigate potential risks.

144. A project manager is developing a project charter for a new software development project. Which of the following elements is NOT typically included in a project charter?
a. Project purpose or justification
b. Detailed project schedule
c. High-level project requirements
d. Summary budget

Answer: b. Detailed project schedule. Explanation: The project charter includes the project purpose or justification, high-level project requirements, and summary budget, but it does not include a detailed project schedule, which is developed later in the project planning phase.

145. While developing the Project Management Plan, a project manager wants to ensure that all aspects of the project are covered. Which component specifically addresses how changes to project scope will be managed?
a. Scope Management Plan
b. Change Control Plan
c. Risk Management Plan
d. Communications Management Plan

Answer: a. Scope Management Plan. Explanation: The Scope Management Plan is a component of the Project Management Plan that describes how the project scope will be defined, validated, and controlled. It includes processes for managing changes to the project scope.

146. A project manager is executing the project work and realizes that the team's productivity can be improved by implementing lessons learned from previous projects. Which process is the project manager utilizing?
a. Monitor and Control Project Work
b. Perform Integrated Change Control
c. Manage Project Knowledge
d. Direct and Manage Project Work

Answer: c. Manage Project Knowledge. Explanation: Manage Project Knowledge involves using existing knowledge and creating new knowledge to achieve project objectives and contribute to organizational learning. This includes applying lessons learned from previous projects to improve current project performance.

147. During the Monitor and Control Project Work process, a project manager identifies a variance from the project plan. What is the first step the project manager should take to address this variance?
a. Implement corrective actions
b. Update the project plan
c. Identify the root cause of the variance
d. Inform the project sponsor

Answer: c. Identify the root cause of the variance. Explanation: Before taking corrective actions or updating the project plan, the project manager should first identify the root cause of the variance. Understanding the cause helps in determining the appropriate corrective measures.

148. A stakeholder requests a change to the project scope, which could significantly impact the project schedule and budget. Which process should the project manager follow to evaluate and implement this change?
a. Monitor and Control Project Work
b. Perform Integrated Change Control
c. Direct and Manage Project Work
d. Manage Stakeholder Engagement

Answer: b. Perform Integrated Change Control. Explanation: Perform Integrated Change Control is the process used to review, evaluate, approve, defer, or reject changes to the project scope, schedule, and budget. This process ensures that all changes are managed in a coordinated way.

149. As part of the project closure process, a project manager needs to document the lessons learned. Which document should be updated with this information?
a. Project Charter
b. Project Management Plan
c. Lessons Learned Register
d. Stakeholder Register

Answer: c. Lessons Learned Register. Explanation: The Lessons Learned Register is a document that is updated throughout the project and finalized during project closure. It captures valuable insights and experiences that can be used to improve future projects.

150. A project manager is tasked with closing a project phase. What is the main objective of the Close Project or Phase process?
a. To reallocate project resources
b. To ensure all project work is complete and formalize acceptance
c. To update the project management plan
d. To conduct a performance review of the project team

Answer: b. To ensure all project work is complete and formalize acceptance. Explanation: The main objective of the Close Project or Phase process is to finalize all activities, ensure that the project or phase deliverables meet the acceptance criteria, and formalize acceptance by stakeholders.

151. During the Direct and Manage Project Work process, a project manager needs to ensure that all project team members have access to the necessary project information. Which tool or technique is most appropriate for this purpose?
a. Expert Judgment
b. Project Management Information System (PMIS)
c. Earned Value Management (EVM)
d. Monte Carlo Simulation

Answer: b. Project Management Information System (PMIS). Explanation: A Project Management Information System (PMIS) is used to collect, integrate, and disseminate project information. It ensures that all team members have access to the necessary information to perform their tasks effectively.

152. A project manager is monitoring project performance and notices that the earned value (EV) is lower than the planned value (PV). What does this indicate about the project's performance?
a. The project is ahead of schedule

b. The project is behind schedule
c. The project is under budget
d. The project is over budget

Answer: b. The project is behind schedule. Explanation: If the earned value (EV) is lower than the planned value (PV), it indicates that less work has been completed than planned, meaning the project is behind schedule.

153. During project execution, a critical issue arises that requires immediate attention. Which process allows the project manager to implement a corrective action to address this issue?
a. Direct and Manage Project Work
b. Monitor and Control Project Work
c. Perform Integrated Change Control
d. Manage Project Knowledge

Answer: a. Direct and Manage Project Work. Explanation: Direct and Manage Project Work involves leading and performing the work defined in the project management plan and implementing approved changes, including corrective actions, to address issues that arise during project execution.

154. A project manager is developing the scope management plan. Which of the following is not typically included in the scope management plan?
a. Process for preparing a detailed project scope statement
b. Procedures for scope validation and control
c. Process for defining, validating, and controlling the project schedule
d. Guidelines for managing scope changes

Answer: c. Process for defining, validating, and controlling the project schedule. Explanation: The scope management plan focuses on processes related to defining, validating, and controlling the project scope. Processes for managing the project schedule are included in the schedule management plan.

155. During the Collect Requirements process, the project manager uses a technique to gather ideas and solutions from stakeholders. Which technique is being described?
a. Delphi technique
b. Brainstorming
c. Benchmarking
d. Mind mapping

Answer: b. Brainstorming. Explanation: Brainstorming is a group creativity technique used to generate ideas and solutions from stakeholders. It is an effective way to gather diverse perspectives and identify potential requirements for the project.

156. A project manager is defining the project scope and needs to include the project boundaries, deliverables, acceptance criteria, and constraints. Which document should be created to capture this information?
a. Project charter
b. Project scope statement
c. Requirements traceability matrix
d. Work breakdown structure (WBS)

Answer: b. Project scope statement. Explanation: The project scope statement details the project boundaries, deliverables, acceptance criteria, and constraints. It serves as a comprehensive description of the project scope, providing a foundation for project planning and execution.

157. The project team is creating the WBS for a new project. Which principle should they follow to ensure that the WBS is effective?
a. The WBS should include only the project deliverables, not the activities.
b. The WBS should be organized by project phases rather than deliverables.
c. Each WBS element should be assigned a unique identifier.
d. The WBS should be limited to three levels of decomposition.

Answer: c. Each WBS element should be assigned a unique identifier. Explanation: Assigning a unique identifier to each WBS element ensures clear tracking and management of project deliverables and work packages. This helps in maintaining consistency and traceability throughout the project lifecycle.

158. During the Validate Scope process, the project manager needs to obtain formal acceptance of the completed project deliverables. Who is responsible for providing this acceptance?
a. Project sponsor
b. Project team
c. Functional manager
d. Customer or stakeholder

Answer: d. Customer or stakeholder. Explanation: The customer or stakeholder is responsible for providing formal acceptance of the completed project deliverables during the Validate Scope process. This ensures that the deliverables meet the agreed-upon requirements and expectations.

159. A project is experiencing scope creep, leading to uncontrolled changes in project scope. What action should the project manager take to address this issue?
a. Implement a more detailed WBS
b. Use a change control system to manage scope changes
c. Reassign team members to manage additional scope
d. Increase project budget to accommodate changes

Answer: b. Use a change control system to manage scope changes. Explanation: A change control system is essential for managing scope changes systematically. It ensures that any proposed changes are evaluated, approved, or rejected, preventing uncontrolled changes and scope creep.

160. A project manager is using a requirements traceability matrix (RTM) to manage project scope. Which benefit does the RTM provide?
a. It outlines the project schedule and milestones.
b. It ensures that all requirements are linked to their origin and tracked throughout the project.
c. It provides a detailed description of the project deliverables.
d. It captures lessons learned from previous projects.

Answer: b. It ensures that all requirements are linked to their origin and tracked throughout the project. Explanation: The requirements traceability matrix (RTM) links each requirement to its origin and tracks its status throughout the project lifecycle. This helps ensure that all requirements are addressed and managed effectively.

161. During the Control Scope process, the project manager identifies a variance between the planned and actual project scope. What should be the next step?
a. Ignore the variance if it is minor
b. Update the project scope statement
c. Perform integrated change control
d. Reassign resources to address the variance

Answer: c. Perform integrated change control. Explanation: When a variance in project scope is identified, the project manager should perform integrated change control to evaluate the impact, obtain necessary approvals, and update project documents as required. This ensures that changes are managed systematically.

162. A project manager is working on a complex project with multiple stakeholders. To ensure that all requirements are collected and managed effectively, which tool or technique should be used?
a. Monte Carlo simulation
b. Focus groups
c. Gantt chart
d. SWOT analysis

Answer: b. Focus groups. Explanation: Focus groups involve gathering a representative group of stakeholders to discuss and capture their requirements and expectations. This technique is effective for collecting diverse perspectives and ensuring that all requirements are considered.

163. The project team has completed the initial project deliverables, and the project manager needs to verify that they meet the agreed-upon requirements. Which process should be followed?
a. Control Quality
b. Validate Scope
c. Define Scope

d. Plan Scope Management

Answer: b. Validate Scope. Explanation: The Validate Scope process involves reviewing the completed deliverables with the customer or stakeholder to ensure they meet the agreed-upon requirements. This process results in formal acceptance of the deliverables, confirming that they meet project objectives.

164. A project manager is leading a team through the execution phase of a complex project. During a weekly status meeting, a team member raises concerns about a potential risk that was not identified during the planning phase. What should the project manager do next?
a. Ignore the risk and focus on the planned work to avoid delays
b. Update the risk register and develop a risk response strategy
c. Escalate the risk to the project sponsor for immediate resolution
d. Postpone the risk assessment until the next phase of the project

Answer: b. Update the risk register and develop a risk response strategy. Explanation: When a new risk is identified during project execution, the project manager should promptly address it to mitigate its potential impact on the project. The first step is to update the risk register with the new risk, including its description, probability, impact, and priority. Next, the project manager should work with the team to develop an appropriate risk response strategy, such as avoidance, transfer, mitigation, or acceptance. Ignoring the risk or postponing its assessment can lead to uncontrolled risk exposure and potential project failures, while immediate escalation may not always be necessary if the risk can be effectively managed at the project level.

165. During the execution phase, a project team member approaches the project manager with a suggestion for improving the project's deliverables. The suggestion is not part of the original project scope but could add significant value to the end users. How should the project manager handle this situation?
a. Implement the suggestion immediately to improve customer satisfaction
b. Reject the suggestion outright to avoid scope creep
c. Evaluate the suggestion's impact on the project constraints and initiate a change request if necessary
d. Defer the suggestion to the next phase of the project

Answer: c. Evaluate the suggestion's impact on the project constraints and initiate a change request if necessary. Explanation: When a change to the project scope is proposed during execution, the project manager should follow the integrated change control process. This involves evaluating the suggestion's impact on the project constraints (scope, schedule, cost, quality, resources, and risks) and determining whether the change is feasible and beneficial. If the change is deemed valuable, the project manager should initiate a change request and seek approval from the change control board (CCB) or project sponsor. Implementing the suggestion without proper evaluation and approval can lead to scope creep and jeopardize the project's success, while rejecting valuable suggestions outright may lead to missed opportunities for improvement.

166. A project manager is using a Gantt chart to monitor the progress of project activities. During the execution phase, the project manager notices that a critical path activity is running behind schedule. Which of the following techniques is most appropriate to bring the activity back on track?
a. Crashing

b. Fast tracking
c. Leveling
d. Monte Carlo analysis

Answer: a. Crashing. Explanation: When a critical path activity is behind schedule, it directly impacts the project's completion date. To bring the activity back on track and minimize the delay, the project manager can use schedule compression techniques. Crashing is a technique that involves adding additional resources (e.g., personnel, equipment, or budget) to an activity to reduce its duration. By allocating more resources to the critical path activity, the project manager can accelerate its completion and bring the project back on schedule. Fast tracking, which involves performing activities in parallel, is not applicable in this case since the activity is already on the critical path. Leveling is used to resolve resource overallocation, while Monte Carlo analysis is a risk assessment technique.

167. During the execution phase, a project team member approaches the project manager with concerns about the performance of a vendor. The vendor is not meeting the agreed-upon quality standards, which is causing rework and delays. What should the project manager do to address this issue?
a. Terminate the vendor's contract immediately
b. Ignore the issue and focus on completing the project on time
c. Schedule a meeting with the vendor to discuss the performance issues and develop a corrective action plan
d. Escalate the issue to the project sponsor and request additional funding to cover the rework

Answer: c. Schedule a meeting with the vendor to discuss the performance issues and develop a corrective action plan. Explanation: When a vendor is not meeting the agreed-upon quality standards, the project manager should address the issue promptly and constructively. The first step is to schedule a meeting with the vendor to discuss the performance issues and understand the root causes of the problem. During the meeting, the project manager should clearly communicate the project's quality expectations and work with the vendor to develop a corrective action plan. This plan should outline the specific steps the vendor will take to improve their performance, along with timelines and measurable goals. Terminating the vendor's contract without attempting to resolve the issues can lead to further delays and legal complications, while ignoring the problem will only exacerbate the quality issues and impact the project's success.

168. A project manager is leading a cross-functional team with members from different departments and backgrounds. During the execution phase, the project manager notices that team members are not communicating effectively, leading to misunderstandings and delays. Which of the following is the most appropriate action for the project manager to improve team communication?
a. Replace underperforming team members with new ones
b. Establish clear communication protocols and conduct regular team-building activities
c. Escalate the issue to the functional managers and request their intervention
d. Reduce the frequency of team meetings to minimize confusion

Answer: b. Establish clear communication protocols and conduct regular team-building activities. Explanation: Effective communication is essential for the success of any project, particularly when working with a diverse, cross-functional team. To improve team communication, the project manager should establish clear communication protocols, such as defining the frequency and format of team meetings, specifying the tools and channels for information sharing, and setting expectations for response times and feedback. Additionally, the project manager should organize regular team-building activities to foster trust, collaboration, and open communication among team members. These activities can include icebreakers, problem-solving exercises, or social events that allow team members to interact in a more informal setting. Replacing team members or reducing the frequency of meetings may not address the underlying communication issues, while escalating the problem to functional managers should only be done if the communication challenges persist despite the project manager's efforts.

169. During the execution phase, a project manager receives a change request from a key stakeholder. The change request involves adding a new feature to the project deliverables, which will require additional time and resources. The project is already behind schedule and over budget. How should the project manager handle this situation?
a. Implement the change request immediately to satisfy the stakeholder
b. Reject the change request outright due to the project's time and budget constraints
c. Evaluate the change request's impact on the project objectives and present a recommendation to the change control board
d. Postpone the change request until the next phase of the project

Answer: c. Evaluate the change request's impact on the project objectives and present a recommendation to the change control board. Explanation: When a change request is received during project execution, the project manager should follow the integrated change control process, regardless of the project's current time and budget performance. This process involves evaluating the change request's impact on the project objectives, constraints, and deliverables. The project manager should analyze the additional time, resources, and costs required to implement the change and assess its potential benefits and risks. Based on this analysis, the project manager should present a recommendation to the change control board (CCB) or project sponsor, who will make the final decision on whether to approve, reject, or defer the change. Implementing the change without proper evaluation can further exacerbate the project's time and budget issues, while rejecting or postponing the change outright may lead to stakeholder dissatisfaction and missed opportunities for improvement.

170. A project manager is reviewing the project's progress during the execution phase and notices that the actual cost is higher than the planned budget. Which of the following earned value management (EVM) metrics would help the project manager determine the project's cost efficiency?
a. Schedule Variance (SV)
b. Cost Variance (CV)
c. Schedule Performance Index (SPI)
d. Cost Performance Index (CPI)

Answer: d. Cost Performance Index (CPI). Explanation: The Cost Performance Index (CPI) is an earned value management metric that measures the cost efficiency of a project. It is calculated by dividing the earned value (EV) by the actual cost (AC). A CPI value greater than 1 indicates that the project is running under budget, while a CPI less than 1 suggests that the project is over budget. In this scenario, where the actual cost is higher than the planned budget, the CPI would be less than 1, indicating poor cost efficiency. The Schedule Variance (SV) and Schedule Performance Index (SPI) are used to assess the project's schedule performance, while the Cost Variance (CV) measures the difference between the earned value and the actual cost but does not provide a direct measure of cost efficiency.

171. During the execution phase, a project team member informs the project manager that they have discovered a more efficient way to complete a critical task. The new approach requires a change in the project's technology stack, which may impact other tasks and team members. What should the project manager do to address this situation?
a. Implement the new approach immediately to realize the efficiency gains
b. Reject the new approach outright to avoid any changes to the project plan
c. Conduct a feasibility analysis and impact assessment before making a decision
d. Delegate the decision to the team member who proposed the new approach

Answer: c. Conduct a feasibility analysis and impact assessment before making a decision. Explanation: When a potential process improvement or change in approach is identified during project execution, the project manager should carefully evaluate its feasibility and impact before making a decision. The first step is to conduct a feasibility analysis to determine whether the new approach is technically viable, cost-effective, and aligned with the project's objectives. Next, the project manager should assess the impact of the change on other project tasks, deliverables, and team members. This includes identifying any dependencies, estimating the additional time and resources required for implementation, and evaluating the potential risks and benefits. Based on this analysis, the project manager can make an informed decision on whether to adopt the new approach, modify it, or maintain the current course of action. Implementing the change without proper evaluation can lead to unforeseen consequences and project disruptions, while rejecting innovative ideas outright may lead to missed opportunities for improvement.

172. A project manager is leading a team through the execution phase of a project. During a risk review meeting, the team identifies a new risk that could significantly impact the project's schedule and budget. The risk has a high probability of occurrence and a high potential impact. What should the project manager do to address this risk?
a. Ignore the risk and focus on executing the project as planned
b. Develop a risk response strategy that includes both risk mitigation and contingency planning
c. Transfer the risk to a third party, such as a subcontractor or insurance provider
d. Escalate the risk to the project sponsor and request additional resources to address it

Answer: b. Develop a risk response strategy that includes both risk mitigation and contingency planning. Explanation: When a high-probability, high-impact risk is identified during project execution, the project manager should proactively address it to minimize its potential effects on the project's objectives. Ignoring the risk or focusing solely on execution can lead to significant schedule delays, cost overruns, and potential project failure. Developing a comprehensive risk response strategy is the most appropriate approach in this situation. This strategy should include risk mitigation actions, which are proactive measures taken to reduce the likelihood or impact of the risk. Examples of risk mitigation actions include implementing process improvements, allocating additional resources, or modifying the project scope. In addition to mitigation, the risk response strategy should also include contingency planning, which involves developing a set of predefined actions to be taken if the risk event occurs. Contingency plans help the project team respond quickly and effectively to minimize the risk's impact on the project. Transferring the risk to a third party or escalating it to the sponsor may be considered as part of the overall risk response strategy, but they should not be the sole actions taken.

173. A project manager is using earned value management (EVM) to monitor the project's performance during the execution phase. The project's current EVM metrics are as follows:- Budget at Completion (BAC): $500,000 - Planned Value (PV): $300,000 - Earned Value (EV): $250,000 - Actual Cost (AC): $350,000. Based on these metrics, what is the project's schedule variance (SV), and what does it indicate about the project's schedule performance?
a. SV = $50,000; the project is ahead of schedule
b. SV = -$50,000; the project is behind schedule

c. SV = $100,000; the project is ahead of schedule
d. SV = -$100,000; the project is behind schedule

Answer: b. SV = -$50,000; the project is behind schedule. Explanation: The schedule variance (SV) is an earned value management metric that measures the difference between the earned value (EV) and the planned value (PV). It indicates whether the project is ahead of or behind schedule. A positive SV means that the project has accomplished more work than planned, while a negative SV indicates that the project has accomplished less work than planned. In this scenario, the SV is calculated as follows: SV = EV - PV = $250,000 - $300,000 = -$50,000. The negative SV of -$50,000 indicates that the project has earned $50,000 less value than planned at this point in time, suggesting that the project is behind schedule. To get the project back on track, the project manager should analyze the causes of the schedule variance, such as resource constraints, scope changes, or unforeseen risks, and take corrective actions to accelerate the remaining work.

174. A project manager is developing the Schedule Management Plan. Which of the following is NOT typically included in the Schedule Management Plan?
a. Control thresholds
b. Level of accuracy
c. Project schedule network diagram
d. Reporting formats

Answer: c. Project schedule network diagram. Explanation: The Schedule Management Plan typically includes control thresholds, the level of accuracy, and reporting formats, but it does not include the project schedule network diagram, which is a separate document created during schedule development.

175. In defining project activities, a project manager uses a technique to break down work packages into smaller components. What is this technique called?
a. Rolling wave planning
b. Decomposition
c. Analogous estimating
d. Bottom-up estimating

Answer: b. Decomposition. Explanation: Decomposition is the technique used to break down work packages into smaller, more manageable components called activities. This helps in defining the specific tasks needed to complete the project work.

176. A project manager is sequencing activities and needs to account for dependencies where one activity cannot start until another has finished. What type of dependency is this?
a. Start-to-Start (SS)
b. Finish-to-Start (FS)
c. Start-to-Finish (SF)
d. Finish-to-Finish (FF)

Answer: b. Finish-to-Start (FS). Explanation: A Finish-to-Start (FS) dependency means that one activity cannot start until another activity has finished. This is the most common type of dependency in project scheduling.

177. A project manager uses three-point estimating to determine the duration of a critical activity. The optimistic estimate is 5 days, the most likely estimate is 10 days, and the pessimistic estimate is 20 days. What is the expected duration of the activity using the PERT formula?
a. 10 days
b. 11 days
c. 12 days
d. 15 days

Answer: c. 12 days. Explanation: The PERT (Program Evaluation and Review Technique) formula for three-point estimating is (Optimistic + 4Most Likely + Pessimistic) / 6. Using the given estimates: (5 + 410 + 20) / 6 = 12 days.

178. During the Develop Schedule process, a project manager identifies that some tasks can be performed in parallel instead of sequentially to shorten the project timeline. What is this technique called?
a. Fast tracking
b. Crashing
c. Resource leveling
d. Critical chain method

Answer: a. Fast tracking. Explanation: Fast tracking is a schedule compression technique where activities that were initially planned to be performed sequentially are re-planned to be performed in parallel, thus shortening the project timeline.

179. A project manager is controlling the project schedule and discovers that the project is behind schedule. Which of the following techniques can be used to bring the project back on track?
a. Analogous estimating
b. Schedule baseline
c. Critical path method
d. Monte Carlo simulation

Answer: c. Critical path method. Explanation: The Critical Path Method (CPM) can be used to identify the longest path of activities and determine where adjustments can be made to bring the project back on track, such as by fast-tracking or crashing critical path activities.

180. A project team is estimating activity durations and decides to use historical data from similar past projects. What type of estimating technique are they using?
a. Parametric estimating
b. Analogous estimating
c. Three-point estimating

d. Bottom-up estimating

Answer: b. Analogous estimating. Explanation: Analogous estimating uses historical data from similar past projects to estimate activity durations. It is a top-down estimating technique and is typically less accurate than other methods.

181. During schedule development, the project manager needs to account for a limited number of key resources that are shared across multiple activities. Which technique should be used to address this constraint?
a. Resource leveling
b. Fast tracking
c. Crashing
d. Parametric estimating

Answer: a. Resource leveling. Explanation: Resource leveling is a technique used to adjust the project schedule to account for resource constraints. It ensures that the demand for resources does not exceed their availability, even if it means extending the project duration.

182. A project manager is using a Gantt chart to develop the project schedule. What is the primary purpose of a Gantt chart?
a. To identify project risks
b. To display project milestones and deadlines
c. To allocate project resources
d. To calculate project costs

Answer: b. To display project milestones and deadlines. Explanation: A Gantt chart is a visual tool used to display the project schedule, showing the start and finish dates of activities, as well as project milestones and deadlines. It helps in tracking project progress and managing timelines.

183. While monitoring the project schedule, a project manager calculates the Schedule Performance Index (SPI) and finds it to be 0.85. What does this indicate about the project's schedule performance?
a. The project is ahead of schedule
b. The project is behind schedule
c. The project is on schedule
d. The project is over budget

Answer: b. The project is behind schedule. Explanation: The Schedule Performance Index (SPI) is calculated as EV/PV (Earned Value/Planned Value). An SPI of less than 1.0 indicates that the project is behind schedule, as the work performed is less than the work planned.

184. A project manager is preparing the cost management plan for a new project. Which of the following should not be included in the cost management plan?

a. Units of measure for reporting costs
b. Control thresholds for variances
c. Funding decisions and financing requirements
d. Earned value management (EVM) guidelines

Answer: c. Funding decisions and financing requirements. Explanation: The cost management plan includes details on how to measure and report costs, manage variances, and guidelines for using EVM. Funding decisions and financing requirements are typically addressed in the project charter or financial plan, not the cost management plan.

185. During the Estimate Costs process, the project manager is using historical data from previous projects to predict the costs of current project activities. Which estimating technique is being used?
a. Bottom-up estimating
b. Analogous estimating
c. Parametric estimating
d. Three-point estimating

Answer: b. Analogous estimating. Explanation: Analogous estimating uses historical data from similar projects to predict the costs of current project activities. It is less time-consuming and provides a quick estimate, though it may be less accurate than other methods.

186. A project manager needs to develop a detailed budget for the project. Which process will help in aggregating the estimated costs of individual activities or work packages to establish an authorized cost baseline?
a. Plan Cost Management
b. Estimate Costs
c. Determine Budget
d. Control Costs

Answer: c. Determine Budget. Explanation: The Determine Budget process aggregates the estimated costs of individual activities or work packages to establish an authorized cost baseline, which is used to monitor and control project costs.

187. During project execution, the project manager notices that the project is running over budget. Which earned value management (EVM) metric should be calculated to understand the project's cost performance?
a. Cost Performance Index (CPI)
b. Schedule Performance Index (SPI)
c. Estimate at Completion (EAC)
d. To-Complete Performance Index (TCPI)

Answer: a. Cost Performance Index (CPI). Explanation: The Cost Performance Index (CPI) is an EVM metric that measures cost efficiency by comparing the earned value (EV) to the actual cost (AC). It is calculated as CPI = EV / AC. A CPI less than 1 indicates that the project is over budget.

188. A project has an earned value (EV) of $100,000, an actual cost (AC) of $120,000, and a planned value (PV) of $110,000. What is the project's schedule variance (SV), and what does it indicate?
a. SV = -$20,000, indicating the project is behind schedule
b. SV = $10,000, indicating the project is ahead of schedule
c. SV = -$10,000, indicating the project is behind schedule
d. SV = $20,000, indicating the project is ahead of schedule

Answer: c. SV = -$10,000, indicating the project is behind schedule. Explanation: Schedule variance (SV) is calculated as SV = EV - PV. In this case, SV = $100,000 - $110,000 = -$10,000. A negative SV indicates that the project is behind schedule.

189. The project manager needs to forecast the total cost of the project based on current performance. Which EVM metric should be used to calculate this forecast?
a. Cost Performance Index (CPI)
b. Schedule Performance Index (SPI)
c. Estimate at Completion (EAC)
d. To-Complete Performance Index (TCPI)

Answer: c. Estimate at Completion (EAC). Explanation: Estimate at Completion (EAC) is a forecast of the total cost of the project based on current performance. It can be calculated using various formulas, depending on the project's cost performance and remaining work.

190. During the Control Costs process, the project manager identifies a significant cost overrun. Which action should be taken first to address this issue?
a. Revise the project budget
b. Implement corrective actions
c. Update the cost management plan
d. Perform a root cause analysis

Answer: d. Perform a root cause analysis. Explanation: The first step in addressing a significant cost overrun is to perform a root cause analysis to understand the underlying reasons for the overrun. This helps in identifying appropriate corrective actions and preventing similar issues in the future.

191. A project manager is using parametric estimating to predict the costs of project activities. Which of the following is an example of parametric estimating?
a. Using historical data from a similar project to estimate costs
b. Estimating costs by multiplying the quantity of work by a unit rate
c. Breaking down the project into smaller components and estimating costs for each component
d. Estimating costs using a range of values for optimistic, pessimistic, and most likely scenarios

Answer: b. Estimating costs by multiplying the quantity of work by a unit rate. Explanation: Parametric estimating uses statistical relationships between historical data and other variables to predict costs. An example is estimating costs by multiplying the quantity of work by a unit rate.

192. The project manager needs to set a baseline for measuring project performance. Which document will provide this baseline?
a. Cost management plan
b. Work breakdown structure (WBS)
c. Project charter
d. Project budget

Answer: d. Project budget. Explanation: The project budget provides the cost baseline, which is used to measure project performance. It includes the aggregated costs of all project activities and is essential for monitoring and controlling costs.

193. A project has an earned value (EV) of $50,000, a planned value (PV) of $60,000, and an actual cost (AC) of $55,000. What is the Cost Performance Index (CPI), and what does it indicate?
a. CPI = 0.83, indicating the project is over budget
b. CPI = 0.91, indicating the project is over budget
c. CPI = 1.09, indicating the project is under budget
d. CPI = 1.20, indicating the project is under budget

Answer: b. CPI = 0.91, indicating the project is over budget. Explanation: The Cost Performance Index (CPI) is calculated as CPI = EV / AC. In this case, CPI = $50,000 / $55,000 = 0.91. A CPI less than 1 indicates that the project is over budget.

194. A project manager is developing the Plan Quality Management process for a new product launch. Which of the following tools is most appropriate for identifying potential defects and their causes in the production process?
a. Histogram
b. Pareto Chart
c. Fishbone Diagram
d. Control Chart

Answer: c. Fishbone Diagram. Explanation: A Fishbone Diagram, also known as a cause-and-effect diagram or Ishikawa diagram, is used to identify potential causes of defects and helps in categorizing these causes to find the root cause of a problem.

195. During the Manage Quality process, the project manager needs to ensure that the project follows established quality standards. Which activity is most relevant to this process?
a. Conducting quality audits
b. Implementing corrective actions

c. Validating scope
d. Performing variance analysis

Answer: a. Conducting quality audits. Explanation: Quality audits are part of the Manage Quality process and involve a systematic review of project activities to ensure they comply with organizational and project policies, processes, and procedures.

196. A project manager is monitoring quality control data using control charts. If a data point falls outside the control limits, what should be the immediate next step?
a. Ignore the data point as a one-time occurrence
b. Investigate the cause of the variation
c. Adjust the control limits
d. Report the issue to the project sponsor

Answer: b. Investigate the cause of the variation. Explanation: When a data point falls outside the control limits on a control chart, it indicates a potential issue in the process. The immediate next step is to investigate the cause of the variation to determine if corrective actions are needed.

197. A project team is implementing Six Sigma methodology to improve process quality. Which of the following best describes the primary goal of Six Sigma?
a. Reducing project costs
b. Eliminating defects by reducing process variation
c. Accelerating project timelines
d. Enhancing stakeholder satisfaction

Answer: b. Eliminating defects by reducing process variation. Explanation: Six Sigma is a data-driven methodology aimed at improving quality by identifying and eliminating defects and reducing process variation, leading to more consistent and predictable process performance.

198. In the Control Quality process, a project manager uses a Pareto chart. What is the primary purpose of this tool?
a. To identify the most common sources of defects
b. To display the distribution of data points
c. To track project schedule performance
d. To measure the impact of risk events

Answer: a. To identify the most common sources of defects. Explanation: A Pareto chart is used in quality control to identify the most significant factors contributing to a problem. It helps prioritize issues based on their frequency or impact, focusing efforts on the most critical areas.

199. A project manager is assessing the cost of quality (COQ) for a manufacturing project. Which of the following is considered an appraisal cost?
a. Training employees on quality standards
b. Conducting inspections and testing
c. Reworking defective products
d. Implementing preventive measures

Answer: b. Conducting inspections and testing. Explanation: Appraisal costs are associated with measuring and monitoring activities to ensure that products or services meet quality standards. This includes activities like inspections and testing.

200. During a quality control review, the project manager uses a histogram. What type of information does a histogram provide?
a. The relationship between two variables
b. The distribution of data points over specified intervals
c. The sequence of process steps
d. The root cause of a problem

Answer: b. The distribution of data points over specified intervals. Explanation: A histogram is a bar chart that represents the frequency distribution of data points over specified intervals. It helps visualize the distribution and identify patterns or trends in the data.

201. A project manager is analyzing quality data to determine the stability of a process. Which tool is most appropriate for this analysis?
a. Scatter Diagram
b. Flowchart
c. Control Chart
d. Checklist

Answer: c. Control Chart. Explanation: A control chart is used to monitor the stability of a process over time by plotting data points and identifying any variations that fall outside the control limits. It helps determine if a process is stable and in control.

202. In the context of quality management, what is the primary purpose of a quality management plan?
a. To outline the project's quality policies, objectives, and responsibilities
b. To define the project scope and deliverables
c. To estimate the project budget
d. To schedule project activities

Answer: a. To outline the project's quality policies, objectives, and responsibilities. Explanation: A quality management plan outlines the quality policies, objectives, criteria, and responsibilities for ensuring that the project meets the required quality standards and customer satisfaction.

203. A project manager is using statistical sampling as part of the Control Quality process. What is the main advantage of using statistical sampling?
a. It ensures 100% inspection of all deliverables
b. It reduces the time and cost of quality control
c. It eliminates the need for quality audits
d. It guarantees defect-free products

Answer: b. It reduces the time and cost of quality control. Explanation: Statistical sampling involves inspecting a subset of the total output rather than 100% inspection, which reduces the time and cost associated with quality control while still providing reliable information about the overall quality of the deliverables.

204. A project manager is developing a resource management plan for a new project. Which of the following should not be included in the resource management plan?
a. Roles and responsibilities
b. Resource calendars
c. Project organization charts
d. Work breakdown structure (WBS)

Answer: d. Work breakdown structure (WBS). Explanation: The resource management plan includes information on roles and responsibilities, resource calendars, and project organization charts. The WBS is a separate document that breaks down the project scope into manageable work packages.

205. During the Estimate Activity Resources process, the project manager is determining the types and quantities of resources required for each activity. Which technique is most appropriate for this process?
a. Delphi technique
b. Analogous estimating
c. Resource leveling
d. Expert judgment

Answer: d. Expert judgment. Explanation: Expert judgment involves using specialized knowledge or expertise to estimate the types and quantities of resources needed for each activity. It is a common technique used in the Estimate Activity Resources process.

206. A project team is in the process of acquiring resources. Which document should be consulted to understand the procedures for acquiring and managing these resources?
a. Project charter
b. Resource management plan
c. Stakeholder register

d. Risk management plan

Answer: b. Resource management plan. Explanation: The resource management plan outlines the procedures for acquiring and managing project resources. It provides guidance on resource allocation, roles, and responsibilities, and resource management throughout the project lifecycle.

207. The project manager needs to improve team performance and cohesion. Which process involves developing individual and team skills to enhance project performance?
a. Develop Team
b. Manage Team
c. Acquire Resources
d. Control Resources

Answer: a. Develop Team. Explanation: The Develop Team process focuses on improving team performance and cohesion by developing individual and team skills. This includes training, team-building activities, and performance assessments to enhance overall project performance.

208. During the Manage Team process, the project manager notices a conflict between two team members. What is the first step the project manager should take to resolve this conflict?
a. Reassign one of the team members
b. Conduct a private meeting with each team member
c. Implement a formal conflict resolution procedure
d. Escalate the issue to the project sponsor

Answer: b. Conduct a private meeting with each team member. Explanation: The first step in resolving a conflict is to understand the perspectives of the individuals involved. Conducting private meetings with each team member allows the project manager to gather information and address the issue constructively.

209. A project manager is using resource leveling to address resource overallocation. What is the primary impact of resource leveling on the project schedule?
a. It shortens the project duration
b. It increases resource utilization
c. It balances the workload among resources
d. It extends the project duration

Answer: d. It extends the project duration. Explanation: Resource leveling aims to balance resource allocation by adjusting the project schedule to prevent overallocation. This often results in extending the project duration to ensure that resources are used efficiently without overloading them.

210. During the Control Resources process, the project manager needs to ensure that physical resources are available as planned. Which action is most appropriate for this process?
a. Conducting performance appraisals
b. Implementing resource allocation changes
c. Monitoring resource utilization
d. Updating the risk register

Answer: c. Monitoring resource utilization. Explanation: The Control Resources process involves monitoring resource utilization to ensure that physical resources are available as planned. This includes tracking resource performance, identifying variances, and taking corrective actions as needed.

211. The project manager is evaluating the effectiveness of team-building activities. Which tool or technique can be used to assess team performance and development?
a. Resource leveling
b. Performance assessments
c. Analogous estimating
d. Stakeholder analysis

Answer: b. Performance assessments. Explanation: Performance assessments are used to evaluate the effectiveness of team-building activities and overall team performance. They help identify areas for improvement and provide feedback on team development efforts.

212. A project manager is developing a resource management plan and needs to identify the reporting relationships among project team members. Which component of the resource management plan should be created?
a. Roles and responsibilities
b. Resource breakdown structure (RBS)
c. Project organization charts
d. Resource calendars

Answer: c. Project organization charts. Explanation: Project organization charts visually depict the reporting relationships among project team members. They help clarify roles, responsibilities, and lines of communication within the project team.

213. The project manager needs to allocate resources to various project activities. Which tool or technique is most suitable for assigning resources to tasks?
a. Monte Carlo simulation
b. RACI matrix
c. Responsibility assignment matrix (RAM)
d. Earned value management (EVM)

Answer: c. Responsibility assignment matrix (RAM). Explanation: The Responsibility Assignment Matrix (RAM) is a tool used to assign resources to tasks by mapping project activities to specific team members responsible for completing them. It helps ensure that all tasks are assigned and accountability is clear.

214. A project manager is developing the Plan Communications Management process and needs to identify the information needs of the project stakeholders. Which tool or technique is most appropriate for this task?
a. Communication technology
b. Communication requirements analysis
c. Performance reporting
d. Communication methods

Answer: b. Communication requirements analysis. Explanation: Communication requirements analysis is used to determine the information needs of the project stakeholders and define the type and frequency of communication. It helps ensure that stakeholders receive the necessary information at the right time.

215. During the Manage Communications process, a project manager needs to distribute project performance reports to stakeholders. Which method of communication is best for ensuring that all stakeholders receive the same information simultaneously?
a. Interactive communication
b. Push communication
c. Pull communication
d. Face-to-face meetings

Answer: b. Push communication. Explanation: Push communication involves sending information to stakeholders, ensuring that everyone receives the same information simultaneously. This can be done through emails, memos, reports, or other written formats.

216. A project manager notices that team members often misunderstand written instructions, leading to errors. Which communication model can help improve the clarity of instructions by ensuring feedback and confirmation?
a. Basic sender-receiver model
b. Interactive communication model
c. Transactional communication model
d. Linear communication model

Answer: b. Interactive communication model. Explanation: The interactive communication model involves a two-way exchange where feedback is provided, and confirmation is received. This helps ensure that the message is understood correctly and reduces misunderstandings.

217. During the Monitor Communications process, a project manager finds that stakeholders are not satisfied with the current communication frequency. What is the first step the project manager should take to address this issue?
a. Update the communication management plan
b. Conduct a stakeholder analysis

c. Schedule additional meetings
d. Analyze the feedback to understand specific concerns

Answer: d. Analyze the feedback to understand specific concerns. Explanation: The first step is to analyze the feedback from stakeholders to understand their specific concerns regarding communication frequency. This helps in identifying the root cause and making informed adjustments to the communication plan.

218. A project manager needs to share complex project data with stakeholders who have different levels of understanding and expertise. Which communication method is most appropriate for this situation?
a. Written reports
b. Interactive meetings
c. Emails
d. Instant messaging

Answer: b. Interactive meetings. Explanation: Interactive meetings allow the project manager to explain complex data in detail, address questions, and ensure that all stakeholders, regardless of their level of understanding and expertise, have a clear and accurate understanding of the information.

219. Which of the following is a primary benefit of implementing a communication management plan in a project?
a. Ensuring all project tasks are completed on time
b. Aligning project objectives with organizational strategy
c. Facilitating efficient and effective communication among stakeholders
d. Reducing the project budget

Answer: c. Facilitating efficient and effective communication among stakeholders. Explanation: A communication management plan outlines how project information will be communicated, ensuring that stakeholders receive timely, accurate, and relevant information, which facilitates efficient and effective communication.

220. A project manager is using a pull communication method to provide stakeholders with access to project documents. Which of the following tools is commonly used for this purpose?
a. Email
b. Intranet site
c. Face-to-face meetings
d. Video conferencing

Answer: b. Intranet site. Explanation: Pull communication methods make information available for stakeholders to access at their convenience. An intranet site is a common tool used for this purpose, providing a central repository for project documents.

221. During a project status meeting, a stakeholder expresses concern about the lack of visibility into project progress. What is the most appropriate action for the project manager to take?
a. Schedule more frequent status meetings
b. Provide access to real-time project dashboards
c. Send detailed progress reports via email
d. Update the project charter to include more communication requirements

Answer: b. Provide access to real-time project dashboards. Explanation: Providing access to real-time project dashboards allows stakeholders to monitor project progress and gain visibility at any time, addressing their concerns about the lack of visibility.

222. A project manager needs to ensure that sensitive project information is communicated securely to stakeholders. Which communication technology should be used to achieve this?
a. Public social media platforms
b. Encrypted email
c. Shared document repository without access controls
d. Open discussion forums

Answer: b. Encrypted email. Explanation: Encrypted email ensures that sensitive project information is communicated securely, protecting it from unauthorized access and ensuring confidentiality.

223. In the context of project communication, what is the primary purpose of a communication model?
a. To define the project scope
b. To describe the flow of information between the sender and receiver
c. To outline the project budget
d. To manage project risks

Answer: b. To describe the flow of information between the sender and receiver. Explanation: A communication model describes the flow of information between the sender and receiver, including encoding, transmission, decoding, and feedback, ensuring that the message is effectively communicated and understood.

224. During the Plan Risk Management process, the project manager needs to define how to conduct risk management activities for the project. Which document is created as a result of this process?
a. Risk register
b. Risk management plan
c. Risk breakdown structure (RBS)
d. Risk mitigation plan

Answer: b. Risk management plan. Explanation: The risk management plan outlines how risk management activities will be structured and performed. It includes methodologies, roles and responsibilities, budgeting, timing, and risk categories, among other elements.

225. The project team is identifying risks that could impact the project. Which technique involves using a group of experts to anonymously provide their opinions on potential project risks?
a. Brainstorming
b. Delphi technique
c. SWOT analysis
d. Root cause analysis

Answer: b. Delphi technique. Explanation: The Delphi technique involves using a group of experts who provide their opinions on potential project risks anonymously. This method helps avoid bias and ensures a wide range of expert insights.

226. During the Perform Qualitative Risk Analysis process, the project manager needs to prioritize risks for further analysis. Which tool or technique is most appropriate for this task?
a. Monte Carlo simulation
b. Probability and impact matrix
c. Decision tree analysis
d. Expected monetary value (EMV) analysis

Answer: b. Probability and impact matrix. Explanation: The probability and impact matrix is used to prioritize risks by assessing their likelihood of occurrence and potential impact on project objectives. This helps in identifying the most significant risks that require further analysis.

227. A project manager is performing quantitative risk analysis and needs to evaluate the potential impact of identified risks on project objectives. Which technique is most suitable for this purpose?
a. SWOT analysis
b. Sensitivity analysis
c. Risk data quality assessment
d. Risk categorization

Answer: b. Sensitivity analysis. Explanation: Sensitivity analysis evaluates the potential impact of identified risks on project objectives by analyzing how variations in risk factors affect project outcomes. It helps in understanding the relative importance of different risks.

228. The project team is developing responses for identified risks. Which strategy involves reducing the probability and/or impact of a risk to an acceptable threshold?
a. Avoidance
b. Mitigation
c. Transfer
d. Acceptance

Answer: b. Mitigation. Explanation: Mitigation involves taking actions to reduce the probability and/or impact of a risk to an acceptable threshold. This strategy aims to minimize the adverse effects of risks on project objectives.

229. During the Implement Risk Responses process, the project manager realizes that a previously identified risk has occurred. What should be the next step?
a. Update the risk register
b. Perform qualitative risk analysis
c. Revise the project management plan
d. Execute the planned risk response

Answer: d. Execute the planned risk response. Explanation: When a previously identified risk occurs, the project manager should execute the planned risk response as outlined in the risk management plan. This ensures that the risk is managed according to the agreed-upon strategy.

230. The project manager is monitoring risks and needs to track identified risks, monitor residual risks, and identify new risks. Which document should be updated regularly during this process?
a. Risk management plan
b. Risk register
c. Risk breakdown structure (RBS)
d. Risk response plan

Answer: b. Risk register. Explanation: The risk register is updated regularly during the Monitor Risks process. It includes information on identified risks, risk owners, risk responses, and status updates, ensuring that risks are tracked and managed throughout the project lifecycle.

231. A project team is conducting a risk review and needs to ensure that all identified risks are adequately addressed. Which tool or technique is commonly used for this purpose?
a. Risk audit
b. Monte Carlo simulation
c. Ishikawa diagram
d. Decision tree analysis

Answer: a. Risk audit. Explanation: A risk audit is a tool used to assess the effectiveness of risk management processes and ensure that all identified risks are adequately addressed. It involves reviewing risk management activities, documentation, and outcomes.

232. The project manager is using Monte Carlo simulation to perform quantitative risk analysis. What is the primary benefit of using this technique?
a. It provides a qualitative assessment of risks.
b. It determines the root cause of risks.
c. It models the combined effects of individual project risks.

d. It categorizes risks based on their sources.

Answer: c. It models the combined effects of individual project risks. Explanation: Monte Carlo simulation models the combined effects of individual project risks by running multiple simulations to predict the overall impact on project objectives. This technique helps in understanding the cumulative effect of risks on project outcomes.

233. A project manager needs to decide on a risk response strategy for a high-impact risk. The strategy should involve shifting the impact of the risk to a third party. Which strategy is most appropriate?
a. Mitigation
b. Avoidance
c. Transfer
d. Acceptance

Answer: c. Transfer. Explanation: The transfer strategy involves shifting the impact of a risk to a third party, such as through insurance, warranties, or outsourcing. This approach reduces the project's exposure to the risk by making another entity responsible for managing it.

234. A project manager is developing the Plan Procurement Management process and needs to determine the types of contracts to be used for different procurements. Which of the following is NOT a type of contract typically considered in this process?
a. Fixed-price contract
b. Cost-reimbursable contract
c. Time and material contract
d. Performance-based contract

Answer: d. Performance-based contract. Explanation: The primary types of contracts considered in Plan Procurement Management are fixed-price, cost-reimbursable, and time and material contracts. Performance-based contracts are not typically categorized in the same way as these three main types.

235. During the Conduct Procurements process, the project manager needs to evaluate proposals from various sellers. Which of the following techniques is most appropriate for this evaluation?
a. Expert judgment
b. Independent estimates
c. Proposal evaluation techniques
d. Bidder conferences

Answer: c. Proposal evaluation techniques. Explanation: Proposal evaluation techniques are used to assess proposals from sellers based on predefined criteria, ensuring that the selected proposal meets the project's requirements and offers the best value.

236. A project manager is controlling procurements and notices that a vendor is consistently delivering materials late, impacting the project schedule. What is the first step the project manager should take to address this issue?
a. Terminate the contract with the vendor
b. Update the procurement management plan
c. Conduct a performance review meeting with the vendor
d. Implement corrective actions without notifying the vendor

Answer: c. Conduct a performance review meeting with the vendor. Explanation: The first step is to conduct a performance review meeting with the vendor to discuss the issues and develop a plan to address the delays. This collaborative approach helps in resolving the issue and maintaining a good working relationship.

237. In the context of Plan Procurement Management, what is the primary purpose of a make-or-buy analysis?
a. To determine the project schedule
b. To decide whether to produce goods internally or purchase them externally
c. To evaluate the quality of project deliverables
d. To assess the risk management plan

Answer: b. To decide whether to produce goods internally or purchase them externally. Explanation: A make-or-buy analysis is conducted to determine whether project needs can be met internally or should be procured from external sources. It helps in making informed decisions about procurement strategies.

238. A project manager is conducting procurements and needs to clarify project requirements and answer questions from potential sellers. Which activity is most appropriate for this purpose?
a. Advertising
b. Bidder conferences
c. Procurement audits
d. Market research

Answer: b. Bidder conferences. Explanation: Bidder conferences are meetings held with potential sellers to clarify project requirements, answer questions, and ensure that all sellers have a clear understanding of the procurement needs. This helps in obtaining accurate and competitive proposals.

239. A project manager is reviewing contract performance and identifies a significant cost overrun. Which type of contract is most likely to have a cost overrun risk for the buyer?
a. Fixed-price contract
b. Cost-reimbursable contract
c. Time and material contract
d. Lump sum contract

Answer: b. Cost-reimbursable contract. Explanation: In a cost-reimbursable contract, the buyer bears the risk of cost overruns because they agree to reimburse the seller for allowable costs incurred during the project, plus a fee. This can lead to higher costs if not properly managed.

240. During the Control Procurements process, the project manager needs to ensure that all contractual obligations are being met. Which document is most useful for tracking this information?
a. Risk register
b. Procurement statement of work (SOW)
c. Stakeholder register
d. Change log

Answer: b. Procurement statement of work (SOW). Explanation: The procurement statement of work (SOW) defines the work to be performed by the seller and serves as a key document for tracking contractual obligations and ensuring that the work meets the project requirements.

241. A project manager is planning to procure specialized equipment for a project. To ensure a fair and competitive bidding process, what document should be prepared and distributed to potential sellers?
a. Request for proposal (RFP)
b. Project charter
c. Risk management plan
d. Communications management plan

Answer: a. Request for proposal (RFP). Explanation: A Request for Proposal (RFP) is a document used to solicit proposals from potential sellers for specialized goods or services. It outlines the project requirements and evaluation criteria, ensuring a fair and competitive bidding process.

242. A project manager is evaluating the performance of a vendor and finds that the delivered products do not meet the agreed-upon quality standards. What is the most appropriate action to take?
a. Accept the products and continue with the project
b. Request a change order to modify the quality standards
c. Issue a formal notice to the vendor to address the quality issues
d. Increase the project budget to accommodate the lower quality

Answer: c. Issue a formal notice to the vendor to address the quality issues. Explanation: The project manager should issue a formal notice to the vendor to address the quality issues and ensure that the products meet the agreed-upon standards. This helps in maintaining quality control and holding the vendor accountable.

243. During the Control Procurements process, a project manager identifies that the project is facing delays due to slow procurement activities. Which technique can be used to expedite the procurement process?
a. Make-or-buy analysis
b. Crashing
c. Fast tracking

d. Negotiation

Answer: d. Negotiation. Explanation: Negotiation can be used to expedite the procurement process by reaching agreements with sellers on faster delivery times, improved terms, or resolving any issues causing delays. It involves direct communication with sellers to achieve a mutually acceptable solution.

244. A project manager is in the process of identifying stakeholders. Which tool or technique should they use to classify stakeholders based on their power, interest, and influence?
a. Stakeholder register
b. Power/interest grid
c. Stakeholder engagement plan
d. Communications management plan

Answer: b. Power/interest grid. Explanation: The power/interest grid is a tool used to classify stakeholders based on their level of power and interest in the project. It helps the project manager develop appropriate strategies for engaging stakeholders according to their influence and impact on the project.

245. During the Plan Stakeholder Engagement process, a project manager needs to analyze the current level of stakeholder engagement and develop strategies to improve it. Which document will provide this information?
a. Stakeholder register
b. Stakeholder engagement assessment matrix
c. Issue log
d. Risk register

Answer: b. Stakeholder engagement assessment matrix. Explanation: The stakeholder engagement assessment matrix compares the current and desired levels of stakeholder engagement. It helps the project manager understand where changes are needed and develop strategies to improve stakeholder engagement.

246. A project manager is managing stakeholder engagement and notices that a key stakeholder is becoming increasingly resistant to the project. What is the first step the project manager should take?
a. Escalate the issue to the project sponsor
b. Conduct a private meeting with the stakeholder to understand their concerns
c. Update the stakeholder engagement plan
d. Reassign the stakeholder to a different project

Answer: b. Conduct a private meeting with the stakeholder to understand their concerns. Explanation: The first step in managing a resistant stakeholder is to understand their concerns. A private meeting allows the project manager to address the stakeholder's issues directly and find ways to mitigate their resistance.

247. The project manager needs to ensure that stakeholder engagement activities are effective and that stakeholder expectations are being met. Which process involves regularly reviewing stakeholder engagement and adjusting strategies as needed?
a. Identify Stakeholders
b. Plan Stakeholder Engagement
c. Manage Stakeholder Engagement
d. Monitor Stakeholder Engagement

Answer: d. Monitor Stakeholder Engagement. Explanation: The Monitor Stakeholder Engagement process involves regularly reviewing stakeholder engagement activities and adjusting strategies as needed to ensure that stakeholder expectations are being met. It ensures continuous engagement and satisfaction of stakeholders.

248. A project is in the execution phase, and the project manager needs to communicate project progress to a diverse group of stakeholders. Which document outlines the methods and frequency of communication with stakeholders?
a. Communications management plan
b. Stakeholder engagement plan
c. Project management plan
d. Stakeholder register

Answer: a. Communications management plan. Explanation: The communications management plan outlines the methods, frequency, and responsibilities for communicating with stakeholders. It ensures that the right information is delivered to the right stakeholders at the right time.

249. During the stakeholder identification process, a project manager discovers that some stakeholders have conflicting interests. How should the project manager handle this situation?
a. Prioritize the interests of the most powerful stakeholders
b. Use stakeholder engagement strategies to address and balance conflicting interests
c. Ignore the conflicting interests and proceed with the project plan
d. Escalate the conflict to the project sponsor for resolution

Answer: b. Use stakeholder engagement strategies to address and balance conflicting interests. Explanation: The project manager should use stakeholder engagement strategies to address and balance conflicting interests. This involves understanding the needs and expectations of different stakeholders and finding a compromise that satisfies all parties involved.

250. The project manager is planning stakeholder engagement for a highly complex project. Which tool or technique is most suitable for analyzing the relationships and interactions among project stakeholders?
a. Stakeholder register
b. Stakeholder engagement assessment matrix
c. Social network analysis
d. Responsibility assignment matrix (RAM)

Answer: c. Social network analysis. Explanation: Social network analysis is a tool used to analyze the relationships and interactions among project stakeholders. It helps the project manager understand the influence patterns and identify key stakeholders who can impact the project's success.

251. A project manager needs to update the stakeholder engagement plan. Which of the following should not be included in this document?
a. Stakeholder communication requirements
b. Stakeholder engagement strategies
c. Stakeholder identification information
d. Stakeholder influence and impact assessment

Answer: c. Stakeholder identification information. Explanation: Stakeholder identification information is included in the stakeholder register, not the stakeholder engagement plan. The stakeholder engagement plan focuses on communication requirements, engagement strategies, and influence and impact assessments.

252. During the Manage Stakeholder Engagement process, a project manager identifies a new stakeholder who was not previously considered. What should the project manager do next?
a. Update the stakeholder register and engagement plan
b. Ignore the new stakeholder as they were not part of the original plan
c. Escalate the issue to the project sponsor
d. Conduct a stakeholder analysis for the new stakeholder

Answer: a. Update the stakeholder register and engagement plan. Explanation: When a new stakeholder is identified, the project manager should update the stakeholder register and the stakeholder engagement plan to ensure that the new stakeholder is appropriately engaged and managed throughout the project.

253. The project manager is conducting a performance review and needs to assess the effectiveness of stakeholder engagement strategies. Which technique can be used for this assessment?
a. Monte Carlo simulation
b. Variance analysis
c. Stakeholder engagement assessment matrix
d. Delphi technique

Answer: c. Stakeholder engagement assessment matrix. Explanation: The stakeholder engagement assessment matrix compares the current and desired levels of stakeholder engagement. It helps the project manager assess the effectiveness of engagement strategies and make necessary adjustments.

254. A project manager is offered a gift by a vendor who is bidding on a contract for the project. The gift is a weekend getaway at a luxury resort, valued at $1,500. According to the PMI Code of Ethics and Professional Conduct, what should the project manager do in this situation?
a. Accept the gift and disclose it to the project sponsor and procurement team

b. Accept the gift and keep it confidential to avoid any perception of bias
c. Politely decline the gift and inform the vendor of the organization's policies on gifts and gratuities
d. Accept the gift and recuse themselves from the vendor selection process

Answer: c. Politely decline the gift and inform the vendor of the organization's policies on gifts and gratuities. Explanation: The PMI Code of Ethics and Professional Conduct states that project managers should avoid conflicts of interest and the appearance of impropriety. Accepting a high-value gift from a vendor who is bidding on a project contract creates a clear conflict of interest and can be perceived as an attempt to influence the project manager's decision. The most appropriate action is to politely decline the gift and inform the vendor of the organization's policies on gifts and gratuities. This helps maintain the project manager's integrity, objectivity, and fairness in the procurement process. Accepting the gift, whether disclosed or kept confidential, can still be seen as a breach of ethics and may lead to disciplinary action or legal consequences.

255. During a project team meeting, a team member makes a derogatory comment about a colleague's age and suggests that they are too old to understand new technologies. According to the PMI Code of Ethics and Professional Conduct, what should the project manager do in response to this situation?
a. Ignore the comment and move on with the meeting agenda
b. Privately reprimand the team member after the meeting
c. Immediately address the inappropriate comment and reinforce the importance of respect and inclusivity
d. Escalate the issue to the HR department for disciplinary action

Answer: c. Immediately address the inappropriate comment and reinforce the importance of respect and inclusivity. Explanation: The PMI Code of Ethics and Professional Conduct emphasizes the importance of respect, fairness, and non-discrimination in the workplace. When a team member makes a derogatory comment based on age or any other protected characteristic, it is the project manager's responsibility to address the issue promptly and clearly. The project manager should immediately intervene and state that such comments are inappropriate and unacceptable. They should reinforce the organization's values of respect, inclusivity, and equal opportunity, and remind the team of their obligation to maintain a harassment-free work environment. Ignoring the comment or addressing it privately after the meeting may send the message that such behavior is tolerated, while escalating it to HR without first attempting to resolve it at the team level may be seen as an overreaction. The project manager should document the incident and follow up with the offending team member to ensure understanding and prevent future occurrences.

256. A project manager is reviewing expense reports submitted by team members and notices that one team member has been consistently claiming reimbursement for personal expenses unrelated to the project, such as meals and entertainment. What should the project manager do according to the PMI Code of Ethics and Professional Conduct?
a. Approve the expense reports to avoid confrontation with the team member
b. Discuss the issue with the team member and give them a warning
c. Investigate the expense reports, document the findings, and report the misconduct to the appropriate authorities
d. Deduct the personal expenses from the team member's next paycheck

Answer: c. Investigate the expense reports, document the findings, and report the misconduct to the appropriate authorities. Explanation: The PMI Code of Ethics and Professional Conduct requires project managers to act with honesty, responsibility, and fairness in their professional activities. Submitting false or inflated expense reports constitutes fraud and is a clear violation of ethical standards. When a project manager suspects or discovers fraudulent behavior, they have an obligation to investigate the matter thoroughly, document the findings, and report the misconduct to the appropriate authorities, such as their supervisor, the compliance department, or the legal team. Approving the expense reports or giving the team member a mere warning would be a breach of the project manager's ethical duties and could expose the organization to legal and financial risks. Deducting the personal expenses from the team member's paycheck without due process would also be inappropriate and could lead to legal challenges.

257. A project manager is approached by a team member who confides that they have been struggling with a substance abuse problem that is affecting their work performance. The team member asks for the project manager's help and confidentiality in seeking treatment. What should the project manager do in this situation, according to the PMI Code of Ethics and Professional Conduct?
a. Immediately report the team member's substance abuse problem to HR and request their termination
b. Maintain strict confidentiality and do not take any action to help the team member
c. Offer support and resources to the team member while maintaining confidentiality, unless there is a legal or ethical obligation to report
d. Inform the entire project team about the team member's substance abuse problem to ensure transparency

Answer: c. Offer support and resources to the team member while maintaining confidentiality, unless there is a legal or ethical obligation to report. Explanation: The PMI Code of Ethics and Professional Conduct emphasizes the importance of acting with compassion, respect, and professionalism when dealing with sensitive personal issues. When a team member confides in the project manager about a substance abuse problem and requests help, the project manager should respond with empathy and support. They should maintain the team member's confidentiality and privacy, as long as there is no legal or ethical obligation to report the issue (e.g., if the substance abuse poses a safety risk to others). The project manager should provide the team member with information about the organization's employee assistance program (EAP) or other relevant resources for treatment and recovery. They should also work with the team member to develop a plan for managing their work responsibilities while seeking help, which may involve temporary accommodations or reassignments. Reporting the issue to HR without the team member's consent or disclosing it to the entire team would be a breach of trust and could deter the team member from seeking needed assistance.

258. A project manager overhears a conversation between two team members discussing confidential client information in a public area. What should the project manager do to address this situation, according to the PMI Code of Ethics and Professional Conduct?
a. Ignore the conversation and assume that the team members will maintain client confidentiality
b. Immediately reprimand the team members in front of others to set an example
c. Schedule a private meeting with the team members to discuss the importance of confidentiality and the potential consequences of a breach
d. Report the team members to the client for violating their confidentiality agreement

Answer: c. Schedule a private meeting with the team members to discuss the importance of confidentiality and the potential consequences of a breach. Explanation: The PMI Code of Ethics and Professional Conduct requires project managers to protect confidential information and respect the privacy of clients, stakeholders, and team members. When a project manager becomes aware of a potential breach of confidentiality, such as team members discussing sensitive client information in a public area, they should address the issue promptly and professionally. The most appropriate action is to schedule a private meeting with the team members involved to discuss the incident and reinforce the importance of maintaining confidentiality. The project manager should explain the potential consequences of a confidentiality breach, such as damage to client trust, legal liabilities, and disciplinary action. They should also provide guidance on how to handle and discuss confidential information appropriately, such as using secure communication channels and avoiding public discussions. Ignoring the conversation or publicly reprimanding the team members would not effectively address the issue, while reporting the team members to the client without first attempting to resolve the matter internally could escalate the situation unnecessarily.

259. A project manager is invited to speak at a conference about a successful project they recently completed. The project manager's presentation includes several slides containing confidential client data and proprietary company information. According to the PMI Code of Ethics and Professional Conduct, what should the project manager do?
a. Present the slides as-is, assuming that the conference attendees will maintain confidentiality
b. Remove all confidential and proprietary information from the slides before presenting
c. Cancel the speaking engagement to avoid any potential breach of confidentiality
d. Seek written permission from the client and company to include the confidential information in the presentation

Answer: b. Remove all confidential and proprietary information from the slides before presenting. Explanation: The PMI Code of Ethics and Professional Conduct emphasizes the importance of protecting confidential and proprietary information in all professional activities, including public presentations and speaking engagements. When preparing a presentation about a project, the project manager should carefully review the content to ensure that it does not include any sensitive client data or company intellectual property. If the slides contain confidential information, the project manager should remove or redact that information before presenting, even if they assume that the audience will maintain confidentiality. Presenting the slides as-is would be a breach of the project manager's ethical obligations and could expose the client and company to risks. Canceling the speaking engagement altogether may be an overreaction and could result in missed opportunities for knowledge sharing and professional development. Seeking written permission to include the confidential information may be appropriate in some cases, but it is generally best to err on the side of caution and avoid sharing sensitive information in public forums.

260. During a project bidding process, a project manager receives an anonymous email alleging that one of the bidding vendors has engaged in unethical practices, such as bribery and collusion, in previous projects. What should the project manager do in this situation, according to the PMI Code of Ethics and Professional Conduct?
a. Ignore the anonymous email and proceed with the bidding process as planned
b. Immediately disqualify the accused vendor from the bidding process
c. Forward the anonymous email to all other bidding vendors to ensure transparency
d. Investigate the allegations while maintaining confidentiality and take appropriate action based on the findings

Answer: d. Investigate the allegations while maintaining confidentiality and take appropriate action based on the findings. Explanation: The PMI Code of Ethics and Professional Conduct requires project managers to uphold the highest standards of integrity, fairness, and transparency in the bidding and procurement process. When a project manager receives credible information about potential unethical practices by a bidding vendor, they have an obligation to investigate the allegations thoroughly and objectively. The project manager should maintain the confidentiality of the anonymous email and the investigation process to avoid any undue influence or retaliation. They should gather and review relevant evidence, such as documentation, interviews, and public records, to determine the validity of the allegations. If the investigation confirms that the vendor has engaged in unethical practices, the project manager should take appropriate action, such as disqualifying the vendor from the bidding process, reporting the misconduct to relevant authorities, and implementing measures to prevent future occurrences. Ignoring the email, immediately disqualifying the vendor without investigation, or sharing the email with other vendors would be premature and could lead to unfair or biased decision-making.

261. A project manager is reviewing the project's financial records and discovers that a team member has been falsifying timesheets and expense reports to receive additional compensation. The team member is a close friend of the project manager and has been going through personal financial difficulties. What should the project manager do in this situation, according to the PMI Code of Ethics and Professional Conduct?
a. Overlook the falsified records and continue to approve the team member's timesheets and expense reports
b. Confront the team member privately and ask them to stop falsifying records, without reporting the issue
c. Report the fraudulent activity to the appropriate authorities, regardless of the personal relationship or circumstances
d. Offer to cover the team member's expenses out of their own pocket to help them through their financial difficulties

Answer: c. Report the fraudulent activity to the appropriate authorities, regardless of the personal relationship or circumstances. Explanation: The PMI Code of Ethics and Professional Conduct requires project managers to act with honesty, integrity, and objectivity in all project-related activities, including financial management and reporting. Falsifying timesheets and expense reports constitutes fraud and is a serious breach of ethical standards, regardless of the motivations or personal circumstances of the individual involved. When a project manager discovers fraudulent activity, they have an obligation to report it to the appropriate authorities, such as their supervisor, the finance department, or the legal team, even if the perpetrator is a close friend or colleague. Overlooking the falsified records or asking the team member to stop without reporting would be a violation of the project manager's ethical duties and could expose the project and the organization to financial and legal risks. Offering to cover the team member's expenses personally would also be inappropriate and could be seen as enabling or condoning the fraudulent behavior. The project manager should maintain objectivity and professionalism, report the issue through the proper channels, and seek guidance on how to handle the personal relationship separately.

262. A project manager is approached by a senior executive who asks them to manipulate the project's financial data to make the project appear more profitable than it actually is. The executive suggests that this will help secure additional funding and resources for the project. What should the project manager do in this situation, according to the PMI Code of Ethics and Professional Conduct?
a. Comply with the executive's request to ensure the project's success and protect the team's jobs
b. Negotiate with the executive to find an alternative solution that does not involve manipulating data
c. Refuse to manipulate the financial data and report the executive's request to the appropriate authorities
d. Resign from the project to avoid being involved in any unethical behavior

Answer: c. Refuse to manipulate the financial data and report the executive's request to the appropriate authorities. Explanation: The PMI Code of Ethics and Professional Conduct requires project managers to maintain the highest standards of integrity, honesty, and accuracy in all project communications and reporting. Manipulating financial data to misrepresent the project's profitability is a form of fraud and a clear violation of ethical standards, even if it is requested by a senior executive or justified as a means to secure additional resources. The project manager has a professional and ethical obligation to refuse to engage in any fraudulent or deceptive practices and to report the executive's inappropriate request to the relevant authorities, such as the compliance department, the audit committee, or the board of directors. Complying with the request or negotiating an alternative solution that still involves unethical behavior would be a breach of the project manager's integrity and could lead to serious legal and reputational consequences for the project manager and the organization. Resigning from the project without reporting the issue would also be an abdication of the project manager's ethical responsibilities and could allow the unethical behavior to continue unchecked.

263. A project manager is leading a project team that includes members from different countries and cultural backgrounds. During a team-building exercise, one team member makes a joke that relies on cultural stereotypes and offends another team member. What should the project manager do to address this situation, according to the PMI Code of Ethics and Professional Conduct?
a. Ignore the incident and hope that the team members will resolve it among themselves
b. Publicly reprimand the team member who made the joke and demand an apology
c. Schedule a private meeting with the offended team member to express support and understand their concerns
d. Facilitate a team discussion about cultural sensitivity, respect, and the impact of stereotypes in the workplace

Answer: d. Facilitate a team discussion about cultural sensitivity, respect, and the impact of stereotypes in the workplace. Explanation: The PMI Code of Ethics and Professional Conduct emphasizes the importance of fostering a diverse, inclusive, and respectful work environment that values the contributions and dignity of all individuals. When a team member makes a joke that relies on cultural stereotypes and offends another team member, it is the project manager's responsibility to address the issue promptly and constructively. Ignoring the incident or hoping that the team members will resolve it themselves may send the message that such behavior is acceptable and could lead to further conflict and disengagement. Publicly reprimanding the team member who made the joke may embarrass them and create a hostile or retaliatory atmosphere. While expressing support to the offended team member is important, addressing the issue only in private may not prevent similar incidents from occurring in the future. The most effective approach is to facilitate a team discussion about cultural sensitivity, respect, and the impact of stereotypes in the workplace. The project manager should create a safe space for open and honest dialogue, encourage team members to share their perspectives and experiences, and establish clear expectations for respectful communication and behavior. This approach helps build mutual understanding, empathy, and trust among team members and reinforces the project manager's commitment to creating an inclusive team culture.

264. A project team is transitioning from a traditional Waterfall approach to Agile. According to the Agile Manifesto, what should the team prioritize?
a. Following a strict project plan
b. Comprehensive documentation
c. Customer collaboration
d. Contract negotiation

Answer: c. Customer collaboration. Explanation: The Agile Manifesto emphasizes customer collaboration over contract negotiation. This principle prioritizes ongoing engagement with customers to ensure their needs and feedback are continuously incorporated into the project.

265. In Agile methodologies, which role is responsible for maximizing the value of the product and managing the product backlog?
a. Scrum Master
b. Development Team
c. Product Owner
d. Project Sponsor

Answer: c. Product Owner. Explanation: The Product Owner is responsible for maximizing the value of the product by managing the product backlog, prioritizing features, and ensuring the development team understands the requirements.

266. During a sprint planning meeting, the team decides which items from the product backlog will be worked on during the sprint. What principle from the Agile Manifesto does this meeting best represent?
a. Responding to change over following a plan
b. Individuals and interactions over processes and tools
c. Customer collaboration over contract negotiation
d. Working software over comprehensive documentation

Answer: b. Individuals and interactions over processes and tools. Explanation: Sprint planning meetings emphasize collaboration among team members to determine what can be accomplished during the sprint, embodying the Agile principle of individuals and interactions over processes and tools.

267. A Scrum Master notices that the team is struggling with self-organization and effective communication. What type of leadership should the Scrum Master adopt to help the team improve?
a. Directive leadership
b. Servant leadership
c. Authoritative leadership
d. Transactional leadership

Answer: b. Servant leadership. Explanation: Servant leadership focuses on supporting and empowering the team to self-organize and improve communication. The Scrum Master should adopt this style to help the team develop these capabilities.

268. An Agile team is using a burndown chart to track progress during a sprint. What information does a burndown chart typically display?
a. The amount of work completed over time
b. The velocity of the team
c. The quality metrics of the product
d. The budget spent over time

Answer: a. The amount of work completed over time. Explanation: A burndown chart shows the amount of work remaining in a sprint or project over time, helping the team visualize their progress and predict whether they will complete the work on schedule.

269. During a sprint review, the team demonstrates the completed work to stakeholders. Which Agile principle is best represented by this practice?
a. Continuous attention to technical excellence
b. Welcome changing requirements, even late in development
c. Deliver working software frequently

d. Simplicity—the art of maximizing the amount of work not done

Answer: c. Deliver working software frequently. Explanation: Sprint reviews focus on demonstrating working software to stakeholders at the end of each sprint, aligning with the Agile principle of delivering working software frequently to ensure continuous feedback and improvement.

270. In an Agile project, who is primarily responsible for removing impediments that hinder the team's progress?
a. Product Owner
b. Project Manager
c. Scrum Master
d. Team Member

Answer: c. Scrum Master. Explanation: The Scrum Master is responsible for removing impediments that hinder the team's progress, enabling the team to focus on delivering value without unnecessary obstacles.

271. A product owner decides to prioritize a new feature based on customer feedback received during the previous sprint review. Which Agile principle does this action best reflect?
a. Simplicity—the art of maximizing the amount of work not done
b. Welcome changing requirements, even late in development
c. Build projects around motivated individuals
d. Business people and developers must work together daily

Answer: b. Welcome changing requirements, even late in development. Explanation: The decision to prioritize a new feature based on customer feedback aligns with the Agile principle of welcoming changing requirements, even late in development, to enhance customer satisfaction and product value.

272. The Agile team conducts a retrospective at the end of each sprint. What is the primary purpose of a sprint retrospective?
a. To plan the work for the next sprint
b. To review the product increment with stakeholders
c. To identify and implement improvements in the team's processes
d. To update the product backlog with new requirements

Answer: c. To identify and implement improvements in the team's processes. Explanation: A sprint retrospective focuses on reflecting on the team's processes, identifying what went well and what could be improved, and implementing changes to enhance future performance.

273. In an Agile project lifecycle, which event is time-boxed and aims to align the team on the daily plan and identify any impediments?
a. Sprint planning

b. Daily stand-up
c. Sprint review
d. Sprint retrospective

Answer: b. Daily stand-up. Explanation: The daily stand-up, also known as the daily scrum, is a time-boxed event where the team aligns on the daily plan, discusses progress, and identifies any impediments that need to be addressed.

274. A project manager is leading a team using the Scrum framework. Which of the following is not one of the core roles in Scrum?
a. Product Owner
b. Scrum Master
c. Development Team
d. Project Manager

Answer: d. Project Manager. Explanation: Scrum has three core roles: Product Owner, Scrum Master, and Development Team. The Project Manager role is not a part of the Scrum framework, as responsibilities are distributed among the three core roles.

275. In Kanban, what is the primary purpose of setting work-in-progress (WIP) limits?
a. To increase the speed of task completion
b. To limit the number of tasks a team can handle in a sprint
c. To identify bottlenecks and improve workflow
d. To prioritize tasks based on their complexity

Answer: c. To identify bottlenecks and improve workflow. Explanation: Setting WIP limits in Kanban helps identify bottlenecks in the workflow and encourages a smooth and efficient process by limiting the amount of work in progress at any given time.

276. A team practicing Extreme Programming (XP) decides to implement pair programming. What is the primary benefit of this practice?
a. Faster completion of tasks
b. Reduced number of defects
c. Improved stakeholder communication
d. Increased project documentation

Answer: b. Reduced number of defects. Explanation: Pair programming involves two developers working together at one workstation, leading to higher code quality and reduced defects due to continuous code review and collaboration.

277. In Lean methodology, which principle focuses on delivering value to the customer as quickly as possible?
a. Eliminate waste
b. Amplify learning
c. Deliver fast
d. Empower the team

Answer: c. Deliver fast. Explanation: The Lean principle of "Deliver fast" focuses on delivering value to the customer quickly and efficiently by optimizing the flow of work and minimizing delays.

278. A project team is using Feature-Driven Development (FDD) to manage their project. Which activity is the first step in FDD's five basic activities?
a. Develop an overall model
b. Build a feature list
c. Plan by feature
d. Design by feature

Answer: a. Develop an overall model. Explanation: The first step in Feature-Driven Development (FDD) is to develop an overall model, which provides a high-level understanding of the system and its key components.

279. In Dynamic Systems Development Method (DSDM), which principle emphasizes the importance of involving stakeholders throughout the project?
a. Focus on frequent delivery of products
b. Collaborative and cooperative approach
c. Prioritize requirements based on business need
d. Incremental and iterative development

Answer: b. Collaborative and cooperative approach. Explanation: The DSDM principle of a collaborative and cooperative approach emphasizes involving stakeholders throughout the project to ensure their needs and expectations are met.

280. A Scrum team is conducting a Sprint Retrospective. What is the primary goal of this event?
a. To plan the work for the next sprint
b. To review the product increment and get feedback from stakeholders
c. To reflect on the past sprint and identify improvements
d. To refine the product backlog

Answer: c. To reflect on the past sprint and identify improvements. Explanation: The primary goal of the Sprint Retrospective is to reflect on the past sprint, discuss what went well and what didn't, and identify improvements for the next sprint to enhance team performance and processes.

281. In Kanban, what is a cumulative flow diagram (CFD) used for?
a. To visualize the progress of tasks through the workflow
b. To estimate the duration of future tasks
c. To prioritize tasks based on their impact
d. To manage stakeholder expectations

Answer: a. To visualize the progress of tasks through the workflow. Explanation: A cumulative flow diagram (CFD) is used in Kanban to visualize the progress of tasks through the workflow. It shows the quantity of tasks in each stage over time, helping identify bottlenecks and improve flow efficiency.

282. An Agile team is using the MoSCoW method to prioritize requirements. What does the "C" in MoSCoW stand for?
a. Critical
b. Could have
c. Continuous
d. Cost-effective

Answer: b. Could have. Explanation: In the MoSCoW method, the "C" stands for "Could have," which represents requirements that are desirable but not essential for the current delivery, allowing for flexibility in prioritization.

283. A team using Scrum has completed the sprint planning and is now in the middle of the sprint. The team realizes that a critical task was missed during planning. What should they do?
a. Add the task to the current sprint backlog
b. Wait until the next sprint to address the task
c. Escalate the issue to the Scrum Master
d. Cancel the current sprint and re-plan

Answer: a. Add the task to the current sprint backlog. Explanation: In Scrum, if a critical task is identified during a sprint, the team should add it to the current sprint backlog. The Scrum framework is flexible and allows the team to adapt to changes during the sprint to ensure critical tasks are completed.

284. A product owner and the Agile team are planning the release of a new software feature. They need to determine the overall goals and high-level timeline for delivering the feature. What type of planning are they performing?
a. Iteration planning
b. Sprint planning
c. Release planning
d. Daily stand-up planning

Answer: c. Release planning. Explanation: Release planning involves setting overall goals, defining a high-level timeline, and identifying key milestones for delivering a new software feature or product increment. It provides a strategic roadmap for the release.

285. During iteration planning, the team commits to completing a set of user stories in the upcoming sprint. What is the primary purpose of this planning activity?
a. To allocate resources for the project
b. To define the scope of work for the iteration
c. To review the project budget
d. To update the project schedule

Answer: b. To define the scope of work for the iteration. Explanation: Iteration planning, also known as sprint planning, involves defining the scope of work for the upcoming iteration. The team commits to completing a set of user stories, which forms the basis of the work to be done during the sprint.

286. In a daily stand-up meeting, each team member answers three key questions. Which of the following is NOT one of these questions?
a. What did I do yesterday?
b. What will I do today?
c. What impediments are in my way?
d. How much budget is remaining?

Answer: d. How much budget is remaining? Explanation: The three key questions in a daily stand-up meeting are: What did I do yesterday? What will I do today? What impediments are in my way? These questions help the team stay aligned and identify any obstacles to progress.

287. A Scrum team is conducting a sprint review at the end of the sprint. Which of the following best describes the purpose of the sprint review?
a. To plan the next sprint
b. To demonstrate the work completed during the sprint to stakeholders
c. To identify process improvements
d. To allocate resources for the next sprint

Answer: b. To demonstrate the work completed during the sprint to stakeholders. Explanation: The sprint review is a meeting where the Scrum team demonstrates the work completed during the sprint to stakeholders. It provides an opportunity for feedback and ensures the product is meeting expectations.

288. During a sprint retrospective, the team discusses what went well and what could be improved. What is the primary goal of this meeting?
a. To plan the next sprint
b. To review the product backlog
c. To identify and implement process improvements
d. To assign tasks for the next sprint

Answer: c. To identify and implement process improvements. Explanation: The primary goal of a sprint retrospective is to reflect on the team's processes, identify what went well and what could be improved, and implement changes to enhance future performance and team collaboration.

289. A product owner needs to prioritize user stories for the upcoming sprint. Which Agile principle is most relevant to this activity?
a. Continuous attention to technical excellence
b. Welcome changing requirements, even late in development
c. Deliver working software frequently
d. The highest priority is to satisfy the customer through early and continuous delivery of valuable software

Answer: d. The highest priority is to satisfy the customer through early and continuous delivery of valuable software. Explanation: Prioritizing user stories aligns with the Agile principle that the highest priority is to satisfy the customer through early and continuous delivery of valuable software. This ensures that the most important and valuable features are developed first.

290. During a release planning session, the team uses velocity to estimate how many iterations will be needed to complete the release. What does velocity measure in Agile projects?
a. The number of user stories completed per iteration
b. The team's capacity to perform work in a given iteration
c. The total effort required to complete the project
d. The speed at which the team delivers code

Answer: a. The number of user stories completed per iteration. Explanation: Velocity measures the amount of work (typically in user stories or story points) that a team can complete in a single iteration. It helps in estimating the number of iterations needed to complete the release.

291. In Agile planning, which artifact is used to capture all the work items and requirements for a product?
a. Sprint backlog
b. Product backlog
c. Burndown chart
d. Task board

Answer: b. Product backlog. Explanation: The product backlog is an ordered list of all the work items and requirements for a product. It includes user stories, features, and technical tasks, and it is maintained by the product owner.

292. A Scrum Master facilitates a daily stand-up meeting. What is the recommended duration for this meeting?
a. 15 minutes
b. 30 minutes
c. 45 minutes

d. 60 minutes

Answer: a. 15 minutes. Explanation: The daily stand-up meeting, also known as the daily scrum, is time-boxed to 15 minutes. This short duration ensures that the meeting remains focused and efficient, allowing the team to quickly synchronize and identify any impediments.

293. During iteration planning, the team decides to break down a complex user story into smaller tasks. What is the primary benefit of this approach?
a. It reduces the overall project cost
b. It increases the team's velocity
c. It makes the work more manageable and trackable
d. It eliminates the need for a product backlog

Answer: c. It makes the work more manageable and trackable. Explanation: Breaking down a complex user story into smaller tasks makes the work more manageable and trackable. This allows the team to better estimate, assign, and monitor progress on individual tasks, leading to more accurate planning and execution.

294. During a sprint planning meeting, the team uses Planning Poker to estimate the effort required for user stories. Which of the following is a key advantage of using Planning Poker for estimation?
a. It provides a precise numerical estimate of effort.
b. It eliminates the need for further discussion once an estimate is chosen.
c. It encourages team collaboration and consensus-building.
d. It speeds up the estimation process by avoiding lengthy discussions.

Answer: c. It encourages team collaboration and consensus-building. Explanation: Planning Poker is a collaborative estimation technique that encourages team discussion and consensus-building. It helps ensure that all team members contribute their perspectives, leading to more accurate and agreed-upon estimates.

295. A project manager wants to track the team's progress using a burndown chart. What does the y-axis typically represent on a burndown chart?
a. Time remaining in the sprint
b. Effort remaining in story points or hours
c. Number of completed tasks
d. Team velocity

Answer: b. Effort remaining in story points or hours. Explanation: The y-axis on a burndown chart typically represents the effort remaining, measured in story points or hours. The x-axis represents time, showing the progression of effort remaining over the duration of the sprint.

296. A team estimates a user story to be 8 story points. During the sprint, they realize it was more complex than anticipated and requires additional effort. What should the team do regarding the story points?
a. Increase the story points for the user story
b. Split the user story into smaller tasks and re-estimate
c. Complete the user story without changing the story points
d. Move the user story to the next sprint and re-estimate

Answer: c. Complete the user story without changing the story points. Explanation: Once a user story is estimated and committed to a sprint, the story points should not be changed. The team should complete the user story and use the experience to inform future estimates. Adjusting story points retroactively can distort velocity measurements.

297. The team's velocity for the last three sprints was 30, 25, and 35 story points. What is the team's average velocity?
a. 25 story points
b. 30 story points
c. 35 story points
d. 40 story points

Answer: b. 30 story points. Explanation: The average velocity is calculated by adding the total story points completed in the last three sprints and dividing by the number of sprints. (30 + 25 + 35) / 3 = 30 story points.

298. A product owner is concerned about the accuracy of the team's estimates. Which Agile estimation technique uses historical data from past sprints to improve future estimates?
a. Planning Poker
b. Relative sizing
c. Affinity estimation
d. Velocity tracking

Answer: d. Velocity tracking. Explanation: Velocity tracking uses historical data from past sprints to understand the team's capacity and improve the accuracy of future estimates. It helps in predicting how much work the team can complete in upcoming sprints.

299. During a sprint, the team discovers that several user stories were underestimated. How should this be addressed in future sprint planning sessions?
a. Adjust the story points for completed user stories in the current sprint.
b. Use the knowledge gained to improve estimation accuracy for future sprints.
c. Extend the sprint duration to accommodate the additional work.
d. Reduce the number of user stories planned for each sprint.

Answer: b. Use the knowledge gained to improve estimation accuracy for future sprints. Explanation: The team should use the knowledge gained from the underestimations to improve estimation accuracy in future sprint planning sessions. This helps in better predicting the effort required for user stories and planning more effectively.

300. A team is using a burndown chart to monitor sprint progress. Halfway through the sprint, the chart shows that the team is behind schedule. What should the team do?
a. Re-estimate all remaining tasks
b. Increase the team's working hours
c. Identify and address any impediments
d. Extend the sprint duration

Answer: c. Identify and address any impediments. Explanation: If the burndown chart shows that the team is behind schedule, the team should identify and address any impediments that might be slowing down progress. Removing obstacles can help the team get back on track without extending the sprint duration.

301. The team has consistently been unable to complete all planned user stories within a sprint. Which action is most appropriate to take during sprint planning to address this issue?
a. Increase the number of user stories planned for the sprint to build momentum
b. Assign more story points to each user story
c. Plan fewer user stories based on the team's average velocity
d. Change the definition of done to make tasks easier to complete

Answer: c. Plan fewer user stories based on the team's average velocity. Explanation: The team should plan fewer user stories based on their average velocity to ensure that they can complete all planned work within the sprint. This helps in setting realistic expectations and improving the team's ability to meet sprint goals.

302. A project manager is reviewing the team's use of story points for estimation. Which statement best describes the purpose of using story points in Agile estimation?
a. Story points measure the exact time required to complete a task.
b. Story points provide a relative measure of effort and complexity.
c. Story points are used to prioritize tasks by importance.
d. Story points are assigned based on the skill level of the team members.

Answer: b. Story points provide a relative measure of effort and complexity. Explanation: Story points are a relative measure of the effort and complexity required to complete a user story. They help the team estimate work based on past experiences and comparisons, rather than exact time measurements.

303. A development team is using user stories to capture requirements. Which component of a user story ensures it is valuable to the end user?
a. The acceptance criteria
b. The story points
c. The definition of done

d. The INVEST criteria

Answer: a. The acceptance criteria. Explanation: Acceptance criteria define the conditions that must be met for a user story to be considered complete and ensure that the story delivers value to the end user by meeting their needs and expectations.

304. During backlog grooming, the product owner works with the team to refine and prioritize user stories. Which of the following activities is NOT typically part of backlog grooming?
a. Estimating the effort required for user stories
b. Adding detailed tasks for each user story
c. Reprioritizing user stories based on current priorities
d. Breaking down large stories into smaller ones

Answer: b. Adding detailed tasks for each user story. Explanation: Backlog grooming involves refining user stories, estimating effort, reprioritizing, and breaking down large stories. Adding detailed tasks is usually done during sprint planning, not backlog grooming.

305. A team practicing continuous integration ensures that code changes are frequently merged into the main codebase. What is the primary benefit of continuous integration?
a. Reducing the time needed for code reviews
b. Preventing integration problems and defects
c. Increasing the speed of development
d. Simplifying the deployment process

Answer: b. Preventing integration problems and defects. Explanation: Continuous integration helps prevent integration problems and defects by ensuring that code changes are frequently merged and tested, allowing issues to be identified and fixed early in the development process.

306. In test-driven development (TDD), what is the correct order of steps for implementing a new feature?
a. Write tests, write code, refactor code
b. Write code, write tests, refactor code
c. Refactor code, write tests, write code
d. Write code, refactor code, write tests

Answer: a. Write tests, write code, refactor code. Explanation: In TDD, the correct order is to write tests first, then write the code to pass the tests, and finally refactor the code to improve its structure while ensuring that all tests still pass.

307. Behavior-driven development (BDD) uses natural language to describe test cases. Which format is commonly used in BDD to write these test cases?

a. Given-When-Then
b. Arrange-Act-Assert
c. Setup-Test-Teardown
d. Precondition-Action-Postcondition

Answer: a. Given-When-Then. Explanation: BDD uses the Given-When-Then format to describe test cases in natural language, making them understandable to both technical and non-technical stakeholders and ensuring clear communication of requirements.

308. A product owner wants to ensure that user stories are well-defined and actionable. Which criteria should be used to evaluate the quality of user stories?
a. SMART criteria
b. MoSCoW criteria
c. INVEST criteria
d. RACI criteria

Answer: c. INVEST criteria. Explanation: The INVEST criteria (Independent, Negotiable, Valuable, Estimable, Small, Testable) help ensure that user stories are well-defined, actionable, and of high quality, making them easier to manage and implement.

309. The development team is using continuous deployment to automatically release new code to production. What is a key challenge associated with continuous deployment?
a. Maintaining code quality
b. Reducing deployment costs
c. Increasing code complexity
d. Managing customer feedback

Answer: a. Maintaining code quality. Explanation: Continuous deployment requires rigorous automated testing and monitoring to ensure that code quality is maintained and that defects do not reach production, as changes are deployed automatically and frequently.

310. In a BDD scenario, what role does the "Then" clause typically represent?
a. The initial state before an action
b. The action taken by the user
c. The expected outcome after the action
d. The setup required for the test

Answer: c. The expected outcome after the action. Explanation: In BDD, the "Then" clause represents the expected outcome after the action specified in the "When" clause has been performed, validating that the system behaves as expected.

311. During backlog grooming, the team identifies a user story that is too large to be completed in a single sprint. What is the recommended approach to handle this situation?
a. Postpone the story to a later sprint
b. Break the story into smaller, more manageable stories
c. Increase the sprint duration
d. Assign more team members to the story

Answer: b. Break the story into smaller, more manageable stories. Explanation: The recommended approach is to break down the large user story into smaller, more manageable stories that can be completed within a single sprint, ensuring better progress tracking and deliverability.

312. A team practicing TDD is working on a new feature. They notice that their tests cover most of the functionality but are missing some edge cases. What should the team do next?
a. Refactor the code to improve coverage
b. Add tests for the edge cases and then refactor the code
c. Deploy the feature and add edge case tests later
d. Focus on writing more code and less on testing

Answer: b. Add tests for the edge cases and then refactor the code. Explanation: The team should add tests for the edge cases to ensure comprehensive coverage and then refactor the code. TDD emphasizes writing tests for all cases, including edge cases, before refactoring to maintain high-quality code.

313. A project manager is analyzing the team's efficiency using cycle time. Which of the following best defines cycle time in an Agile project?
a. The total time from the start to the end of the project
b. The time taken to complete one iteration or sprint
c. The time taken from the start of work on a task to its completion
d. The total time taken to plan and execute a project

Answer: c. The time taken from the start of work on a task to its completion. Explanation: Cycle time measures the time taken from the moment work starts on a task until it is completed. It is a key metric in Agile for evaluating the efficiency of the team's workflow.

314. In a Kanban system, what does lead time measure?
a. The time taken to complete the entire project
b. The time taken for a task to move through the entire workflow from request to delivery
c. The time taken for the team to plan and prioritize tasks
d. The time taken to complete a single iteration

Answer: b. The time taken for a task to move through the entire workflow from request to delivery. Explanation: Lead time measures the total time taken for a task to move from the initial request through the entire workflow to delivery. It helps in understanding the overall efficiency of the process from a customer's perspective.

315. A project manager uses a cumulative flow diagram (CFD) to analyze the team's workflow. Which key insight can be gained from a CFD?
a. The team's average velocity
b. The distribution of work across different workflow stages
c. The specific causes of defects in the product
d. The team's ability to complete sprints on time

Answer: b. The distribution of work across different workflow stages. Explanation: A cumulative flow diagram (CFD) visualizes the distribution of work across different stages of the workflow over time. It helps identify bottlenecks and understand the flow of tasks through the system.

316. The team is concerned about a bottleneck in their workflow. Which part of the cumulative flow diagram should the project manager examine to identify this issue?
a. The area where the bands are widest
b. The total height of the diagram
c. The point where the bands converge
d. The rate of increase in the bands

Answer: a. The area where the bands are widest. Explanation: In a cumulative flow diagram, a bottleneck can be identified where the bands representing different workflow stages are widest. This indicates that tasks are accumulating in that stage and not progressing efficiently.

317. A project manager wants to reduce the lead time for user stories. Which of the following strategies would be most effective?
a. Increase the team's velocity
b. Limit the work in progress (WIP)
c. Extend the length of iterations
d. Increase the number of team members

Answer: b. Limit the work in progress (WIP). Explanation: Limiting the work in progress (WIP) helps reduce lead time by ensuring that the team focuses on completing tasks before starting new ones. This reduces bottlenecks and improves workflow efficiency.

318. During a sprint review, the team notices that their cycle time has increased. What is the most likely cause of this increase?
a. The team has increased the number of user stories in the sprint
b. The team has reduced the sprint length
c. The complexity of tasks has increased

d. The team has improved their estimation accuracy

Answer: c. The complexity of tasks has increased. Explanation: An increase in cycle time is often due to an increase in the complexity of tasks. More complex tasks take longer to complete, resulting in longer cycle times.

319. A project manager is comparing cycle time and lead time metrics. Which statement accurately describes the difference between these two metrics?
a. Cycle time includes waiting time, while lead time does not
b. Lead time includes the entire process from request to delivery, while cycle time only includes the active work time
c. Cycle time is measured in story points, while lead time is measured in hours
d. Lead time is always shorter than cycle time

Answer: b. Lead time includes the entire process from request to delivery, while cycle time only includes the active work time. Explanation: Lead time measures the total time from the initial request to delivery, including any waiting time. Cycle time measures the time taken for active work on a task from start to completion.

320. A cumulative flow diagram shows that the "in-progress" band is steadily increasing. What does this indicate about the team's workflow?
a. The team is completing tasks faster than new tasks are being added
b. The team is struggling to complete tasks, leading to an accumulation of work in progress
c. The team has a consistent velocity
d. The team is adding more tasks to the backlog

Answer: b. The team is struggling to complete tasks, leading to an accumulation of work in progress. Explanation: An increasing "in-progress" band in a cumulative flow diagram indicates that tasks are accumulating in the in-progress stage, suggesting a bottleneck or inefficiency in completing tasks.

321. To improve cycle time, a project manager decides to analyze the workflow. Which metric should they focus on to identify the stages causing delays?
a. Velocity
b. Throughput
c. WIP limits
d. Touch time

Answer: d. Touch time. Explanation: Touch time refers to the actual time spent working on a task, excluding waiting time. Analyzing touch time can help identify stages in the workflow that are causing delays and areas where efficiency can be improved.

322. A project manager wants to visualize the progress of tasks and identify bottlenecks in the workflow. Which tool should they use?

a. Gantt chart
b. Burndown chart
c. Cumulative flow diagram
d. Velocity chart

Answer: c. Cumulative flow diagram. Explanation: A cumulative flow diagram (CFD) is used to visualize the progress of tasks through different stages of the workflow and identify bottlenecks. It provides a clear picture of the flow of work and helps in identifying areas for improvement.

323. A project manager is considering using an Agile approach for a new software development project. Which of the following is not one of the four core values of the Agile Manifesto?
a. Individuals and interactions over processes and tools
b. Working software over comprehensive documentation
c. Customer collaboration over contract negotiation
d. Following a plan over responding to change

Answer: d. Following a plan over responding to change. Explanation: The Agile Manifesto, a guiding set of principles for Agile software development, emphasizes four core values: individuals and interactions over processes and tools, working software over comprehensive documentation, customer collaboration over contract negotiation, and responding to change over following a plan. Agile methodologies prioritize flexibility, adaptability, and continuous improvement, recognizing that requirements and circumstances may evolve throughout the project lifecycle. The manifesto does not value following a rigid plan over responding to change; in fact, it advocates for embracing change and adjusting plans accordingly to deliver the most value to the customer.

324. In Scrum, a product backlog item is considered "Done" when:
a. The development team has completed coding the item
b. The product owner has approved the item
c. The item has been fully tested and meets the defined acceptance criteria
d. The item has been added to the sprint backlog

Answer: c. The item has been fully tested and meets the defined acceptance criteria. Explanation: In Scrum, the concept of "Done" refers to the shared understanding and agreement among the team members about what constitutes a complete, releasable increment of work. A product backlog item is considered "Done" when it has been fully developed, tested, and meets the predefined acceptance criteria, which are specific conditions that the item must satisfy to be accepted by the product owner and stakeholders. Completing the coding alone does not make an item "Done," as it may still contain defects or fail to meet the required quality standards. The product owner's approval is important, but it is based on the item meeting the acceptance criteria. Adding an item to the sprint backlog does not make it "Done," as it still needs to be developed and tested during the sprint.

325. Which of the following is not one of the three main roles in Scrum?
a. Scrum Master
b. Product Owner
c. Development Team

d. Project Manager

Answer: d. Project Manager. Explanation: Scrum, an Agile framework for managing complex projects, defines three core roles: the Scrum Master, the Product Owner, and the Development Team. The Scrum Master is responsible for ensuring that the Scrum process is followed, facilitating team communication and collaboration, and removing any impediments to progress. The Product Owner represents the stakeholders' interests, defines and prioritizes the product backlog, and ensures that the team delivers value to the business. The Development Team is a cross-functional, self-organizing group of professionals who are responsible for developing and delivering the product increment in each sprint. Scrum does not include a traditional Project Manager role, as the responsibilities of project management are distributed among the Scrum roles, with the team collectively managing and adapting their work.

326. In Kanban, what is the purpose of setting Work in Progress (WIP) limits?
a. To ensure that the team always has a backlog of tasks to work on
b. To maximize resource utilization and keep everyone busy
c. To create a pull system and improve the flow of work through the process
d. To track the time spent on each task and identify bottlenecks

Answer: c. To create a pull system and improve the flow of work through the process. Explanation: Kanban is an Agile method that focuses on visualizing the workflow, limiting work in progress (WIP), and optimizing the flow of work through the system. WIP limits are constraints placed on the number of tasks that can be in progress at each stage of the workflow. The purpose of setting WIP limits is to create a pull system, where new work is started only when there is capacity available, rather than pushing work onto the team based on a predefined schedule. By limiting WIP, the team can focus on completing existing tasks before starting new ones, reducing context switching and improving the overall flow of work. WIP limits also help identify bottlenecks and constraints in the process, as tasks will accumulate before a bottleneck, signaling the need for process improvement. The goal is not to keep everyone busy or maximize resource utilization, but rather to optimize the throughput and minimize the lead time for delivering value to the customer.

327. Which of the following is not one of the five values of Extreme Programming (XP)?
a. Communication
b. Simplicity
c. Feedback
d. Individualism

Answer: d. Individualism. Explanation: Extreme Programming (XP) is an Agile methodology that emphasizes five core values: communication, simplicity, feedback, courage, and respect. Communication refers to the importance of open, honest, and frequent communication among team members, customers, and stakeholders. Simplicity means focusing on the essentials, writing clean and maintainable code, and avoiding unnecessary complexity. Feedback involves continuous testing, regular customer reviews, and embracing change based on feedback. Courage refers to the willingness to make difficult decisions, admit mistakes, and adapt to changing circumstances. Respect means valuing and trusting each team member's contributions, promoting a collaborative and inclusive environment. Individualism, which emphasizes personal autonomy and independence, is not one of the core values of XP. Instead, XP stresses the importance of teamwork, collective ownership, and a shared commitment to delivering high-quality software.

328. Which of the following best describes the role of the product owner in Scrum?
a. Writing user stories and acceptance criteria
b. Facilitating daily stand-up meetings and removing impediments
c. Prioritizing the product backlog and representing the stakeholders' interests
d. Designing and implementing the technical architecture of the product

Answer: c. Prioritizing the product backlog and representing the stakeholders' interests. Explanation: In Scrum, the product owner is a key role responsible for maximizing the value of the product and representing the interests of stakeholders, including customers, users, and the business. The primary responsibilities of the product owner include defining and prioritizing the product backlog, which is an ordered list of features, requirements, and improvements that the team will work on. The product owner ensures that the backlog items are clearly defined, prioritized based on value and risk, and aligned with the overall product vision and strategy. While the product owner may collaborate with the team in writing user stories and acceptance criteria, this is not their sole responsibility. The Scrum Master is responsible for facilitating meetings, removing impediments, and ensuring the team follows the Scrum process. The development team is responsible for designing, implementing, and testing the product increment. The product owner provides guidance, makes decisions, and adapts the backlog based on feedback and changing business needs.

329. In the context of Agile estimation, what is the purpose of planning poker?
a. To assign tasks to individual team members based on their skills and availability
b. To estimate the relative size and complexity of user stories using consensus-based sizing
c. To determine the project budget and allocate resources across sprints
d. To track the team's velocity and predict the completion date of the project

Answer: b. To estimate the relative size and complexity of user stories using consensus-based sizing. Explanation: Planning poker, also known as Scrum poker or pointing poker, is a consensus-based estimation technique used in Agile methodologies, particularly in Scrum. The purpose of planning poker is to estimate the relative size and complexity of user stories or backlog items, rather than estimating the absolute time required to complete them. In a planning poker session, each team member has a deck of cards with values representing relative sizes, such as Fibonacci numbers or t-shirt sizes (e.g., XS, S, M, L, XL). For each user story, the team members privately select a card that represents their estimate of the story's size. The cards are then revealed simultaneously, and if there is a wide divergence in estimates, the team discusses the reasons for the differences and reaches a consensus on the final estimate. Planning poker promotes collaboration, knowledge sharing, and a shared understanding of the work to be done. It helps surface assumptions, uncertainties, and dependencies that may impact the estimate. The goal is not to assign tasks, determine the budget, or track velocity, but rather to establish a relative sizing of the work that can be used for prioritization and sprint planning.

330. What is the main purpose of a sprint retrospective in Scrum?
a. To demonstrate the completed work to stakeholders and gather feedback
b. To plan the next sprint and estimate the user stories to be included
c. To reflect on the previous sprint and identify improvements for the next sprint
d. To update the product backlog and reprioritize the remaining user stories

Answer: c. To reflect on the previous sprint and identify improvements for the next sprint. Explanation: In Scrum, the sprint retrospective is a meeting held at the end of each sprint where the team reflects on their process, teamwork, and performance during the previous sprint and identifies areas for improvement. The purpose of the sprint retrospective is to foster continuous improvement, adapt the team's practices, and enhance their effectiveness in future sprints. During the retrospective, the team discusses what went well, what didn't go well, and what can be improved in the next sprint. They may use techniques like "Start, Stop, Continue" or "Glad, Sad, Mad" to structure the conversation and gather insights. The outcome of the retrospective is a set of actionable improvements that the team commits to implementing in the upcoming sprint. The retrospective is not focused on demonstrating work to stakeholders, planning the next sprint, or updating the product backlog, as these activities are covered in other Scrum events like the sprint review and sprint planning. The retrospective is a crucial opportunity for the team to learn, adapt, and continuously improve their Agile practices.

331. Which of the following is not a typical artifact in Scrum?
a. Product backlog
b. Sprint backlog
c. Increment
d. Gantt chart

Answer: d. Gantt chart. Explanation: In Scrum, there are three primary artifacts that provide transparency and enable inspection and adaptation: the product backlog, the sprint backlog, and the increment. The product backlog is an ordered list of features, requirements, and improvements that define the product's future state. It is maintained and prioritized by the product owner and serves as the single source of work for the development team. The sprint backlog is a subset of the product backlog that the team commits to delivering in a sprint. It includes the specific user stories, tasks, and deliverables that the team will work on during the sprint. The increment is the sum of all the completed product backlog items at the end of a sprint. It represents a potentially shippable product that meets the definition of "Done" and can be released to users if desired. A Gantt chart, which is a visual representation of a project schedule with tasks, dependencies, and timelines, is not a typical artifact in Scrum. Scrum emphasizes flexibility, adaptability, and self-organization, rather than detailed upfront planning and rigid timelines. While a Gantt chart may be used in traditional project management, it is not a core artifact in the Scrum framework.

332. Which of the following best describes the concept of "timeboxing" in Agile methodologies?
a. Allocating a fixed amount of time for each user story based on its complexity
b. Limiting the duration of meetings to ensure they are productive and focused
c. Setting a fixed end date for the project and working backwards to determine the scope
d. Dedicating a fixed period of time to complete a specific set of work, such as a sprint

Answer: d. Dedicating a fixed period of time to complete a specific set of work, such as a sprint. Explanation: Timeboxing is a core principle in Agile methodologies that involves allocating a fixed, maximum duration for an activity, event, or iteration. The purpose of timeboxing is to create a sense of urgency, focus, and discipline, and to prevent work from expanding indefinitely. In Scrum, timeboxing is applied to sprints, which are fixed-duration iterations (usually 1-4 weeks) in which the team commits to delivering a potentially releasable increment of work. The team works within the constraints of the sprint timebox to complete the agreed-upon set of user stories and tasks. Timeboxing is also applied to Scrum events, such as the daily stand-up meeting, which is typically limited to 15 minutes, and the sprint planning meeting, which is usually timeboxed to 8 hours for a one-month sprint. Timeboxing helps the team prioritize, make trade-offs, and deliver value incrementally, rather than aiming for perfection or spending excessive time on a single task. While timeboxing can be used to limit the duration of meetings or set a fixed end date for the project, its primary application in Agile is to dedicate a fixed period of time to complete a specific set of work, such as a sprint.

333. A project manager is planning the business analysis approach for a new project. Which of the following is a key consideration in this planning process?
a. The project budget
b. The stakeholders' availability and location
c. The project timeline
d. The technical complexity of the solution

Answer: b. The stakeholders' availability and location. Explanation: When planning the business analysis approach, it is crucial to consider the stakeholders' availability and location. This ensures effective communication and collaboration throughout the project.

334. During stakeholder analysis, a business analyst needs to identify the influence and interest of stakeholders. Which tool or technique is most appropriate for this task?
a. SWOT analysis
b. RACI matrix
c. Stakeholder register
d. Stakeholder mapping

Answer: d. Stakeholder mapping. Explanation: Stakeholder mapping is a technique used to analyze stakeholders by plotting their level of influence and interest. This helps in identifying key stakeholders and planning appropriate engagement strategies.

335. A business analyst is developing the Business Analysis Communication Plan. What is the primary purpose of this document?
a. To outline the project budget and resource allocation
b. To define how information will be communicated to stakeholders
c. To detail the technical requirements of the project
d. To establish the project timeline and milestones

Answer: b. To define how information will be communicated to stakeholders. Explanation: The Business Analysis Communication Plan outlines how information will be communicated to stakeholders, ensuring that they receive timely, relevant, and accurate information throughout the project.

336. In the Requirements Management Plan, which element describes how changes to requirements will be managed and tracked?
a. Requirements traceability matrix
b. Change control process
c. Requirements validation
d. Risk management plan

Answer: b. Change control process. Explanation: The change control process in the Requirements Management Plan describes how changes to requirements will be managed and tracked, ensuring that any modifications are documented and approved.

337. A business analyst is conducting a stakeholder analysis and needs to determine each stakeholder's communication needs. Which of the following is NOT a typical output of this analysis?
a. Stakeholder engagement plan
b. Communication requirements
c. Stakeholder register
d. Project scope statement

Answer: d. Project scope statement. Explanation: The project scope statement is not a typical output of stakeholder analysis. Stakeholder analysis focuses on identifying communication requirements, stakeholder register, and stakeholder engagement plan.

338. During the planning phase, a business analyst creates a RACI matrix. What is the primary purpose of this document?
a. To define the project budget and resources
b. To assign roles and responsibilities for project tasks
c. To document technical requirements
d. To develop the project schedule

Answer: b. To assign roles and responsibilities for project tasks. Explanation: A RACI matrix is used to assign roles and responsibilities for project tasks, ensuring clarity on who is Responsible, Accountable, Consulted, and Informed for each task.

339. When developing the Business Analysis Communication Plan, a business analyst needs to consider the frequency and format of communication. Which factor is most important to ensure effective communication?
a. The project budget
b. The stakeholders' preferences and needs
c. The project timeline
d. The technical complexity of the solution

Answer: b. The stakeholders' preferences and needs. Explanation: To ensure effective communication, it is crucial to consider the stakeholders' preferences and needs regarding the frequency and format of communication. This ensures that stakeholders receive information in a way that is most useful to them.

340. A business analyst is creating a requirements traceability matrix. What is the primary purpose of this document?
a. To outline the project timeline and milestones

b. To ensure all requirements are linked to their origins and tracked throughout the project lifecycle
c. To allocate resources and define the project budget
d. To document the technical specifications of the project

Answer: b. To ensure all requirements are linked to their origins and tracked throughout the project lifecycle. Explanation: The requirements traceability matrix links requirements to their origins and tracks them throughout the project lifecycle, ensuring that all requirements are addressed and met.

341. In the Requirements Management Plan, the business analyst defines how requirements will be prioritized. Which technique is commonly used for this purpose?
a. MoSCoW analysis
b. SWOT analysis
c. Root cause analysis
d. Monte Carlo simulation

Answer: a. MoSCoW analysis. Explanation: MoSCoW analysis is a technique used to prioritize requirements by categorizing them as Must have, Should have, Could have, and Won't have. This helps in focusing on the most critical requirements first.

342. A business analyst is preparing a communication plan for a project with multiple stakeholders, including senior executives and end-users. Which of the following is a key consideration when tailoring the communication plan for these different stakeholder groups?
a. The project budget
b. The complexity of the technical solution
c. The specific information needs and preferences of each stakeholder group
d. The geographical location of the project team

Answer: c. The specific information needs and preferences of each stakeholder group. Explanation: Tailoring the communication plan involves considering the specific information needs and preferences of each stakeholder group to ensure that they receive relevant and understandable information.

343. A project manager is conducting interviews with stakeholders to gather requirements for a new project. Which of the following is a key advantage of using interviews as a requirements elicitation technique?
a. They provide quantitative data that is easy to analyze.
b. They allow for in-depth exploration of stakeholder needs.
c. They are quick to conduct and require minimal preparation.
d. They are suitable for gathering requirements from large groups simultaneously.

Answer: b. They allow for in-depth exploration of stakeholder needs. Explanation: Interviews are beneficial for gaining a deep understanding of stakeholder needs, preferences, and expectations. They enable the project manager to ask follow-up questions and clarify responses, leading to more detailed and accurate requirements.

344. During a requirements elicitation workshop, the project manager uses brainstorming to generate ideas. Which of the following best describes the primary benefit of brainstorming in this context?
a. It ensures that all participants agree on the requirements.
b. It generates a large number of ideas quickly.
c. It provides a structured format for documenting requirements.
d. It allows for anonymous input from stakeholders.

Answer: b. It generates a large number of ideas quickly. Explanation: Brainstorming is an effective technique for generating a large number of ideas in a short period. It encourages creativity and participation from all workshop attendees, helping to identify a wide range of requirements.

345. A project team is using document analysis to identify requirements for a software upgrade. Which type of document would be least useful for this purpose?
a. Current system documentation
b. User manuals for the existing software
c. Market research reports on competitor products
d. Organizational process assets

Answer: d. Organizational process assets. Explanation: Organizational process assets, while useful for general project management practices, are not directly relevant for identifying specific requirements for a software upgrade. Current system documentation, user manuals, and market research reports provide more specific and relevant information.

346. Prototyping is being used to gather requirements for a new user interface. What is the main advantage of using prototyping in requirements elicitation?
a. It reduces the overall project timeline.
b. It provides a working model for stakeholders to interact with.
c. It eliminates the need for detailed requirements documentation.
d. It ensures all technical requirements are met.

Answer: b. It provides a working model for stakeholders to interact with. Explanation: Prototyping allows stakeholders to interact with a working model of the product, providing valuable feedback on design and functionality. This helps in refining and validating requirements based on actual user experience.

347. A project manager is using surveys and questionnaires to gather requirements from a large group of stakeholders. What is the primary challenge associated with this technique?
a. Ensuring that the questions are unbiased and clear.
b. Analyzing qualitative data from open-ended responses.
c. Engaging stakeholders in face-to-face discussions.
d. Managing the logistical aspects of scheduling interviews.

Answer: a. Ensuring that the questions are unbiased and clear. Explanation: When using surveys and questionnaires, it is crucial to design questions that are unbiased and clear to avoid misinterpretation and ensure that the data collected is reliable and accurate.

348. In a requirements elicitation session, stakeholders frequently change their minds about their needs and priorities. Which elicitation technique can best handle such dynamic inputs?
a. Document analysis
b. Focus groups
c. Workshops
d. Prototyping

Answer: d. Prototyping. Explanation: Prototyping is well-suited for handling dynamic inputs because it allows stakeholders to see and interact with a tangible model of the product. This helps them better understand their needs and make informed decisions, even if their priorities change.

349. A project manager is facilitating a workshop to gather requirements for a new project. Which role should the project manager primarily play during the workshop?
a. Active participant contributing ideas
b. Neutral facilitator guiding the discussion
c. Technical expert providing solutions
d. Decision-maker finalizing the requirements

Answer: b. Neutral facilitator guiding the discussion. Explanation: The project manager should act as a neutral facilitator during a requirements elicitation workshop, guiding the discussion, encouraging participation from all stakeholders, and ensuring that the session remains focused on achieving its objectives.

350. When conducting document analysis, the project manager encounters conflicting information in different documents. What should be the next step?
a. Choose the information from the most recent document.
b. Consult with stakeholders to clarify the discrepancies.
c. Ignore the conflicting information and proceed with the majority view.
d. Update all documents to reflect a single version of the truth.

Answer: b. Consult with stakeholders to clarify the discrepancies. Explanation: When encountering conflicting information during document analysis, the project manager should consult with stakeholders to clarify the discrepancies and ensure that the requirements are accurately understood and documented.

351. A project manager is using focus groups to gather requirements. What is the primary disadvantage of this technique?
a. It provides limited opportunities for in-depth discussion.
b. It is difficult to facilitate and requires specialized skills.

c. It is not suitable for gathering detailed quantitative data.
d. It involves only a small number of stakeholders at a time.

Answer: d. It involves only a small number of stakeholders at a time. Explanation: The primary disadvantage of focus groups is that they involve a small number of stakeholders at a time, which may not provide a comprehensive view of the requirements. However, they are effective for gaining qualitative insights and understanding stakeholder perspectives.

352. The project manager is conducting interviews to gather requirements and wants to ensure that the process is efficient. Which approach should the project manager take to achieve this goal?
a. Prepare a detailed interview guide with specific questions.
b. Allow the conversation to flow naturally without a predefined structure.
c. Focus on technical details rather than stakeholder needs.
d. Limit each interview to no more than 15 minutes.

Answer: a. Prepare a detailed interview guide with specific questions. Explanation: Preparing a detailed interview guide with specific questions ensures that the interview process is structured and efficient. It helps the project manager cover all relevant topics and gather comprehensive information from stakeholders.

353. A project manager is using a requirements traceability matrix (RTM) to ensure that all project requirements are fulfilled. Which of the following is NOT typically included in an RTM?
a. Requirement ID
b. Test cases
c. Change requests
d. Requirement status

Answer: c. Change requests. Explanation: A requirements traceability matrix (RTM) typically includes requirement ID, test cases, and requirement status to ensure all project requirements are tracked and met. Change requests are managed separately through change control processes.

354. During the requirements prioritization process, a business analyst uses MoSCoW analysis. What does the "S" in MoSCoW stand for?
a. Significant
b. Should have
c. Secondary
d. Supportive

Answer: b. Should have. Explanation: MoSCoW analysis is a prioritization technique where "S" stands for Should have. It categorizes requirements as Must have, Should have, Could have, and Won't have, helping prioritize the most critical requirements.

355. A business analyst is monitoring the status of requirements throughout the project lifecycle. Which document is most useful for this purpose?
a. Project charter
b. Requirements traceability matrix
c. Risk management plan
d. Stakeholder register

Answer: b. Requirements traceability matrix. Explanation: The requirements traceability matrix (RTM) is used to monitor the status of requirements throughout the project lifecycle, ensuring that all requirements are addressed and fulfilled.

356. A project team is using the Kano model to prioritize requirements. Which of the following best describes the Kano model?
a. It classifies requirements into mandatory, optional, and nice-to-have categories
b. It prioritizes requirements based on their impact on customer satisfaction
c. It ranks requirements based on their technical complexity
d. It assigns scores to requirements based on cost and benefit

Answer: b. It prioritizes requirements based on their impact on customer satisfaction. Explanation: The Kano model prioritizes requirements based on their impact on customer satisfaction, classifying them into categories such as basic needs, performance needs, and excitement needs.

357. The project manager is seeking formal approval of the project requirements from stakeholders. Which process is primarily involved in obtaining this approval?
a. Validate scope
b. Control scope
c. Define scope
d. Collect requirements

Answer: a. Validate scope. Explanation: The Validate Scope process involves obtaining formal acceptance of the completed project deliverables from stakeholders, including the formal approval of project requirements.

358. In managing the requirements lifecycle, which activity ensures that requirements are clearly defined and understood by all stakeholders before project work begins?
a. Requirements validation
b. Requirements traceability
c. Requirements elicitation
d. Requirements prioritization

Answer: a. Requirements validation. Explanation: Requirements validation ensures that requirements are clearly defined, complete, and understood by all stakeholders before project work begins. This activity helps prevent misunderstandings and scope creep.

359. A business analyst needs to prioritize requirements for a new software development project. Which of the following criteria is least likely to be used in requirements prioritization?
a. Business value
b. Technical feasibility
c. Stakeholder influence
d. Project schedule

Answer: d. Project schedule. Explanation: While project schedule is important, it is not typically a primary criterion for prioritizing requirements. Requirements prioritization usually focuses on factors like business value, technical feasibility, and stakeholder influence.

360. The project team discovers that some requirements are not linked to their original business objectives. Which technique should they use to address this issue?
a. Root cause analysis
b. Requirements traceability
c. Impact analysis
d. Stakeholder analysis

Answer: b. Requirements traceability. Explanation: Requirements traceability ensures that each requirement is linked to its original business objective, helping the project team address any gaps and ensure that all requirements are aligned with the project's goals.

361. A stakeholder requests a change to an already approved requirement. What is the first step the project manager should take to manage this change?
a. Implement the change immediately
b. Update the requirements traceability matrix
c. Assess the impact of the change
d. Reject the change request

Answer: c. Assess the impact of the change. Explanation: The first step in managing a change request is to assess its impact on the project. This includes evaluating the change's effect on scope, schedule, cost, and quality before making a decision.

362. The project team needs to ensure that all requirements are correctly implemented in the final deliverable. Which process is used to confirm this?
a. Validate scope
b. Control quality
c. Verify requirements

d. Conduct procurements

Answer: a. Validate scope. Explanation: Validate Scope is the process used to confirm that all requirements are correctly implemented in the final deliverable. It involves reviewing deliverables with stakeholders to ensure they meet the agreed-upon requirements.

363. A project manager is performing a SWOT analysis to develop a strategy for a new project. Which of the following best describes the purpose of SWOT analysis?
a. To evaluate project risks and develop mitigation plans
b. To assess the project's internal strengths and weaknesses and external opportunities and threats
c. To create a detailed project schedule and budget
d. To identify the root causes of project issues

Answer: b. To assess the project's internal strengths and weaknesses and external opportunities and threats. Explanation: SWOT analysis is used to identify and analyze the internal strengths and weaknesses of a project, as well as the external opportunities and threats. This helps in developing strategies that leverage strengths and opportunities while mitigating weaknesses and threats.

364. During a root cause analysis, the project manager uses the "5 Whys" technique. What is the primary objective of this technique?
a. To develop a detailed project plan
b. To identify the root cause of a problem by repeatedly asking why the problem occurs
c. To create a list of potential project risks
d. To generate a wide range of solutions to a problem

Answer: b. To identify the root cause of a problem by repeatedly asking why the problem occurs. Explanation: The "5 Whys" technique involves repeatedly asking "why" to drill down into the underlying cause of a problem. This helps identify the root cause, enabling the project manager to address the issue effectively.

365. A business case is being developed for a new project. Which of the following is not typically included in a business case?
a. Project objectives and benefits
b. Detailed project schedule
c. Financial analysis and cost-benefit analysis
d. Risk assessment

Answer: b. Detailed project schedule. Explanation: A business case typically includes project objectives and benefits, financial analysis, cost-benefit analysis, and risk assessment. A detailed project schedule is usually developed later during the project planning phase.

366. A project manager is conducting a SWOT analysis and identifies a potential new market for the project's product. How should this information be categorized in the SWOT analysis?
a. Strength
b. Weakness
c. Opportunity
d. Threat

Answer: c. Opportunity. Explanation: A potential new market for the project's product represents an external opportunity. Opportunities are external factors that can be leveraged to achieve project objectives and improve outcomes.

367. During the development of a business case, the project manager needs to justify the project's financial viability. Which financial metric is most commonly used to assess the return on investment (ROI) of the project?
a. Net present value (NPV)
b. Internal rate of return (IRR)
c. Payback period
d. Cost variance (CV)

Answer: a. Net present value (NPV). Explanation: Net present value (NPV) is a financial metric that calculates the difference between the present value of cash inflows and outflows over a project's life. It is commonly used to assess the return on investment (ROI) and determine the project's financial viability.

368. A root cause analysis reveals that a recurring issue in a project is due to inadequate training of team members. What is the most appropriate action for the project manager to take?
a. Replace the team members with more experienced individuals
b. Provide additional training and support to the team members
c. Increase the project budget to account for potential delays
d. Ignore the issue and continue with the project plan

Answer: b. Provide additional training and support to the team members. Explanation: Addressing the root cause of inadequate training by providing additional training and support helps resolve the issue and prevent it from recurring. This action improves team performance and project outcomes.

369. A project manager is developing a business case for a project aimed at reducing operational costs. Which element should be emphasized to justify the project's approval?
a. Project milestones and timeline
b. Estimated cost savings and return on investment (ROI)
c. Potential risks and mitigation strategies
d. Stakeholder engagement plan

Answer: b. Estimated cost savings and return on investment (ROI). Explanation: For a project aimed at reducing operational costs, the business case should emphasize the estimated cost savings and return on investment (ROI). This information justifies the project's approval by demonstrating its financial benefits.

370. In a root cause analysis, the project manager uses a fishbone diagram. What is the primary purpose of this tool?
a. To identify all possible causes of a problem and categorize them
b. To develop a detailed project schedule
c. To prioritize project tasks based on their impact
d. To create a risk management plan

Answer: a. To identify all possible causes of a problem and categorize them. Explanation: A fishbone diagram, also known as an Ishikawa diagram, is used to identify and categorize all possible causes of a problem. It helps in visually organizing potential causes to facilitate root cause analysis.

371. During a SWOT analysis, a project manager identifies a competitor's recent technological advancement that could impact the project's success. How should this information be categorized?
a. Strength
b. Weakness
c. Opportunity
d. Threat

Answer: d. Threat. Explanation: A competitor's recent technological advancement represents an external threat. Threats are external factors that could negatively impact the project's success and need to be addressed in the project strategy.

372. A business case includes a risk assessment that identifies several potential risks to the project's success. What should be the next step in developing the business case?
a. Develop risk mitigation strategies for the identified risks
b. Create a detailed project schedule and budget
c. Conduct a stakeholder analysis
d. Perform a cost-benefit analysis for the project

Answer: a. Develop risk mitigation strategies for the identified risks. Explanation: After identifying potential risks in the business case, the next step is to develop risk mitigation strategies. This ensures that risks are managed proactively, increasing the project's chances of success.

373. A business analyst is specifying and modeling requirements for a new software application. Which technique is most appropriate for visualizing the interactions between the system and its users?
a. Data flow diagram
b. Entity-relationship diagram
c. Use case diagram
d. Gantt chart

Answer: c. Use case diagram. Explanation: A use case diagram is used to visualize the interactions between the system and its users, showing how users (actors) interact with different parts of the system to achieve specific goals.

374. During the requirements verification process, a business analyst needs to ensure that all requirements are complete and consistent. Which of the following activities is NOT typically part of requirements verification?
a. Reviewing requirements with stakeholders
b. Ensuring requirements are traceable
c. Conducting peer reviews
d. Prioritizing requirements

Answer: d. Prioritizing requirements. Explanation: Requirements verification involves reviewing requirements with stakeholders, ensuring they are complete, consistent, and traceable, and conducting peer reviews. Prioritizing requirements is part of requirements prioritization, not verification.

375. In the process of validating requirements, which of the following is the primary objective?
a. To ensure requirements are feasible and achievable
b. To confirm that the requirements meet the needs of the stakeholders
c. To determine the cost of implementing the requirements
d. To develop a project schedule

Answer: b. To confirm that the requirements meet the needs of the stakeholders. Explanation: The primary objective of validating requirements is to ensure that they meet the needs and expectations of the stakeholders, ensuring that the final product will be accepted.

376. A project team is defining solution options for a new project. What is the main purpose of this activity?
a. To select the vendor for the project
b. To identify different ways to meet the business requirements
c. To allocate resources to project tasks
d. To develop the project budget

Answer: b. To identify different ways to meet the business requirements. Explanation: Defining solution options involves identifying different approaches or solutions that can meet the business requirements, allowing stakeholders to evaluate and select the best option.

377. During solution evaluation, the project team needs to assess whether the implemented solution meets the specified requirements. Which technique is most appropriate for this assessment?
a. SWOT analysis
b. Benchmarking
c. User acceptance testing

d. Stakeholder analysis

Answer: c. User acceptance testing. Explanation: User acceptance testing (UAT) is used to assess whether the implemented solution meets the specified requirements and is ready for deployment. UAT involves stakeholders testing the solution in real-world scenarios to ensure it works as expected.

378. A business analyst is specifying and modeling requirements and needs to capture detailed functional requirements. Which technique is best suited for this purpose?
a. Brainstorming
b. Use case diagram
c. Functional decomposition
d. Delphi technique

Answer: c. Functional decomposition. Explanation: Functional decomposition is a technique used to break down complex processes and systems into smaller, more manageable parts, capturing detailed functional requirements for each component.

379. During the verification of requirements, a discrepancy is found between the documented requirements and stakeholder expectations. What is the first step the business analyst should take to resolve this issue?
a. Update the requirements documentation
b. Escalate the issue to the project manager
c. Conduct a meeting with stakeholders to clarify expectations
d. Perform a root cause analysis

Answer: c. Conduct a meeting with stakeholders to clarify expectations. Explanation: The first step is to conduct a meeting with stakeholders to clarify their expectations and resolve any discrepancies between the documented requirements and their needs.

380. A project team is evaluating multiple solution options to determine the best approach for meeting business requirements. Which of the following criteria is LEAST likely to be used in this evaluation?
a. Cost of implementation
b. Technical feasibility
c. Historical performance of the project team
d. Alignment with business objectives

Answer: c. Historical performance of the project team. Explanation: While historical performance of the project team may be relevant in some contexts, it is not typically a primary criterion for evaluating solution options. The focus is usually on cost, technical feasibility, and alignment with business objectives.

381. In the process of validating requirements, the team discovers that some requirements are not testable. What should the business analyst do to address this issue?
a. Remove the non-testable requirements
b. Redefine the requirements to make them testable
c. Ignore the issue and proceed with development
d. Document the issue in the risk register

Answer: b. Redefine the requirements to make them testable. Explanation: Non-testable requirements should be redefined to make them clear, measurable, and testable. This ensures that the final solution can be verified against these requirements.

382. A business analyst needs to ensure that the solution meets the business needs and provides the expected value. Which activity is most relevant to this goal?
a. Functional decomposition
b. Solution evaluation
c. Requirements traceability
d. Risk analysis

Answer: b. Solution evaluation. Explanation: Solution evaluation involves assessing the implemented solution to ensure it meets the business needs and provides the expected value. This includes comparing the solution's performance against the specified requirements and business objectives.

383. A project manager is evaluating the performance of a newly implemented software solution. Which metric would be most appropriate to measure solution performance in terms of user satisfaction?
a. Number of bugs reported
b. User acceptance test (UAT) results
c. Average response time of the software
d. Net Promoter Score (NPS)

Answer: d. Net Promoter Score (NPS). Explanation: The Net Promoter Score (NPS) measures user satisfaction by asking users how likely they are to recommend the software to others. It provides insight into user sentiment and satisfaction with the solution.

384. During the analysis of performance measures, a project manager finds that the solution is not meeting the expected performance levels. What should be the first step in addressing this issue?
a. Conduct a root cause analysis to identify underlying problems
b. Increase the project budget to improve performance
c. Replace the current solution with a new one
d. Ignore the performance issue and focus on other areas

Answer: a. Conduct a root cause analysis to identify underlying problems. Explanation: The first step in addressing performance issues is to conduct a root cause analysis. This helps identify the underlying problems causing the performance shortfall, allowing for targeted and effective corrective actions.

385. The project manager needs to assess the limitations of a new software solution that has been implemented. Which approach would be most effective in identifying these limitations?
a. Reviewing the original project scope
b. Conducting user feedback sessions and surveys
c. Comparing the solution to competitor products
d. Analyzing the project's financial reports

Answer: b. Conducting user feedback sessions and surveys. Explanation: User feedback sessions and surveys are effective in identifying limitations of a new software solution. Users can provide insights into issues and challenges they encounter, which helps in understanding the solution's limitations from a practical perspective.

386. After implementing a new solution, the project manager discovers that the solution does not align well with existing enterprise processes. What should be the next step?
a. Recommend abandoning the solution and reverting to the old system
b. Assess the enterprise limitations to identify necessary adjustments
c. Increase training for employees to adapt to the new solution
d. Focus on improving the solution's technical performance

Answer: b. Assess the enterprise limitations to identify necessary adjustments. Explanation: When a solution does not align well with existing enterprise processes, the next step is to assess enterprise limitations. This involves understanding how the current processes and infrastructure may need to be adjusted to better integrate the new solution.

387. A project manager is tasked with recommending actions to increase the value of an underperforming solution. Which recommendation would be most appropriate?
a. Extend the project timeline to allow for more thorough testing
b. Implement additional features based on user feedback
c. Increase the budget to hire more developers
d. Reduce the scope of the solution to focus on core functionalities

Answer: b. Implement additional features based on user feedback. Explanation: Implementing additional features based on user feedback can increase the value of an underperforming solution. It ensures that the solution better meets user needs and enhances user satisfaction and usability.

388. The project manager is measuring the performance of a new CRM system by tracking key performance indicators (KPIs). Which KPI would best indicate the system's effectiveness in improving customer relationships?
a. Number of new customers acquired
b. Customer retention rate

c. Average time to resolve customer issues
d. Total sales revenue

Answer: b. Customer retention rate. Explanation: The customer retention rate is a key indicator of a CRM system's effectiveness in improving customer relationships. A higher retention rate suggests that the system is helping to maintain and enhance customer loyalty.

389. During a solution evaluation, the project manager identifies several functional limitations that hinder the solution's performance. What should be the primary focus to address these limitations?
a. Enhancing the solution's user interface design
b. Conducting additional training sessions for users
c. Developing and implementing a workaround strategy
d. Modifying the solution to eliminate the functional limitations

Answer: d. Modifying the solution to eliminate the functional limitations. Explanation: The primary focus should be on modifying the solution to eliminate the functional limitations. This ensures that the solution performs as intended and meets the project's objectives.

390. A project manager is analyzing performance measures of a recently implemented solution and finds that it has led to increased operational costs. What action should the project manager take to increase the solution's value?
a. Recommend discontinuing the solution
b. Conduct a cost-benefit analysis to identify cost-saving opportunities
c. Increase the project's budget to cover the additional costs
d. Extend the project timeline to allow for further optimization

Answer: b. Conduct a cost-benefit analysis to identify cost-saving opportunities. Explanation: Conducting a cost-benefit analysis helps identify opportunities to reduce operational costs and increase the solution's value. It allows the project manager to make informed decisions on cost-saving measures.

391. The project manager needs to recommend actions to enhance the value of a solution that has been underutilized by the organization. Which approach is most likely to increase user adoption?
a. Increase the project's marketing efforts
b. Provide additional user training and support
c. Reduce the complexity of the solution
d. Extend the project deadline

Answer: b. Provide additional user training and support. Explanation: Providing additional user training and support can enhance user adoption by ensuring that users are comfortable and proficient in using the solution. This can lead to increased utilization and value realization.

392. During the assessment of solution limitations, the project manager identifies that the solution is not scalable to accommodate future growth. What recommendation should the project manager make?
a. Continue using the solution until scalability becomes an issue
b. Implement a scalable architecture to support future growth
c. Limit the use of the solution to its current capacity
d. Develop a new project to replace the solution

Answer: b. Implement a scalable architecture to support future growth. Explanation: Implementing a scalable architecture ensures that the solution can accommodate future growth and changing business needs. This proactive approach prevents scalability issues from hindering the solution's effectiveness in the long term.

393. A business analyst is defining the business needs for a new project aimed at improving customer satisfaction. Which of the following is the primary purpose of this activity?
a. To develop the project schedule
b. To identify the underlying problems or opportunities
c. To allocate resources to project tasks
d. To establish the project budget

Answer: b. To identify the underlying problems or opportunities. Explanation: Defining business needs involves identifying the underlying problems or opportunities that the project aims to address. This activity helps in setting clear objectives and justifying the project's value.

394. During the assessment of capability gaps, the project team identifies that the current system lacks the functionality to automate certain processes. What is the next step in this analysis?
a. Define the solution scope
b. Develop the project schedule
c. Conduct a cost-benefit analysis
d. Create a risk management plan

Answer: a. Define the solution scope. Explanation: After identifying capability gaps, the next step is to define the solution scope, which outlines the boundaries and high-level requirements of the solution needed to address the identified gaps.

395. A project team is determining the solution approach for a new product launch. Which factor is LEAST likely to influence the selection of the solution approach?
a. Available budget
b. Stakeholder preferences
c. Project manager's experience
d. Technical feasibility

Answer: c. Project manager's experience. Explanation: While the project manager's experience is valuable, it is not a primary factor in determining the solution approach. The selection is more influenced by the available budget, stakeholder preferences, and technical feasibility.

396. In defining the solution scope, which document typically provides a detailed description of the solution's boundaries and deliverables?
a. Project charter
b. Business case
c. Solution scope statement
d. Requirements management plan

Answer: c. Solution scope statement. Explanation: The solution scope statement provides a detailed description of the solution's boundaries, deliverables, and high-level requirements, ensuring that all stakeholders have a clear understanding of what the solution will encompass.

397. A business analyst is conducting enterprise analysis and needs to prioritize business needs. Which technique is most appropriate for this task?
a. MoSCoW analysis
b. SWOT analysis
c. Fishbone diagram
d. RACI matrix

Answer: a. MoSCoW analysis. Explanation: MoSCoW analysis is a prioritization technique used to categorize business needs and requirements into Must have, Should have, Could have, and Won't have, helping to focus on the most critical needs first.

398. During the assessment of capability gaps, the project team identifies several areas where current capabilities do not meet business needs. Which of the following is the primary goal of this assessment?
a. To determine the project timeline
b. To identify the resources required
c. To understand the limitations of the current state
d. To develop the project budget

Answer: c. To understand the limitations of the current state. Explanation: The primary goal of assessing capability gaps is to understand the limitations of the current state and identify areas where improvements are needed to meet business needs.

399. A business analyst is determining the solution approach for an enterprise-wide software implementation. Which factor is MOST critical in this decision-making process?
a. The organization's strategic goals
b. The color scheme of the software interface
c. The number of team members available

d. The office location of the project team

Answer: a. The organization's strategic goals. Explanation: The most critical factor in determining the solution approach is how well it aligns with the organization's strategic goals, ensuring that the solution supports long-term objectives and adds value.

400. In defining the solution scope, the project team must ensure alignment with which of the following?
a. The project manager's preferences
b. The current IT infrastructure
c. The project charter
d. The project team's skills

Answer: c. The project charter. Explanation: The solution scope must align with the project charter, which outlines the project's objectives, constraints, and high-level requirements, ensuring that the solution supports the overall project goals.

401. During the enterprise analysis, a business analyst uses a SWOT analysis. What does the "T" in SWOT stand for, and what is its relevance?
a. Trends; to identify market trends affecting the project
b. Tactics; to outline strategic actions for the project
c. Threats; to identify external risks that could impact the project
d. Technology; to assess the technological capabilities of the organization

Answer: c. Threats; to identify external risks that could impact the project. Explanation: The "T" in SWOT stands for Threats, which are external risks or factors that could negatively impact the project. Identifying these threats is crucial for developing strategies to mitigate them.

402. A project team is defining business needs and has identified several key stakeholders. What is the next step to ensure these needs are accurately captured and addressed?
a. Develop a communication plan
b. Conduct stakeholder interviews
c. Create a risk register
d. Develop a work breakdown structure (WBS)

Answer: b. Conduct stakeholder interviews. Explanation: Conducting stakeholder interviews is the next step to accurately capture and address business needs. This helps gather detailed information and insights directly from stakeholders, ensuring their needs are well understood and considered.

403. A business analyst is conducting a feasibility study for a proposed project. Which of the following is the primary purpose of a feasibility study?

a. To determine the project's scope, schedule, and budget
b. To identify and prioritize the project's risks and mitigation strategies
c. To assess the project's viability and likelihood of success
d. To select the project team and assign roles and responsibilities

Answer: c. To assess the project's viability and likelihood of success. Explanation: A feasibility study is an evaluation of a proposed project to determine its practicality and potential for success. The primary purpose of a feasibility study is to assess the project's viability from various perspectives, such as technical, economic, legal, and operational feasibility. By conducting a thorough analysis of the project's requirements, constraints, and benefits, the business analyst can provide decision-makers with the information they need to determine whether to proceed with the project, modify its scope or approach, or abandon it altogether. While a feasibility study may touch on aspects like project scope, risks, and team composition, its main focus is on determining the overall likelihood of the project's success before committing significant resources to its execution.

404. Which of the following techniques is most appropriate for eliciting requirements from a large group of stakeholders with diverse needs and perspectives?
a. One-on-one interviews
b. Surveys and questionnaires
c. Observation and shadowing
d. Facilitated workshops

Answer: d. Facilitated workshops. Explanation: When dealing with a large group of stakeholders with diverse needs and perspectives, facilitated workshops are often the most effective technique for eliciting requirements. Facilitated workshops bring together key stakeholders in a structured, collaborative environment to discuss, brainstorm, and reach consensus on the project's requirements. The business analyst acts as a facilitator, guiding the discussion, encouraging participation, and ensuring that all stakeholders have an opportunity to contribute. Workshops allow for real-time feedback, clarification of issues, and alignment of expectations, which can be more difficult to achieve through one-on-one interviews or surveys. Observation and shadowing are useful for understanding existing processes and workflows but may not capture the full range of stakeholder needs and insights. Facilitated workshops promote a shared understanding of the project's goals and requirements, helping to build consensus and buy-in among stakeholders.

405. A business analyst is using the MoSCoW prioritization technique to prioritize requirements. Which of the following best describes the "Won't Have" category?
a. Requirements that are critical to the project's success and must be included
b. Requirements that are important but not essential and could be included if time and resources permit
c. Requirements that are desirable but not necessary and will not be included in the current scope
d. Requirements that are out of scope and will not be considered for the project

Answer: d. Requirements that are out of scope and will not be considered for the project. Explanation: The MoSCoW prioritization technique is a method for categorizing and prioritizing requirements based on their importance and urgency. The four categories in MoSCoW are Must Have (non-negotiable requirements), Should Have (important but not critical), Could Have (desirable but not necessary), and Won't Have. The "Won't Have" category represents requirements that are explicitly out of scope for the current project and will not be considered or included in the deliverables. These requirements may be documented for future reference or deferred to later phases or projects, but they are not part of the current project's scope. It's important to clarify the "Won't Have" requirements to manage stakeholder expectations and ensure that the project team focuses on delivering the most essential features and functionalities.

406. Which of the following is the primary benefit of using a traceability matrix in requirements management?
a. To prioritize requirements based on their importance and urgency
b. To track the status and progress of each requirement throughout the project lifecycle
c. To identify and resolve conflicts or dependencies between requirements
d. To ensure that each requirement is linked to a specific business objective or stakeholder need

Answer: d. To ensure that each requirement is linked to a specific business objective or stakeholder need. Explanation: A traceability matrix is a tool used in requirements management to map and trace the relationships between requirements, design elements, test cases, and other project artifacts. The primary benefit of using a traceability matrix is to ensure that each requirement is traceable back to a specific business objective, stakeholder need, or regulatory compliance. By establishing and maintaining these traceability links, the business analyst can demonstrate that the project deliverables align with the intended outcomes and stakeholder expectations. Traceability helps to prevent scope creep, identify gaps or inconsistencies in requirements, and facilitate impact analysis when changes occur. While a traceability matrix can be used to track requirement status, resolve conflicts, and aid in prioritization, its main purpose is to provide a clear line of sight between project requirements and the underlying business goals and stakeholder needs they support.

407. A company is considering two project proposals with the following financial projections: Project A: Initial investment of $100,000, expected annual cash inflows of $40,000 for 5 years Project B: Initial investment of $150,000, expected annual cash inflows of $50,000 for 4 years The company's required rate of return is 10%. Which project should the company choose based on the net present value (NPV) criterion?
a. Project A, because it has a lower initial investment
b. Project B, because it has higher annual cash inflows
c. Project A, because it has a higher NPV at the 10% discount rate
d. Project B, because it has a shorter payback period

Answer: c. Project A, because it has a higher NPV at the 10% discount rate. Explanation: The net present value (NPV) is a financial metric used to evaluate the profitability and feasibility of investment projects. NPV calculates the present value of a project's future cash inflows and outflows, discounted at the required rate of return. A positive NPV indicates that the project is expected to generate a return higher than the discount rate and create value for the company. To calculate the NPV, the business analyst should use the following formula: NPV = (Cash Inflow / $(1+r)^t$) - Initial Investment, where r is the discount rate and t is the time period. For Project A, the NPV at a 10% discount rate is $38,137, while for Project B, the NPV is $35,061. Therefore, based on the NPV criterion, the company should choose Project A, as it has a higher NPV and is expected to create more value. The initial investment, annual cash inflows, and payback period are important factors to consider, but the NPV provides a more comprehensive assessment of a project's financial worth, taking into account the time value of money.

408. A business analyst is using a decision tree to evaluate the expected monetary value (EMV) of a proposed project. The project has two possible outcomes: success (probability 60%, payoff $200,000) and failure (probability 40%, loss $80,000). What is the project's EMV?

a. $72,000
b. $88,000
c. $120,000
d. $160,000

Answer: b. $88,000. Explanation: A decision tree is a visual tool used to analyze decisions under uncertainty by mapping out the possible outcomes, their probabilities, and associated payoffs or costs. The expected monetary value (EMV) is a statistical concept that calculates the average outcome of a decision, considering the probability and value of each possible result. In a decision tree, the EMV is determined by multiplying the probability of each outcome by its respective payoff or loss and summing the results. For the given project, the EMV is calculated as follows: EMV = (0.60 × $200,000) + (0.40 × -$80,000) = $120,000 - $32,000 = $88,000. This means that, on average, the project is expected to generate a net value of $88,000, considering the potential for both success and failure. The EMV helps decision-makers assess the risk and potential return of a project, but it should not be the sole criterion for decision-making, as it does not account for factors such as strategic alignment, resource constraints, or stakeholder preferences.

409. A business analyst is conducting a stakeholder analysis for a new software development project. Which of the following is the primary purpose of a stakeholder analysis?
a. To identify the project's scope, objectives, and deliverables
b. To determine the project's budget, schedule, and resource requirements
c. To assess the project's risks, assumptions, and constraints
d. To identify and understand the individuals and groups who can influence or be affected by the project

Answer: d. To identify and understand the individuals and groups who can influence or be affected by the project. Explanation: Stakeholder analysis is the process of identifying, assessing, and managing the individuals, groups, or organizations that have a vested interest in a project or can influence its outcomes. The primary purpose of stakeholder analysis is to gain a clear understanding of who the project stakeholders are, their roles, interests, expectations, and potential impact on the project. By conducting a thorough stakeholder analysis, the business analyst can develop strategies for engaging and communicating with each stakeholder group, anticipating and managing their concerns, and leveraging their support and expertise. Stakeholder analysis helps to align the project's objectives with stakeholder needs, minimize resistance to change, and build a coalition of support for the project. While stakeholder analysis may inform other aspects of project planning, such as scope definition, risk assessment, and resource allocation, its main focus is on identifying and understanding the people and groups who have a stake in the project's success.

410. A business analyst is using the RACI matrix to define the roles and responsibilities of project stakeholders. What does the "I" in RACI stand for?
a. Informed
b. Involved
c. Influential
d. Impacted

Answer: a. Informed. Explanation: The RACI matrix is a responsibility assignment chart that maps out the roles and responsibilities of stakeholders in a project or process. RACI is an acronym that stands for Responsible, Accountable, Consulted, and Informed. The "I" in RACI represents "Informed," which refers to the stakeholders who need to be kept up-to-date on the project's progress, decisions, and outcomes, but do not have a direct role in the work or decision-making. Informed stakeholders are typically those who are affected by the project's results or have a general interest in its success, such as senior management, external partners, or end-users. The business analyst should ensure that informed stakeholders receive regular, timely, and relevant communication about the project, such as status reports, meeting minutes, or key milestones. Keeping stakeholders informed helps to maintain transparency, build trust, and manage expectations throughout the project lifecycle.

411. Which of the following is the primary benefit of using a use case diagram in requirements gathering?
a. To prioritize requirements based on their complexity and business value
b. To identify and model the functional requirements and system interactions from a user's perspective
c. To document the non-functional requirements, such as performance, security, and usability
d. To map the relationships and dependencies between requirements and project deliverables

Answer: b. To identify and model the functional requirements and system interactions from a user's perspective. Explanation: A use case diagram is a visual representation of a system's functional requirements, depicting how users (actors) interact with the system to achieve specific goals. The primary benefit of using a use case diagram in requirements gathering is to identify, clarify, and communicate the system's functionality from the perspective of its end-users. By modeling the different use cases (tasks or processes) that actors perform, the business analyst can gain a clear understanding of what the system needs to do, what inputs and outputs are involved, and what exceptions or alternative flows may occur. Use case diagrams help to focus the requirements gathering process on the user's needs and objectives, ensuring that the system being developed is aligned with its intended purpose and value proposition. While use case diagrams can inform other aspects of requirements management, such as prioritization, non-functional requirements, and traceability, their main strength lies in capturing and communicating the system's functional behavior and user interactions.

412. A company is considering investing in a new customer relationship management (CRM) system. The initial cost of the system is $200,000, and the company expects it to generate incremental cash inflows of $60,000 per year for the next 5 years. The company's required rate of return is 12%. What is the project's internal rate of return (IRR)?
a. 12%
b. 15%
c. 18%
d. 21%

Answer: b. 15%. Explanation: The internal rate of return (IRR) is a financial metric used to evaluate the profitability and feasibility of investment projects. IRR is the discount rate that makes the net present value (NPV) of a project's cash inflows and outflows equal to zero. In other words, it represents the expected annual rate of return that the project will generate, considering the time value of money. A project is considered financially viable if its IRR is higher than the company's required rate of return or cost of capital. To calculate the IRR, the business analyst should use the IRR function in a spreadsheet or financial calculator, inputting the project's initial cost and expected cash inflows. For the given CRM project, the IRR is approximately 15%, which is higher than the company's required rate of return of 12%. This indicates that the project is expected to generate a sufficient return on investment and create value for the company. However, the IRR should not be the sole criterion for decision-making, as it does not account for factors such as project risk, strategic fit, or opportunity costs.

413. A project manager is conducting a risk identification workshop with the project team. Which tool or technique is most appropriate for identifying risks during this workshop?
a. Monte Carlo simulation
b. SWOT analysis
c. Probability and impact matrix
d. Decision tree analysis

Answer: b. SWOT analysis. Explanation: SWOT analysis (Strengths, Weaknesses, Opportunities, Threats) is a useful tool for identifying risks by analyzing internal and external factors that could impact the project. It helps in identifying potential threats and opportunities.

414. After identifying risks, a project manager needs to prioritize them based on their potential impact and likelihood. Which tool is best suited for this purpose?
a. Pareto chart
b. Risk register
c. Probability and impact matrix
d. RACI matrix

Answer: c. Probability and impact matrix. Explanation: A probability and impact matrix is used to prioritize risks by assessing their likelihood of occurrence and potential impact on the project. It helps in identifying which risks need more attention and resources.

415. A project manager is planning risk responses for a high-priority risk that could significantly delay the project. Which risk response strategy involves changing the project plan to eliminate the risk entirely?
a. Mitigation
b. Avoidance
c. Transfer
d. Acceptance

Answer: b. Avoidance. Explanation: Risk avoidance involves changing the project plan to eliminate the risk entirely, thereby preventing it from impacting the project. This strategy is used for high-priority risks that have a significant impact.

416. During a risk assessment, the project team uses qualitative analysis to evaluate the identified risks. Which of the following is a key characteristic of qualitative risk analysis?
a. It uses numerical data to calculate risk exposure
b. It focuses on the probability and impact of risks
c. It involves complex mathematical modeling
d. It requires detailed cost and schedule data

Answer: b. It focuses on the probability and impact of risks. Explanation: Qualitative risk analysis evaluates risks based on their probability of occurrence and impact on project objectives. It is a subjective assessment that prioritizes risks for further analysis or action.

417. The project manager is developing a risk response plan and decides to use risk mitigation for a specific risk. What is the primary objective of risk mitigation?
a. To eliminate the risk entirely
b. To reduce the probability or impact of the risk
c. To transfer the risk to a third party
d. To accept the risk without any action

Answer: b. To reduce the probability or impact of the risk. Explanation: Risk mitigation aims to reduce the likelihood or impact of a risk to acceptable levels by implementing measures to address the risk proactively.

418. A project team identifies a risk that a key supplier may fail to deliver critical components on time. Which risk response strategy involves outsourcing the risk to another party, such as a third-party supplier or insurer?
a. Avoidance
b. Mitigation
c. Transfer
d. Acceptance

Answer: c. Transfer. Explanation: Risk transfer involves outsourcing the risk to another party, such as through a contract or insurance. This strategy shifts the responsibility and potential impact of the risk to the third party.

419. During a project review, the project manager identifies a risk that was not previously documented. What should be the first step to address this new risk?
a. Implement an immediate response
b. Add the risk to the risk register
c. Perform a quantitative risk analysis
d. Escalate the risk to the project sponsor

Answer: b. Add the risk to the risk register. Explanation: The first step in addressing a new risk is to document it in the risk register. This ensures that the risk is formally recognized and can be analyzed and managed appropriately.

420. In a risk assessment meeting, the team decides to perform a quantitative risk analysis. Which technique is commonly used in quantitative risk analysis to assess the impact of risks on project objectives?
a. SWOT analysis
b. Monte Carlo simulation
c. Probability and impact matrix
d. Risk audit

Answer: b. Monte Carlo simulation. Explanation: Monte Carlo simulation is a quantitative risk analysis technique that uses statistical modeling to assess the impact of risks on project objectives. It provides a range of possible outcomes and their probabilities.

421. A project manager decides to accept a low-priority risk without taking any immediate action. Which of the following best describes this risk response strategy?
a. Avoidance
b. Mitigation
c. Transfer
d. Acceptance

Answer: d. Acceptance. Explanation: Risk acceptance is a strategy where the project manager decides to accept the risk without taking any immediate action. This is usually done for low-priority risks with minimal impact.

422. The project team is monitoring risks and discovers that a previously identified risk has increased in severity. What is the most appropriate action for the project manager to take?
a. Re-evaluate the risk response plan
b. Ignore the change and continue as planned
c. Remove the risk from the risk register
d. Increase the project budget to cover potential impacts

Answer: a. Re-evaluate the risk response plan. Explanation: When a risk increases in severity, the project manager should re-evaluate the risk response plan to determine if additional actions are needed to manage the risk effectively.

423. A project manager is conducting a cost-benefit analysis for a new project. Which of the following should be considered a benefit in this analysis?
a. The initial investment required to start the project
b. The ongoing maintenance costs of the project
c. The increased revenue generated by the project
d. The depreciation of equipment used in the project

Answer: c. The increased revenue generated by the project. Explanation: Benefits in a cost-benefit analysis are positive outcomes such as increased revenue, cost savings, or other gains that the project will generate. Increased revenue generated by the project is a direct benefit that should be included in the analysis.

424. A project manager is evaluating a project with an Internal Rate of Return (IRR) of 12%. What does the IRR indicate?
a. The project's annual growth rate
b. The project's average return over its lifetime
c. The discount rate at which the project's NPV is zero
d. The project's break-even point in years

Answer: c. The discount rate at which the project's NPV is zero. Explanation: IRR is the discount rate that makes the NPV of a project zero. It represents the project's expected rate of return and is used to evaluate the attractiveness of a project.

425. A business case includes the calculation of Return on Investment (ROI). Which formula is used to calculate ROI?
a. ROI = (Net Profit / Total Investment) x 100
b. ROI = (Total Revenue / Total Costs) x 100
c. ROI = (Total Investment / Net Profit) x 100
d. ROI = (Total Costs / Total Revenue) x 100

Answer: a. ROI = (Net Profit / Total Investment) x 100. Explanation: ROI measures the profitability of an investment by comparing the net profit to the total investment. It is calculated using the formula ROI = (Net Profit / Total Investment) x 100.

426. When comparing two mutually exclusive projects, Project A has a higher NPV but a lower IRR than Project B. Which project should be selected based on financial analysis, and why?
a. Project A, because it adds more value to the firm
b. Project B, because it has a higher rate of return
c. Project A, because it has a longer payback period
d. Project B, because it has a lower initial investment

Answer: a. Project A, because it adds more value to the firm. Explanation: NPV is generally considered a more reliable indicator of a project's value because it measures the absolute value added to the firm. A higher NPV means the project contributes more to the firm's wealth.

427. A project manager is evaluating the financial viability of a project using NPV. Which of the following factors is not directly considered in the NPV calculation?
a. Initial investment
b. Annual cash inflows
c. Discount rate
d. Project duration

Answer: d. Project duration. Explanation: While project duration indirectly affects the NPV by determining the number of periods over which cash flows are received, it is not directly considered in the NPV formula. The NPV calculation focuses on the initial investment, annual cash inflows, and the discount rate.

428. A company is considering a project that requires an initial investment of $200,000 and is expected to generate cash inflows of $50,000 annually for 6 years. If the company's required rate of return is 8%, should the project be accepted based on its NPV?

a. Yes, because the NPV is positive
b. No, because the NPV is negative
c. Yes, because the IRR is greater than the required rate of return
d. No, because the payback period is too long

Answer: a. Yes, because the NPV is positive. Explanation: To determine whether the project should be accepted, calculate the NPV using the given discount rate. Since the NPV is positive, it means the project is expected to generate more value than the cost of investment, and therefore, it should be accepted.

429. A project manager needs to choose between two projects with different payback periods. Project X has a payback period of 3 years, and Project Y has a payback period of 5 years. Which project should be selected based on the payback period criterion, and why?
a. Project X, because it recovers the investment faster
b. Project Y, because it has a longer duration
c. Project X, because it has a higher IRR
d. Project Y, because it has a higher NPV

Answer: a. Project X, because it recovers the investment faster. Explanation: Based on the payback period criterion, the project with the shorter payback period is preferred because it recovers the initial investment faster, reducing the risk and improving liquidity.

430. When conducting a cost-benefit analysis, which of the following should be included as a cost?
a. Increased customer satisfaction
b. Reduced operational expenses
c. Initial project investment
d. Higher market share

Answer: c. Initial project investment. Explanation: In a cost-benefit analysis, costs include the initial project investment, ongoing operational expenses, and any other expenditures required to implement and maintain the project. Increased customer satisfaction and higher market share are considered benefits.

431. During the initial phase of a project, the project manager identifies a new stakeholder who has significant influence over the project. What should the project manager do first?
a. Include the stakeholder in the project charter
b. Conduct a stakeholder analysis to understand the stakeholder's interests and influence
c. Assign the stakeholder a low-priority status due to their late identification
d. Inform the project team about the new stakeholder

Answer: b. Conduct a stakeholder analysis to understand the stakeholder's interests and influence. Explanation: The first step in engaging a newly identified stakeholder is to conduct a stakeholder analysis. This will help the project manager understand the stakeholder's interests, influence, and potential impact on the project.

432. A project manager is analyzing stakeholder needs and determines that some stakeholders have conflicting interests. What should be the project manager's next step?
a. Ignore the conflicting interests and proceed with the project plan
b. Use stakeholder engagement strategies to address and balance the conflicting interests
c. Prioritize the interests of the most influential stakeholders
d. Document the conflicts and monitor them throughout the project

Answer: b. Use stakeholder engagement strategies to address and balance the conflicting interests. Explanation: The project manager should use stakeholder engagement strategies to address and balance conflicting interests. This approach helps ensure that all stakeholders feel heard and valued, reducing potential conflicts and enhancing project success.

433. During a stakeholder meeting, a key stakeholder expresses concerns about the project's impact on their department. How should the project manager respond?
a. Dismiss the concerns if they are not aligned with the project goals
b. Address the concerns by explaining how the project benefits their department
c. Postpone the discussion until the next meeting
d. Note the concerns and continue with the planned agenda

Answer: b. Address the concerns by explaining how the project benefits their department. Explanation: The project manager should address the stakeholder's concerns by explaining how the project benefits their department. This approach helps build trust and ensures stakeholder buy-in and support for the project.

434. A project manager needs to manage stakeholder relationships throughout the project lifecycle. Which tool or technique is most appropriate for this task?
a. RACI matrix
b. Stakeholder engagement assessment matrix
c. Gantt chart
d. Monte Carlo simulation

Answer: b. Stakeholder engagement assessment matrix. Explanation: The stakeholder engagement assessment matrix is a tool used to manage stakeholder relationships. It helps assess the current and desired levels of stakeholder engagement and provides strategies to move from the current to the desired state.

435. A project team is conducting a stakeholder analysis and needs to categorize stakeholders based on their power, interest, and influence. Which tool should they use?
a. Work breakdown structure (WBS)
b. Responsibility assignment matrix (RAM)
c. Power/interest grid
d. SWOT analysis

Answer: c. Power/interest grid. Explanation: The power/interest grid is a tool used to categorize stakeholders based on their level of power, interest, and influence. It helps the project team develop strategies for engaging stakeholders according to their influence and impact on the project.

436. During a project review, the project manager finds that some stakeholders are not as engaged as planned. What action should the project manager take?
a. Update the stakeholder engagement plan
b. Replace the disengaged stakeholders with new ones
c. Reduce the project's scope to align with stakeholder interest
d. Escalate the issue to the project sponsor

Answer: a. Update the stakeholder engagement plan. Explanation: If stakeholders are not as engaged as planned, the project manager should update the stakeholder engagement plan. This involves identifying new engagement strategies to increase stakeholder involvement and support.

437. A project manager is identifying stakeholders for a new project. Which document is most useful for this process?
a. Project charter
b. Risk register
c. Communication plan
d. Issue log

Answer: a. Project charter. Explanation: The project charter is a key document that outlines the project's objectives, scope, and key stakeholders. It is useful for identifying stakeholders during the initial phase of the project.

438. The project manager is tasked with ensuring that stakeholder needs are aligned with project objectives. Which approach is most effective for achieving this alignment?
a. Conduct regular stakeholder meetings to discuss project progress and issues
b. Assign stakeholders to project tasks based on their expertise
c. Limit stakeholder involvement to the planning phase of the project
d. Focus solely on the requirements provided in the project charter

Answer: a. Conduct regular stakeholder meetings to discuss project progress and issues. Explanation: Regular stakeholder meetings are effective for ensuring that stakeholder needs are aligned with project objectives. These meetings provide a platform for discussing progress, addressing concerns, and making necessary adjustments to keep the project on track.

439. A project manager is managing stakeholder relationships and wants to measure the effectiveness of their engagement strategies. Which metric is most appropriate for this purpose?
a. Stakeholder satisfaction index
b. Project cost variance

c. Number of completed tasks
d. Project schedule adherence

Answer: a. Stakeholder satisfaction index. Explanation: The stakeholder satisfaction index is a metric used to measure the effectiveness of stakeholder engagement strategies. It provides insights into how well stakeholders' needs and expectations are being met.

440. The project manager discovers that a key stakeholder has become less supportive of the project. What should the project manager do to re-engage this stakeholder?
a. Exclude the stakeholder from future meetings to minimize disruption
b. Meet with the stakeholder to understand their concerns and address them
c. Delegate the stakeholder's responsibilities to other team members
d. Focus on more supportive stakeholders and ignore the disengaged one

Answer: b. Meet with the stakeholder to understand their concerns and address them. Explanation: To re-engage a less supportive stakeholder, the project manager should meet with them to understand their concerns and address them. This helps build trust and ensures the stakeholder feels valued and heard.

441. A business analyst is modeling a process using Business Process Model and Notation (BPMN). Which of the following BPMN elements represents an external participant or system that interacts with the process?
a. Pool
b. Lane
c. Gateway
d. Event

Answer: a. Pool. Explanation: In BPMN, a pool is a graphical container that represents a participant in a process, typically an external entity or system that interacts with the process being modeled. A pool can be either a "black box," hiding its internal details, or a "white box," showing the process steps and flows within it. Pools are used to define the boundaries and interfaces between different process participants, such as organizations, departments, or roles. Lanes, on the other hand, are sub-partitions within a pool that represent internal roles, teams, or systems involved in the process. Gateways are decision points that control the divergence and convergence of process flows based on specified conditions, while events represent triggers or results that occur during the process. By using pools to model external participants, the business analyst can clearly delineate the interactions and information exchanges between the process and its external stakeholders.

442. Which of the following is the primary goal of business process reengineering (BPR)?
a. To automate existing processes using technology
b. To make incremental improvements to process efficiency
c. To fundamentally rethink and radically redesign processes for dramatic improvements
d. To standardize processes across different business units

Answer: c. To fundamentally rethink and radically redesign processes for dramatic improvements. Explanation: Business process reengineering (BPR) is a management approach that aims to achieve dramatic improvements in process performance by fundamentally rethinking and radically redesigning business processes. Unlike incremental process improvement, which focuses on making small, continuous enhancements, BPR involves a complete overhaul of existing processes to achieve significant breakthroughs in efficiency, quality, and customer satisfaction. The primary goal of BPR is to align processes with the organization's strategic objectives and customer needs, eliminating non-value-added activities, reducing costs, and improving agility and responsiveness. BPR often involves the use of technology as an enabler, but automation alone is not the primary focus. Standardization may be an outcome of BPR, but it is not the main goal, as processes may need to be tailored to specific business requirements. By fundamentally rethinking and redesigning processes, BPR aims to achieve transformative improvements in organizational performance.

443. A company is considering two alternative processes for fulfilling customer orders. Process A has an average cycle time of 5 days and a defect rate of 2%, while Process B has an average cycle time of 3 days and a defect rate of 5%. The company's priority is to minimize defects. Which process should the company choose based on the given information?
a. Process A, because it has a lower defect rate
b. Process B, because it has a shorter cycle time
c. Process A, because it has a longer cycle time
d. Process B, because it has a higher defect rate

Answer: a. Process A, because it has a lower defect rate. Explanation: When evaluating alternative processes, the business analyst should consider the company's priorities and objectives. In this case, the company's primary goal is to minimize defects in the order fulfillment process. Process A has a defect rate of 2%, which is lower than Process B's defect rate of 5%. Although Process B has a shorter cycle time of 3 days compared to Process A's 5 days, the difference in cycle time is less critical given the company's focus on defect reduction. By choosing Process A, the company can expect to have fewer defective orders, which can lead to higher customer satisfaction, reduced rework and returns, and lower overall costs. However, the business analyst should also consider other factors, such as the process complexity, resource requirements, and scalability, before making a final recommendation. If the cycle time difference significantly impacts customer service or operational efficiency, a more comprehensive analysis may be needed to determine the optimal process design.

444. A business analyst is leading a process improvement initiative using the Six Sigma methodology. Which of the following is the correct sequence of phases in the Six Sigma DMAIC approach?
a. Define, Measure, Analyze, Improve, Control
b. Design, Measure, Analyze, Implement, Control
c. Define, Measure, Analyze, Control, Improve
d. Design, Measure, Analyze, Improve, Implement

Answer: a. Define, Measure, Analyze, Improve, Control. Explanation: Six Sigma is a data-driven methodology for process improvement that aims to reduce defects and variations in a process. The DMAIC approach is a structured problem-solving framework used in Six Sigma projects, consisting of five phases: Define, Measure, Analyze, Improve, and Control. In the Define phase, the project team identifies the problem, goals, and customer requirements. The Measure phase involves collecting data on the current process performance and establishing a baseline. The Analyze phase focuses on identifying the root causes of defects and variations using statistical tools. The Improve phase develops and implements solutions to address the identified issues and optimize the process. Finally, the Control phase ensures that the improvements are sustained over time by establishing monitoring and control mechanisms. By following the DMAIC sequence, the business analyst can systematically diagnose and improve process performance, reducing defects and enhancing customer satisfaction.

445. A company's procurement process involves multiple handoffs and approval steps, resulting in long cycle times and frequent delays. Which of the following process improvement techniques would be most effective in streamlining the procurement process?
a. Value stream mapping
b. Root cause analysis
c. Pareto analysis
d. Kanban system

Answer: a. Value stream mapping. Explanation: Value stream mapping is a lean technique used to visualize and analyze the flow of materials and information in a process, from the initial request to the final delivery. By creating a detailed map of the current process, including all the steps, handoffs, and decision points, the business analyst can identify non-value-added activities, bottlenecks, and waste in the process. Value stream mapping helps to highlight opportunities for process streamlining, such as eliminating unnecessary steps, reducing wait times, and improving communication and coordination between process participants. In the case of a procurement process with multiple handoffs and approval steps, value stream mapping can reveal the specific points where delays occur and guide the development of a more efficient and streamlined process. While other techniques like root cause analysis, Pareto analysis, and Kanban systems can also contribute to process improvement, value stream mapping is particularly effective for visualizing and optimizing end-to-end process flows.

446. A business analyst is modeling a process for handling customer complaints using BPMN. Which of the following BPMN elements represents a point in the process where a decision is made based on a specific condition?
a. Task
b. Event
c. Gateway
d. Sequence Flow

Answer: c. Gateway. Explanation: In BPMN, a gateway is a modeling element that represents a decision point or a point of divergence or convergence in a process flow. Gateways are used to control the flow of the process based on specific conditions or business rules. There are different types of gateways, such as exclusive (XOR), inclusive (OR), and parallel (AND) gateways, each with its own symbol and behavior. An exclusive gateway, represented by a diamond shape with an "X" inside, is used when the process flow follows one path or another based on a condition. For example, in a customer complaint handling process, an exclusive gateway could be used to decide whether to escalate a complaint based on its severity or priority. By using gateways to model decision points, the business analyst can clearly represent the logic and criteria that govern the process flow, making the process more transparent and understandable to stakeholders.

447. A company has implemented a new customer relationship management (CRM) system to improve its sales process. However, user adoption of the system has been low, and sales performance has not improved as expected. Which of the following actions should the business analyst take to address this issue?
a. Conduct a root cause analysis to identify the barriers to user adoption
b. Redesign the sales process to eliminate the need for the CRM system

c. Provide additional training to users on the features and benefits of the system
d. Implement a performance improvement plan for underperforming sales staff

Answer: a. Conduct a root cause analysis to identify the barriers to user adoption. Explanation: When a new process or system fails to deliver the expected results, it is important for the business analyst to investigate the underlying reasons and identify the root causes of the problem. In this case, the low user adoption of the CRM system suggests that there may be barriers or issues preventing sales staff from effectively using the system. Conducting a root cause analysis involves gathering data from various sources, such as user interviews, surveys, system logs, and performance metrics, to uncover the specific factors contributing to the low adoption. Some common barriers to user adoption include lack of training, complex or non-intuitive user interfaces, data quality issues, and resistance to change. By identifying the root causes, the business analyst can develop targeted solutions to address the barriers, such as providing additional training, simplifying the user experience, improving data management processes, or engaging stakeholders to build support for the system. Redesigning the sales process or implementing performance improvement plans may be necessary steps, but they should be based on a thorough understanding of the root causes of the adoption challenge.

448. A business process has an average cycle time of 10 days and a standard deviation of 2 days. Assuming a normal distribution, what percentage of process instances will be completed within 12 days?
a. 68.27%
b. 84.13%
c. 95.45%
d. 99.73%

Answer: b. 84.13%. Explanation: In a normal distribution, approximately 68.27% of values fall within one standard deviation of the mean, 95.45% fall within two standard deviations, and 99.73% fall within three standard deviations. To determine the percentage of process instances that will be completed within 12 days, we need to calculate how many standard deviations 12 days is from the mean cycle time. Given that the mean cycle time is 10 days and the standard deviation is 2 days, 12 days is one standard deviation above the mean (12 = 10 + 1 × 2). Since 68.27% of values fall within one standard deviation of the mean, half of that percentage (34.135%) will be above the mean. To find the total percentage of process instances completed within 12 days, we add this value to the 50% that fall below the mean: 50% + 34.135% = 84.13%. Understanding the distribution of process cycle times can help the business analyst set realistic expectations, identify improvement opportunities, and monitor process performance over time.

449. A company wants to improve its order fulfillment process, which currently has an average lead time of 7 days. The business analyst has identified several non-value-added activities that can be eliminated, potentially reducing the lead time by 2 days. However, the process also includes a bottleneck operation that takes 3 days to complete. What is the maximum theoretical lead time reduction that can be achieved by eliminating the non-value-added activities?
a. 1 day
b. 2 days
c. 3 days
d. 4 days

Answer: a. 1 day. Explanation: The lead time of a process is determined by the longest sequence of activities, known as the critical path. In this case, the bottleneck operation, which takes 3 days to complete, is on the critical path and limits the overall lead time of the process. Even if all the non-value-added activities are eliminated, the lead time cannot be reduced below the duration of the bottleneck operation. Therefore, the maximum theoretical lead time reduction that can be achieved by eliminating the non-value-added activities is 7 days - 3 days = 4 days. However, since the non-value-added activities only account for 2 days of the lead time, the actual reduction will be limited to 2 days, resulting in a new lead time of 5 days (7 days - 2 days). To further reduce the lead time, the business analyst would need to focus on improving the performance of the bottleneck operation, such as by increasing capacity, reducing setup times, or implementing process innovations. Understanding the concept of critical path and bottleneck analysis is crucial for identifying improvement opportunities and setting realistic targets in process optimization.

450. A business analyst is using a Supplier-Input-Process-Output-Customer (SIPOC) diagram to analyze a process. Which of the following is the correct order of elements in a SIPOC diagram, from left to right?
a. Supplier, Input, Process, Output, Customer
b. Input, Process, Output, Customer, Supplier
c. Process, Input, Output, Supplier, Customer
d. Customer, Output, Process, Input, Supplier

Answer: a. Supplier, Input, Process, Output, Customer. Explanation: A SIPOC diagram is a high-level process map that helps to identify the key elements of a process and its stakeholders. SIPOC stands for Supplier, Input, Process, Output, and Customer, and this is the correct order of elements in the diagram, from left to right. The SIPOC diagram starts with the Suppliers, which are the entities that provide the necessary inputs to the process. Inputs are the materials, information, or resources required to execute the process. The Process is the series of steps or activities that transform the inputs into outputs. Outputs are the products, services, or information that result from the process. Finally, Customers are the recipients or users of the process outputs. By organizing the process elements in this logical order, the SIPOC diagram provides a clear and concise overview of the process flow and the stakeholders involved, helping the business analyst to identify improvement opportunities and communicate the process scope and boundaries to others.

451. A project manager is evaluating different requirements management software tools. Which feature is essential for tracking the relationships between requirements and ensuring they are met throughout the project lifecycle?
a. Risk management module
b. Traceability matrix
c. Gantt chart integration
d. Resource allocation module

Answer: b. Traceability matrix. Explanation: A traceability matrix is essential in requirements management software for tracking the relationships between requirements, ensuring that all requirements are met throughout the project lifecycle, and helping identify the impact of changes.

452. A project team is using a requirements management tool that supports real-time collaboration. What is the primary benefit of this feature?
a. It reduces the need for formal documentation
b. It ensures that all team members have the latest information and can collaborate effectively
c. It minimizes the need for risk management
d. It allows for automatic resource allocation

Answer: b. It ensures that all team members have the latest information and can collaborate effectively. Explanation: Real-time collaboration in requirements management tools ensures that all team members have access to the most up-to-date information, facilitating effective communication and collaboration.

453. The project manager is implementing a new requirements management tool that includes a built-in workflow for approval processes. What is the main advantage of this feature?
a. It automates the project scheduling process
b. It ensures that all requirements go through a formal approval process before implementation
c. It helps track project costs more accurately
d. It enhances team morale by reducing workload

Answer: b. It ensures that all requirements go through a formal approval process before implementation. Explanation: A built-in workflow for approval processes in a requirements management tool ensures that all requirements are formally reviewed and approved before implementation, maintaining quality and alignment with project objectives.

454. A project team is using a collaboration tool to manage requirements. Which of the following features is most beneficial for capturing and addressing stakeholder feedback?
a. Real-time chat
b. Version control
c. Task assignment
d. Commenting and annotation

Answer: d. Commenting and annotation. Explanation: Commenting and annotation features in collaboration tools are beneficial for capturing and addressing stakeholder feedback directly within the context of the requirements, enabling clear communication and easier tracking of changes.

455. A project manager is using a requirements management tool that supports version control. Why is version control important in requirements management?
a. It helps in scheduling project tasks
b. It allows for tracking changes to requirements over time
c. It improves resource allocation
d. It automates risk analysis

Answer: b. It allows for tracking changes to requirements over time. Explanation: Version control is important in requirements management as it allows for tracking changes to requirements over time, providing a clear history of revisions and helping manage changes effectively.

456. The project team needs to ensure that the final deliverables meet all documented requirements. Which tool or technique is most appropriate for verifying this alignment?
a. Traceability matrix
b. Risk register
c. Work breakdown structure (WBS)
d. Communication plan

Answer: a. Traceability matrix. Explanation: A traceability matrix is used to verify that the final deliverables meet all documented requirements by ensuring that each requirement is linked to its corresponding deliverable, facilitating validation and quality assurance.

457. A business analyst is using a requirements management tool to generate reports on the status of requirements. Which feature of the tool is most useful for creating these reports?
a. Dashboard visualization
b. Automated notifications
c. Risk assessment module
d. Time tracking

Answer: a. Dashboard visualization. Explanation: Dashboard visualization in requirements management tools is useful for creating reports on the status of requirements, providing an overview of progress, issues, and other key metrics in an easily understandable format.

458. The project manager wants to ensure that all team members can contribute to the requirements management process. Which feature of collaboration tools is most critical for this purpose?
a. Role-based access control
b. Automated backup
c. Email integration
d. Time tracking

Answer: a. Role-based access control. Explanation: Role-based access control in collaboration tools is critical for ensuring that all team members can contribute to the requirements management process by granting appropriate permissions based on their roles, ensuring security and accountability.

459. A project team is using a requirements management software that integrates with their project management tool. What is the primary benefit of this integration?
a. It reduces the overall project cost
b. It eliminates the need for regular status meetings
c. It ensures seamless alignment between requirements and project tasks
d. It automates the hiring process

Answer: c. It ensures seamless alignment between requirements and project tasks. Explanation: Integration between requirements management software and project management tools ensures seamless alignment between requirements and project tasks, improving coordination and tracking of project progress.

460. A project manager is assessing the need for a new requirements management tool. Which of the following should be the primary consideration in this decision?
a. The tool's ability to generate financial reports
b. The tool's compatibility with existing systems
c. The tool's user interface design
d. The tool's marketing features

Answer: b. The tool's compatibility with existing systems. Explanation: The primary consideration when assessing a new requirements management tool should be its compatibility with existing systems to ensure smooth integration and data consistency across tools and processes.

461. A business analyst is using MoSCoW prioritization to categorize requirements for a new software project. Which of the following represents a "Should Have" requirement?
a. A feature that is necessary for the system to meet regulatory compliance
b. A feature that would significantly enhance user experience but is not critical for the system to function
c. A feature that can be included if there is enough time and resources
d. A feature that would be nice to have but has little impact on the system's overall functionality

Answer: b. A feature that would significantly enhance user experience but is not critical for the system to function. Explanation: In MoSCoW prioritization, "Should Have" requirements are important and add significant value, but they are not critical for the system's basic functionality.

462. During a gap analysis, the project manager identifies a discrepancy between the current capabilities of the organization's IT system and the desired capabilities needed to support a new business process. What should be the next step?
a. Ignore the discrepancy and proceed with the current system
b. Develop a plan to bridge the gap by enhancing the IT system
c. Reduce the scope of the new business process to fit the current capabilities
d. Document the discrepancy and revisit it at the end of the project

Answer: b. Develop a plan to bridge the gap by enhancing the IT system. Explanation: The next step after identifying a gap in capabilities is to develop a plan to bridge the gap. This may involve enhancing the IT system to meet the desired capabilities required to support the new business process.

463. A project manager is creating a use case diagram to capture the functional requirements of a system. Which element represents the interaction between a user and the system?
a. Activity
b. Actor

c. Sequence
d. State

Answer: b. Actor. Explanation: In a use case diagram, an actor represents a user or any entity that interacts with the system. Actors can be people, other systems, or external devices.

464. In a sequence diagram, what does a lifeline represent?
a. The sequence of events that occur in a system
b. The interaction between different components or objects over time
c. The state changes of an object within the system
d. The workflow of a particular business process

Answer: b. The interaction between different components or objects over time. Explanation: A lifeline in a sequence diagram represents an individual participant (object or actor) in the interaction, showing how they communicate with other participants over time.

465. A project manager uses a state diagram to model the behavior of an object. What is the primary purpose of a state diagram?
a. To illustrate the sequence of messages exchanged between objects
b. To describe the states an object can be in and the transitions between those states
c. To show the hierarchical relationship between different system components
d. To outline the use cases and their interactions with actors

Answer: b. To describe the states an object can be in and the transitions between those states. Explanation: A state diagram is used to describe the different states an object can be in during its lifecycle and the transitions between those states based on events.

466. When conducting a gap analysis, which of the following is not typically part of the process?
a. Identifying the current state
b. Defining the desired future state
c. Prioritizing requirements based on business value
d. Developing a strategy to bridge the gap

Answer: c. Prioritizing requirements based on business value. Explanation: Gap analysis focuses on identifying the current state, defining the desired future state, and developing a strategy to bridge the gap. Prioritizing requirements based on business value is part of requirements prioritization techniques like MoSCoW.

467. A business analyst is working on a use case diagram for an online shopping system. Which of the following is likely to be an actor in this use case diagram?
a. Customer

b. Shopping cart
c. Checkout process
d. Payment confirmation

Answer: a. Customer. Explanation: In a use case diagram, an actor is an entity that interacts with the system. In the context of an online shopping system, a customer is a typical actor who interacts with the system to perform various functions like browsing products, adding items to the cart, and making purchases.

468. In a sequence diagram, what is the purpose of a message?
a. To represent a state change in an object
b. To show the flow of control from one object to another
c. To depict the structural relationships between objects
d. To outline the responsibilities of different actors

Answer: b. To show the flow of control from one object to another. Explanation: In a sequence diagram, a message represents the communication between objects, showing the flow of control from one object to another as they interact.

469. A state diagram is being developed for a project. Which of the following best describes what a transition represents in a state diagram?
a. A communication exchange between objects
b. A change from one state to another triggered by an event
c. A sequence of activities within a workflow
d. An interaction between an actor and a use case

Answer: b. A change from one state to another triggered by an event. Explanation: In a state diagram, a transition represents the movement from one state to another, triggered by an event or condition.

470. A business analyst is using MoSCoW prioritization to organize project requirements. Which requirement would be classified as a "Could Have"?
a. A feature essential for the system's basic operation
b. A feature that would improve system performance but is not essential
c. A feature required to meet legal and regulatory standards
d. A feature that users have requested but is not critical

Answer: d. A feature that users have requested but is not critical. Explanation: In MoSCoW prioritization, "Could Have" requirements are desirable but not critical. These features are nice to have and can be included if time and resources permit, but they are not essential for the system's basic operation.

471. A project manager is working in a functional organizational structure. Which of the following characteristics is most typical of this type of structure?
a. The project manager has full authority over the project and resources.
b. Project team members report directly to the project manager.
c. Functional managers have more authority than project managers.
d. Resources are allocated to projects based on the project manager's discretion.

Answer: c. Functional managers have more authority than project managers. Explanation: In a functional organizational structure, functional managers have more authority over resources and decisions than project managers. Project managers typically have limited authority and must work through functional managers to get resources and decisions approved.

472. A project manager is assessing the readiness of an organization for a major change initiative. Which of the following is a key component of a readiness assessment?
a. Project schedule
b. Risk register
c. Stakeholder analysis
d. Communication plan

Answer: c. Stakeholder analysis. Explanation: A readiness assessment evaluates the organization's preparedness for a change initiative, and stakeholder analysis is a key component. It identifies key stakeholders, assesses their support and resistance, and plans strategies for managing their expectations and involvement.

473. In a matrix organizational structure, what is a potential challenge that project managers may face?
a. Lack of resources for the project
b. Limited authority over project team members
c. Difficulty in defining project goals
d. Insufficient project funding

Answer: b. Limited authority over project team members. Explanation: In a matrix organizational structure, project managers share authority with functional managers. This can lead to conflicts and challenges in managing project team members, as the project manager does not have full control over resources.

474. A project manager is implementing a change management plan to ensure successful adoption of a new software system. Which of the following activities is least likely to be part of this plan?
a. Training sessions for end-users
b. Creating a detailed project budget
c. Communication campaigns to inform stakeholders
d. Providing ongoing support after implementation

Answer: b. Creating a detailed project budget. Explanation: While a detailed project budget is important, it is not a primary activity of a change management plan. The plan focuses on activities that facilitate the adoption of the change, such as training, communication, and support.

475. When analyzing the organizational culture, which of the following aspects is most critical to understand for project success?
a. The geographical location of the organization
b. The organization's financial performance
c. The values, beliefs, and behaviors of the organization
d. The technical infrastructure of the organization

Answer: c. The values, beliefs, and behaviors of the organization. Explanation: Understanding the values, beliefs, and behaviors that make up the organizational culture is critical for project success. These aspects influence how projects are received and supported within the organization.

476. A project manager is conducting a readiness assessment for a project that involves significant process changes. Which method is most effective for gathering detailed insights from employees?
a. Surveys
b. Interviews
c. Focus groups
d. Observation

Answer: b. Interviews. Explanation: Interviews are effective for gathering detailed insights from employees. They allow for in-depth discussions and provide an opportunity to explore employees' perspectives, concerns, and readiness for the process changes.

477. In a projectized organizational structure, which of the following statements is true?
a. Project managers have little authority over resources.
b. Project team members report to functional managers.
c. Project managers have high authority and control over projects.
d. Functional managers make key project decisions.

Answer: c. Project managers have high authority and control over projects. Explanation: In a projectized organizational structure, project managers have high authority and control over resources and decision-making for their projects. Team members report directly to the project manager.

478. A project manager is planning to introduce a new project management methodology in an organization. What is the first step in managing this change?
a. Develop a detailed implementation plan
b. Conduct a stakeholder analysis
c. Schedule training sessions for the team
d. Assess the current project management processes

Answer: d. Assess the current project management processes. Explanation: The first step in managing the introduction of a new project management methodology is to assess the current processes. This helps identify gaps, areas for improvement, and the specific changes needed to adopt the new methodology.

479. During a readiness assessment, the project manager identifies that the organization lacks the necessary skills for a new project. What is the most appropriate action to take?
a. Delay the project until the skills are acquired
b. Outsource the project to an external vendor
c. Develop a training plan to build the necessary skills
d. Reallocate resources from other projects

Answer: c. Develop a training plan to build the necessary skills. Explanation: If the organization lacks the necessary skills for a new project, developing a training plan to build those skills is the most appropriate action. This ensures that the team is adequately prepared to undertake the project.

480. A project manager is analyzing the impact of organizational culture on project execution. Which of the following cultural factors is most likely to influence project outcomes?
a. The organization's market share
b. The leadership style of senior management
c. The company's physical office layout
d. The organization's IT infrastructure

Answer: b. The leadership style of senior management. Explanation: The leadership style of senior management significantly influences project outcomes. It affects decision-making, communication, and the overall support for the project within the organization.

481. A project manager is conducting a competitive analysis for a new product launch. Which of the following should be the primary focus of this analysis?
a. Identifying potential new markets for expansion
b. Evaluating the strengths and weaknesses of key competitors
c. Determining the internal resource requirements for the product launch
d. Establishing a project timeline and milestones

Answer: b. Evaluating the strengths and weaknesses of key competitors. Explanation: The primary focus of a competitive analysis is to evaluate the strengths and weaknesses of key competitors. This helps the project manager understand the competitive landscape and develop strategies to position the new product effectively.

482. A project manager is analyzing market trends to inform a strategic decision. Which of the following is the most reliable source of data for understanding current market trends?

a. Internal company reports
b. Customer feedback surveys
c. Industry research reports
d. Anecdotal evidence from sales teams

Answer: c. Industry research reports. Explanation: Industry research reports are a reliable source of data for understanding current market trends. These reports are typically based on comprehensive research and analysis conducted by experts, providing valuable insights into market dynamics.

483. During a customer needs analysis, the project manager discovers that customers are dissatisfied with the current product's user interface. What should be the project manager's next step?
a. Dismiss the feedback as subjective opinions
b. Focus on improving the product's core functionality instead
c. Initiate a redesign of the user interface based on customer feedback
d. Increase marketing efforts to highlight other product features

Answer: c. Initiate a redesign of the user interface based on customer feedback. Explanation: If customers are dissatisfied with the current product's user interface, the project manager should initiate a redesign based on their feedback. This helps improve customer satisfaction and ensures the product meets user needs.

484. In a market analysis, a project manager needs to determine the market size for a new service. Which metric is most appropriate for this purpose?
a. Customer satisfaction score
b. Market share
c. Total addressable market (TAM)
d. Net promoter score (NPS)

Answer: c. Total addressable market (TAM). Explanation: The total addressable market (TAM) is the most appropriate metric for determining the market size for a new service. TAM represents the total revenue opportunity available if the service captures 100% of the market.

485. A project manager is conducting a SWOT analysis as part of a market analysis. Which of the following would be classified as an opportunity?
a. A strong brand reputation
b. High production costs
c. Emerging market trends favoring the product
d. Intense competition in the market

Answer: c. Emerging market trends favoring the product. Explanation: Opportunities in a SWOT analysis are external factors that can be leveraged to achieve project objectives. Emerging market trends favoring the product represent an opportunity for growth and success.

486. During a competitive analysis, the project manager identifies a competitor with a superior distribution network. What strategy should the project manager consider to counter this competitive advantage?
a. Improve the quality of the product
b. Reduce the price of the product
c. Develop partnerships to enhance the distribution network
d. Increase spending on marketing and advertising

Answer: c. Develop partnerships to enhance the distribution network. Explanation: To counter a competitor's superior distribution network, the project manager should consider developing partnerships to enhance their own distribution network. This strategy helps improve market reach and competitiveness.

487. A project manager is assessing customer needs through focus groups. Which advantage does this method offer compared to surveys?
a. It provides quantitative data
b. It allows for anonymous feedback
c. It enables in-depth discussions and insights
d. It reaches a larger audience quickly

Answer: c. It enables in-depth discussions and insights. Explanation: Focus groups offer the advantage of enabling in-depth discussions and insights. They allow participants to express their views and experiences in detail, providing richer qualitative data compared to surveys.

488. In evaluating market trends, a project manager observes a shift towards eco-friendly products. How should this trend influence the project strategy?
a. Increase production of existing products
b. Develop and market eco-friendly product options
c. Focus on reducing operational costs
d. Expand into unrelated markets

Answer: b. Develop and market eco-friendly product options. Explanation: Observing a shift towards eco-friendly products should influence the project strategy by developing and marketing eco-friendly product options. This aligns with market trends and meets customer demands for sustainable products.

489. A project manager is using customer segmentation to tailor marketing efforts. Which segmentation criteria is most relevant for a high-end luxury product?
a. Geographic location
b. Demographic factors such as income level
c. Behavioral factors such as purchase history
d. Psychographic factors such as lifestyle and values

Answer: d. Psychographic factors such as lifestyle and values. Explanation: For a high-end luxury product, psychographic factors such as lifestyle and values are most relevant for customer segmentation. These factors help identify customers who prioritize luxury and are willing to pay a premium for high-end products.

490. In a market analysis, the project manager identifies a declining trend in a key market segment. What should be the project manager's next step?
a. Increase investment in the declining segment
b. Explore alternative market segments for growth opportunities
c. Maintain the current strategy without changes
d. Reduce marketing efforts to minimize costs

Answer: b. Explore alternative market segments for growth opportunities. Explanation: If a key market segment is declining, the project manager should explore alternative market segments for growth opportunities. This helps ensure the project's long-term success by diversifying and tapping into new markets.

491. A project manager is working on a software development project and needs to define the product scope. Which of the following best describes product scope?
a. The work required to deliver the product with the specified features and functions
b. The process of managing changes to the project scope
c. The time and cost estimates for the project
d. The roles and responsibilities of the project team

Answer: a. The work required to deliver the product with the specified features and functions. Explanation: Product scope refers to the features and functions that characterize a product, including the work required to deliver the product as specified.

492. During the project execution phase, a key stakeholder requests a significant change to the project scope. What should the project manager do first?
a. Implement the change immediately
b. Update the project schedule
c. Evaluate the impact of the change on the project
d. Reject the change request

Answer: c. Evaluate the impact of the change on the project. Explanation: The project manager should first evaluate the impact of the requested change on the project's scope, schedule, cost, and quality before deciding whether to implement the change.

493. A project manager needs to balance product scope and project scope to ensure project success. What is a primary consideration when balancing these two scopes?
a. Ensuring all stakeholder requirements are met, regardless of cost
b. Maintaining the project schedule at all costs

c. Aligning the product scope with the project's objectives and constraints
d. Minimizing the project team's workload

Answer: c. Aligning the product scope with the project's objectives and constraints. Explanation: Balancing product scope and project scope involves aligning the product's features and functions with the project's objectives and constraints, such as time, cost, and resources.

494. Which document is most useful for defining and managing the product scope?
a. Project charter
b. Work breakdown structure (WBS)
c. Requirements traceability matrix
d. Product scope statement

Answer: d. Product scope statement. Explanation: The product scope statement provides a detailed description of the product scope, including the product's features and functions. It is essential for defining and managing the product scope throughout the project.

495. A project manager is managing scope changes using a change control process. Which of the following is a key component of this process?
a. Project budget estimation
b. Quality assurance activities
c. Impact analysis of changes
d. Resource allocation planning

Answer: c. Impact analysis of changes. Explanation: Impact analysis is a key component of the change control process. It involves assessing the effects of proposed changes on the project's scope, schedule, cost, and quality before approving or rejecting the changes.

496. During a project review, the project manager realizes that the project scope has expanded beyond the original plan, a situation known as scope creep. What is the best way to prevent scope creep?
a. Allow stakeholders to add new requirements at any time
b. Implement a strict change control process
c. Focus solely on the project schedule
d. Increase the project budget to accommodate changes

Answer: b. Implement a strict change control process. Explanation: To prevent scope creep, a strict change control process should be implemented. This process ensures that all changes to the project scope are carefully reviewed and approved before being incorporated into the project plan.

497. The project team has completed the requirements gathering phase and needs to ensure that all requirements are included in the project scope. Which tool can help verify this alignment?
a. Gantt chart
b. Risk register
c. Requirements traceability matrix
d. Communications management plan

Answer: c. Requirements traceability matrix. Explanation: The requirements traceability matrix links requirements to their origins and tracks them throughout the project lifecycle. It helps verify that all requirements are included in the project scope and met by the deliverables.

498. A project manager is working on a project with a fixed budget and tight deadlines. How should they handle a request for additional features that would increase the project's scope?
a. Automatically approve the request to satisfy the customer
b. Reject the request to stay within budget and deadlines
c. Evaluate the impact on the project's objectives and constraints before making a decision
d. Delay the decision until more resources become available

Answer: c. Evaluate the impact on the project's objectives and constraints before making a decision. Explanation: The project manager should evaluate the impact of the request on the project's objectives and constraints, such as budget and deadlines, before making a decision to approve or reject the request.

499. Which of the following best describes the relationship between project scope and product scope?
a. Project scope defines the product scope
b. Product scope is independent of project scope
c. Project scope encompasses product scope
d. Product scope includes the project scope

Answer: c. Project scope encompasses product scope. Explanation: Project scope encompasses product scope, meaning that the project scope includes all the work required to deliver the product with its specified features and functions.

500. A project manager is balancing the need to meet stakeholder requirements with the constraints of time, budget, and resources. Which approach is most effective for achieving this balance?
a. Accepting all stakeholder requirements to ensure satisfaction
b. Prioritizing requirements based on their alignment with project objectives and constraints
c. Extending the project timeline to accommodate all requirements
d. Increasing the project budget to include all requested features

Answer: b. Prioritizing requirements based on their alignment with project objectives and constraints. Explanation: Prioritizing requirements based on their alignment with project objectives and constraints helps achieve a balance between meeting stakeholder needs and adhering to project limitations, ensuring a successful outcome.

501. A project manager is conducting a value stream mapping exercise to identify areas of waste in the production process. Which of the following steps should be taken first?
a. Analyze the flow of value through each process step
b. Identify the customer requirements and value stream
c. Implement changes to eliminate identified waste
d. Create a future state map based on the current process

Answer: b. Identify the customer requirements and value stream. Explanation: The first step in a value stream mapping exercise is to identify the customer requirements and value stream. This helps in understanding what constitutes value from the customer's perspective and defining the boundaries of the value stream.

502. During a value stream mapping session, the team identifies several bottlenecks in the production process. What is the primary goal of analyzing these bottlenecks?
a. To reduce the number of production steps
b. To identify areas where automation can be implemented
c. To improve the flow of value by addressing constraints
d. To eliminate non-essential activities

Answer: c. To improve the flow of value by addressing constraints. Explanation: The primary goal of analyzing bottlenecks is to improve the flow of value by addressing constraints that slow down the process. This helps in achieving a smoother, more efficient production flow.

503. In value stream mapping, what is the purpose of creating a future state map?
a. To document the current process in detail
b. To visualize the ideal process flow with improvements
c. To identify potential new markets for the product
d. To track the progress of ongoing projects

Answer: b. To visualize the ideal process flow with improvements. Explanation: A future state map is created to visualize the ideal process flow after improvements have been made. It helps in planning and implementing changes to achieve a more efficient and effective value stream.

504. A project manager notices that a particular process step adds no value to the customer but is necessary for compliance reasons. How should this step be categorized in the value stream map?
a. Value-adding
b. Non-value-adding but necessary
c. Pure waste
d. Value-enabling

Answer: b. Non-value-adding but necessary. Explanation: A process step that adds no value to the customer but is required for compliance reasons is categorized as non-value-adding but necessary. It cannot be eliminated but should be minimized to the extent possible.

505. When analyzing the flow of value in a manufacturing process, the project manager finds that work-in-progress (WIP) inventory is frequently piling up between two stages. What is the most likely cause of this issue?
a. The upstream process is faster than the downstream process
b. The downstream process is faster than the upstream process
c. There is a lack of skilled workers in the upstream process
d. There is insufficient raw material supply

Answer: a. The upstream process is faster than the downstream process. Explanation: When WIP inventory piles up between two stages, it is usually because the upstream process is faster than the downstream process, causing a bottleneck. The downstream process cannot keep up with the inflow of work, leading to inventory buildup.

506. In a value stream mapping workshop, the team identifies several activities that do not contribute to customer value. What should be the project manager's approach to these activities?
a. Document and continue the activities as they are
b. Eliminate or reduce these activities to streamline the process
c. Increase the resources allocated to these activities
d. Shift these activities to a later stage in the process

Answer: b. Eliminate or reduce these activities to streamline the process. Explanation: The project manager should aim to eliminate or reduce activities that do not contribute to customer value. This helps streamline the process, reduce waste, and improve overall efficiency.

507. A project manager is mapping a value stream and identifies a step where multiple handoffs occur between departments. What is the potential impact of this on the process?
a. Increased process efficiency
b. Enhanced communication and collaboration
c. Increased risk of errors and delays
d. Reduced need for quality checks

Answer: c. Increased risk of errors and delays. Explanation: Multiple handoffs between departments can increase the risk of errors and delays. Each handoff is an opportunity for miscommunication and mistakes, which can slow down the process and reduce quality.

508. During the creation of a value stream map, the project manager includes a timeline showing the lead time and processing time for each step. What is the main purpose of this timeline?

a. To identify the total time taken to complete the value stream
b. To allocate resources more effectively
c. To compare different value streams
d. To determine the cost of each process step

Answer: a. To identify the total time taken to complete the value stream. Explanation: The main purpose of including a timeline in a value stream map is to identify the total time taken to complete the value stream, including both lead time and processing time. This helps in understanding delays and opportunities for improvement.

509. A project manager is working to eliminate waste in a value stream. Which type of waste is characterized by excess inventory that exceeds customer demand?
a. Overproduction
b. Waiting
c. Defects
d. Overprocessing

Answer: a. Overproduction. Explanation: Overproduction refers to producing more inventory than is needed to meet customer demand. This type of waste ties up resources, increases storage costs, and can lead to obsolescence.

510. In value stream mapping, what is the primary benefit of involving cross-functional teams in the mapping process?
a. Ensuring that only senior management's perspective is considered
b. Gaining a comprehensive understanding of the entire process
c. Accelerating the decision-making process
d. Reducing the overall cost of the project

Answer: b. Gaining a comprehensive understanding of the entire process. Explanation: Involving cross-functional teams in the value stream mapping process ensures that different perspectives are considered, leading to a comprehensive understanding of the entire process. This helps in identifying and addressing issues more effectively.

511. A project manager is using a data flow diagram (DFD) to model the processes in an information system. Which of the following elements is NOT typically included in a DFD?
a. Data stores
b. Processes
c. Actors
d. Network paths

Answer: d. Network paths. Explanation: A data flow diagram (DFD) includes data stores, processes, and actors (external entities) but does not include network paths, which are related to physical network diagrams.

512. During the creation of an entity-relationship diagram (ERD), the project team identifies entities and their relationships. What is the primary purpose of an ERD?
a. To model the flow of data within a system
b. To define the hardware components of a system
c. To visually represent the data structure and relationships between entities
d. To describe the user interface of a system

Answer: c. To visually represent the data structure and relationships between entities. Explanation: An entity-relationship diagram (ERD) is used to visually represent the data structure and relationships between entities in a database, helping to define how data is stored and interrelated.

513. A business analyst is updating the data dictionary for a new project. Which of the following best describes the purpose of a data dictionary?
a. To define the logical and physical structure of a database
b. To document the details and descriptions of data elements
c. To track changes to project requirements
d. To outline the project budget and schedule

Answer: b. To document the details and descriptions of data elements. Explanation: A data dictionary provides detailed descriptions and definitions of data elements, including their attributes, types, and relationships, ensuring consistency and clarity in data usage.

514. A project team is creating a data flow diagram (DFD) to understand the flow of information in an existing system. Which of the following best represents the flow of data between processes in a DFD?
a. Data stores
b. Data flows
c. External entities
d. Control flows

Answer: b. Data flows. Explanation: In a data flow diagram (DFD), data flows represent the movement of data between processes, data stores, and external entities, showing how information flows through the system.

515. While designing an entity-relationship diagram (ERD), the team needs to model a one-to-many relationship between two entities. Which of the following best describes this relationship?
a. Each instance of the first entity is associated with exactly one instance of the second entity
b. Each instance of the first entity is associated with zero or more instances of the second entity
c. Each instance of the first entity is associated with exactly one instance of the second entity, and vice versa
d. Each instance of the first entity is associated with one or more instances of the second entity, and each instance of the second entity is associated with zero or more instances of the first entity

Answer: b. Each instance of the first entity is associated with zero or more instances of the second entity. Explanation: A one-to-many relationship in an entity-relationship diagram (ERD) means that each instance of the first entity can be associated with zero or more instances of the second entity, but each instance of the second entity is associated with only one instance of the first entity.

516. A project manager needs to ensure that all team members understand the meaning and usage of specific data elements in the project. Which tool or document should they refer to?
a. Project charter
b. Data flow diagram
c. Data dictionary
d. Work breakdown structure

Answer: c. Data dictionary. Explanation: The data dictionary provides detailed descriptions and definitions of data elements, ensuring that all team members have a consistent understanding of their meaning and usage.

517. During a requirements gathering session, the project team decides to use data flow diagrams (DFDs) to capture system requirements. What is a primary advantage of using DFDs for this purpose?
a. They provide a detailed physical layout of the system's hardware
b. They visually depict how data moves through the system, facilitating understanding
c. They offer a step-by-step guide for system implementation
d. They track project progress and milestones

Answer: b. They visually depict how data moves through the system, facilitating understanding. Explanation: Data flow diagrams (DFDs) visually depict the flow of data within a system, making it easier for stakeholders to understand how information is processed and transferred.

518. A project team is developing an entity-relationship diagram (ERD) for a customer database. Which of the following is an example of an entity in an ERD?
a. Customer name
b. Order processing
c. Customer
d. Data flow

Answer: c. Customer. Explanation: In an entity-relationship diagram (ERD), an entity represents a real-world object or concept, such as Customer, which has attributes (e.g., Customer name) and relationships with other entities.

519. A data dictionary entry includes the data element "Order Date." Which attribute is LEAST likely to be included in the data dictionary for this element?
a. Data type (e.g., date, string, integer)
b. Default value
c. Related processes
d. Validation rules

Answer: c. Related processes. Explanation: A data dictionary entry typically includes attributes such as data type, default value, and validation rules for a data element like "Order Date." Related processes are not typically part of the data dictionary but rather part of process documentation.

520. The project team is using a data flow diagram (DFD) to model a new system. They need to represent an external entity that interacts with the system. Which symbol is used in a DFD to represent an external entity?
a. Circle
b. Rectangle
c. Arrow
d. Diamond

Answer: b. Rectangle. Explanation: In a data flow diagram (DFD), an external entity is typically represented by a rectangle, indicating sources or destinations of data that interact with the system but are outside its boundaries.

521. A project manager is overseeing the solution testing and evaluation phase of a new software implementation. Which of the following activities should be prioritized during this phase?
a. Developing the project charter
b. Conducting user acceptance testing (UAT)
c. Creating a work breakdown structure (WBS)
d. Performing a SWOT analysis

Answer: b. Conducting user acceptance testing (UAT). Explanation: During the solution testing and evaluation phase, conducting user acceptance testing (UAT) is critical. UAT ensures that the software meets the business requirements and that end users find it functional and satisfactory.

522. In assessing organizational readiness for a new system implementation, which factor is most critical to evaluate?
a. The current state of the IT infrastructure
b. The market trends in the industry
c. The financial stability of the organization
d. The readiness of stakeholders to adopt the new system

Answer: d. The readiness of stakeholders to adopt the new system. Explanation: Assessing organizational readiness involves evaluating how prepared stakeholders are to adopt the new system. This includes their willingness, training levels, and overall support for the change.

523. A project manager needs to determine the transition requirements for moving from the current system to the new system. Which of the following should be included in the transition plan?
a. Detailed project scope
b. Training materials for end users

c. Historical market data
d. Future state process maps

Answer: b. Training materials for end users. Explanation: The transition plan should include training materials for end users to ensure they understand how to use the new system. This helps facilitate a smooth transition and reduces resistance to change.

524. During the solution assessment, the project manager identifies several critical issues with the solution's performance. What is the next step to address these issues?
a. Document the issues and proceed with implementation
b. Communicate the issues to the project sponsor and halt implementation
c. Develop and implement corrective actions to resolve the issues
d. Ignore the issues if they do not impact the project schedule

Answer: c. Develop and implement corrective actions to resolve the issues. Explanation: The project manager should develop and implement corrective actions to resolve critical issues identified during the solution assessment. This ensures the solution meets performance standards before full implementation.

525. In evaluating the effectiveness of a new solution, which metric is most useful for measuring user satisfaction?
a. Mean time to repair (MTTR)
b. Net promoter score (NPS)
c. Return on investment (ROI)
d. Cost variance (CV)

Answer: b. Net promoter score (NPS). Explanation: The net promoter score (NPS) is a metric used to measure user satisfaction by gauging how likely users are to recommend the solution to others. It provides valuable insights into user acceptance and satisfaction.

526. A project manager is preparing for the deployment of a new solution. Which activity is essential to ensure a smooth transition?
a. Conducting a thorough risk assessment
b. Reviewing the project charter
c. Finalizing the project budget
d. Developing a stakeholder engagement plan

Answer: a. Conducting a thorough risk assessment. Explanation: Conducting a thorough risk assessment is essential to identify potential issues that could impact the deployment and to develop mitigation strategies. This helps ensure a smooth transition to the new solution.

527. To validate that a solution meets business requirements, a project manager uses a set of predefined criteria. What is this process called?
a. Risk management
b. Scope verification
c. Requirements traceability
d. Quality assurance

Answer: c. Requirements traceability. Explanation: Requirements traceability involves using predefined criteria to validate that a solution meets business requirements. It ensures that all requirements are accounted for and addressed in the final solution.

528. The project manager needs to assess whether the organization is ready to accept the new solution. Which technique is best suited for this assessment?
a. SWOT analysis
b. Benchmarking
c. Readiness assessment survey
d. Cost-benefit analysis

Answer: c. Readiness assessment survey. Explanation: A readiness assessment survey is a technique used to evaluate the organization's preparedness to accept the new solution. It gathers feedback from stakeholders on their readiness, training needs, and any concerns they may have.

529. During the transition phase, the project manager identifies a gap in the training provided to end users. What should be the next step?
a. Delay the transition until all users are fully trained
b. Update the training materials and provide additional training sessions
c. Ignore the gap if it does not impact critical users
d. Assign the responsibility of training to team leads

Answer: b. Update the training materials and provide additional training sessions. Explanation: The project manager should update the training materials and provide additional training sessions to ensure all users are adequately prepared to use the new system. This helps ensure a smooth transition and effective use of the solution.

530. A project manager is evaluating the performance of a recently implemented solution. Which method should be used to collect feedback from end users?
a. Focus groups
b. Earned value analysis (EVA)
c. Delphi technique
d. Monte Carlo simulation

Answer: a. Focus groups. Explanation: Focus groups are an effective method for collecting detailed feedback from end users. They allow for in-depth discussions and insights into the users' experiences with the implemented solution.

531. A business analyst is preparing a communication plan for a project with multiple stakeholders. Which of the following strategies is most effective for ensuring clear and consistent communication with all stakeholders?
a. Using a single communication method for all stakeholders
b. Tailoring communication methods to the preferences and needs of different stakeholder groups
c. Limiting communication to formal meetings only
d. Sending detailed reports to stakeholders on a monthly basis

Answer: b. Tailoring communication methods to the preferences and needs of different stakeholder groups. Explanation: Tailoring communication methods to the preferences and needs of different stakeholder groups ensures that each stakeholder receives information in a format that is most effective for them, leading to better understanding and engagement.

532. During a project meeting, the business analyst notices that one team member is dominating the discussion, preventing others from contributing. Which facilitation technique should the business analyst use to ensure balanced participation?
a. Encourage open-ended questions
b. Allow the dominant team member to continue
c. Use a round-robin approach
d. Schedule a separate meeting with the dominant team member

Answer: c. Use a round-robin approach. Explanation: Using a round-robin approach ensures that each team member has an equal opportunity to speak and contribute to the discussion, promoting balanced participation and diverse perspectives.

533. A business analyst is mediating a conflict between two stakeholders with opposing views on a project requirement. What is the first step the business analyst should take in resolving this conflict?
a. Determine which stakeholder has more influence
b. Identify the underlying interests and concerns of each stakeholder
c. Choose a solution that satisfies both stakeholders
d. Escalate the conflict to the project sponsor

Answer: b. Identify the underlying interests and concerns of each stakeholder. Explanation: The first step in resolving a conflict is to understand the underlying interests and concerns of each stakeholder. This helps in finding a mutually acceptable solution that addresses the root cause of the conflict.

534. A business analyst is leading a requirements workshop with a diverse group of stakeholders. Which of the following is an effective strategy for facilitating this workshop?
a. Presenting all information in a lecture format
b. Encouraging active participation through interactive activities

c. Limiting discussion to avoid disagreements
d. Allowing the loudest voices to drive the discussion

Answer: b. Encouraging active participation through interactive activities. Explanation: Encouraging active participation through interactive activities, such as brainstorming sessions or group discussions, ensures that all stakeholders are engaged and contribute to the workshop, leading to more comprehensive and well-rounded requirements.

535. During a negotiation session, the business analyst aims to reach an agreement that benefits both parties. Which negotiation strategy is most appropriate for achieving a win-win outcome?
a. Competitive negotiation
b. Avoidance
c. Compromise
d. Collaborative negotiation

Answer: d. Collaborative negotiation. Explanation: Collaborative negotiation focuses on finding mutually beneficial solutions that satisfy the interests of both parties, aiming for a win-win outcome. It involves open communication, trust-building, and problem-solving.

536. A business analyst is preparing a presentation for senior executives. Which of the following communication strategies is most effective for this audience?
a. Using detailed technical jargon to demonstrate expertise
b. Focusing on high-level summaries and key insights
c. Providing extensive background information
d. Using informal language and humor

Answer: b. Focusing on high-level summaries and key insights. Explanation: Senior executives typically prefer high-level summaries and key insights that provide a clear overview of the important information without getting bogged down in technical details.

537. During a project review meeting, a conflict arises between two team members over resource allocation. What is the most appropriate conflict resolution technique for the business analyst to use in this situation?
a. Forcing a decision
b. Avoiding the conflict
c. Compromising
d. Collaborating

Answer: d. Collaborating. Explanation: Collaborating involves working together to find a solution that satisfies the needs and concerns of both parties. It promotes open communication and problem-solving, leading to a more sustainable and mutually acceptable resolution.

538. A business analyst needs to communicate complex technical information to a non-technical stakeholder. Which communication technique is most effective for this purpose?
a. Using technical jargon to ensure accuracy
b. Simplifying the information and using analogies
c. Providing detailed technical documentation
d. Avoiding technical information altogether

Answer: b. Simplifying the information and using analogies. Explanation: Simplifying complex technical information and using analogies helps non-technical stakeholders understand the content without overwhelming them with jargon and technical details.

539. A project team is experiencing low morale due to unclear communication of project goals. What is the most effective communication strategy for the business analyst to improve team morale?
a. Sending weekly progress reports via email
b. Holding regular team meetings to discuss project goals and progress
c. Assigning individual tasks without explanation
d. Reducing the frequency of communication

Answer: b. Holding regular team meetings to discuss project goals and progress. Explanation: Regular team meetings provide an opportunity to discuss project goals and progress, clarify any uncertainties, and ensure that all team members are aligned and motivated.

540. A business analyst is facilitating a brainstorming session to generate ideas for a new product feature. Which of the following rules is most important to ensure the effectiveness of the session?
a. Criticize ideas to ensure only the best ones are discussed
b. Encourage all ideas, no matter how unconventional
c. Limit the number of ideas generated
d. Allow only senior team members to contribute

Answer: b. Encourage all ideas, no matter how unconventional. Explanation: Encouraging all ideas, no matter how unconventional, fosters creativity and ensures that a wide range of potential solutions are considered. Criticism should be avoided during the brainstorming phase to promote open and free thinking.

541. A project team is facing a complex issue with conflicting stakeholder requirements. The project manager decides to use an analytical technique to identify the root cause. Which technique should be used?
a. Brainstorming
b. Pareto analysis
c. Ishikawa (fishbone) diagram
d. SWOT analysis

Answer: c. Ishikawa (fishbone) diagram. Explanation: The Ishikawa diagram, also known as a fishbone diagram, is an analytical technique used to identify the root cause of a problem by categorizing potential causes into different areas. It helps the team systematically explore all possible causes of the issue.

542. During a brainstorming session, the team generates a large number of ideas to solve a problem. What should be the project manager's next step?
a. Implement the most popular idea immediately
b. Evaluate and prioritize the ideas based on feasibility and impact
c. Discard the ideas that seem too complex
d. Seek approval from the project sponsor for all the ideas

Answer: b. Evaluate and prioritize the ideas based on feasibility and impact. Explanation: After generating ideas in a brainstorming session, the next step is to evaluate and prioritize them based on their feasibility and potential impact. This helps the team focus on the most effective solutions.

543. A project manager needs to make a decision that will impact the project's schedule and budget. Which decision-making process is most appropriate for ensuring a thorough and unbiased evaluation of options?
a. Intuition-based decision-making
b. Multi-criteria decision analysis (MCDA)
c. Authority-based decision-making
d. Random selection

Answer: b. Multi-criteria decision analysis (MCDA). Explanation: Multi-criteria decision analysis (MCDA) is a structured decision-making process that evaluates multiple options based on various criteria. It ensures a thorough and unbiased evaluation by considering different factors and their relative importance.

544. A project manager is faced with a problem that requires a creative solution. Which technique is best suited for generating innovative ideas?
a. Delphi technique
b. Mind mapping
c. Cost-benefit analysis
d. Work breakdown structure (WBS)

Answer: b. Mind mapping. Explanation: Mind mapping is a creative problem-solving technique that helps generate innovative ideas by visually organizing information and exploring connections between different concepts. It encourages free thinking and creativity.

545. The project team is using the "5 Whys" technique to address a recurring issue. What is the primary objective of this technique?
a. To create a detailed project plan
b. To identify the root cause of the problem by repeatedly asking "why"
c. To prioritize project tasks based on urgency

d. To develop a risk management plan

Answer: b. To identify the root cause of the problem by repeatedly asking "why". Explanation: The "5 Whys" technique involves repeatedly asking "why" to drill down into the underlying cause of a problem. This helps identify the root cause, allowing the team to address the issue effectively.

546. A project manager needs to analyze a large dataset to identify trends and patterns. Which analytical technique is most appropriate for this task?
a. SWOT analysis
b. Regression analysis
c. Scenario planning
d. Nominal group technique

Answer: b. Regression analysis. Explanation: Regression analysis is an analytical technique used to identify trends and patterns in large datasets by examining the relationships between variables. It helps the project manager understand how different factors influence the outcomes.

547. During a decision-making process, the project manager wants to ensure that all team members have an equal opportunity to contribute their ideas. Which technique should be used?
a. Brainstorming
b. Nominal group technique (NGT)
c. Delphi technique
d. SWOT analysis

Answer: b. Nominal group technique (NGT). Explanation: The nominal group technique (NGT) is a structured decision-making process that ensures all team members have an equal opportunity to contribute their ideas. It involves generating ideas individually, discussing them as a group, and then prioritizing the ideas.

548. A project manager is using scenario planning to prepare for potential future challenges. What is the primary benefit of this technique?
a. It provides a detailed project schedule
b. It helps anticipate and plan for different future scenarios
c. It identifies the root cause of current problems
d. It prioritizes tasks based on business value

Answer: b. It helps anticipate and plan for different future scenarios. Explanation: Scenario planning involves creating and analyzing multiple potential future scenarios to anticipate and plan for different challenges. It helps the project manager develop strategies to address various possible outcomes.

549. The project team is experiencing difficulty in reaching a consensus on a critical decision. Which decision-making technique can help facilitate consensus?
a. Random selection
b. Voting
c. Delphi technique
d. Cost-benefit analysis

Answer: c. Delphi technique. Explanation: The Delphi technique is a structured decision-making process that uses multiple rounds of anonymous input from experts to reach a consensus. It helps facilitate agreement by allowing participants to provide their opinions and refine their responses based on feedback.

550. A project manager needs to solve a problem quickly and efficiently. Which problem-solving approach is most appropriate for this situation?
a. Creative problem-solving
b. Analytical problem-solving
c. Trial and error
d. Intuitive problem-solving

Answer: b. Analytical problem-solving. Explanation: Analytical problem-solving involves systematically analyzing the problem, identifying root causes, and developing a structured solution. It is most appropriate for quickly and efficiently solving problems by using logical and data-driven approaches.

551. A business analyst is preparing requirements documentation for a new project. Which of the following is a key component that should be included in this documentation?
a. Project schedule
b. Resource allocation plan
c. Acceptance criteria for each requirement
d. Detailed budget estimates

Answer: c. Acceptance criteria for each requirement. Explanation: Requirements documentation should include acceptance criteria for each requirement, which define the conditions that must be met for the requirement to be considered fulfilled. This ensures clear understanding and agreement on what constitutes successful completion.

552. During a project review, the business analyst needs to present a summary of the project's progress and key issues. Which type of report is most appropriate for this purpose?
a. Detailed technical report
b. Executive summary report
c. Financial report
d. Risk management report

Answer: b. Executive summary report. Explanation: An executive summary report provides a concise overview of the project's progress, key issues, and critical information, making it ideal for presenting to stakeholders who need a high-level understanding without delving into technical details.

553. A project team is using visual models to document requirements. Which visual model is best suited for showing the sequence of activities in a process?
a. Entity-relationship diagram
b. Use case diagram
c. Process flowchart
d. Data flow diagram

Answer: c. Process flowchart. Explanation: A process flowchart is a visual model that shows the sequence of activities in a process, making it an effective tool for documenting and understanding the steps involved in a particular workflow.

554. The business analyst is responsible for creating a business analysis report. What is the primary purpose of this report?
a. To allocate project resources
b. To communicate findings, recommendations, and conclusions
c. To define the project's technical specifications
d. To establish the project's timeline

Answer: b. To communicate findings, recommendations, and conclusions. Explanation: The primary purpose of a business analysis report is to communicate the findings, recommendations, and conclusions of the analysis. It helps stakeholders make informed decisions based on the analysis.

555. A business analyst is documenting requirements for a complex software system. Which technique can help ensure that all requirements are clearly defined and understood by stakeholders?
a. Holding informal conversations with team members
b. Using formal requirements documentation templates
c. Conducting unstructured interviews with stakeholders
d. Avoiding the use of diagrams or visual aids

Answer: b. Using formal requirements documentation templates. Explanation: Using formal requirements documentation templates helps ensure that all requirements are clearly defined, structured, and understood by stakeholders. It provides a consistent format for capturing and communicating requirements.

556. In a requirements documentation, which section typically includes the business needs and objectives the project aims to address?
a. Project scope statement
b. Business requirements section
c. Technical requirements section

d. Risk management plan

Answer: b. Business requirements section. Explanation: The business requirements section of the documentation includes the business needs and objectives that the project aims to address. It provides context for why the project is being undertaken and what it seeks to achieve.

557. A business analyst uses a data flow diagram (DFD) to illustrate the flow of information within a system. What is the primary purpose of a DFD?
a. To model the relationships between data entities
b. To define the physical layout of a system
c. To show how data moves through a system and how it is processed
d. To outline the project's timeline and milestones

Answer: c. To show how data moves through a system and how it is processed. Explanation: A data flow diagram (DFD) illustrates how data moves through a system and how it is processed by depicting data sources, processes, data stores, and data flows.

558. When preparing a business analysis report, the business analyst needs to ensure that the document is clear and concise. Which of the following practices helps achieve this goal?
a. Including all technical details, regardless of their relevance
b. Using jargon and technical terms extensively
c. Structuring the report with headings, subheadings, and bullet points
d. Writing long paragraphs without breaks

Answer: c. Structuring the report with headings, subheadings, and bullet points. Explanation: Structuring the report with headings, subheadings, and bullet points helps make the document clear and concise. It improves readability and allows stakeholders to quickly find and understand the key information.

559. A project manager asks the business analyst to create a visual model to help stakeholders understand the interactions between different system components. Which visual model is most appropriate for this purpose?
a. Gantt chart
b. Entity-relationship diagram
c. Use case diagram
d. Fishbone diagram

Answer: c. Use case diagram. Explanation: A use case diagram visually represents the interactions between different system components and their users (actors). It helps stakeholders understand how various parts of the system interact to achieve specific goals.

560. During a requirements gathering session, the business analyst documents all inputs, processes, and outputs for a system. Which visual model is typically used to represent this information?
a. Process flowchart
b. Fishbone diagram
c. Data flow diagram
d. Entity-relationship diagram

Answer: c. Data flow diagram. Explanation: A data flow diagram (DFD) is typically used to represent the inputs, processes, and outputs of a system. It shows how data flows between different components and how it is processed within the system.

561. A project manager discovers that a team member has manipulated project data to meet a critical deadline. What should the project manager do first?
a. Ignore the issue since the deadline was met
b. Confront the team member privately and address the manipulation
c. Report the incident to senior management immediately
d. Adjust future project deadlines to avoid similar issues

Answer: b. Confront the team member privately and address the manipulation. Explanation: The project manager should first address the issue directly with the team member to understand the reasons behind the manipulation and to reinforce the importance of ethical behavior and data integrity. This approach helps maintain trust and accountability within the team.

562. During a project review meeting, a stakeholder offers the project manager a gift to ensure their requirements are prioritized. What is the most appropriate course of action for the project manager?
a. Accept the gift and prioritize the stakeholder's requirements
b. Politely decline the gift and report the incident to the ethics committee
c. Accept the gift but ensure all requirements are treated equally
d. Decline the gift and ignore the incident

Answer: b. Politely decline the gift and report the incident to the ethics committee. Explanation: Accepting gifts that could influence project decisions is unethical. The project manager should decline the gift and report the incident to the ethics committee to maintain transparency and integrity in the project.

563. A project manager is faced with a decision that could benefit the project but might harm the environment. How should the project manager approach this decision?
a. Proceed with the decision since it benefits the project
b. Evaluate the environmental impact and seek alternative solutions
c. Ignore the environmental concerns if they are not legally binding
d. Make the decision privately to avoid stakeholder objections

Answer: b. Evaluate the environmental impact and seek alternative solutions. Explanation: The project manager should consider the environmental impact and seek alternative solutions that benefit the project while minimizing harm to the environment. Ethical decision-making involves balancing project benefits with broader social and environmental responsibilities.

564. A business analyst notices that a colleague is consistently overestimating project costs to build in extra budget. What should the business analyst do?
a. Ignore the behavior since it benefits the project
b. Discuss the issue with the colleague privately
c. Report the behavior to the project manager
d. Document the issue and wait for it to resolve on its own

Answer: b. Discuss the issue with the colleague privately. Explanation: The business analyst should first address the issue with the colleague privately to understand their motivations and to emphasize the importance of accurate and ethical cost estimation. If the behavior continues, it should be reported to the project manager.

565. A project manager realizes that the project deliverables may not meet the client's expectations due to a misunderstanding in requirements. What is the most ethical action to take?
a. Deliver the current product and address issues if the client complains
b. Inform the client about the potential shortfall and discuss possible solutions
c. Proceed with the deliverables as planned and hope for the best
d. Adjust the deliverables without informing the client

Answer: b. Inform the client about the potential shortfall and discuss possible solutions. Explanation: The project manager should inform the client about the misunderstanding and discuss potential solutions to meet their expectations. This approach maintains transparency and trust with the client.

566. During a project, a team member accesses confidential information not related to their tasks. What should the project manager do?
a. Ignore the issue since no harm was done
b. Reprimand the team member publicly to set an example
c. Address the issue privately with the team member and remind them of confidentiality policies
d. Change the team member's role to limit their access to information

Answer: c. Address the issue privately with the team member and remind them of confidentiality policies. Explanation: The project manager should address the issue privately with the team member, emphasizing the importance of adhering to confidentiality policies. This approach helps prevent future breaches and reinforces professional conduct.

567. A project manager is considering cutting corners on quality to meet a tight deadline. What should be the primary consideration in this decision?
a. The impact on the project schedule

b. The potential risks to stakeholder satisfaction and safety
c. The cost savings from reduced quality assurance
d. The likelihood of receiving a performance bonus

Answer: b. The potential risks to stakeholder satisfaction and safety. Explanation: The primary consideration should be the potential risks to stakeholder satisfaction and safety. Cutting corners on quality can lead to significant issues, including reduced product performance, safety hazards, and loss of stakeholder trust.

568. A business analyst is asked to provide a positive report on a project's progress, even though the project is behind schedule. What is the ethical course of action?
a. Comply with the request to avoid conflict
b. Provide an honest report reflecting the actual project status
c. Alter the report slightly to make the progress appear better
d. Delay the report to gather more positive data

Answer: b. Provide an honest report reflecting the actual project status. Explanation: The ethical course of action is to provide an honest report reflecting the actual project status. Transparency and accuracy in reporting are crucial for informed decision-making and maintaining professional integrity.

569. A project manager discovers that a supplier is using child labor. What should be the project manager's response?
a. Continue working with the supplier to avoid project delays
b. Report the issue to the appropriate authorities and seek alternative suppliers
c. Negotiate a lower price with the supplier due to their unethical practices
d. Ignore the issue if the supplier provides quality materials

Answer: b. Report the issue to the appropriate authorities and seek alternative suppliers. Explanation: The project manager should report the issue to the appropriate authorities and seek alternative suppliers. Supporting suppliers that use unethical practices, such as child labor, is against professional responsibility and ethical standards.

570. A team member suggests using pirated software to reduce project costs. What should the project manager do?
a. Approve the use of pirated software to save costs
b. Reject the suggestion and explain the legal and ethical implications
c. Consider the suggestion if it significantly reduces costs
d. Use the software but keep the decision confidential

Answer: b. Reject the suggestion and explain the legal and ethical implications. Explanation: The project manager should reject the suggestion and explain the legal and ethical implications of using pirated software. Using pirated software is illegal and unethical, and it can lead to severe consequences for the project and the organization.

571. A project manager is analyzing the customer journey to improve the user experience of a new mobile application. Which of the following steps is most crucial for identifying pain points in the customer journey?
a. Mapping the project milestones
b. Conducting stakeholder interviews
c. Creating a customer journey map
d. Developing a project budget

Answer: c. Creating a customer journey map. Explanation: Creating a customer journey map is crucial for identifying pain points in the customer journey. It visually represents the customer's experience with the product, highlighting areas where improvements are needed.

572. During a project to enhance customer satisfaction, the project manager decides to map customer touchpoints. Which of the following best describes a customer touchpoint?
a. The budget allocated for customer service
b. Any interaction a customer has with the company
c. The project schedule milestones
d. Internal meetings to discuss customer feedback

Answer: b. Any interaction a customer has with the company. Explanation: A customer touchpoint is any interaction a customer has with the company, including interactions through various channels such as phone, email, website, or in-person.

573. A project team is working on improving customer satisfaction for an online retail store. Which metric is most appropriate for measuring customer satisfaction?
a. Net Promoter Score (NPS)
b. Return on Investment (ROI)
c. Cost Performance Index (CPI)
d. Schedule Performance Index (SPI)

Answer: a. Net Promoter Score (NPS). Explanation: The Net Promoter Score (NPS) is a widely used metric for measuring customer satisfaction. It assesses how likely customers are to recommend the company's products or services to others.

574. A business analyst is mapping the customer journey for a financial services company. Which tool or technique can best capture the emotions and perceptions of customers at various touchpoints?
a. SWOT analysis
b. Pareto chart
c. Empathy map
d. Gantt chart

Answer: c. Empathy map. Explanation: An empathy map captures the emotions and perceptions of customers at various touchpoints, providing insights into their feelings, thoughts, and motivations, which is essential for understanding the customer experience.

575. To enhance the customer experience, a project manager needs to gather detailed feedback from customers about their interactions with the company's support team. Which method is most effective for collecting this feedback?
a. Internal team meetings
b. Customer satisfaction surveys
c. Budget analysis
d. Project status reports

Answer: b. Customer satisfaction surveys. Explanation: Customer satisfaction surveys are an effective method for collecting detailed feedback from customers about their interactions with the company's support team. Surveys can provide valuable insights into customer experiences and areas for improvement.

576. A project team is working on reducing customer complaints about the billing process. What is the first step in addressing this issue?
a. Analyze the current billing process
b. Increase the customer service budget
c. Implement a new billing system
d. Schedule more frequent team meetings

Answer: a. Analyze the current billing process. Explanation: The first step in addressing customer complaints about the billing process is to analyze the current billing process to identify root causes and areas for improvement.

577. A company wants to improve the overall customer experience by reducing the time it takes to resolve customer issues. Which key performance indicator (KPI) should they focus on?
a. Average Handle Time (AHT)
b. Cost Variance (CV)
c. Budget at Completion (BAC)
d. Earned Value (EV)

Answer: a. Average Handle Time (AHT). Explanation: Average Handle Time (AHT) is a key performance indicator that measures the average time taken to handle customer issues. Reducing AHT can improve the overall customer experience by resolving issues more quickly.

578. A project manager needs to ensure that all customer touchpoints provide a consistent and positive experience. Which approach is most effective for achieving this goal?
a. Standardizing customer service scripts
b. Increasing marketing efforts
c. Developing a detailed project budget

d. Scheduling more frequent project status meetings

Answer: a. Standardizing customer service scripts. Explanation: Standardizing customer service scripts ensures that all customer touchpoints provide a consistent and positive experience by guiding customer service representatives on how to interact with customers effectively.

579. During a customer journey mapping session, the project team identifies a key touchpoint where customers frequently encounter issues. What should be the next step to address these issues?
a. Implementing immediate changes without further analysis
b. Prioritizing the touchpoint for a detailed root cause analysis
c. Ignoring the issues to focus on other areas
d. Reducing the project scope to exclude the problematic touchpoint

Answer: b. Prioritizing the touchpoint for a detailed root cause analysis. Explanation: The next step is to prioritize the touchpoint for a detailed root cause analysis to understand why customers are encountering issues and to develop effective solutions.

580. A company wants to ensure that the improvements made to customer touchpoints are sustainable over the long term. Which strategy should they employ?
a. Conducting regular customer feedback sessions
b. Reducing the customer service team size
c. Focusing only on short-term gains
d. Ignoring negative feedback from customers

Answer: a. Conducting regular customer feedback sessions. Explanation: Conducting regular customer feedback sessions helps ensure that improvements to customer touchpoints are sustainable over the long term by continuously gathering insights and making necessary adjustments based on customer feedback.

581. A project manager is leading a digital transformation initiative to incorporate artificial intelligence (AI) into the company's customer service operations. Which of the following is a critical first step in this initiative?
a. Develop a detailed project schedule
b. Assess the current state of customer service operations
c. Hire a new team of AI specialists
d. Purchase the latest AI software

Answer: b. Assess the current state of customer service operations. Explanation: Assessing the current state of customer service operations is a critical first step. This assessment helps identify existing pain points, processes that can be improved with AI, and the readiness of the organization for digital transformation.

582. In evaluating emerging technologies for a new project, which factor is most important to consider?

a. The popularity of the technology in the industry
b. The cost of implementing the technology
c. The potential to provide a competitive advantage
d. The ease of integrating the technology with existing systems

Answer: c. The potential to provide a competitive advantage. Explanation: When evaluating emerging technologies, the potential to provide a competitive advantage is crucial. Technologies that can differentiate the company from competitors and offer unique benefits are highly valuable in a digital transformation strategy.

583. A company is transitioning to a digital business model by offering subscription-based services. What is a key benefit of this model?
a. Increased one-time sales
b. Predictable recurring revenue
c. Reduced customer acquisition costs
d. Simplified product development

Answer: b. Predictable recurring revenue. Explanation: A subscription-based business model provides predictable recurring revenue, which improves cash flow stability and allows for better financial planning and investment in customer retention strategies.

584. The project manager is tasked with fostering innovation within the team. Which approach is most effective for encouraging innovative ideas?
a. Implementing strict guidelines for idea submission
b. Providing incentives for creative solutions
c. Limiting brainstorming sessions to senior management
d. Requiring all ideas to be approved by the project sponsor

Answer: b. Providing incentives for creative solutions. Explanation: Providing incentives for creative solutions encourages team members to think innovatively and propose new ideas. This approach fosters a culture of innovation and motivates employees to contribute their best ideas.

585. A project manager is considering using blockchain technology for enhancing supply chain transparency. What is a primary benefit of using blockchain in this context?
a. Reduced supply chain costs
b. Enhanced data security and transparency
c. Simplified regulatory compliance
d. Faster product development cycles

Answer: b. Enhanced data security and transparency. Explanation: Blockchain technology enhances supply chain transparency by providing a secure, immutable record of transactions. This improves trust and accountability among all parties involved in the supply chain.

586. In the context of innovation management, what is the role of a minimum viable product (MVP)?
a. A fully developed product ready for market launch
b. A prototype used for internal testing only
c. The simplest version of a product that can be released to gather user feedback
d. A detailed business plan for a new product

Answer: c. The simplest version of a product that can be released to gather user feedback. Explanation: An MVP is the simplest version of a product that includes only the essential features needed to test the product in the market and gather user feedback. This approach helps validate assumptions and make improvements before a full-scale launch.

587. A project manager is using big data analytics to improve decision-making. Which capability of big data is most relevant in this context?
a. Processing large volumes of data quickly
b. Reducing data storage costs
c. Enhancing data visualization techniques
d. Improving cybersecurity measures

Answer: a. Processing large volumes of data quickly. Explanation: Big data analytics enables the processing of large volumes of data quickly, providing valuable insights that improve decision-making. This capability allows organizations to analyze trends, patterns, and relationships that inform strategic decisions.

588. The project manager is evaluating the adoption of a digital twin technology for a manufacturing process. What is a digital twin?
a. A virtual representation of a physical object or system
b. A digital marketing strategy for promoting products
c. An AI-driven customer service chatbot
d. A cloud-based data storage solution

Answer: a. A virtual representation of a physical object or system. Explanation: A digital twin is a virtual representation of a physical object or system that is used to simulate, analyze, and optimize performance. It allows for real-time monitoring and predictive maintenance, improving operational efficiency.

589. In the context of digital transformation, what is a primary advantage of adopting cloud computing?
a. Increased capital expenditures
b. Enhanced physical security of data centers
c. Improved scalability and flexibility
d. Simplified software development processes

Answer: c. Improved scalability and flexibility. Explanation: Cloud computing offers improved scalability and flexibility, allowing organizations to adjust resources based on demand. This reduces the need for large upfront investments in IT infrastructure and enables more agile responses to changing business needs.

590. A project manager is responsible for ensuring that the organization's digital transformation aligns with its strategic goals. What is the best approach to achieve this alignment?
a. Developing a separate digital strategy independent of the overall business strategy
b. Ensuring that digital initiatives are directly linked to the organization's strategic objectives
c. Focusing solely on implementing the latest technologies
d. Delegating digital transformation efforts to the IT department

Answer: b. Ensuring that digital initiatives are directly linked to the organization's strategic objectives. Explanation: To achieve alignment, digital initiatives must be directly linked to the organization's strategic objectives. This ensures that the digital transformation supports the broader goals of the organization and delivers meaningful value.

591. A project team is using the DMAIC process to improve a manufacturing process. During which phase of DMAIC is the root cause of defects identified?
a. Define
b. Measure
c. Analyze
d. Improve

Answer: c. Analyze. Explanation: In the Analyze phase of the DMAIC process, the team identifies the root causes of defects by analyzing data collected during the Measure phase. This analysis helps to pinpoint where improvements are needed.

592. In Lean Six Sigma, which tool is most commonly used to visually represent the flow of a process and identify areas of waste?
a. Fishbone diagram
b. Pareto chart
c. Value stream map
d. Control chart

Answer: c. Value stream map. Explanation: A value stream map is used in Lean Six Sigma to visually represent the flow of a process, highlighting areas where waste occurs. It helps teams identify and eliminate non-value-added activities.

593. A project manager is implementing Lean principles to reduce cycle time in a production process. Which of the following is a core Lean principle?
a. Increasing inventory levels
b. Focusing on customer value
c. Maximizing equipment utilization
d. Reducing employee training

Answer: b. Focusing on customer value. Explanation: A core Lean principle is to focus on delivering value to the customer. This involves identifying and eliminating activities that do not add value from the customer's perspective.

594. During the Improve phase of DMAIC, which tool is commonly used to generate ideas for potential solutions?
a. Histogram
b. Brainstorming
c. Scatter plot
d. SIPOC diagram

Answer: b. Brainstorming. Explanation: During the Improve phase, brainstorming is often used to generate a wide range of ideas for potential solutions to address the root causes of defects identified in the Analyze phase.

595. Which Six Sigma tool is used to prioritize problems or causes based on their frequency of occurrence?
a. Control chart
b. Pareto chart
c. Flowchart
d. Cause-and-effect diagram

Answer: b. Pareto chart. Explanation: A Pareto chart is used to prioritize problems or causes based on their frequency of occurrence, following the Pareto principle that a small number of causes often account for the majority of problems.

596. In the Control phase of DMAIC, a project team wants to ensure that improvements are sustained over time. Which tool should they use to monitor the process performance?
a. Control chart
b. Process map
c. Fishbone diagram
d. Affinity diagram

Answer: a. Control chart. Explanation: A control chart is used in the Control phase to monitor the performance of a process over time, ensuring that the improvements are sustained and any variations are within acceptable limits.

597. Lean Six Sigma emphasizes the elimination of waste. Which of the following is NOT considered one of the eight types of waste in Lean?
a. Overproduction
b. Defects
c. Transportation
d. Training

Answer: d. Training. Explanation: Training is not considered one of the eight types of waste in Lean. The eight types of waste include overproduction, defects, transportation, waiting, inventory, motion, overprocessing, and unused talent.

598. A Six Sigma project aims to improve customer satisfaction by reducing the variation in service delivery times. Which statistical tool can the team use to measure and analyze this variation?
a. SIPOC diagram
b. Histogram
c. Affinity diagram
d. Pareto chart

Answer: b. Histogram. Explanation: A histogram is a statistical tool used to measure and analyze the variation in a process. It visually represents the distribution of data points, helping the team identify patterns and areas for improvement.

599. During the Define phase of DMAIC, the project team creates a SIPOC diagram. What does SIPOC stand for?
a. Suppliers, Inputs, Process, Outputs, Customers
b. Strategy, Implementation, Performance, Outcomes, Control
c. Systems, Integration, Planning, Operations, Compliance
d. Stakeholders, Information, Processes, Objectives, Criteria

Answer: a. Suppliers, Inputs, Process, Outputs, Customers. Explanation: SIPOC stands for Suppliers, Inputs, Process, Outputs, Customers. It is a high-level map used in the Define phase to identify the key elements of a process and ensure that all stakeholders understand the process boundaries.

600. In Lean Six Sigma, what is the primary purpose of using a fishbone diagram (Ishikawa diagram)?
a. To display the frequency of defects
b. To map the steps of a process
c. To identify potential causes of a problem
d. To track the performance of a process over time

Answer: c. To identify potential causes of a problem. Explanation: A fishbone diagram, or Ishikawa diagram, is used to identify potential causes of a problem. It visually organizes and categorizes the possible causes, helping teams to analyze and address the root causes systematically.

601. A business analyst is working with an Agile development team on a new software project. Which of the following best describes the role of the business analyst in an Agile environment?
a. To create detailed requirements documentation upfront and ensure strict adherence to the plan
b. To work closely with the product owner and development team to continuously refine and prioritize the product backlog
c. To act as a gatekeeper between the business stakeholders and the development team

d. To manage the project schedule and budget, ensuring that all deadlines are met

Answer: b. To work closely with the product owner and development team to continuously refine and prioritize the product backlog. Explanation: In an Agile environment, the role of the business analyst is to collaborate with the product owner and development team to ensure that the product backlog accurately reflects the business needs and priorities. The business analyst helps to elicit, analyze, and communicate requirements, but instead of creating extensive documentation upfront, they focus on iterative and incremental delivery. The business analyst works closely with the product owner to refine user stories, acceptance criteria, and prioritization, ensuring that the most valuable features are delivered first. They also facilitate communication between the business stakeholders and the development team, helping to clarify requirements, answer questions, and provide feedback throughout the development process. Agile emphasizes flexibility, collaboration, and adaptability, rather than strict adherence to a predefined plan or formal gatekeeping between business and development.

602. In Scrum, which of the following ceremonies provides an opportunity for the development team to showcase the work completed during the sprint and receive feedback from stakeholders?
a. Sprint Planning
b. Daily Stand-up
c. Sprint Review
d. Sprint Retrospective

Answer: c. Sprint Review. Explanation: The Sprint Review is a ceremony held at the end of each sprint where the development team demonstrates the work they have completed during the sprint to the product owner, stakeholders, and other interested parties. The purpose of the Sprint Review is to showcase the increment of working software, receive feedback, and collaborate with stakeholders to ensure that the product is meeting their needs and expectations. During the Sprint Review, the team presents the features and functionalities developed during the sprint, and the stakeholders have the opportunity to ask questions, provide input, and suggest improvements. The feedback gathered during the Sprint Review helps the team to validate their work, identify areas for improvement, and adapt their plans for future sprints. The Sprint Planning is held at the beginning of each sprint to define the sprint goal and select the backlog items to be completed. The Daily Stand-up is a brief meeting held every day to synchronize the team's activities and identify any obstacles. The Sprint Retrospective is a meeting held at the end of each sprint to reflect on the team's process and identify opportunities for continuous improvement.

603. Which of the following is a key benefit of involving business analysts in the continuous feedback and iteration process in Agile?
a. To ensure that the original project scope and requirements remain unchanged
b. To minimize the need for communication between the development team and stakeholders
c. To help the team adapt to changing business needs and priorities
d. To reduce the frequency of product demos and user feedback sessions

Answer: c. To help the team adapt to changing business needs and priorities. Explanation: One of the core principles of Agile is to welcome changing requirements, even late in the development process, to ensure that the product remains aligned with the evolving needs of the business and customers. By involving business analysts in the continuous feedback and iteration process, Agile teams can effectively adapt to these changes and deliver the most value to the stakeholders. Business analysts play a crucial role in facilitating communication between the development team and the business stakeholders, helping to gather feedback, clarify requirements, and translate business needs into actionable user stories. They participate in regular product demos, user testing sessions, and stakeholder reviews to validate the team's work and identify areas for improvement. By continuously incorporating feedback and iterating on the product, business analysts help the team to stay responsive to changing priorities, market conditions, and customer preferences. Agile does not aim to keep the original scope and requirements static, minimize communication, or reduce the frequency of feedback loops, but rather embraces change, collaboration, and continuous improvement.

604. A business analyst is facilitating a user story mapping session with the Agile team and stakeholders. What is the primary purpose of user story mapping?
a. To create a detailed project plan and assign tasks to individual team members
b. To visualize the user journey and prioritize features based on their value to the customer
c. To estimate the effort required for each user story and calculate the project budget
d. To document the technical architecture and design decisions for the product

Answer: b. To visualize the user journey and prioritize features based on their value to the customer. Explanation: User story mapping is a collaborative technique used in Agile to create a visual representation of the user journey and the features required to support that journey. The primary purpose of user story mapping is to help the team understand the end-to-end user experience, identify the key activities and goals of the users, and prioritize the features and functionalities that will deliver the most value to the customer. During a user story mapping session, the business analyst facilitates a discussion with the team and stakeholders to break down the user journey into a series of steps or activities, such as "search for a product," "add to cart," "checkout," etc. For each step, the team identifies the user stories or features that are needed to support that activity, and arranges them in a horizontal timeline. The user stories are then prioritized based on their importance to the user and their business value, using techniques like the MoSCoW method or relative sizing. User story mapping helps the team to create a shared understanding of the product vision, focus on delivering value incrementally, and make informed decisions about scope and prioritization. It is not primarily used for detailed project planning, effort estimation, or technical design, although it can inform those activities.

605. Which of the following is a key characteristic of the "definition of ready" in Agile?
a. It defines the criteria for accepting a user story as complete and releasable
b. It specifies the technical design and architecture for each user story
c. It outlines the skills and experience required for each team member
d. It describes the conditions that must be met before a user story can be considered for development

Answer: d. It describes the conditions that must be met before a user story can be considered for development. Explanation: In Agile, the "definition of ready" (DoR) is a set of criteria that a user story must meet before it can be considered ready for development in a sprint. The DoR helps to ensure that user stories are well-defined, actionable, and feasible, reducing the risk of delays, rework, and scope creep during the sprint. Typical criteria in a DoR may include: - The user story has a clear and concise description of the desired functionality - The acceptance criteria are well-defined and testable - The story has been broken down into small, independent, and deliverable increments - The story has been estimated by the team and fits within the sprint capacity - The dependencies, risks, and assumptions associated with the story have been identified - The story has been reviewed and approved by the product owner and stakeholders By ensuring that user stories meet the DoR before being accepted into a sprint, Agile teams can improve the flow of work, reduce waste, and increase the likelihood of delivering a potentially shippable product increment at the end of each sprint. The DoR is different from the "definition of done" (DoD), which defines the criteria for accepting a user story as complete and releasable, such as passing all tests, meeting the acceptance criteria, and being properly documented.

606. In an Agile project, a business analyst is responsible for facilitating the backlog refinement process. Which of the following is not a typical activity performed during backlog refinement?
a. Splitting large user stories into smaller, more manageable pieces
b. Estimating the relative size or complexity of user stories
c. Assigning user stories to individual developers based on their skills and experience
d. Clarifying the acceptance criteria and requirements for each user story

Answer: c. Assigning user stories to individual developers based on their skills and experience. Explanation: Backlog refinement, also known as backlog grooming, is a collaborative process in which the Agile team regularly reviews, updates, and prioritizes the product backlog to ensure that it reflects the current understanding of the project scope, requirements, and priorities. The business analyst plays a key role in facilitating this process, working closely with the product owner, development team, and stakeholders to maintain a healthy and actionable backlog. Typical activities performed during backlog refinement include: - Splitting large, complex user stories (epics) into smaller, more manageable stories that can be completed within a single sprint - Estimating the relative size or complexity of user stories, using techniques like story points or t-shirt sizes, to help with sprint planning and forecasting - Clarifying the acceptance criteria, requirements, and business rules for each user story, to ensure a shared understanding among the team and stakeholders - Identifying and resolving dependencies, risks, and impediments that may impact the delivery of the user stories - Prioritizing the user stories based on their value, urgency, and alignment with the product vision and roadmap Assigning user stories to individual developers is not a typical activity performed during backlog refinement, as Agile emphasizes collective ownership and self-organization. The team collaborates to select the user stories for each sprint based on the priority, capacity, and skills available, but the individual assignment of tasks is usually done during the sprint planning meeting or through the team's self-organization.

607. Which of the following collaborative techniques is most effective for generating a large number of ideas and solutions in a short amount of time?
a. Brainstorming
b. Focus groups
c. Interviews
d. Surveys

Answer: a. Brainstorming. Explanation: Brainstorming is a collaborative technique that is particularly effective for generating a large number of ideas and solutions in a short amount of time. In a brainstorming session, a group of people comes together to generate as many ideas as possible, without judging or critiquing them. The goal is to create a safe and open environment where participants feel encouraged to think creatively and share their ideas freely. Brainstorming sessions typically follow a set of guidelines, such as: - Encouraging wild and unconventional ideas - Building on each other's ideas and combining them in new ways - Deferring judgment and criticism until the end of the session - Aiming for quantity over quality in the initial stage - Capturing all ideas visually, using tools like whiteboards, sticky notes, or mind maps By fostering a culture of creativity, collaboration, and rapid ideation, brainstorming can help Agile teams to quickly generate a wide range of potential solutions to complex problems, identify new opportunities, and drive innovation. Focus groups, interviews, and surveys are also valuable techniques for gathering insights and feedback, but they are typically more structured and focused on eliciting specific information from participants, rather than generating a large volume of ideas in a short timeframe.

608. Which of the following is a key benefit of using the "planning poker" technique for estimating user stories in Agile?
a. It ensures that the estimates are always accurate and precise
b. It allows the team to assign user stories to specific developers based on their skills
c. It promotes group consensus and shared understanding of the work involved
d. It eliminates the need for any discussion or clarification of the user stories

Answer: c. It promotes group consensus and shared understanding of the work involved. Explanation: Planning poker, also known as Scrum poker or estimation poker, is a collaborative estimation technique used in Agile to estimate the relative size or complexity of user stories. In a planning poker session, each team member has a deck of cards with values representing different story point estimates, such as the Fibonacci sequence (1, 2, 3, 5, 8, 13, etc.) or t-shirt sizes (XS, S, M, L, XL). For each user story, the team members individually select a card that represents their estimate, and then reveal their cards simultaneously. If there is a wide divergence in the estimates, the team discusses the reasons behind the differences, clarifies any assumptions or uncertainties, and reaches a consensus on the final estimate. One of the key benefits of planning poker is that it promotes group consensus and shared understanding of the work involved in each user story. By encouraging open discussion and collaboration, planning poker helps to surface different perspectives, identify potential risks or dependencies, and ensure that everyone is on the same page regarding the scope and complexity of the work. It also helps to prevent individual biases or dominant personalities from unduly influencing the estimates. However, planning poker does not guarantee perfectly accurate or precise estimates, as estimation is inherently uncertain and dependent on many factors, such as the team's experience, the project's complexity, and the availability of information. It also does not eliminate the need for discussion or clarification of the user stories, but rather facilitates a structured and productive conversation around the work to be done.

609. A business analyst is working with an Agile team to define the acceptance criteria for a user story. Which of the following is the most important characteristic of well-written acceptance criteria?
a. They are long and detailed, covering every possible scenario and edge case
b. They are written in technical jargon and programming language
c. They are focused on the underlying technical implementation details
d. They are clear, concise, and testable, describing the desired outcome from a user's perspective

Answer: d. They are clear, concise, and testable, describing the desired outcome from a user's perspective. Explanation: Acceptance criteria are a set of conditions or requirements that a user story must meet to be considered complete and acceptable by the customer or stakeholder. They define the boundaries of the user story and provide a clear and measurable definition of "done." Well-written acceptance criteria are essential for ensuring that the development team has a shared understanding of the desired functionality, and for providing a basis for testing and validation. The most important characteristic of well-written acceptance criteria is that they are clear, concise, and testable, describing the desired outcome from a user's perspective. They should focus on the observable behavior and business value of the feature, rather than the underlying technical implementation details. Good acceptance criteria typically follow the "Given/When/Then" format, which specifies the initial context (Given), the action or event that triggers the behavior (When), and the expected outcome or result (Then). For example: "Given that a user has added items to their shopping cart, when they click the 'Checkout' button, then they should be redirected to the payment page." Acceptance criteria should not be long, detailed, or exhaustive, as they are not meant to replace the conversation and collaboration between the team and the stakeholders. They should also avoid technical jargon or programming language, as they should be understandable by all members of the Agile team, including non-technical stakeholders. By defining clear, concise, and testable acceptance criteria, business analysts can help Agile teams to deliver software that meets the customer's needs and expectations, and to avoid misunderstandings, rework, and delays.

610. Which of the following is a key principle of the Agile Manifesto?
a. Comprehensive documentation over working software
b. Contract negotiation over customer collaboration
c. Responding to change over following a plan
d. Processes and tools over individuals and interactions

Answer: c. Responding to change over following a plan. Explanation: The Agile Manifesto is a set of guiding principles for Agile software development, first published in 2001. It emphasizes four core values: 1. Individuals and interactions over processes and tools 2. Working software over comprehensive documentation 3. Customer collaboration over contract negotiation 4. Responding to change over following a plan While all of these values are important, the principle of "responding to change over following a plan" is particularly crucial in Agile. It recognizes that in a complex and rapidly changing business environment, it is more important to be flexible and adaptable than to adhere rigidly to a predefined plan. Agile teams embrace change as an opportunity to learn, improve, and deliver value to the customer. They work in short iterations, delivering working software frequently and seeking feedback early and often. They prioritize continuous improvement, inspect and adapt their processes, and make decisions based on empirical evidence rather than speculation or assumption. By valuing responding to change over following a plan, Agile teams can avoid the pitfalls of traditional, plan-driven approaches, such as scope creep, delays, and delivering solutions that no longer meet the customer's needs. They can react quickly to new information, changing priorities, and evolving requirements, and deliver software that is more closely aligned with the customer's goals and expectations.

611. A project manager is addressing a recurring issue in a project using a systems thinking approach. Which of the following best describes systems thinking in this context?
a. Analyzing individual components in isolation to identify the root cause
b. Considering the project as a whole and understanding how components interact
c. Focusing on short-term solutions to resolve the immediate issue
d. Implementing a top-down management approach to control the project

Answer: b. Considering the project as a whole and understanding how components interact. Explanation: Systems thinking involves viewing the project as an integrated whole, understanding how individual components interact and influence each other. This approach helps identify underlying patterns and root causes of issues.

612. A project manager is using a feedback loop to monitor project performance. Which of the following best describes a feedback loop?
a. A linear process with a clear start and end point
b. A method for providing regular updates to stakeholders
c. A circular process where outputs are fed back into the system as inputs
d. A one-time assessment conducted at the end of the project

Answer: c. A circular process where outputs are fed back into the system as inputs. Explanation: A feedback loop is a circular process where the outputs of a system are fed back into the system as inputs. This helps in continuously monitoring and adjusting project performance based on real-time data and feedback.

613. The project manager is analyzing interdependencies in a complex project. Which tool is most appropriate for mapping out these interdependencies?
a. Gantt chart
b. Work breakdown structure (WBS)
c. Network diagram
d. Risk register

Answer: c. Network diagram. Explanation: A network diagram is a tool used to map out interdependencies between tasks and activities in a project. It helps visualize how tasks are connected and the sequence in which they need to be completed, making it easier to manage complex interdependencies.

614. During a project review, the team identifies a reinforcing feedback loop that is causing project delays. What is the primary characteristic of a reinforcing feedback loop?
a. It stabilizes the system by balancing inputs and outputs
b. It amplifies changes, leading to exponential growth or decline
c. It operates independently of other system components
d. It eliminates all external influences on the system

Answer: b. It amplifies changes, leading to exponential growth or decline. Explanation: A reinforcing feedback loop amplifies changes in a system, leading to exponential growth or decline. It can create positive or negative outcomes depending on the nature of the feedback.

615. A project manager is addressing interconnections within a project team to improve collaboration. What is the most effective approach to manage these interconnections?
a. Isolating team members to focus on individual tasks
b. Encouraging open communication and regular team meetings
c. Assigning all tasks to a single team member to ensure consistency
d. Limiting the flow of information to avoid confusion

Answer: b. Encouraging open communication and regular team meetings. Explanation: Encouraging open communication and regular team meetings is the most effective approach to manage interconnections within a project team. It ensures that team members are aligned, share information, and collaborate effectively.

616. A project manager is using a holistic approach to problem-solving. Which of the following best describes this approach?
a. Solving problems by addressing each issue in isolation
b. Focusing on the most visible symptoms of a problem
c. Considering the entire system and how different elements interact

d. Implementing quick fixes to resolve immediate issues

Answer: c. Considering the entire system and how different elements interact. Explanation: A holistic approach to problem-solving involves considering the entire system and how different elements interact. This approach helps identify the root cause of problems and develop comprehensive solutions.

617. During project planning, the project manager identifies a balancing feedback loop. What is the primary function of a balancing feedback loop in a project system?
a. To create exponential growth
b. To stabilize the system by counteracting changes
c. To introduce new variables into the system
d. To disrupt the system and drive innovation

Answer: b. To stabilize the system by counteracting changes. Explanation: A balancing feedback loop functions to stabilize the system by counteracting changes. It helps maintain equilibrium within the system by reducing fluctuations and promoting steady progress.

618. A project team is using system dynamics to model project performance. What is the main advantage of using system dynamics in project management?
a. It simplifies the project by focusing on individual tasks
b. It provides a static view of the project at a single point in time
c. It allows for the simulation of different scenarios to understand potential outcomes
d. It eliminates the need for stakeholder involvement

Answer: c. It allows for the simulation of different scenarios to understand potential outcomes. Explanation: The main advantage of using system dynamics in project management is that it allows for the simulation of different scenarios to understand potential outcomes. This helps in making informed decisions and planning for various contingencies.

619. A project manager is examining the cause-and-effect relationships within a project. Which tool is most suitable for this analysis?
a. Pareto chart
b. Fishbone diagram (Ishikawa diagram)
c. Histogram
d. Scatter plot

Answer: b. Fishbone diagram (Ishikawa diagram). Explanation: A fishbone diagram, also known as an Ishikawa diagram, is most suitable for analyzing cause-and-effect relationships. It helps identify the root causes of a problem by categorizing potential factors into different areas.

620. A project manager needs to address a delay caused by a dependency between two tasks. What is the best approach to mitigate this issue?
a. Ignore the dependency and focus on other tasks
b. Reassign the tasks to different team members
c. Adjust the project schedule to account for the dependency
d. Increase the project budget to expedite the tasks

Answer: c. Adjust the project schedule to account for the dependency. Explanation: The best approach to mitigate a delay caused by a dependency between two tasks is to adjust the project schedule to account for the dependency. This ensures that the tasks are completed in the correct sequence and reduces the impact of delays on the overall project timeline.

621. A project manager is developing Key Performance Indicators (KPIs) to measure the success of a new product launch. Which of the following is the most appropriate KPI for tracking customer satisfaction?
a. Number of units sold
b. Customer retention rate
c. Employee turnover rate
d. Marketing spend

Answer: b. Customer retention rate. Explanation: Customer retention rate is a key indicator of customer satisfaction, as it measures how many customers continue to do business with the company over time, reflecting their satisfaction with the product or service.

622. A project manager uses a performance dashboard to monitor project progress. What is the primary benefit of using a performance dashboard?
a. It provides a detailed financial analysis
b. It visualizes project metrics and performance in real time
c. It documents project risks and issues
d. It outlines the project's scope and objectives

Answer: b. It visualizes project metrics and performance in real time. Explanation: A performance dashboard visualizes key project metrics and performance indicators in real time, allowing project managers and stakeholders to quickly assess progress and make informed decisions.

623. A project team is conducting benchmarking to improve their project management processes. Which of the following best describes benchmarking?
a. Setting arbitrary performance targets
b. Comparing current performance against industry best practices
c. Conducting internal performance reviews
d. Analyzing past project failures

Answer: b. Comparing current performance against industry best practices. Explanation: Benchmarking involves comparing an organization's current performance against industry best practices or standards to identify areas for improvement and implement strategies to enhance performance.

624. During a project review, the project manager identifies a gap between current performance and the project's KPIs. What is the first step the project manager should take to address this gap?
a. Increase the project budget
b. Adjust the KPIs to match current performance
c. Conduct a root cause analysis to identify the underlying issues
d. Extend the project timeline

Answer: c. Conduct a root cause analysis to identify the underlying issues. Explanation: The first step to address a performance gap is to conduct a root cause analysis to identify the underlying issues causing the gap. This analysis helps in developing targeted strategies to improve performance.

625. A project manager is using a balanced scorecard to track project performance. Which of the following perspectives is NOT typically included in a balanced scorecard?
a. Financial perspective
b. Customer perspective
c. Internal business processes perspective
d. Legal compliance perspective

Answer: d. Legal compliance perspective. Explanation: The balanced scorecard typically includes four perspectives: financial, customer, internal business processes, and learning and growth. Legal compliance is not one of the standard perspectives in a balanced scorecard.

626. The project team wants to benchmark their project management practices against those of leading companies in the industry. What is the primary goal of this benchmarking exercise?
a. To adopt the exact practices of leading companies
b. To identify areas where the project team can improve
c. To demonstrate superiority over competitors
d. To justify increasing the project budget

Answer: b. To identify areas where the project team can improve. Explanation: The primary goal of benchmarking is to identify areas where the project team can improve by learning from the best practices of leading companies in the industry.

627. A project manager needs to ensure that the KPIs selected are effective in measuring project performance. Which characteristic is most important for an effective KPI?
a. Broad and general
b. Complex and detailed
c. Relevant and measurable

d. Vague and flexible

Answer: c. Relevant and measurable. Explanation: Effective KPIs should be relevant to the project objectives and measurable so that performance can be quantitatively assessed and tracked over time.

628. The project manager has identified that the project is not meeting its performance targets. Which tool is most appropriate for visually analyzing the cause-and-effect relationships of performance issues?
a. Pareto chart
b. Fishbone diagram
c. Histogram
d. Control chart

Answer: b. Fishbone diagram. Explanation: A fishbone diagram, also known as an Ishikawa diagram, is used to visually analyze the cause-and-effect relationships of performance issues, helping to identify potential root causes and areas for improvement.

629. A project team uses benchmarking best practices to improve their time management processes. Which step is essential in the benchmarking process?
a. Ignoring competitor practices
b. Identifying performance metrics and collecting data
c. Reducing the project scope
d. Increasing the project's budget

Answer: b. Identifying performance metrics and collecting data. Explanation: Identifying performance metrics and collecting data is essential in the benchmarking process. This step provides the necessary information to compare current performance against best practices and identify improvement opportunities.

630. To improve project performance, a project manager wants to implement continuous monitoring of KPIs. What is a key benefit of continuous monitoring?
a. It eliminates the need for regular project meetings
b. It allows for real-time adjustments to keep the project on track
c. It reduces the overall project cost
d. It guarantees project success without additional effort

Answer: b. It allows for real-time adjustments to keep the project on track. Explanation: Continuous monitoring of KPIs allows for real-time adjustments to project activities, helping to keep the project on track by quickly identifying and addressing performance issues as they arise.

631. A project manager is explaining the importance of requirements traceability to the project team. Which of the following best describes a key benefit of requirements traceability?

a. It ensures all stakeholders are satisfied with the final deliverable
b. It helps in tracking the status of project tasks
c. It ensures that all requirements are addressed and aligned with project objectives
d. It reduces the overall project cost by eliminating unnecessary tasks

Answer: c. It ensures that all requirements are addressed and aligned with project objectives. Explanation: Requirements traceability ensures that all project requirements are tracked throughout the project lifecycle and are aligned with the project objectives. This helps in verifying that the final deliverable meets the intended requirements and stakeholder expectations.

632. A project manager is creating a requirements traceability matrix (RTM). Which of the following elements is most crucial to include in the RTM?
a. Project budget
b. Stakeholder contact information
c. Requirement ID, source, and verification method
d. Project timeline

Answer: c. Requirement ID, source, and verification method. Explanation: The most crucial elements to include in an RTM are the requirement ID, the source of the requirement, and the verification method. These elements help track each requirement from its origin through its implementation and validation.

633. During a project review, the project manager finds that some requirements have not been adequately addressed. What is the primary purpose of maintaining requirements traceability throughout the project?
a. To monitor project costs
b. To ensure project timelines are met
c. To identify and resolve gaps in requirement coverage
d. To manage stakeholder communications

Answer: c. To identify and resolve gaps in requirement coverage. Explanation: Maintaining requirements traceability throughout the project helps identify and resolve gaps in requirement coverage. This ensures that all requirements are properly addressed and implemented in the final deliverable.

634. In the context of requirements traceability, what is the role of a traceability matrix?
a. To document project risks and mitigation strategies
b. To track the progress of project tasks and milestones
c. To map requirements to their corresponding test cases and design elements
d. To allocate project resources and budget

Answer: c. To map requirements to their corresponding test cases and design elements. Explanation: A traceability matrix maps requirements to their corresponding test cases and design elements. This helps ensure that each requirement is properly tested and implemented, facilitating comprehensive validation and verification.

635. A project manager needs to update the requirements traceability matrix after a change request is approved. What is the first step in this process?
a. Notify all stakeholders of the change
b. Update the project schedule to reflect the change
c. Identify the impacted requirements and update the RTM
d. Conduct a risk assessment for the change

Answer: c. Identify the impacted requirements and update the RTM. Explanation: The first step in updating the requirements traceability matrix after a change request is approved is to identify the impacted requirements and update the RTM accordingly. This ensures that all changes are tracked and managed effectively.

636. The project team is using the requirements traceability matrix to track compliance with regulatory requirements. Which of the following best describes how the RTM facilitates this process?
a. It documents the project's overall compliance strategy
b. It links each regulatory requirement to its implementation and verification steps
c. It provides a high-level overview of the project scope
d. It allocates resources to compliance-related tasks

Answer: b. It links each regulatory requirement to its implementation and verification steps. Explanation: The RTM facilitates tracking compliance with regulatory requirements by linking each regulatory requirement to its implementation and verification steps. This ensures that all regulatory requirements are met and properly documented.

637. A stakeholder requests a report on the status of specific project requirements. How can the project manager use the requirements traceability matrix to generate this report?
a. By filtering the RTM to show only the relevant requirements and their current status
b. By creating a new document that summarizes the project progress
c. By using the project budget to estimate requirement completion
d. By consulting the project timeline to determine the status

Answer: a. By filtering the RTM to show only the relevant requirements and their current status. Explanation: The project manager can generate a report on the status of specific project requirements by filtering the RTM to show only the relevant requirements and their current status. This provides a clear and concise overview of the progress for each requirement.

638. During the final phase of a project, the project manager reviews the requirements traceability matrix. What is the main purpose of this review?
a. To finalize the project budget
b. To ensure that all requirements have been met and validated
c. To allocate resources for future projects
d. To develop a project schedule

Answer: b. To ensure that all requirements have been met and validated. Explanation: The main purpose of reviewing the requirements traceability matrix during the final phase of a project is to ensure that all requirements have been met and validated. This confirms that the project deliverables are complete and meet stakeholder expectations.

639. A project manager is training a new team on the importance of requirements traceability. Which example best illustrates the use of a traceability matrix?
a. A chart that outlines the project milestones and deadlines
b. A document that maps each requirement to its source, design, and testing activities
c. A list of project stakeholders and their contact information
d. A report that tracks the project's overall budget and expenditures

Answer: b. A document that maps each requirement to its source, design, and testing activities. Explanation: An example that best illustrates the use of a traceability matrix is a document that maps each requirement to its source, design, and testing activities. This ensures that all requirements are tracked throughout the project lifecycle.

640. The project team has identified several new requirements during the project execution phase. What should be the project manager's approach to maintaining requirements traceability for these new requirements?
a. Add the new requirements to the RTM and update the related design and test cases
b. Document the new requirements separately and review them at the end of the project
c. Ignore the new requirements if they were not part of the original scope
d. Adjust the project timeline to accommodate the new requirements

Answer: a. Add the new requirements to the RTM and update the related design and test cases. Explanation: The project manager should add the new requirements to the RTM and update the related design and test cases. This ensures that all new requirements are properly tracked and integrated into the project plan.

641. A project manager is planning a workshop to gather requirements from key stakeholders. Which of the following activities should be performed first during the workshop?
a. Brainstorming potential solutions
b. Defining the workshop objectives and agenda
c. Building consensus on the final requirements
d. Conducting a risk assessment for the project

Answer: b. Defining the workshop objectives and agenda. Explanation: Defining the workshop objectives and agenda should be the first activity performed to ensure that all participants understand the purpose and structure of the workshop, leading to more effective and focused discussions.

642. During a brainstorming session, a few participants are dominating the conversation. What facilitation technique should the project manager use to ensure balanced participation?

a. Allowing the dominant participants to continue
b. Using a round-robin approach
c. Ignoring contributions from dominant participants
d. Extending the session duration

Answer: b. Using a round-robin approach. Explanation: Using a round-robin approach ensures that each participant has an equal opportunity to contribute ideas, preventing any single participant from dominating the conversation and encouraging balanced participation.

643. The project team is conducting a consensus-building session to agree on the project's critical success factors. Which technique is most effective for achieving consensus among diverse stakeholders?
a. Voting without discussion
b. Brainstorming
c. Multi-voting
d. Lecture-style presentations

Answer: c. Multi-voting. Explanation: Multi-voting is an effective technique for achieving consensus among diverse stakeholders. It allows participants to prioritize and narrow down options through multiple rounds of voting and discussion, leading to a more democratic decision-making process.

644. In preparation for a workshop, the project manager wants to ensure that all participants are actively engaged and contributing. Which of the following strategies is most effective for fostering engagement?
a. Providing detailed pre-workshop materials
b. Scheduling the workshop for a full day without breaks
c. Limiting the number of participants to only senior managers
d. Using a lecture-based format for the entire workshop

Answer: a. Providing detailed pre-workshop materials. Explanation: Providing detailed pre-workshop materials helps participants understand the context and come prepared, fostering engagement and ensuring more productive discussions during the workshop.

645. A project manager is facilitating a workshop to identify risks associated with a new project. Which technique is best suited for generating a comprehensive list of potential risks?
a. Role-playing
b. Brainstorming
c. SWOT analysis
d. Root cause analysis

Answer: b. Brainstorming. Explanation: Brainstorming is an effective technique for generating a comprehensive list of potential risks, as it encourages participants to think creatively and contribute a wide range of ideas in a collaborative setting.

646. During a consensus-building workshop, some stakeholders strongly disagree on a critical requirement. What should the project manager do to resolve the disagreement and build consensus?
a. Make an executive decision without further discussion
b. Escalate the issue to senior management
c. Facilitate a discussion to understand the underlying concerns and find common ground
d. Ignore the disagreement and proceed with the majority opinion

Answer: c. Facilitate a discussion to understand the underlying concerns and find common ground. Explanation: The project manager should facilitate a discussion to understand the underlying concerns of the stakeholders and find common ground. This approach helps to address the root causes of the disagreement and build consensus.

647. The project team is conducting a workshop to develop a project charter. What is the primary purpose of this workshop?
a. To allocate project resources
b. To define the project scope, objectives, and deliverables
c. To create a detailed project schedule
d. To conduct a risk assessment

Answer: b. To define the project scope, objectives, and deliverables. Explanation: The primary purpose of a workshop to develop a project charter is to define the project scope, objectives, and deliverables. This document provides a high-level overview of the project and serves as a foundation for planning and execution.

648. A project manager is using a fishbone diagram during a workshop to identify potential causes of a recurring issue. Which of the following best describes the fishbone diagram's function?
a. To prioritize risks based on their impact
b. To map out the sequence of project tasks
c. To identify and categorize the root causes of a problem
d. To allocate resources to project activities

Answer: c. To identify and categorize the root causes of a problem. Explanation: A fishbone diagram, also known as an Ishikawa diagram, is used to identify and categorize the root causes of a problem. It visually organizes potential causes into categories, helping teams analyze and address the underlying issues.

649. In a brainstorming session aimed at generating innovative solutions, what rule should the project manager enforce to ensure creativity and participation?
a. Criticize ideas to refine them immediately
b. Limit the number of ideas each participant can suggest
c. Encourage all ideas, no matter how unconventional
d. Focus only on feasible and practical solutions

Answer: c. Encourage all ideas, no matter how unconventional. Explanation: Encouraging all ideas, no matter how unconventional, fosters creativity and participation in a brainstorming session. This approach allows for a broad range of potential solutions, which can be evaluated and refined later.

650. A project manager is planning a workshop to align team members on project goals and objectives. Which of the following is an effective strategy for achieving alignment?
a. Allowing team members to work independently
b. Using facilitated group discussions to ensure everyone's input is considered
c. Focusing solely on technical details
d. Limiting the workshop to only the project manager and sponsor

Answer: b. Using facilitated group discussions to ensure everyone's input is considered. Explanation: Using facilitated group discussions helps ensure that all team members have the opportunity to contribute and understand the project goals and objectives, fostering alignment and a shared vision.

651. A project manager is overseeing the design of a new IT solution. Which of the following is the most important architectural consideration to ensure the solution's scalability?
a. Selecting the latest programming language
b. Designing a modular architecture
c. Implementing strict access controls
d. Reducing initial development costs

Answer: b. Designing a modular architecture. Explanation: A modular architecture allows for scalability by enabling the addition of new modules without affecting existing components. This ensures the solution can grow and adapt to future needs.

652. During the solution design phase, the project team is considering various options for integrating the new solution with existing systems. Which approach should be prioritized to ensure seamless integration?
a. Using proprietary interfaces for integration
b. Developing custom connectors for each system
c. Implementing standard APIs and protocols
d. Replacing all existing systems with new ones

Answer: c. Implementing standard APIs and protocols. Explanation: Standard APIs and protocols ensure seamless integration by providing a consistent and well-documented interface for communication between the new solution and existing systems.

653. A project manager is tasked with designing a solution that requires high availability. Which architectural feature is most critical to achieve this requirement?
a. Single server deployment
b. Redundant systems and failover mechanisms

c. Manual backup processes
d. Reduced development time

Answer: b. Redundant systems and failover mechanisms. Explanation: High availability requires redundant systems and failover mechanisms to ensure that if one component fails, another can take over without disrupting the service.

654. In the context of solution design, what is the primary benefit of using a microservices architecture?
a. Simplified project documentation
b. Enhanced performance through monolithic design
c. Increased flexibility and easier maintenance
d. Lower initial setup costs

Answer: c. Increased flexibility and easier maintenance. Explanation: Microservices architecture divides a solution into smaller, independent services that can be developed, deployed, and maintained separately, providing increased flexibility and easier maintenance.

655. A project manager needs to ensure that a new solution is secure. Which architectural consideration should be given the highest priority?
a. Implementing strong encryption for data at rest and in transit
b. Using the fastest network protocols
c. Ensuring all team members have administrative access
d. Prioritizing user experience over security

Answer: a. Implementing strong encryption for data at rest and in transit. Explanation: Implementing strong encryption for data at rest and in transit ensures that sensitive information is protected from unauthorized access and breaches, which is a critical aspect of solution security.

656. The project team is integrating a new solution with an existing legacy system. What is the primary challenge they are likely to face?
a. Ensuring the new solution has a modern user interface
b. Aligning the new solution's functionality with outdated technologies
c. Reducing the overall project budget
d. Increasing the project timeline

Answer: b. Aligning the new solution's functionality with outdated technologies. Explanation: Integrating a new solution with an existing legacy system often involves aligning the new solution's functionality with outdated technologies, which can be complex and time-consuming.

657. A project manager is evaluating cloud-based solutions for a new project. Which architectural consideration is most relevant for cloud-based solutions?

a. Ensuring physical proximity of servers
b. Assessing the cloud provider's service-level agreements (SLAs)
c. Developing a custom in-house data center
d. Avoiding the use of virtualized resources

Answer: b. Assessing the cloud provider's service-level agreements (SLAs). Explanation: When evaluating cloud-based solutions, it is crucial to assess the cloud provider's SLAs to ensure they meet the project's requirements for availability, performance, and support.

658. During the design phase, the project manager decides to use containerization for deploying the solution. What is the main advantage of containerization?
a. Simplified licensing requirements
b. Improved portability and consistency across environments
c. Enhanced user interface design
d. Reduced need for testing

Answer: b. Improved portability and consistency across environments. Explanation: Containerization encapsulates an application and its dependencies into a container, ensuring that it runs consistently across different environments, thereby improving portability and consistency.

659. A project manager is integrating a new CRM system with existing sales and marketing tools. Which integration method would best ensure real-time data synchronization between these systems?
a. Batch processing
b. Manual data entry
c. Real-time API integration
d. Weekly data exports

Answer: c. Real-time API integration. Explanation: Real-time API integration ensures that data is synchronized in real-time between the new CRM system and existing sales and marketing tools, providing up-to-date information across systems.

660. The project team needs to design a solution that can handle large volumes of data efficiently. Which architectural consideration should be prioritized?
a. Choosing a relational database with extensive indexing
b. Implementing a NoSQL database that can scale horizontally
c. Using a single server with high processing power
d. Reducing the overall data volume

Answer: b. Implementing a NoSQL database that can scale horizontally. Explanation: A NoSQL database that can scale horizontally is suitable for handling large volumes of data efficiently, as it allows for the addition of more servers to distribute the load and improve performance.

661. A project manager is working on the development of a new software application. During which phase of the project life cycle is the project's feasibility and alignment with organizational goals typically assessed?
a. Initiating
b. Planning
c. Executing
d. Closing

Answer: a. Initiating. Explanation: In the initiating phase of the project life cycle, the project's feasibility and alignment with organizational goals are assessed. This phase includes activities such as developing the project charter and identifying stakeholders.

662. A project manager is transitioning from the development phase to the deployment phase in a product life cycle. What is the primary focus during this transition?
a. Finalizing the project budget
b. Ensuring the product meets quality standards and is ready for release
c. Conducting team performance reviews
d. Closing all project contracts

Answer: b. Ensuring the product meets quality standards and is ready for release. Explanation: During the transition from development to deployment in a product life cycle, the primary focus is on ensuring that the product meets quality standards and is ready for release to the market.

663. Which of the following best describes the difference between a project life cycle and a product life cycle?
a. A project life cycle is longer than a product life cycle
b. A product life cycle includes the phases of a project life cycle and extends beyond to include market introduction, growth, maturity, and decline
c. A project life cycle focuses on sustaining product value, while a product life cycle focuses on project execution
d. A product life cycle is used only in manufacturing, while a project life cycle is used in all industries

Answer: b. A product life cycle includes the phases of a project life cycle and extends beyond to include market introduction, growth, maturity, and decline. Explanation: A product life cycle encompasses the entire duration from the market introduction of a product to its decline, whereas a project life cycle includes phases from initiation to project closure, focusing on the creation and delivery of the project deliverables.

664. A project manager needs to ensure the ongoing value of a product after its release. Which phase of the product life cycle is primarily concerned with sustaining product value?
a. Introduction
b. Growth
c. Maturity
d. Decline

Answer: c. Maturity. Explanation: During the maturity phase of the product life cycle, the focus is on sustaining the product's value, maximizing its market share, and maintaining customer satisfaction while managing costs and optimizing operations.

665. During which phase of the project life cycle are detailed project plans, such as the schedule, budget, and resource allocation, typically developed?
a. Initiating
b. Planning
c. Executing
d. Monitoring and Controlling

Answer: b. Planning. Explanation: Detailed project plans, including the schedule, budget, and resource allocation, are typically developed during the planning phase of the project life cycle. This phase involves setting the direction and scope of the project to ensure successful execution.

666. A project manager is closing a project and transitioning the product to the operations team. What is a key activity during this phase of the project life cycle?
a. Developing the project charter
b. Conducting stakeholder analysis
c. Finalizing project deliverables and obtaining formal acceptance
d. Creating a detailed work breakdown structure (WBS)

Answer: c. Finalizing project deliverables and obtaining formal acceptance. Explanation: During the closing phase of the project life cycle, the key activities include finalizing project deliverables, obtaining formal acceptance from stakeholders, and transitioning the product to the operations team.

667. A product manager is analyzing the market to determine when to introduce a new version of an existing product. Which phase of the product life cycle is most likely being evaluated for this decision?
a. Introduction
b. Growth
c. Maturity
d. Decline

Answer: d. Decline. Explanation: The decline phase of the product life cycle is characterized by decreasing sales and market share. A product manager would evaluate this phase to determine the right time to introduce a new version or replace the existing product to maintain competitiveness.

668. During the project life cycle, what is the primary purpose of the Monitoring and Controlling phase?
a. To initiate the project and define its objectives
b. To execute the project plan and produce deliverables

c. To track project performance and make necessary adjustments
d. To close the project and finalize deliverables

Answer: c. To track project performance and make necessary adjustments. Explanation: The primary purpose of the Monitoring and Controlling phase is to track project performance against the plan, identify any variances, and make necessary adjustments to ensure the project stays on track.

669. A project team is working on a product that has reached the growth phase of its life cycle. What should be the team's primary focus during this phase?
a. Increasing production capacity to meet rising demand
b. Conducting a feasibility study for the product
c. Planning the project scope and objectives
d. Finalizing the project deliverables and closing contracts

Answer: a. Increasing production capacity to meet rising demand. Explanation: During the growth phase of the product life cycle, the primary focus is on increasing production capacity and improving processes to meet the rising demand for the product, while also expanding market reach and increasing sales.

670. A project manager is preparing for the transition from the project to product management. Which document is most critical in ensuring that the operations team understands the product's maintenance and support requirements?
a. Project charter
b. Product roadmap
c. Operations manual
d. Risk management plan

Answer: c. Operations manual. Explanation: The operations manual is critical for ensuring that the operations team understands the product's maintenance and support requirements. It provides detailed instructions and guidelines for managing and sustaining the product after the project has been completed.

671. A project manager is evaluating potential vendors for a critical project component. Which criterion is most important to consider when selecting a vendor?
a. The vendor's marketing materials
b. The vendor's past performance and reliability
c. The vendor's proximity to the project site
d. The vendor's social media presence

Answer: b. The vendor's past performance and reliability. Explanation: Evaluating a vendor's past performance and reliability is crucial because it provides insight into their ability to deliver quality products or services on time, which is critical for the success of the project.

672. During contract negotiations with a new supplier, the project manager wants to ensure favorable payment terms. Which of the following terms should the project manager prioritize?
a. Upfront payment before delivery
b. Net 30 payment terms
c. Payment upon order placement
d. Payment after project completion

Answer: b. Net 30 payment terms. Explanation: Net 30 payment terms provide a reasonable timeframe for the project team to evaluate the delivered goods or services before making payment, balancing cash flow management and supplier relations.

673. A project manager is managing a long-term relationship with a key supplier. What is the most effective strategy to maintain a positive relationship?
a. Regularly switching suppliers to ensure competitive pricing
b. Maintaining open and transparent communication
c. Limiting interactions to formal contract reviews
d. Focusing solely on price negotiations

Answer: b. Maintaining open and transparent communication. Explanation: Open and transparent communication helps build trust and fosters a collaborative relationship, ensuring that any issues are addressed promptly and the supplier remains aligned with project goals.

674. A project manager is assessing a vendor's proposal that includes a detailed project timeline and cost breakdown. Which aspect is most critical to validate before proceeding with the vendor?
a. The aesthetic design of the proposal
b. The alignment of the proposed timeline with project milestones
c. The number of pages in the proposal
d. The vendor's logo and branding

Answer: b. The alignment of the proposed timeline with project milestones. Explanation: Ensuring that the vendor's proposed timeline aligns with the project's milestones is critical to maintaining the overall project schedule and avoiding delays.

675. During a vendor performance review, the project manager identifies several areas where the vendor has not met the agreed-upon service levels. What should be the project manager's next step?
a. Terminate the contract immediately
b. Document the performance issues and discuss them with the vendor
c. Ignore the issues if they are minor
d. Reduce the scope of work assigned to the vendor

Answer: b. Document the performance issues and discuss them with the vendor. Explanation: Documenting the performance issues and discussing them with the vendor allows for a constructive dialogue to address and resolve the issues, helping to improve future performance.

676. A project manager needs to evaluate multiple suppliers for a new project. Which tool or technique is most appropriate for comparing the suppliers objectively?
a. SWOT analysis
b. Pareto chart
c. Weighted scoring model
d. Delphi technique

Answer: c. Weighted scoring model. Explanation: A weighted scoring model allows the project manager to evaluate multiple suppliers objectively by assigning weights to various criteria and scoring each supplier based on these criteria, facilitating an informed decision.

677. In contract negotiations, the project manager wants to mitigate potential risks associated with delivery delays. Which contract clause is most effective for this purpose?
a. Force majeure clause
b. Liquidated damages clause
c. Confidentiality clause
d. Termination for convenience clause

Answer: b. Liquidated damages clause. Explanation: A liquidated damages clause specifies a predetermined amount that the vendor must pay if delivery is delayed, providing a financial incentive for the vendor to meet deadlines and mitigating the risk of delays.

678. A project manager is developing a vendor management plan. Which element is most critical to include in this plan?
a. The vendor's marketing strategy
b. The vendor's holiday schedule
c. Performance metrics and evaluation criteria
d. A list of vendor's competitors

Answer: c. Performance metrics and evaluation criteria. Explanation: Including performance metrics and evaluation criteria in the vendor management plan is critical to objectively assess the vendor's performance and ensure they meet the project's requirements and standards.

679. During the procurement process, the project manager receives bids from several vendors. What is the most important factor to consider when selecting the best bid?
a. The lowest price offered
b. The vendor's compliance with project specifications
c. The number of bids received

d. The format of the bid document

Answer: b. The vendor's compliance with project specifications. Explanation: Ensuring the vendor's compliance with project specifications is the most important factor, as it guarantees that the vendor can deliver the required goods or services that meet the project's needs.

680. A project manager is negotiating a contract with a new supplier. What is the primary goal of the negotiation process?
a. To achieve the lowest possible price
b. To establish a win-win agreement that benefits both parties
c. To secure long-term exclusivity with the supplier
d. To finalize the contract as quickly as possible

Answer: b. To establish a win-win agreement that benefits both parties. Explanation: The primary goal of contract negotiation is to establish a win-win agreement that benefits both parties, fostering a positive and collaborative relationship that supports the project's success.

681. A project manager is working on a project that must comply with specific industry regulations. Which of the following is the most critical first step in ensuring compliance?
a. Developing a detailed project schedule
b. Conducting a regulatory compliance audit
c. Identifying all applicable regulations and requirements
d. Allocating budget for compliance-related activities

Answer: c. Identifying all applicable regulations and requirements. Explanation: The first step in ensuring compliance is to identify all applicable regulations and requirements. This ensures that the project team is aware of the compliance obligations and can plan accordingly to meet them.

682. During a project review, the project manager discovers that a key deliverable does not meet regulatory standards. What should be the project manager's next course of action?
a. Ignore the issue and proceed with the project
b. Document the non-compliance and escalate it to the project sponsor
c. Modify the deliverable to meet regulatory standards
d. Revise the project schedule to accommodate compliance checks

Answer: c. Modify the deliverable to meet regulatory standards. Explanation: The project manager should ensure that the deliverable is modified to meet regulatory standards. Compliance is crucial, and delivering non-compliant products can result in legal and financial repercussions.

683. A project manager needs to ensure ongoing compliance with regulatory requirements throughout the project lifecycle. Which tool is most appropriate for monitoring compliance?
a. Gantt chart
b. Risk register
c. Compliance checklist
d. Project charter

Answer: c. Compliance checklist. Explanation: A compliance checklist is an effective tool for monitoring regulatory requirements throughout the project lifecycle. It helps ensure that all necessary compliance activities are completed and documented.

684. The project team is developing a new medical device that must comply with stringent health and safety regulations. Which phase of the project should focus heavily on regulatory compliance?
a. Initiating
b. Planning
c. Executing
d. Closing

Answer: b. Planning. Explanation: The planning phase should focus heavily on regulatory compliance to ensure that all requirements are identified, understood, and incorporated into the project plan. This helps prevent compliance issues later in the project.

685. A project manager is responsible for ensuring that the project complies with environmental regulations. Which activity is most critical during the planning phase to address this requirement?
a. Scheduling regular team meetings
b. Conducting an environmental impact assessment
c. Creating a project budget
d. Developing a communication plan

Answer: b. Conducting an environmental impact assessment. Explanation: Conducting an environmental impact assessment during the planning phase is critical for identifying potential environmental risks and ensuring that the project complies with environmental regulations.

686. During a regulatory audit, the auditor requests documentation demonstrating compliance with industry standards. Which document is most likely to provide this information?
a. Project charter
b. Stakeholder register
c. Compliance audit report
d. Work breakdown structure

Answer: c. Compliance audit report. Explanation: A compliance audit report provides documentation demonstrating that the project meets industry standards and regulatory requirements. It is a key document for regulatory audits.

687. A project manager must ensure that the project team understands the impact of regulations on the project. Which method is most effective for achieving this understanding?
a. Conducting a one-time training session
b. Sending out periodic email reminders
c. Integrating compliance training into regular team meetings
d. Assigning compliance responsibilities to a single team member

Answer: c. Integrating compliance training into regular team meetings. Explanation: Integrating compliance training into regular team meetings ensures that the project team consistently understands and adheres to regulatory requirements, fostering ongoing awareness and compliance.

688. A business analyst is assessing the impact of new regulations on a project's business requirements. What is the most appropriate action to take?
a. Updating the project schedule to include compliance activities
b. Revising the business requirements to align with the new regulations
c. Increasing the project budget to cover compliance costs
d. Delegating the compliance assessment to the legal department

Answer: b. Revising the business requirements to align with the new regulations. Explanation: The business analyst should revise the business requirements to ensure they align with the new regulations, ensuring that the project deliverables meet all necessary compliance standards.

689. A project is nearing completion when a new regulatory requirement is introduced. What should the project manager do to address this change?
a. Ignore the new requirement as the project is nearly complete
b. Conduct a change impact analysis and update the project plan
c. Delay the project until the regulation is fully understood
d. Allocate additional resources to complete the project faster

Answer: b. Conduct a change impact analysis and update the project plan. Explanation: The project manager should conduct a change impact analysis to understand how the new regulatory requirement affects the project and update the project plan accordingly to ensure compliance.

690. A project manager is ensuring that all project activities comply with data protection regulations. What is a key component of this compliance effort?
a. Developing a risk management plan
b. Implementing data encryption and access controls
c. Increasing the project budget
d. Scheduling more frequent project reviews

Answer: b. Implementing data encryption and access controls. Explanation: Implementing data encryption and access controls is a key component of ensuring compliance with data protection regulations. These measures help protect sensitive information and ensure that the project adheres to legal requirements.

691. A project manager is defining business rules for a new financial application. Which of the following best describes a business rule?
a. A detailed technical specification for the application
b. A statement that defines or constrains some aspect of the business
c. A timeline for project implementation
d. A list of user interface design guidelines

Answer: b. A statement that defines or constrains some aspect of the business. Explanation: A business rule is a statement that defines or constrains some aspect of the business, ensuring that the business operates in a consistent and controlled manner.

692. The project team needs to ensure that new business rules align with existing organizational policies. Which approach should the project manager use?
a. Develop business rules independently of organizational policies
b. Review and map business rules to relevant organizational policies
c. Focus solely on stakeholder requirements
d. Implement business rules first and adjust organizational policies later

Answer: b. Review and map business rules to relevant organizational policies. Explanation: To ensure alignment, the project manager should review and map business rules to relevant organizational policies, ensuring that the new rules support and are consistent with existing policies.

693. A project manager is assessing the impact of new business rules on project requirements. Which factor is most critical to consider?
a. The cost of implementing the business rules
b. The project's completion date
c. The compatibility of the business rules with stakeholder preferences
d. The extent to which the business rules affect the project's scope

Answer: d. The extent to which the business rules affect the project's scope. Explanation: It is critical to consider how the new business rules affect the project's scope, as they may introduce new requirements or constraints that need to be addressed in the project plan.

694. During a project review, a stakeholder raises concerns that a newly implemented business rule is not aligned with regulatory requirements. What should the project manager do?

a. Ignore the concern and proceed with the project
b. Review the business rule and ensure compliance with regulatory requirements
c. Remove the business rule from the project scope
d. Delegate the concern to the legal department without further action

Answer: b. Review the business rule and ensure compliance with regulatory requirements. Explanation: The project manager should review the business rule and ensure it complies with regulatory requirements, making any necessary adjustments to align with legal standards.

695. A project team is defining business rules for an e-commerce website. Which of the following is an example of a business rule for this project?
a. The website must load within 3 seconds
b. Users must be able to filter products by category
c. Orders over $50 qualify for free shipping
d. The homepage should feature the latest promotions

Answer: c. Orders over $50 qualify for free shipping. Explanation: This is a business rule that defines a specific condition under which customers receive free shipping, impacting the operations and policies of the e-commerce website.

696. The project manager is tasked with managing changes to business rules during the project lifecycle. Which process is most appropriate for this task?
a. Scope verification
b. Change control management
c. Quality assurance
d. Risk management

Answer: b. Change control management. Explanation: Change control management is the process used to manage changes to business rules during the project lifecycle, ensuring that changes are reviewed, approved, and documented systematically.

697. A project manager is evaluating the impact of a new business rule on an existing system. Which type of analysis is most useful for this evaluation?
a. Cost-benefit analysis
b. Gap analysis
c. SWOT analysis
d. Root cause analysis

Answer: b. Gap analysis. Explanation: Gap analysis is used to evaluate the impact of new business rules on an existing system by identifying differences between the current state and the desired future state, highlighting areas that need to be addressed.

698. A stakeholder requests a new business rule that conflicts with an existing rule. What is the project manager's best course of action?
a. Implement both rules and monitor for conflicts
b. Prioritize the stakeholder's request over existing rules
c. Analyze the conflict and work with stakeholders to resolve it
d. Reject the new rule to avoid complications

Answer: c. Analyze the conflict and work with stakeholders to resolve it. Explanation: The project manager should analyze the conflict and work with stakeholders to resolve it, ensuring that all business rules are consistent and do not contradict each other.

699. The project team is documenting business rules for an inventory management system. Which format is most appropriate for documenting these rules?
a. Detailed technical specifications
b. User interface wireframes
c. Structured natural language or decision tables
d. Project budget breakdown

Answer: c. Structured natural language or decision tables. Explanation: Documenting business rules in structured natural language or decision tables ensures they are clear, understandable, and easily referenced, facilitating their implementation and management.

700. During project execution, a project manager notices that a key business rule has been violated. What should be the immediate next step?
a. Ignore the violation if it does not impact the project schedule
b. Notify the project sponsor and stakeholders of the violation
c. Review and correct the processes to ensure compliance with the business rule
d. Adjust the project scope to accommodate the violation

Answer: c. Review and correct the processes to ensure compliance with the business rule. Explanation: The immediate next step is to review and correct the processes to ensure compliance with the business rule, maintaining project integrity and alignment with organizational policies.

701. A project manager is planning User Acceptance Testing (UAT) for a new software application. Which of the following activities should be performed first in the UAT process?
a. Developing test scripts
b. Identifying and training UAT participants
c. Creating the UAT schedule
d. Defining acceptance criteria

Answer: d. Defining acceptance criteria. Explanation: Defining acceptance criteria is the first step in the UAT process as it sets the standards and conditions that the software must meet to be accepted by the users. This ensures that the testing is focused and aligned with user expectations.

702. During UAT, a critical issue is discovered that prevents the system from functioning as intended. What is the most appropriate next step for the project manager?
a. Proceed with the deployment as planned
b. Document the issue and proceed with testing other functionalities
c. Halt the UAT process and escalate the issue to the development team for resolution
d. Ignore the issue and instruct users to find a workaround

Answer: c. Halt the UAT process and escalate the issue to the development team for resolution. Explanation: When a critical issue is discovered during UAT, the process should be halted, and the issue should be escalated to the development team for resolution. This ensures that the system meets the necessary requirements before proceeding with further testing or deployment.

703. The project team is conducting UAT for a new financial reporting system. Which type of testing is most critical to ensure the accuracy of financial data?
a. Performance testing
b. Functional testing
c. Usability testing
d. Security testing

Answer: b. Functional testing. Explanation: Functional testing is most critical in UAT for a financial reporting system as it ensures that the system's functions operate correctly and produce accurate financial data, which is essential for the system's reliability and compliance.

704. A project manager needs to document the results of UAT. Which information is most important to include in the UAT results documentation?
a. Project budget and resource allocation
b. Test scripts and detailed financial analysis
c. Test cases, actual results, and any discrepancies or issues found
d. Development team structure and project timeline

Answer: c. Test cases, actual results, and any discrepancies or issues found. Explanation: UAT results documentation should include the test cases executed, actual results, and any discrepancies or issues found during testing. This provides a clear record of the testing process and outcomes, facilitating issue resolution and final acceptance decisions.

705. The criteria for acceptance in UAT should be based on which of the following?
a. The preferences of the development team

b. The budget constraints of the project
c. The requirements and expectations of the end-users
d. The technical specifications of the software

Answer: c. The requirements and expectations of the end-users. Explanation: The criteria for acceptance in UAT should be based on the requirements and expectations of the end-users, as UAT aims to ensure that the software meets their needs and is ready for deployment.

706. During the UAT planning phase, the project manager must ensure that all relevant stakeholders are involved. Which stakeholders are most critical to include in UAT?
a. Senior management and financial analysts
b. End-users and business analysts
c. Software developers and IT support staff
d. Marketing team and external consultants

Answer: b. End-users and business analysts. Explanation: End-users and business analysts are most critical to include in UAT because they represent the primary users of the system and have a deep understanding of the business requirements and processes that the software needs to support.

707. A project manager is preparing the UAT schedule. What is a key factor to consider when developing this schedule?
a. The availability of end-users for testing
b. The development team's vacation plans
c. The marketing campaign launch date
d. The length of the project initiation phase

Answer: a. The availability of end-users for testing. Explanation: When developing the UAT schedule, it is crucial to consider the availability of end-users for testing, as their participation is essential for validating that the system meets their requirements and is user-friendly.

708. A project team discovers during UAT that a critical functionality is missing from the software. What is the best course of action?
a. Document the missing functionality and proceed with UAT
b. Halt UAT, address the missing functionality, and then resume UAT
c. Ignore the missing functionality and complete UAT as planned
d. Request additional budget to cover the missing functionality

Answer: b. Halt UAT, address the missing functionality, and then resume UAT. Explanation: If a critical functionality is missing, UAT should be halted, the missing functionality should be addressed, and then UAT should be resumed. This ensures that the software is fully functional and meets all necessary requirements.

709. The project manager needs to ensure that UAT is thorough and covers all necessary aspects of the software. Which approach is most effective for achieving this?
a. Limiting UAT to the most frequently used features
b. Involving a diverse group of users and scenarios in UAT
c. Conducting UAT in a single session with all participants
d. Focusing UAT only on the system's performance

Answer: b. Involving a diverse group of users and scenarios in UAT. Explanation: Involving a diverse group of users and scenarios in UAT ensures that the testing is thorough and covers all necessary aspects of the software, leading to a more comprehensive validation of the system's functionality and usability.

710. A project manager is conducting the final review of UAT results. What is the primary objective of this review?
a. To finalize the project budget
b. To determine if the software meets the defined acceptance criteria
c. To create the project schedule
d. To assess the performance of the project team

Answer: b. To determine if the software meets the defined acceptance criteria. Explanation: The primary objective of the final review of UAT results is to determine if the software meets the defined acceptance criteria. This decision is crucial for approving the software for deployment and ensuring it is ready for use by end-users.

711. A project manager is preparing for the implementation of a new software solution. Which of the following activities should be prioritized to ensure operational readiness?
a. Developing a marketing plan for the solution
b. Conducting end-user training sessions
c. Redesigning the company website
d. Finalizing the project budget

Answer: b. Conducting end-user training sessions. Explanation: Conducting end-user training sessions ensures that users are familiar with the new software and can operate it effectively, which is crucial for operational readiness.

712. During the transition to a new system, the project manager encounters resistance from employees. Which change management strategy is most effective in addressing this resistance?
a. Ignoring the resistance and proceeding with the implementation
b. Mandating the change without providing explanations
c. Communicating the benefits of the change and involving employees in the process
d. Delaying the implementation until all resistance is eliminated

Answer: c. Communicating the benefits of the change and involving employees in the process. Explanation: Communicating the benefits of the change and involving employees helps address resistance by ensuring that employees understand the reasons for the change and feel included in the process.

713. A project manager needs to ensure that operational support is in place for a new application. What is the most critical step to take before the application goes live?
a. Conducting a risk assessment for the project
b. Creating a detailed support plan with defined roles and responsibilities
c. Holding a project kickoff meeting
d. Finalizing the project scope statement

Answer: b. Creating a detailed support plan with defined roles and responsibilities. Explanation: A detailed support plan with defined roles and responsibilities ensures that operational support is ready to address any issues that arise once the application goes live.

714. The project team is preparing to deploy a new infrastructure system. Which of the following is an essential component of the operational readiness checklist?
a. Reviewing the project's business case
b. Testing the system under production-like conditions
c. Conducting a market analysis
d. Drafting a project charter

Answer: b. Testing the system under production-like conditions. Explanation: Testing the system under production-like conditions is essential to identify and address any potential issues before the system goes live, ensuring operational readiness.

715. A project manager is implementing a change management strategy to support the deployment of a new process. Which of the following actions best supports this strategy?
a. Providing comprehensive documentation and training to all impacted employees
b. Keeping the implementation plan confidential until the deployment date
c. Reducing the project timeline to minimize disruption
d. Limiting communication to only senior management

Answer: a. Providing comprehensive documentation and training to all impacted employees. Explanation: Providing comprehensive documentation and training ensures that all impacted employees are well-prepared for the new process, facilitating a smooth transition and supporting the change management strategy.

716. During a project to upgrade an existing system, the project manager identifies a potential risk to operational readiness. What should be the project manager's next step?
a. Ignore the risk and focus on the project timeline
b. Document the risk and develop a mitigation plan
c. Accelerate the project schedule to complete early

d. Inform stakeholders of the risk but take no further action

Answer: b. Document the risk and develop a mitigation plan. Explanation: Documenting the risk and developing a mitigation plan helps address potential issues proactively, ensuring that the project remains on track and operational readiness is maintained.

717. A project manager is responsible for ensuring that all necessary resources are in place for a new system implementation. Which resource is most critical for operational readiness?
a. An updated company logo
b. A dedicated support team
c. A new marketing campaign
d. A redesigned office space

Answer: b. A dedicated support team. Explanation: A dedicated support team is critical for operational readiness, as they will address any technical issues and provide ongoing support to ensure the system operates smoothly after implementation.

718. The project manager needs to ensure that the new solution is fully integrated with existing systems. What is the best approach to achieve this?
a. Conducting integration testing to validate compatibility
b. Implementing the solution in isolation and testing later
c. Focusing on the new solution's features and deferring integration concerns
d. Minimizing communication with existing system owners

Answer: a. Conducting integration testing to validate compatibility. Explanation: Conducting integration testing ensures that the new solution works seamlessly with existing systems, validating compatibility and preventing integration issues after deployment.

719. A project manager is implementing a new enterprise resource planning (ERP) system. What is a key activity to ensure operational support for the ERP system?
a. Training the IT support team on the new system's functionalities
b. Distributing marketing materials about the new system
c. Redesigning the company's organizational structure
d. Increasing the project budget to account for unforeseen costs

Answer: a. Training the IT support team on the new system's functionalities. Explanation: Training the IT support team on the new system's functionalities ensures that they are prepared to provide effective support, addressing any technical issues that may arise.

720. The project team is preparing for a system go-live event. Which action is most important to ensure a successful go-live?
a. Finalizing the project documentation
b. Conducting a final round of user acceptance testing (UAT)
c. Holding a celebratory event for the team
d. Completing a market analysis for future projects

Answer: b. Conducting a final round of user acceptance testing (UAT). Explanation: Conducting a final round of UAT ensures that the system meets user requirements and functions as expected, addressing any last-minute issues before going live and ensuring a smooth deployment.

721. A project manager is leading a healthcare software development project and needs to comply with HIPAA regulations. Which of the following processes is most crucial for ensuring compliance?
a. Quality management
b. Risk management
c. Procurement management
d. Scope management

Answer: b. Risk management. Explanation: Risk management is crucial for identifying and mitigating risks related to HIPAA compliance, ensuring that patient data is protected throughout the project.

722. During a financial services project, the project manager notices a significant variance in the budget. What should be the project manager's first step?
a. Update the budget baseline
b. Perform a root cause analysis
c. Request additional funds
d. Inform stakeholders immediately

Answer: b. Perform a root cause analysis. Explanation: The first step is to identify the cause of the budget variance to understand if it's a one-time issue or an ongoing problem that needs corrective action.

723. A healthcare project is in the execution phase, and new regulatory requirements have been introduced. What should the project manager do first?
a. Ignore the new requirements
b. Update the project management plan
c. Assess the impact on project scope, schedule, and budget
d. Inform the project sponsor

Answer: c. Assess the impact on project scope, schedule, and budget. Explanation: The project manager should first evaluate how the new regulations will affect the project's constraints before updating plans or communicating changes.

724. In an IT project, a project manager wants to ensure all deliverables meet the customer's expectations. Which process should be primarily used to achieve this?
a. Perform Integrated Change Control
b. Validate Scope
c. Control Quality
d. Monitor and Control Project Work

Answer: b. Validate Scope. Explanation: Validate Scope involves formalizing acceptance of the completed project deliverables, ensuring they meet customer expectations.

725. A project manager in a financial services company is using earned value management (EVM) to track project performance. The project has a planned value (PV) of $200,000, an earned value (EV) of $180,000, and an actual cost (AC) of $210,000. What is the cost performance index (CPI), and what does it indicate?
a. 0.86, the project is under budget
b. 0.86, the project is over budget
c. 1.17, the project is under budget
d. 1.17, the project is over budget

Answer: b. 0.86, the project is over budget. Explanation: CPI is calculated as EV/AC = $180,000/$210,000 = 0.86. A CPI less than 1 indicates the project is over budget.

726. A project manager is managing a software development project and the team is experiencing high levels of defects in the code. Which quality tool should the project manager use to prioritize the most critical defects?
a. Fishbone diagram
b. Pareto chart
c. Control chart
d. Histogram

Answer: b. Pareto chart. Explanation: A Pareto chart helps prioritize the most significant defects, based on the 80/20 rule, allowing the team to focus on the most critical issues first.

727. In a healthcare project, the project manager needs to procure specialized medical equipment. Which contract type would best minimize the buyer's risk?
a. Fixed-price contract
b. Cost-plus-fixed-fee contract
c. Time and materials contract
d. Cost-plus-incentive-fee contract

Answer: a. Fixed-price contract. Explanation: A fixed-price contract minimizes the buyer's risk by setting a fixed total price for the procurement, making the seller responsible for cost overruns.

728. An IT project is nearing completion, and the project manager needs to ensure that all project deliverables are formally accepted. Which document should be referred to for acceptance criteria?
a. Project charter
b. Project management plan
c. Scope statement
d. Requirements traceability matrix

Answer: d. Requirements traceability matrix. Explanation: The requirements traceability matrix includes the acceptance criteria and ensures that each deliverable meets the requirements outlined by the stakeholders.

729. A project in the financial services industry involves significant data analysis and reporting. The project manager wants to ensure data integrity and accuracy. Which process group should the project manager focus on to establish controls for data quality?
a. Initiating
b. Planning
c. Executing
d. Monitoring and Controlling

Answer: d. Monitoring and Controlling. Explanation: The Monitoring and Controlling process group focuses on tracking, reviewing, and regulating the progress and performance of the project, ensuring data integrity and accuracy through quality control measures.

730. During a healthcare project, a team member reports a potential risk related to patient data security. Which risk response strategy should the project manager consider if the risk cannot be avoided or transferred?
a. Mitigation
b. Acceptance
c. Escalation
d. Exploitation

Answer: a. Mitigation. Explanation: Mitigation involves taking actions to reduce the likelihood or impact of a risk, which is appropriate when the risk cannot be avoided or transferred.

731. A project is initiated to develop a new software application that aligns with the company's strategic goal of entering the healthcare market. Which of the following activities is most critical during the initiation phase to ensure strategic alignment?
a. Defining the project's scope
b. Identifying key stakeholders
c. Developing the project schedule
d. Creating the Work Breakdown Structure (WBS)

Answer: b. Identifying key stakeholders. Explanation: Identifying key stakeholders is crucial during the initiation phase to ensure that the project aligns with the strategic goals and objectives of the organization. Engaging stakeholders early helps in understanding their needs and expectations, which is essential for strategic alignment.

732. A project manager is assessing a new project proposal to determine its alignment with organizational strategy. Which tool or technique would be most effective for this assessment?
a. SWOT analysis
b. Earned Value Management (EVM)
c. Monte Carlo simulation
d. Critical Path Method (CPM)

Answer: a. SWOT analysis. Explanation: SWOT analysis (Strengths, Weaknesses, Opportunities, Threats) is an effective tool for assessing how a project aligns with organizational strategy. It helps in identifying the internal and external factors that can impact the strategic fit of the project.

733. The leadership team has defined a strategic objective to reduce operational costs by 15% over the next year. Which project outcome would most likely support this strategic objective?
a. Implementing a new marketing campaign
b. Developing a new product line
c. Upgrading the company's IT infrastructure
d. Enhancing customer service training programs

Answer: c. Upgrading the company's IT infrastructure. Explanation: Upgrading the IT infrastructure can streamline operations, improve efficiency, and reduce operational costs, directly supporting the strategic objective of cost reduction.

734. A project manager needs to ensure that the proposed solutions for a project align with the strategic objectives of the organization. Which document should be reviewed to confirm this alignment?
a. Project charter
b. Stakeholder register
c. Risk management plan
d. Project management plan

Answer: a. Project charter. Explanation: The project charter outlines the project's objectives and how they align with the organization's strategic goals. Reviewing the project charter ensures that the proposed solutions support these objectives.

735. During the planning phase, a project manager is tasked with ensuring the project's deliverables are strategically aligned with the company's mission. Which planning activity will best help achieve this?

a. Developing the project budget
b. Conducting a feasibility study
c. Creating a detailed project schedule
d. Defining the project's critical success factors

Answer: d. Defining the project's critical success factors. Explanation: Defining critical success factors ensures that the project's deliverables are aligned with the company's mission and strategic goals. These factors are key to measuring the project's success in terms of strategic alignment.

736. A project manager is leading a project to develop a new product that fits the strategic objective of market expansion. To ensure strategic fit, which of the following actions is most important during the execution phase?
a. Monitoring project progress against the schedule
b. Managing stakeholder expectations
c. Conducting regular risk assessments
d. Ensuring quality control of deliverables

Answer: b. Managing stakeholder expectations. Explanation: Managing stakeholder expectations is critical during the execution phase to ensure that the project continues to align with the strategic objective of market expansion. This involves regular communication and engagement with stakeholders to align on project goals.

737. The company's strategic goal is to enhance innovation and market competitiveness. Which project would most likely align with this strategic goal?
a. Developing a customer feedback system
b. Implementing a new financial management system
c. Launching an employee wellness program
d. Creating a research and development (R&D) department

Answer: d. Creating a research and development (R&D) department. Explanation: Establishing an R&D department directly supports the strategic goal of enhancing innovation and market competitiveness by fostering new ideas and product development.

738. A project is undertaken to streamline the supply chain process to support the strategic goal of improving customer satisfaction. Which key performance indicator (KPI) would best measure the project's success in achieving this strategic alignment?
a. Number of new suppliers
b. Reduction in supply chain costs
c. Decrease in order fulfillment time
d. Increase in inventory levels

Answer: c. Decrease in order fulfillment time. Explanation: Reducing order fulfillment time is a direct measure of improved supply chain efficiency, which supports the strategic goal of enhancing customer satisfaction by ensuring quicker delivery of products.

739. The project management office (PMO) is evaluating projects to ensure they align with the company's long-term strategic vision. Which criterion would be least relevant for this evaluation?
a. Potential for short-term financial gain
b. Alignment with strategic objectives
c. Availability of required resources
d. Impact on organizational culture

Answer: a. Potential for short-term financial gain. Explanation: While financial gain is important, it is less relevant when evaluating projects for long-term strategic alignment. The focus should be on how well the project supports strategic objectives, resource availability, and cultural impact.

740. A company's strategic objective is to achieve sustainability and reduce its carbon footprint. Which project outcome would best align with this objective?
a. Increasing the number of retail locations
b. Developing a paperless office initiative
c. Launching a new advertising campaign
d. Expanding the sales team

Answer: b. Developing a paperless office initiative. Explanation: A paperless office initiative directly supports the strategic objective of sustainability and reducing the carbon footprint by minimizing paper usage and promoting digital solutions.

741. A project portfolio manager is reviewing the performance of several projects within a portfolio. Which key performance indicator (KPI) would be most relevant for assessing the alignment of projects with the organization's strategic goals?
a. Cost variance
b. Return on investment (ROI)
c. Schedule variance
d. Number of change requests

Answer: b. Return on investment (ROI). Explanation: ROI measures the profitability and effectiveness of projects in terms of financial returns, aligning with the organization's strategic goals and providing insight into the value generated by the portfolio.

742. During a portfolio review, a stakeholder expresses concern about the resource allocation for a high-priority project that is behind schedule. What is the most appropriate action for the portfolio manager to take?
a. Reallocate resources from lower-priority projects
b. Increase the budget for the high-priority project

c. Extend the project deadline
d. Initiate a change request to reduce the project scope

Answer: a. Reallocate resources from lower-priority projects. Explanation: Reallocating resources ensures that the high-priority project receives the necessary attention to get back on track, reflecting the portfolio's strategic priorities.

743. Which document typically outlines the criteria for project selection and prioritization within a portfolio?
a. Project charter
b. Portfolio management plan
c. Business case
d. Risk management plan

Answer: b. Portfolio management plan. Explanation: The portfolio management plan includes criteria for selecting and prioritizing projects, ensuring alignment with organizational strategy and objectives.

744. A business analyst is conducting a feasibility study for a new project within a portfolio. What aspect should be considered to determine the project's alignment with portfolio priorities?
a. Technical requirements
b. Stakeholder engagement
c. Strategic fit
d. Project deliverables

Answer: c. Strategic fit. Explanation: Strategic fit assesses how well a project aligns with the organization's strategic goals and priorities, which is crucial for ensuring the project's relevance and value within the portfolio.

745. The portfolio manager must balance the competing demands of several projects. What is the primary benefit of conducting a portfolio risk analysis?
a. Identifying high-risk projects for immediate termination
b. Understanding the aggregated risk exposure of the portfolio
c. Ensuring all projects are completed on time
d. Allocating additional resources to all projects

Answer: b. Understanding the aggregated risk exposure of the portfolio. Explanation: Portfolio risk analysis provides insights into the overall risk landscape, helping to manage and mitigate risks at the portfolio level and balance competing demands effectively.

746. In a project portfolio, one of the projects is consistently failing to meet its milestones. What should the portfolio manager consider before deciding to terminate the project?
a. The project's budget remaining

b. The potential impact on other projects in the portfolio
c. The team's performance history
d. The original project plan

Answer: b. The potential impact on other projects in the portfolio. Explanation: Assessing the impact on other projects helps understand the broader implications of terminating a project, ensuring informed decision-making within the portfolio context.

747. A business analyst is defining the value proposition of a new project within a portfolio. Which tool is most effective for aligning the project's benefits with strategic objectives?
a. SWOT analysis
b. Balanced scorecard
c. Fishbone diagram
d. Monte Carlo simulation

Answer: b. Balanced scorecard. Explanation: The balanced scorecard links project benefits to strategic objectives through performance metrics, ensuring alignment and effective communication of the project's value proposition.

748. To ensure optimal resource utilization across a portfolio, what is the most critical aspect a portfolio manager should monitor?
a. Individual project schedules
b. Portfolio resource capacity and demand
c. Project team satisfaction
d. Stakeholder communication plans

Answer: b. Portfolio resource capacity and demand. Explanation: Monitoring resource capacity and demand ensures that resources are allocated efficiently across the portfolio, preventing overallocation or underutilization.

749. During a portfolio review, the portfolio manager identifies several interdependent projects. What approach should be used to manage these interdependencies effectively?
a. Sequential project scheduling
b. Integrated change control
c. Program management
d. Agile methodology

Answer: c. Program management. Explanation: Program management coordinates and manages interdependent projects to achieve benefits and control not available from managing them individually, ensuring effective handling of interdependencies.

750. A portfolio manager needs to report the performance of the portfolio to the executive board. Which metric best represents the overall health of the portfolio?
a. Number of completed projects
b. Portfolio value delivery index
c. Total project budget
d. Number of project milestones achieved

Answer: b. Portfolio value delivery index. Explanation: The portfolio value delivery index measures the portfolio's ability to deliver value against the strategic objectives, providing a comprehensive view of the portfolio's overall health and performance.

751. A project manager is determining the costs associated with ensuring quality in a software development project. Which of the following is an example of prevention cost?
a. Rework due to defects
b. Employee training on quality standards
c. Product testing
d. Customer returns

Answer: b. Employee training on quality standards. Explanation: Prevention costs are incurred to avoid defects in products or services. Employee training on quality standards is a proactive measure to prevent defects from occurring in the first place.

752. During a project review, it is discovered that several deliverables do not meet the quality requirements and need to be reworked. What type of cost is this?
a. Prevention cost
b. Appraisal cost
c. Internal failure cost
d. External failure cost

Answer: c. Internal failure cost. Explanation: Internal failure costs are associated with defects found before the product or service is delivered to the customer. Rework is an example of an internal failure cost because it is necessary to correct defects before delivery.

753. A project manager is analyzing the cost of quality and identifies the expenses related to inspection and testing of deliverables. What type of cost is this?
a. Prevention cost
b. Appraisal cost
c. Internal failure cost
d. External failure cost

Answer: b. Appraisal cost. Explanation: Appraisal costs are incurred to identify defects through inspection and testing. These costs are aimed at ensuring the quality of deliverables before they reach the customer.

754. After delivering the final product to the customer, several complaints are received regarding defects. The company incurs costs to address these complaints and make necessary corrections. What type of cost does this represent?
a. Prevention cost
b. Appraisal cost
c. Internal failure cost
d. External failure cost

Answer: d. External failure cost. Explanation: External failure costs occur after the product or service has been delivered to the customer. These costs include handling customer complaints and making corrections to defective products that have already reached the customer.

755. A project manager wants to minimize the total cost of quality by focusing on prevention. Which of the following actions is most aligned with this strategy?
a. Increasing the frequency of product inspections
b. Investing in employee training and process improvements
c. Implementing more stringent testing procedures
d. Budgeting for potential warranty claims

Answer: b. Investing in employee training and process improvements. Explanation: Focusing on prevention involves taking proactive measures to avoid defects. Investing in employee training and process improvements helps to prevent quality issues from occurring, thereby reducing the total cost of quality.

756. Which of the following best describes the relationship between prevention costs and failure costs?
a. Increasing prevention costs generally decreases failure costs.
b. Increasing prevention costs generally increases failure costs.
c. Prevention costs and failure costs are unrelated.
d. Prevention costs are always higher than failure costs.

Answer: a. Increasing prevention costs generally decreases failure costs. Explanation: By investing in prevention measures, such as training and process improvements, the likelihood of defects is reduced, which in turn decreases the costs associated with failures.

757. A project incurs costs for implementing a quality management system to ensure all deliverables meet the required standards. These costs are categorized under:
a. Prevention costs
b. Appraisal costs
c. Internal failure costs
d. External failure costs

Answer: a. Prevention costs. Explanation: Implementing a quality management system is a proactive measure designed to prevent defects and ensure that deliverables meet quality standards. Therefore, these costs fall under prevention costs.

758. A company experiences a high rate of product returns due to defects. To address this, they implement additional quality checks during production. What type of costs are these additional checks?
a. Prevention costs
b. Appraisal costs
c. Internal failure costs
d. External failure costs

Answer: b. Appraisal costs. Explanation: Additional quality checks during production are aimed at identifying defects before the product reaches the customer. These are appraisal costs because they are associated with inspecting and testing products to ensure quality.

759. The cost of reworking a deliverable after it has failed an internal quality check is an example of:
a. Prevention cost
b. Appraisal cost
c. Internal failure cost
d. External failure cost

Answer: c. Internal failure cost. Explanation: Reworking a deliverable after it has failed an internal quality check is considered an internal failure cost. These costs are incurred to correct defects found before the product is delivered to the customer.

760. In a project, the total cost of quality is calculated by summing which of the following components?
a. Prevention costs, appraisal costs, and failure costs
b. Direct costs, indirect costs, and failure costs
c. Material costs, labor costs, and overhead costs
d. Appraisal costs, internal failure costs, and external failure costs

Answer: a. Prevention costs, appraisal costs, and failure costs. Explanation: The total cost of quality includes prevention costs, appraisal costs, and failure costs (both internal and external). This comprehensive approach ensures all quality-related expenses are accounted for.

761. A project manager is implementing a business intelligence (BI) system to improve decision-making processes. Which of the following is the primary benefit of using BI tools in business analysis?
a. Reducing operational costs
b. Enhancing data visualization

c. Automating routine tasks
d. Increasing data entry speed

Answer: b. Enhancing data visualization. Explanation: BI tools primarily enhance data visualization, enabling better interpretation and analysis of data to support decision-making processes.

762. A company is using data mining techniques to identify patterns in customer purchasing behavior. Which of the following techniques is most appropriate for predicting future purchases based on past behavior?
a. Clustering
b. Association
c. Classification
d. Regression

Answer: d. Regression. Explanation: Regression analysis is used to predict future values based on historical data, making it suitable for forecasting future customer purchases.

763. During the implementation of a BI system, a project manager needs to ensure that the data is accurate and reliable. Which process is critical for achieving this goal?
a. Data cleansing
b. Data warehousing
c. Data modeling
d. Data integration

Answer: a. Data cleansing. Explanation: Data cleansing involves detecting and correcting (or removing) corrupt or inaccurate records from a dataset, ensuring the accuracy and reliability of the data used in the BI system.

764. A business analyst is tasked with developing a dashboard for senior management to monitor key performance indicators (KPIs). Which feature is essential for the dashboard to be effective?
a. Real-time data updates
b. Complex data algorithms
c. Multiple data sources
d. Interactive charts

Answer: a. Real-time data updates. Explanation: Real-time data updates are essential for an effective dashboard, allowing senior management to make timely and informed decisions based on the latest information.

765. In the context of business intelligence, what is the primary purpose of using OLAP (Online Analytical Processing) tools?
a. To process transactions quickly
b. To support complex queries and analysis

c. To store large volumes of raw data
d. To enhance network security

Answer: b. To support complex queries and analysis. Explanation: OLAP tools are designed to support complex queries and analysis, allowing users to interactively explore and analyze large datasets from multiple perspectives.

766. A project manager is evaluating different data mining tools for a BI project. Which factor is most important when selecting a tool for predictive analytics?
a. Cost of the tool
b. Ease of use
c. Scalability
d. Accuracy of predictions

Answer: d. Accuracy of predictions. Explanation: For predictive analytics, the accuracy of the predictions generated by the data mining tool is the most critical factor, as it directly impacts the quality of insights and decisions.

767. A business analyst is using a reporting tool to generate monthly performance reports. What is the main advantage of using automated reporting tools in business intelligence?
a. Reducing the need for skilled analysts
b. Enhancing report aesthetics
c. Ensuring data consistency and accuracy
d. Increasing report generation speed

Answer: c. Ensuring data consistency and accuracy. Explanation: Automated reporting tools help ensure data consistency and accuracy by standardizing the data collection and reporting process, reducing the risk of human error.

768. In a BI project, the project manager is concerned about data security. Which of the following measures is most effective for protecting sensitive data?
a. Data encryption
b. Data replication
c. Data normalization
d. Data aggregation

Answer: a. Data encryption. Explanation: Data encryption is the most effective measure for protecting sensitive data, as it converts the data into a secure format that is unreadable without the decryption key.

769. A company wants to use business intelligence to gain insights into customer satisfaction. Which data mining technique should be used to identify factors that influence customer satisfaction?
a. Decision trees

b. Neural networks
c. Market basket analysis
d. K-means clustering

Answer: a. Decision trees. Explanation: Decision trees are effective for identifying and analyzing factors that influence a particular outcome, such as customer satisfaction, by splitting data into branches based on different criteria.

770. A project manager is implementing a new BI solution and needs to ensure it integrates seamlessly with existing systems. Which integration approach is most suitable for maintaining real-time data flow between systems?
a. Batch processing
b. ETL (Extract, Transform, Load)
c. API (Application Programming Interface)
d. Data archiving

Answer: c. API (Application Programming Interface). Explanation: APIs are most suitable for maintaining real-time data flow between systems, enabling seamless integration and communication in real-time.

771. A project manager is overseeing a construction project and is required to manage the triple constraint. Which elements are included in the triple constraint?
a. Scope, schedule, cost
b. Quality, risk, resources
c. Communication, procurement, stakeholders
d. Initiation, planning, execution

Answer: a. Scope, schedule, cost. Explanation: The triple constraint, also known as the project management triangle, includes scope, schedule, and cost. These three elements are interdependent, and changes to one element can affect the others.

772. During project initiation, which document is created to formally authorize the project and provide the project manager with the authority to apply organizational resources to project activities?
a. Project charter
b. Stakeholder register
c. Risk management plan
d. Project scope statement

Answer: a. Project charter. Explanation: The project charter is a key document created during project initiation. It formally authorizes the project, outlines the project's objectives, and grants the project manager the authority to use organizational resources for project activities.

773. A project manager is using a Work Breakdown Structure (WBS) to plan a project. What is the primary purpose of a WBS?
a. To define the project schedule
b. To break down project deliverables into smaller, manageable components
c. To assign tasks to team members
d. To identify project risks

Answer: b. To break down project deliverables into smaller, manageable components. Explanation: The primary purpose of a WBS is to decompose project deliverables into smaller, more manageable components, making it easier to plan, execute, and control the project.

774. A project team is in the process of identifying risks. Which technique involves visualizing relationships between potential causes of risks and their effects?
a. Monte Carlo simulation
b. Fishbone diagram
c. SWOT analysis
d. Delphi technique

Answer: b. Fishbone diagram. Explanation: The Fishbone diagram, also known as the Ishikawa or cause-and-effect diagram, helps visualize the relationships between potential causes of risks and their effects, aiding in the identification of root causes of problems.

775. A project manager is tracking project performance using Earned Value Management (EVM). The project has an Earned Value (EV) of $150,000, Actual Cost (AC) of $160,000, and Planned Value (PV) of $200,000. What is the Schedule Performance Index (SPI)?
a. 0.75
b. 0.94
c. 1.07
d. 1.33

Answer: a. 0.75. Explanation: SPI is calculated as EV / PV. For this project, SPI = $150,000 / $200,000 = 0.75. An SPI less than 1 indicates the project is behind schedule.

776. Which process group involves coordinating people and resources, as well as integrating and performing project activities in accordance with the project management plan?
a. Initiating
b. Planning
c. Executing
d. Monitoring and Controlling

Answer: c. Executing. Explanation: The Executing process group involves coordinating people and resources, integrating and performing project activities, and ensuring that the project deliverables are produced according to the project management plan.

777. A project manager is using the RACI matrix to define roles and responsibilities. What does RACI stand for?
a. Responsible, Accountable, Consulted, Informed
b. Review, Approve, Communicate, Implement
c. Report, Analyze, Control, Improve
d. Research, Assess, Create, Implement

Answer: a. Responsible, Accountable, Consulted, Informed. Explanation: RACI stands for Responsible, Accountable, Consulted, and Informed. It is a responsibility assignment matrix used to clarify roles and responsibilities in a project.

778. A project manager needs to ensure that all project work is completed within the defined scope. Which process should they use to monitor and control the work being performed?
a. Control Scope
b. Validate Scope
c. Control Quality
d. Monitor and Control Project Work

Answer: a. Control Scope. Explanation: The Control Scope process involves monitoring the status of the project and product scope and managing changes to the scope baseline to ensure that all project work is completed within the defined scope.

779. Which of the following is a key benefit of using a Change Control Board (CCB) in project management?
a. It ensures all changes are approved by the project sponsor
b. It standardizes the process for reviewing and approving change requests
c. It allows team members to implement changes without formal approval
d. It eliminates the need for a project management plan

Answer: b. It standardizes the process for reviewing and approving change requests. Explanation: A Change Control Board (CCB) standardizes the process for reviewing and approving change requests, ensuring that changes are properly evaluated and authorized before implementation.

780. A project manager is closing out a project and needs to ensure that all deliverables meet the required standards. Which process will they use to formally accept the completed deliverables?
a. Validate Scope
b. Control Quality
c. Close Project or Phase
d. Perform Integrated Change Control

Answer: a. Validate Scope. Explanation: The Validate Scope process involves formalizing the acceptance of the completed project deliverables. This process ensures that the deliverables meet the required standards and are formally accepted by the customer or sponsor.

781. A project manager is tasked with creating a detailed Work Breakdown Structure (WBS) for a new software development project. Which of the following best describes the purpose of a WBS?
a. To provide a graphical representation of the project timeline
b. To list all the stakeholders involved in the project
c. To break down the project deliverables into smaller, manageable components
d. To outline the communication plan for the project

Answer: c. To break down the project deliverables into smaller, manageable components. Explanation: The WBS decomposes project deliverables into smaller, more manageable components, providing a structured view of what needs to be accomplished.

782. A project manager notices that the project is behind schedule and over budget. Which Earned Value Management (EVM) metric should be analyzed first to understand the cost performance of the project?
a. Schedule Performance Index (SPI)
b. Cost Performance Index (CPI)
c. Planned Value (PV)
d. Earned Value (EV)

Answer: b. Cost Performance Index (CPI). Explanation: CPI measures cost efficiency by comparing the earned value to actual cost. A CPI less than 1 indicates cost overruns.

783. During the project initiation phase, a project manager needs to identify and document high-level risks. Which document should be created to capture this information?
a. Risk management plan
b. Risk register
c. Project charter
d. Stakeholder register

Answer: c. Project charter. Explanation: The project charter includes high-level risks, project objectives, and other critical information necessary for initiating the project.

784. A business analyst is conducting a needs assessment to identify business problems. Which technique is most suitable for uncovering the root cause of these problems?
a. Brainstorming
b. Fishbone diagram
c. Focus groups
d. Surveys

Answer: b. Fishbone diagram. Explanation: The fishbone diagram helps identify the root causes of problems by visually mapping out potential contributing factors.

785. A project manager is working in a matrix organization and faces resource allocation conflicts. What should be the first step to resolve these conflicts?
a. Escalate the issue to senior management
b. Reassign resources from other projects
c. Negotiate with functional managers
d. Delay the project schedule

Answer: c. Negotiate with functional managers. Explanation: In a matrix organization, functional managers control resources, so negotiating with them is essential for resolving resource allocation conflicts.

786. A project team is using Agile methodology and needs to estimate the effort required for user stories. Which technique is most appropriate for this purpose?
a. Critical Path Method (CPM)
b. Monte Carlo simulation
c. Story points and planning poker
d. Analogous estimating

Answer: c. Story points and planning poker. Explanation: Story points and planning poker are Agile estimation techniques that help teams estimate effort based on complexity and size.

787. A project manager needs to ensure that all project deliverables meet the required quality standards. Which process should be used to achieve this goal?
a. Perform Integrated Change Control
b. Control Quality
c. Validate Scope
d. Manage Quality

Answer: b. Control Quality. Explanation: Control Quality involves monitoring and recording results of executing quality activities to assess performance and recommend necessary changes.

788. During the execution phase of a project, a key stakeholder requests a change that could impact the project scope. What should the project manager do first?
a. Implement the change immediately
b. Update the project charter
c. Assess the impact of the change
d. Communicate the change to the project team

Answer: c. Assess the impact of the change. Explanation: The project manager should first evaluate how the change will affect the project scope, schedule, cost, and quality before taking any further steps.

789. A project manager is developing a communication plan for a complex project with multiple stakeholders. Which factor is most critical to consider when creating this plan?
a. The size of the project team
b. The preferred communication methods of stakeholders
c. The number of project deliverables
d. The project budget

Answer: b. The preferred communication methods of stakeholders. Explanation: Understanding stakeholders' preferred communication methods ensures that information is effectively conveyed and received.

790. A project manager is overseeing a project to implement a new business intelligence (BI) system. The project sponsor is primarily concerned with ensuring that the system provides accurate and timely reports. Which project management knowledge area is most relevant to address the sponsor's concern?
a. Scope management
b. Time management
c. Quality management
d. Risk management

Answer: c. Quality management. Explanation: Quality management ensures that the BI system meets the required standards for accuracy and timeliness in reporting, addressing the sponsor's concern.

791. A project manager is overseeing the development of a new product and needs to ensure that all project deliverables meet the required quality standards. What is the primary purpose of a Quality Management Plan?
a. To outline the project's quality policies and procedures
b. To identify potential risks and develop risk responses
c. To define the project's scope and objectives
d. To create a detailed project schedule

Answer: a. To outline the project's quality policies and procedures. Explanation: The Quality Management Plan describes how the project's quality requirements will be met by outlining quality policies, procedures, and criteria for project deliverables, ensuring that the project's deliverables meet the required standards.

792. A project manager is identifying stakeholders for a new project. Which document should they create to formally record and analyze stakeholder information?
a. Project charter
b. Stakeholder register

c. Risk register
d. Work breakdown structure (WBS)

Answer: b. Stakeholder register. Explanation: The Stakeholder Register is a document that identifies and records information about stakeholders, including their interests, influence, and impact on the project. It is essential for planning and managing stakeholder engagement.

793. During the planning phase, a project manager uses a Responsibility Assignment Matrix (RAM) to assign project tasks. Which element is critical to include in a RAM?
a. Project budget
b. Task durations
c. Resource availability
d. Roles and responsibilities

Answer: d. Roles and responsibilities. Explanation: A Responsibility Assignment Matrix (RAM) is used to define and assign roles and responsibilities for project tasks, ensuring that each task has an accountable owner and that team members understand their responsibilities.

794. A project manager is using the Critical Path Method (CPM) to schedule project activities. What does the critical path represent?
a. The sequence of activities with the lowest risk
b. The shortest path to complete the project
c. The longest path through the project network diagram
d. The path with the most available float

Answer: c. The longest path through the project network diagram. Explanation: The critical path is the sequence of activities that determines the project's minimum duration. It represents the longest path through the project network diagram, and any delay in the critical path activities will delay the project completion.

795. In a matrix organization, a project manager needs to coordinate with functional managers for resource allocation. Which type of matrix structure gives project managers the most authority?
a. Weak matrix
b. Balanced matrix
c. Strong matrix
d. Functional

Answer: c. Strong matrix. Explanation: In a strong matrix structure, the project manager has more authority over resources and project activities compared to functional managers, enabling better coordination and control of project resources.

796. A project manager is conducting a risk assessment and prioritizing risks based on their probability and impact. Which technique would be most appropriate for this analysis?
a. Monte Carlo simulation
b. SWOT analysis
c. Qualitative risk analysis
d. Ishikawa diagram

Answer: c. Qualitative risk analysis. Explanation: Qualitative risk analysis involves assessing the probability and impact of identified risks using qualitative techniques, such as probability and impact matrices, to prioritize risks for further action.

797. During the execution phase, a project manager discovers that a key deliverable is behind schedule. Which process should the project manager use to bring the project back on track?
a. Perform Integrated Change Control
b. Direct and Manage Project Work
c. Monitor and Control Project Work
d. Control Schedule

Answer: d. Control Schedule. Explanation: The Control Schedule process involves monitoring the project schedule, identifying variances, and implementing corrective actions to bring the project back on track and ensure timely completion of deliverables.

798. A project manager is using Earned Value Management (EVM) to track project performance. The project has an Earned Value (EV) of $120,000, Actual Cost (AC) of $100,000, and Planned Value (PV) of $150,000. What is the project's Cost Performance Index (CPI)?
a. 0.80
b. 1.20
c. 1.50
d. 0.67

Answer: b. 1.20. Explanation: CPI is calculated as EV / AC. For this project, CPI = $120,000 / $100,000 = 1.20. A CPI greater than 1 indicates that the project is under budget.

799. A project team is using Agile methodologies and needs to estimate the effort required for user stories. Which technique involves team members assigning points to user stories based on their relative complexity?
a. Planning poker
b. Three-point estimating
c. Delphi technique
d. Analogous estimating

Answer: a. Planning poker. Explanation: Planning poker is an Agile estimation technique where team members assign story points to user stories based on their relative complexity and effort, promoting consensus and accuracy in estimates.

800. A project manager is closing out a project and needs to ensure all project documents are archived. Which document outlines the procedures for closing the project and archiving documents?
a. Project charter
b. Project management plan
c. Close Project or Phase process
d. Project scope statement

Answer: c. Close Project or Phase process. Explanation: The Close Project or Phase process outlines the procedures for finalizing all project activities, obtaining formal acceptance of deliverables, and archiving project documents for future reference and compliance.

801. A business analyst is working in an organization that follows The Open Group Architecture Framework (TOGAF). Which of the following is not one of the main components of the TOGAF framework?
a. Architecture Development Method (ADM)
b. Enterprise Continuum
c. Resource Allocation Diagram (RAD)
d. Architecture Content Framework

Answer: c. Resource Allocation Diagram (RAD). Explanation: The Open Group Architecture Framework (TOGAF) is a widely used enterprise architecture framework that provides a comprehensive approach for designing, planning, implementing, and governing enterprise information technology architecture. TOGAF consists of several main components, including the Architecture Development Method (ADM), a step-by-step process for developing and managing an enterprise architecture; the Enterprise Continuum, a virtual repository of architecture assets and solutions; and the Architecture Content Framework, a structured metamodel for describing architectural artifacts. However, the Resource Allocation Diagram (RAD) is not a component of TOGAF. RAD is a term used in project management to describe a Gantt chart or other visual representation of how resources, such as people or equipment, are allocated to project tasks over time. While resource allocation is an important consideration in enterprise architecture, it is not a specific component of the TOGAF framework.

802. Which of the following best describes the role of a business analyst in the context of enterprise architecture?
a. To design and implement the technical infrastructure of the organization
b. To ensure that business processes and systems are aligned with the organization's strategic goals
c. To manage the budget and financial resources of the enterprise architecture program
d. To develop and maintain the organization's marketing and branding strategy

Answer: b. To ensure that business processes and systems are aligned with the organization's strategic goals. Explanation: Enterprise architecture is a discipline that focuses on aligning an organization's business processes, information systems, and technology infrastructure with its strategic goals and objectives. The role of a business analyst in this context is to act as a bridge between the business and IT domains, ensuring that the organization's processes and systems are designed and implemented in a way that supports its overall strategy. Business analysts contribute to enterprise architecture by: - Analyzing the organization's business model, goals, and requirements - Identifying opportunities for process improvement and optimization - Defining the target state architecture and roadmap for achieving it - Ensuring that individual projects and initiatives are aligned with the enterprise architecture - Facilitating communication and collaboration between business and IT stakeholders - Measuring and reporting on the value and effectiveness of the enterprise architecture Business analysts do not typically have direct responsibility for technical implementation, budgeting, or marketing, although they may collaborate with specialists in these areas. Their primary focus is on understanding the business needs and translating them into architectural requirements that guide the design and development of systems and processes.

803. An organization is considering adopting the Zachman Framework for its enterprise architecture. Which of the following is a key benefit of using the Zachman Framework?
a. It provides a step-by-step methodology for developing and implementing enterprise architecture
b. It offers a comprehensive taxonomy for organizing and classifying architectural artifacts
c. It includes detailed guidelines for selecting and implementing specific technologies and tools
d. It emphasizes the importance of agile and iterative development practices

Answer: b. It offers a comprehensive taxonomy for organizing and classifying architectural artifacts. Explanation: The Zachman Framework is an enterprise architecture framework that provides a structured way of viewing and defining an enterprise from different perspectives. It was developed by John Zachman in the 1980s and has become one of the most widely recognized frameworks in the field of enterprise architecture. One of the key benefits of using the Zachman Framework is that it offers a comprehensive taxonomy for organizing and classifying architectural artifacts. The framework consists of a 6x6 matrix, with six rows representing different perspectives or levels of abstraction (Scope, Business Model, System Model, Technology Model, Detailed Representations, and Functioning Enterprise) and six columns representing different aspects or dimensions of the enterprise (What, How, Where, Who, When, and Why). Each cell in the matrix represents a specific type of architectural artifact, such as a business plan, data model, or network diagram. By organizing artifacts in this way, the Zachman Framework helps to ensure that all relevant aspects of the enterprise are considered and that there is consistency and traceability between different levels of abstraction. However, the Zachman Framework is not a methodology and does not provide specific guidance on how to develop or implement enterprise architecture. It is also neutral with respect to specific technologies, tools, or development practices, such as agile or waterfall.

804. Which of the following is an example of a project that would typically be considered part of an organization's enterprise architecture?
a. Developing a new marketing campaign to promote a product
b. Implementing a company-wide customer relationship management (CRM) system
c. Conducting a financial audit of the organization's accounts
d. Hiring and training new employees in the human resources department

Answer: b. Implementing a company-wide customer relationship management (CRM) system. Explanation: Enterprise architecture is concerned with the design and management of an organization's business processes, information systems, and technology infrastructure. Projects that involve the development, integration, or optimization of these components are typically considered part of an organization's enterprise architecture. Implementing a company-wide customer relationship management (CRM) system is a good example of an enterprise architecture project. CRM systems are designed to manage an organization's interactions with customers, clients, and sales prospects, and they often integrate with other systems such as marketing automation, customer service, and sales force automation.

Implementing a CRM system requires a holistic view of the organization's business processes, data flows, and technology landscape, and it may involve significant changes to the way the organization operates. Other examples of enterprise architecture projects might include: - Developing a master data management strategy - Implementing a service-oriented architecture (SOA) - Migrating applications to the cloud - Consolidating and modernizing legacy systems Marketing campaigns, financial audits, and HR initiatives, while important, are generally not considered part of enterprise architecture because they do not directly involve the design or management of business processes, information systems, or technology infrastructure.

805. A business analyst is working on a project to implement a new enterprise resource planning (ERP) system. Which of the following is the most important factor in ensuring that the project aligns with the organization's enterprise architecture?
a. Involving key stakeholders from across the organization in the project planning and design phases
b. Selecting the ERP vendor with the lowest cost and shortest implementation timeline
c. Customizing the ERP system to match the organization's existing business processes exactly
d. Minimizing communication and collaboration with other projects and initiatives within the organization

Answer: a. Involving key stakeholders from across the organization in the project planning and design phases. Explanation: Enterprise architecture is concerned with ensuring that an organization's business processes, information systems, and technology infrastructure are aligned with its strategic goals and objectives. When implementing a new system or technology, such as an ERP system, it is critical to ensure that the project aligns with the organization's overall enterprise architecture. One of the most important factors in achieving this alignment is involving key stakeholders from across the organization in the project planning and design phases. These stakeholders might include representatives from business units, IT, finance, legal, and other relevant functions. By engaging these stakeholders early and often, the project team can: - Ensure that the project scope and objectives are aligned with the organization's strategic priorities - Identify potential risks, issues, and dependencies that may impact the project or other initiatives - Gather and validate requirements from a broad range of perspectives - Build buy-in and support for the project across the organization - Ensure that the solution is designed to integrate with existing systems and processes Selecting the lowest-cost vendor, customizing the system to match existing processes, and minimizing communication with other projects are not effective strategies for aligning with enterprise architecture. In fact, these approaches may lead to suboptimal outcomes, such as systems that are difficult to maintain, processes that are inefficient or disconnected, and projects that duplicate effort or create conflicts.

806. Which of the following is a common pitfall that organizations may encounter when trying to align projects with their enterprise architecture?
a. Overemphasizing the importance of standardization and consistency across projects
b. Involving too many stakeholders in the project planning and decision-making process
c. Focusing too narrowly on short-term project goals at the expense of long-term strategic alignment
d. Investing too much time and effort in documenting and communicating architectural principles and guidelines

Answer: c. Focusing too narrowly on short-term project goals at the expense of long-term strategic alignment. Explanation: Aligning individual projects with an organization's enterprise architecture is essential for ensuring that the organization's business processes, information systems, and technology infrastructure support its strategic goals and objectives. However, this alignment can be challenging, and organizations may encounter several common pitfalls. One of the most significant pitfalls is focusing too narrowly on short-term project goals at the expense of long-term strategic alignment. This can happen when project teams are under pressure to deliver results quickly and may be tempted to take shortcuts or make decisions that are not fully consistent with the organization's architectural principles and guidelines. For example, a team may choose to implement a solution that meets the immediate needs of their project but is not scalable or interoperable with other systems in the organization. Over time, this can lead to a fragmented and inconsistent technology landscape that is difficult and expensive to maintain. To avoid this pitfall, organizations should: - Ensure that project teams are aware of and understand the organization's enterprise architecture principles and guidelines - Involve enterprise architecture stakeholders in project planning and decision-making - Establish governance processes to review and approve project decisions for alignment with enterprise architecture - Monitor and measure projects for compliance with architectural standards and best practices - Foster a culture that values long-term strategic alignment over short-term tactical gains Overemphasizing standardization, involving too many stakeholders, and investing too much in documentation are not typically major pitfalls in aligning projects with enterprise architecture, although they can be challenges if not managed appropriately. The key is to strike the right balance between consistency and flexibility, collaboration and efficiency, and documentation and action.

807. Which of the following is a key benefit of using the TOGAF Architecture Development Method (ADM) to develop an enterprise architecture?
a. It provides a flexible and adaptable approach that can be customized to the organization's specific needs and goals
b. It emphasizes the importance of agile and iterative development practices over traditional waterfall approaches
c. It includes a comprehensive set of tools and templates for documenting and modeling architectural artifacts
d. It focuses primarily on the technical aspects of enterprise architecture, such as hardware and software components

Answer: a. It provides a flexible and adaptable approach that can be customized to the organization's specific needs and goals. Explanation: The TOGAF Architecture Development Method (ADM) is a step-by-step approach for developing and managing an enterprise architecture. It is one of the core components of the TOGAF framework and is designed to be flexible and adaptable to the specific needs and goals of the organization. One of the key benefits of using the ADM is that it provides a structured yet customizable approach to enterprise architecture development. The ADM consists of eight phases, each of which focuses on a specific aspect of the architecture development process, such as architecture vision, business architecture, information systems architectures, and migration planning. However, the ADM is not prescriptive and allows for iteration and adaptation based on the organization's context and priorities. For example, an organization may choose to focus more heavily on certain phases or activities based on its current challenges and opportunities, or may adapt the terminology and deliverables to align with its existing processes and standards. The ADM also emphasizes the importance of stakeholder engagement and communication throughout the architecture development process, which helps to ensure that the resulting architecture is aligned with the needs and goals of the business. While the ADM does include guidelines and techniques for documenting and modeling architectural artifacts, it is not primarily focused on documentation or technical details. It also does not prescribe a particular development methodology, such as agile or waterfall, although it can be used in conjunction with these approaches. The ADM is a high-level, business-driven approach to enterprise architecture that helps organizations to define and achieve their strategic objectives.

808. A business analyst is working on a project to develop a new mobile application for customers. Which of the following is the most important consideration for ensuring that the project aligns with the organization's enterprise architecture?
a. Choosing the most popular and widely-used mobile development platform and tools
b. Designing the application to have the most advanced and cutting-edge features and functionality
c. Ensuring that the application is developed as quickly and cheaply as possible to meet tight deadlines and budgets
d. Aligning the application with the organization's business and IT strategies, standards, and roadmaps

Answer: d. Aligning the application with the organization's business and IT strategies, standards, and roadmaps. Explanation: When developing a new application or system, it is important to ensure that the project aligns with the organization's overall enterprise architecture. This means considering how the application fits into the broader context of the organization's business processes, information systems, and technology infrastructure. One of the most important considerations for achieving this alignment is to ensure that the application is developed in accordance with the organization's business and IT strategies, standards, and roadmaps. This might include: - Aligning the application's features and functionality with the organization's business goals and customer needs - Ensuring that the application integrates with existing systems and data sources in a way that is consistent with the organization's IT architecture - Following the organization's standards and guidelines for application development, security, performance, and scalability - Considering how the application fits into the organization's long-term technology roadmap and plans for innovation and growth Choosing the most popular development platform, having the most advanced features, or being developed as quickly and cheaply as possible are not the most important considerations for aligning with enterprise architecture. While these factors may be important for the success of the project, they should be balanced against the need for strategic alignment and long-term sustainability. Developing an application that is not aligned with the organization's enterprise architecture can lead to a range of problems, such as integration challenges, security vulnerabilities, and difficulty scaling and maintaining the application over time. By prioritizing alignment with enterprise architecture, organizations can ensure that their applications are developed in a way that supports their overall business objectives and technology strategies.

809. Which of the following is an example of how a business analyst can help to ensure that a project aligns with an organization's enterprise architecture?
a. By identifying opportunities to reduce project costs and timelines by sacrificing quality or scope
b. By ensuring that project team members have the necessary technical skills and certifications
c. By defining clear project roles and responsibilities and holding team members accountable for their work
d. By facilitating communication and collaboration between project stakeholders and enterprise architecture teams

Answer: d. By facilitating communication and collaboration between project stakeholders and enterprise architecture teams. Explanation: Business analysts play a critical role in ensuring that projects align with an organization's enterprise architecture. They act as a bridge between the project team and the broader organization, helping to ensure that the project is developed in a way that supports the organization's overall business and technology strategies. One of the key ways that business analysts can help to ensure this alignment is by facilitating communication and collaboration between project stakeholders and enterprise architecture teams. This might include: - Ensuring that project stakeholders are aware of and understand the organization's enterprise architecture principles, standards, and guidelines - Communicating the project's goals, requirements, and constraints to the enterprise architecture team and seeking their input and feedback - Identifying and managing dependencies and impacts between the project and other initiatives or systems within the organization - Facilitating discussions and decision-making processes to ensure that the project is aligned with the organization's strategic priorities and technology roadmaps - Advocating for the project's needs and requirements while also ensuring that it adheres to the organization's architectural standards and best practices By fostering open and effective communication and collaboration between project teams and enterprise architecture teams, business analysts can help to ensure that projects are developed in a way that is consistent with the organization's overall technology strategy and direction. This can help to reduce risks, improve project outcomes, and deliver value to the organization over the long term. Reducing project costs and timelines by sacrificing quality or scope, ensuring that team members have technical skills and certifications, and defining project roles and responsibilities are all important aspects of project management, but they are not the most critical factors for ensuring alignment with enterprise architecture. The key is to maintain a strategic and holistic perspective that considers the project's fit within the broader organizational context.

810. Which of the following is a common challenge that organizations may face when trying to align projects with their enterprise architecture?
a. Ensuring that all project team members have a deep understanding of the organization's architecture principles and guidelines
b. Managing the complexity and dependencies between projects and other initiatives within the organization
c. Convincing project stakeholders of the importance and value of adhering to architectural standards and best practices
d. Allocating sufficient budget and resources to the enterprise architecture team to support project alignment efforts

Answer: b. Managing the complexity and dependencies between projects and other initiatives within the organization. Explanation: Aligning projects with an organization's enterprise architecture can be a complex and challenging undertaking, particularly in large and diverse organizations with multiple projects and initiatives underway at any given time. One of the most common challenges that organizations face in this regard is managing the complexity and dependencies between projects and other initiatives within the organization. Enterprise architecture is concerned with the overall design and structure of an organization's business processes, information systems, and technology infrastructure. Projects that involve changes or additions to these components can have far-reaching impacts and dependencies that may not be immediately apparent. For example, a project to implement a new customer relationship management (CRM) system may require changes to existing data models, integrations with other systems, and updates to business processes and workflows. These changes may impact other projects or initiatives within the organization, such as a project to develop a new mobile application that relies on customer data from the CRM system. Managing these dependencies and ensuring that projects are aligned and coordinated with each other and with the overall enterprise architecture can be a significant challenge. It requires effective communication, collaboration, and governance processes that involve stakeholders from across the organization. Other challenges, such as ensuring team member understanding of architecture principles, convincing stakeholders of the value of adherence to standards, and allocating sufficient resources to support alignment efforts, can also be significant. However, managing complexity and dependencies is often the most critical and difficult challenge, as it requires a deep understanding of the organization's technology landscape and a ability to think strategically and holistically about the impacts and implications of project decisions.

Conclusion
Congratulations on reaching the end of this CAPM Exam Prep Study Guide! You've embarked on a journey of learning and growth, and you've equipped yourself with the knowledge and skills necessary to tackle the CAPM exam with confidence. Throughout this guide, we've covered everything from the fundamental principles of project management to specific techniques and strategies essential for success.
We've explored the critical aspects of project management, including understanding project stakeholders, mastering the project lifecycle, and delving into the ten knowledge areas. You've learned about essential tools and techniques, such as the Critical Path Method, requirements gathering, and risk management. Along the way, we've provided practice questions with instant feedback to reinforce your learning and boost your retention.
Remember, this journey is about more than just passing an exam. It's about becoming a more effective project manager who can lead teams, manage projects successfully, and contribute positively to your organization. As you move forward, keep these key points in mind:
1. **Stay Focused:** You've done the hard work. Keep revising, practicing, and staying committed to your goal.
2. **Embrace Challenges:** Every challenge is an opportunity to learn and grow. Don't be discouraged by setbacks; use them as stepping stones to success.

3. **Leverage Your Resources:** Use the tools, techniques, and knowledge you've gained from this guide to tackle real-world project management scenarios.
4. **Seek Support:** Reach out to your peers, mentors, and study groups. Sharing knowledge and experiences can provide new insights and keep you motivated.

As you prepare for the CAPM exam, remember that this is just one step in your journey. The skills and knowledge you've acquired will serve you well beyond the exam, helping you to excel in your career and achieve your dreams. Believe in yourself. You've come a long way, and you're capable of great things. Whether you're tackling project challenges, leading teams, or aiming for new heights in your career, know that you have the tools and the determination to succeed.

Best of luck on your CAPM exam! You've got this. Keep pushing forward, stay positive, and remember that every bit of effort you put in now will pay off in your future endeavors. Go out there and make your mark!

Warmest wishes for your success and a bright future ahead!

Made in the USA
Columbia, SC
07 September 2024

SIGMUND AARSETH
Norway Painted in Light and Color

Å få vera med på dette spanande prosjektet er noko eg er verkeleg glad for. Etter fleire andre bokutgjevingar, kjem endeleg ei bok med det som eg vil kalle hovudyrket hans far, friluftsmålar som fester landskap på lerretet.

Det har vore eit utfordrande arbeidsår, der det stundom har dukka opp uventa skjær i sjøen, men med god hjelp frå mange har ting ordna seg.

Eg vil takke Jørgen Dukan for all lærdom og inspirasjon gjennom dei åra eg har vore eleven din, takk til min gode nabo Kent for pc hjelp, spesiell takk til syster Halldis for uvurderleg hjelp, til bror Gudmund for din store arbeidsinnsats.

Takk til mor, det er du som med sikker hand, men stille og varleg samlar alle lause trådar og vev dei saman. Sist, men ikkje minst, takk far.

I am incredibly happy to have had the opportunity to participate on this exciting book. After being involved in a number of other publications, we finally have a book showcasing what I would describe as my father's main occupation – an outdoor painter capturing landscapes on canvas.

It has been a challenging year, with some unexpected hurdles along the way. But with good help from many, all has worked out well.

I would like to thank Jørgen Dukan for all his teaching and inspiration throughout the years that I have been his student; and my good neighbor, Kent, for computer help. A special thank you to my sister Halldis for boundless help, and to my brother Gudmund for his great labor.

Thanks to Mother, who with a steady hand quietly and carefully gathered all the loose threads and wove them together. And last but not least – thanks, Dad.

Marit Aarseth

SIGMUND AARSETH
Norway Painted in Light and Color

WRITTEN BY MARIT AARSETH
DESIGN & REPRODUCTIONS BY GUDMUND AARSETH

Sigmund Aarseth: Norway Painted in Light and Color.
Copyright © 2008 Sigmund Aarseth. Printed in the United States of America. All rights reserved. No part of this book may be reproduced in any form or by any electronic or mechanical means including information storage and retrieval systems without permission in writing from the publisher, except by a reviewer, who may quote brief passages in a review.

Library of Congress Control Number: 2008930887

ISBN: 978-0-9760541-4-6

Written by Marit Aarseth
With additional texts by Sigmund Aarseth
Design and reproductions by Gudmund Aarseth
Translated into English by Kari Bye
Norwegian edited by Halldis Aarseth
English edited by Diane Edwards and Jo Ann B. Winistorfer

Published and marketed by:
Astri My Astri Publishing
Deb Nelson Gourley
602 3rd Ave SW
Waukon, IA 52172 USA
Phone: 563-568-6229
Fax: 563-568-5377
deb@astrimyastri.com
www.astrimyastri.com

Printed by: Sheridan Books, Inc., MI

First printing: 2008
Made in USA

INNHALD ❧ *Contents*

FORORD   6
Forewords by Jørgen Dukan and Douglas A. Eckheart

INTRODUKSJON   9
Introduction by Marit Aarseth

OM OSS   14
About Us

HEIME   15
At Home

PÅ TUR MOT VEST   47
Traveling to the Fjords

VINTER I NORGE   93
Winter in Norway

VÅREN KJEM   131
Spring is Coming

SUMAR   147
Summer

HAUSTFARGAR   183
Autumn Colors

POSTKORT FRÅ UTLANDET   221
Postcards from Abroad

FORORD – FOREWORD

Sigmund Aarseth kan stå med begge føttene på det fagelige grunnfjellet og male vare, skiftende stemninger fra døgnrytme og årstidene, uten å miste den levende spontaniteten. Marit Aarseth har vist en utrolig treffsikkerhet i sine billed-kommentarer, som gjør bildene enda rikere.

Sigmund Aarseth can stand with both feet firmly planted on the professional foundations of art, painting delicate, transient moods from the daily rhythms and changing seasons, without losing the lively spontaneity. Marit Aarseth has shown incredible accuracy in her comments, making the paintings even more rewarding to the viewer.

Jørgen Dukan
Litograf, maler og grafiker
Forfatter av *Fargelære*, Lunde Forlag 2007

Sigmund Aarseth is one of Norway's premier contemporary artists. He embraces the legacy and tradition of his Norwegian forefathers in art, such as Thomas Fearnley, Christian Krogh, Edvard Munch, and especially Fritz Thaulow, one of Norway's first plein air *(outdoor)* painters and poetic colorists and, of course, all the Lillehammer painters.

But then, Sigmund develops his own unique and personal style that transforms everyday and often commonplace objects, places and points in time to brilliant, bold *alla prima (all at once)* brush strokes and a dynamic color palette. His work expresses the heart and soul of the natural world in Norway. Color, shape, texture and light are transformed and modified through his art to portray his Norway, his place, his spirit, and the art spirit of the land and people — Norwegian poetry in color and light.

It was especially rewarding to visit Sigmund and his lovely wife, Ingebjørg, at their home and studio in Valdres, Norway. The most memorable part was to see first hand the many locations in the mountains, fjords, valleys, and vistas where he paints *plein air* in all seasons. These places are his fingerprints in paint. I purchased two of his works and now see his Norge every day in our home.

Mange takk (many thanks), Sigmund, for sharing yourself and your Norge with all of us. You are a gift.

Douglas A. Eckheart
Professor of Art/Artist
Luther College
Decorah, Iowa

Å MÅLE UTE (EN PLEIN AIR) OG IMPRESJONISMEN

Det kan trygt seiast at friluftsmålinga ligg Sigmunds hjarte nær – det å setje ned på lerretet kva du ser der og då. Men med det same, og vel så viktig; freiste å framstille sjølve inntrykket. Det franske ordet l'impression, er uttrykket Monet brukte på det han ville formidle, derav omgrepet «impresjonisme», som vel er den kunstretninga Sigmund reknar seg innanfor.

Historisk sett var det utviklinga av ferdigblanda måling på tuber som sette fart i, og i høg grad gjorde det mogeleg, å ta med seg arbeidsplassen ut. Ein kan berre tenkje seg kor tungvint, tidkrevande, grisete og ikkje minst kostbart det kunne vorte, skulle ein prøvd seg på miksing av pigmentpulver og olje ute i vêr og vind. Kjemisk, industriell pigmentproduksjon hadde også mykje å seie.

Tradisjonelt har pigmenta kunstnarane nyttar vore henta frå ulike naturlege kjelder, frå mineral, plante eller dyreriket. Dei ulike pigmenta har difor naturleg nok variert svært i pris etter tilgjenge, kvalitet, kor kostbare råvarene er og kor mykje arbeid som må leggjast ned før ein har fargepulveret klart. Den eksklusive karminraude fargen, for eksempel, var stort sett reservert for pavekappa, ettersom det skal nokre hundre tusen eksemplar av kaktuslusa cochenille til for å lage eit gram ekte karmosin. Også koboltblått, eit heller sjeldan knallblått mineral som vart levert til heile verda frå gruver i blant anna Modum i Buskerud, var svært kostbart. Den lukrative drifta der fekk imidlertid ein brå slutt sist på attenhundretalet då ein lukkast i å framstille kobolt kjemisk.

Andre pigment var lettare tilgjengelege og såleis mykje billegare. Oker, umbra og sienna er kjende naturlege jordfargar ein lenge har hatt i rimelege og rikelege mengder i sør-Europa, men så veldig lysekte er dei ikkje. Nokre av råmaterialane og framgangsmåtane for å utvinne fargar vitnar om stor fantasi og kløkt. Men det seier og noko om kor viktig fargar har vore i ulike kulturar og til ulike tider.

Så fort veret tillet det, og gradestokken kryp så vidt over null, reiser Sigmund ut med sekken. Årstid og vêr kan nok i stor grad vere med på å bestemme motivvalet, men set gjerne merket sitt like så mykje på det ferdige resultatet. Ei regnskur midt i arbeidet, eller hastverk før neste, kan resultere i fantastisk røffe og spontane ekte uversbilete.

PAINTING OUTDOORS (EN PLEIN AIR) AND IMPRESSIONISM

It is fair to say that outdoor painting is closest to Sigmund's heart: to capture on canvas what you see here and now. But it is equally important for him to present the impression and the emotion of the scene. The French word l'impression explains what he wishes to say in his art, and "impressionism," Sigmund feels, is the category for his painting. Painting a scene alla prima or "all at once" is Sigmund's preferred way of painting outdoors.

Plein air, or outdoor, painting began in the 1850s when paint was first manufactured in tubes, and this made it possible to take the workplace outdoors. One can only imagine the difficulties, and how time-consuming, messy and expensive it would be, if one were to attempt the mixing of pigment powder and oil out in the wind and weather. Chemical and industrial pigment production was also important to that change.

Traditionally, artists have gotten the pigments they need from various natural sources from the mineral, plant, and animal kingdom. The different pigments vary a great deal in cost according to availability, quality, and how costly it is to create the pigment powder.

The exclusive crimson red color was limited to painting the pope's robe, as it took some hundreds of thousands of the tiny cactus lice called cochenille to make 1 gram of genuine crimson. Cobalt blue was also very expensive. It is a rare mineral, found and distributed all over the world from mines in Modum, Norway. This successful industry came to a sudden halt in the late 19th century, when cobalt began to be produced chemically.

Other pigments were more readily available and therefore cheaper. Ocher, umber, and sienna are well-known natural earth colors. For a long time, these have been found in abundance in southern Europe, but they are affected by light and are not color-fast. Some of the raw material and the process of producing colors involved great ingenuity and skill. But it also says something about how important colors have been in various cultures and at different periods in time.

As soon as the weather permits, and the temperature goes above freezing, Sigmund will grab his backpack and head out to paint. When going out painting, planning and having the right equipment are of paramount importance. If you are just outside the door at home, it isn't a problem if you've forgotten a few things and have to return to the studio a couple of times to fetch them. If, on the other hand,

Når ein skal ha med seg målarsaker ut, er rett utstyr og planlegging avgjerande. Om ein er like rundt husveggane er det ikkje så farleg om ein gløymer noko og må springe eit par turar ekstra inn på verkstaden, men er ein langt til fjells med staffeliet klart, ein kilometer frå bilen og eit par mil heimafrå, vil ein helst ikkje oppdage at kvitmålinga ligg att heime!

you are way up in the mountains, with the canvas ready and with a half-hour walk just to get back to the car, you don't want to find out that you've forgotten the white paint at home.

In addition to the rucksack filled with painting equipment, the car is filled up with everything else that may come in handy – anything from luggage straps and rope

I tillegg til sekken med målarutstyr, er bilen fylt med alt ein kan tenkje seg å få bruk for. Alt frå stroppar og reimer til å tjore fast staffeliet ein vindfylt dag, tepper for å skjerme mot sola og paraply mot regn og snø, til ekstra klede eller meir vanleg målarutstyr, som ekstra tuber og lerret. Skal ein måle på Valdresflye ein frisk haustdag, er altså både bilstrikkar og brun teip rekna som uunnverleg målarutstyr.

Det er mange ting å ta omsyn til når ein vil måle ute i friluft, sjølv når veret og årstida kan synest å vera ideell. Å måle inne i studio er nok på mange vis enklare, men på den andre sida, er ein ute kan ein stort sett søle og grise med vatn og måling så mykje ein berre vil, og det er sjeldan plassproblem!

to tie down the easel on a windy day, to extra clothing and umbrellas against rain and snow, in addition to the regular painting equipment such as canvasses and paint. If you go out painting in the mountains on an unsettled autumn day, both rope and parcel tape may prove to be indispensable painting equipment.

Even when the season and the weather may seem optimal, there are many things that have to be taken into consideration when painting out in the open air. Painting indoors, in a studio, is in many ways easier, at least in practical terms. Outside, on the other hand, you never have to worry about spilling water or paint, and there are rarely any space restrictions!

Å MÅLE INNE

Når friluftsmåling ligg hjartet nære, og ein bur i Valdres, Norge, kan ein trygt seia at ein har stilt seg i ein vanskeleg situasjon! Før eller seinare måtte ei anna løysing enn vottar og varmedress tvinge seg fram. Det går alltid å måle ute opp til eit visst punkt, men om det er så kaldt at målinga frys og det knapt er dagslys, står ein maktesl aus.

Tidlegare vart vinteren vart stort sett brukt til ulike interiøroppdrag og ikkje minst rosemåling. I den gamle låven på tunet var tidlegare heile det store atelieret i andre etasje fylt med kister som skulle rosemålast før jul. Men etter at den faste kistemakaren vart eldre og trappa ned, har det vorte mindre av slikt.

For nokre år sidan vart atelieret på låven ombygd frå eit stort ope rom, velegna for måling av store kister og skåp, til to mindre rom pluss lagerplass. Det minste rommet har vorte til eit lite atelier med utstyr for framvising av lysbilete, avtrekk mot målinglukt og løysemiddeldunstar, godt lys og det som elles måtte til.

Det må også seiast at det å stå inne og måle ikkje akkurat er nytt for Sigmund, det har trass alt vorte mange interiør, stilleben og portrett måla innandørs opp gjennom åra. Berre det å måle *landskap* innandørs er forholdsvis nytt, men no strøymer det både bølgjande italienske landskap og frisk vestlandsk sjøsprøyt ut frå det knøttvesle rommet på låven.

Ved å prosjektere lysbilete inn i ein mørk krok i atelieret, kan han måle bileter som det ville vera uråd å måle på staden. Med dagens kamera og lysbiletefilm blir kvaliteten så bra, og formatet kan gjerast så stort, at det nesten kan jamnstillast med å vera på staden, men berre nesten. Kameralinsene kan forvrenge nokså mykje, særleg fører bruken av vidvinkel objektiv til at fjella vert nokså flate, så dei må «reisast opp att» når ein målar, og komposisjonen kan ofte med fordel fortettast. Inntrykket når ein står på staden er alltid meir majestetisk, så ein må overdrive akkurat passe mykje for at verknaden og sluttoppfatninga skal verte rett.

Det gjeld å ikkje berre kopiere det ein ser, men tenkje på korleis hjernen oppfattar heilskapen til slutt. Det er og viktig å bestemme seg for kva ein vil formidle, og plukke ut det ein vil fokusere på i kvart enkelt motiv. Ikkje absolutt alt kan vera i fokus samtidig, så her må det nøye avveging til. Kamera er ei stor hjelp, men ikkje alle slags motiv eignar seg, og det passar best for mindre bilete.

PAINTING INDOORS

When painting directly outdoors is what your artist's heart desires, and you live in Valdres, Norway, it is safe to say that you have probably put yourself into a difficult situation! Sooner or later a solution other than mittens and padded clothing has to emerge. Painting outside is usually possible up to a certain point, but when it gets so cold that the paint freezes and there is hardly any daylight, there is not much you can do.

Earlier, Sigmund's winters were mostly used for commissions of interior decorating and rosemaling. The big studio on the second floor of our old barn was formerly filled with chests to be decorated before Christmas every year. But after the local chest-maker became older and did less woodwork, there's been less of this kind of work.

A few years ago the barn was converted from one big open room, suitable for big chests and cupboards, to two smaller rooms and a storeroom. The smallest room has become a winter studio with equipment for projection of slides, ventilation for paint and solvent smells and fumes, good lighting, and everything else required by a busy artist.

It has to be said that painting indoors as such is nothing new to Sigmund. Over the years there has been a large number of interiors, still lifes and portraits, all produced indoors. It is only landscape painting indoors that is a fairly recent development for Sigmund, but now flowing Italian landscapes, as well as refreshing seascapes of western Norway, emerge from the little studio in the barn.

By projecting photographic slides into a darkened corner of the studio, Sigmund can now create scenes that would have been impossible to paint on the spot. With today's cameras and film, the quality is so good, and the images can be enlarged so much, that it is almost equivalent to being present where the photo was taken, but only almost. The camera lenses can cause some distortion. The use of wide-angle lenses in particular make the mountains long and flat, so they have to be "straightened up again," and the composition can often be compressed and improved upon. The impression when being there is always more majestic, so one must emphasize and exaggerate just enough that the final impression is right. It is not merely a matter of copying what one sees, but of considering how the brain comprehends the total image at the end. It is important to decide what you want to communicate, and to pick out that which you want to focus on in each motif. The camera can be of great help, but not for every type of subject matter; it works best for smaller paintings.

I tillegg til foto, og det må vera lysbilder, så er ofte dei raske skissene med tettskrivne notatar som berre Sigmund sjølv kan forstå, svært viktige. Då noterer han fargenyansar som han ikkje finn att i slides, som varme eller kalde skuggar, svake refleksar i snø og liknande. Særleg om vinteren ute, når det er nesten mørkt, så lagar han desse notata på staden med hjelp av hovudlykt, og så tek han ofte eit polaroid bilete dagen etter i dagslys. Då får han teikninga, og fargane hugsar han att dagen etterpå når han har analysert dei og notert kvelden før. Motiv med faste former, som byar i Syden, er greitt å måle etter slides. Uvêr i fjellet er mykje verre.

In addition to photos in the form of slides, the quick sketches Sigmund does on the spot are a very important part of his painting technique. These are filled with written notes that only he can understand. These describe colors not visible in the slides: warm and cool shadows, pale reflections in the snow, etc. Outdoors in the winter when it is almost dark, he takes notes while wearing a headlight. The next day, he often returns to take a Polaroid photo, which gives him the shapes. He usually remembers the colors, after having taken notes and analyzing them the day before. Motifs with firm shapes, such as buildings in southern Europe, are fairly easy to paint from slides. Rough weather in the mountains is much more difficult.

Fordelane med å arbeide inne er heilt klare. Både lerret og staffeli, vasskopp og palett, og ikkje minst målaren sjølv, sit lunt og godt, verna mot vêr og vind. Forholda kan gjerast stabile og optimale, og det er ikkje langt å gå anten ein har gløymt tuba med kvitmåling, vil ha seg ein matbit, eller må gå endå meir nødvendige ærend. Og ikkje minst held motivet seg uforandra, kor lang tid du enn måtte trenge. Men nett dette er også det Sigmund ser som eit hovudproblem med «studio-målarar» – det er lett å ta seg for god tid. Eg har sett mange som sit med det same biletet dag etter dag, veke etter veke, og det blir berre dårlegare og dårlegare til fleire lag med måling som kjem på.

Nokre nyttar jamvel tidsbruken som eit argument for å selje til høgare pris! Men i kunstlivet finst ikkje timeløn. Det er resultatet som tel. Likevel får eg stadig spørsmål om kor lang tid ein brukar på slike måleri. Stort sett av velmeinande interesserte som gjerne ik-

There are clear advantages to working indoors. The canvas and easel, water-cup and palette, and not least, the painter himself, can stay warm and comfortable while indoors – protected against wind and weather. Conditions can be optimized and stabilized, and you do not have far to go if you have forgotten the tube of white paint, want a bite to eat, or need to make an even more important errand. And, most of all, the motif stays unchanged, no matter how much time you need.

This can also present problems. With "studio painting," Sigmund considers that it can become too easy to spend way too much time. Sometimes painters work on the same painting for days, or even for weeks, and the painting often becomes overworked as more layers of paint are added.

Some artists even base their sales prices on their use of time! There should be no hourly wage in art. It should be the result that creates great art. So often an artist is asked how much time has been spent on a painting – usually by

kje har særskilt tilhøve til eller kunnskap om kunst, og ikkje heilt veit kva dei skal seie, noko som ein kvar av oss kan kome ut for i blant. Men det er vel ingen, særleg ikkje om det gjeld takseringa, som spør etter kva måleri for eksempel Munch brukte lengst tid på!

Det kjem sjølvsagt an på kva slags stilretning ein jobbar innanfor, men mi erfaring er at ein ganske stor del av arbeidet går med til førebuingar og planlegging, legge opp måling på paletten, tenkje, sjå, prioritere kor mykje eller lite å ta med, måle lengder og vinklar med penselen, og så; dei fyrste streka, grunnrisset, komposisjonen, dei viktigaste elementa. Når det er lagt er «resten plankekjøring», brukar Sigmund å seia.

Når sjølve grunnlaget er lagt, er mykje av utfordringa å vite når ein skal slutte. Det er fort gjort å overarbeide eit bilete slik at ein mistar det røffe og spontane uttrykket, og det vert stivt. Og det er sjølvsagt ein risiko for å øydeleggje noko som var bra frå før, fordi ein må bortpå med penselen ein gong til, men dette er eit aspekt Sigmund er særs bevisst på.

Å MÅLE INTERIØR

Det å måle interiør inneber mange av dei fordelane som gjeld ordna og stabile forhold som eg har nemnd når det gjeld å måle inne generelt; men det finst heilt klare ulemper og. Fyrst og fremst er det nok eit spørsmål om plass. Der det gode motivet finst, er det ikkje sagt at det er god plass til staffeli, lerret og palett, for ikkje å nemne kunstnaren sjølv.

Ofte kan det vere fine motiv i tronge gamle stabbur eller naust, men det er ein grunn til at desse oftare har synsvinkel utanfrå og inn gjennom ei dør enn omvendt. Betre vert det ikkje om du skal presse inn ein modell, og kanskje ei blomsterkrukke eller to ein stad.

Eg har sett eit hovudskilje mellom det å måle ute og å måle inne, og ved fyrste augnekast kan det synast som om det er ute-målinga som byr på dei fleste variasjonar og utfordringar, så vel som inspirasjon. Det går nok likevel ganske opp i opp både med fordelar og ulemper.

Marit Aarseth

the well-meaning and interested who do not particularly relate to, or have knowledge of, art, and who do not know quite what to say – something that any one of us can experience sometimes. But there would not be anyone asking which painting by Munch, for example, took the longest time! With the advent of plein air *painting, now the value of style and experience and expertise is much more valued.*

A large part of the work involves preparation. Planning the painting, filling up the palette, thinking, looking, and discerning how much or how little to include takes some time. Then the artist must measure, estimating the lengths and angles using the brush handle. Next come the first sketchy lines – the foundation, the composition – creating the vital elements. Once these are in place, the rest is usually straight-forward, Sigmund says.

When the foundation is there and the painting has taken shape, the main challenge is then knowing when to quit. A painting can quickly become overworked, losing its intended focus and spontaneous expression and becoming stiff. There is also the chance of destroying an element that worked fine before, just because one had to let the brush touch it one more time. This is a situation of which Sigmund is very aware.

PAINTING INTERIORS

Painting interiors entails many of the advantages regarding orderly and stable conditions, just as does indoor painting in general. There are clearly disadvantages to painting interiors as well. First and foremost, there is the issue of space. Where there is a good subject, there may not necessarily be room for an easel, canvas and palette, in addition to the artist himself.

When planning a painting, there can be wonderful settings in crowded old storehouses or boat sheds. However, there is a good reason why these pictures often have a view from the outside – for instance, looking in through a door, rather than the other way around. It certainly does not get easier if one is to add a model to the scene, and perhaps a flower pot or two somewhere.

When considering the principal difference between painting outdoors and painting indoors, it may seem that outdoor painting offers the most variety and challenges, as well as inspiration. However, in general, the advantages and disadvantages are probably very similar.

Marit Aarseth

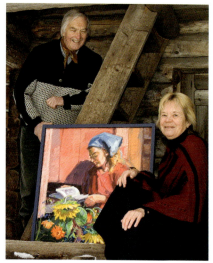

Sigmund Aarseth er fødd i Hjørundfjorden på Sunnmøre i 1936, men busett i Valdres dei siste 45 åra. I seinare år har Sigmund arbeidt mest med biletkunst, men tidlegare varierte det mellom skilt, fanemåling, husteikning, dekorasjonsoppdrag, restaurering og rosemåling. Rosemåling førde han til USA for fyrste gong i 1965. Etter det har han hatt 1-2 turar dit i året og hatt utstillingar, kurs og dekorasjonsoppdrag i 19 statar. Dei fyrste oppdraga kom frå Norges Eksportråd og var knytte til deltaking på messer i store varehus. Deretter vart det kurs for Vesterheim og elles i mange statar frå aust til vest. Det vanka utsmykkingsoppdrag og skaping av spesielle interiør, ikkje minst har det vorte mange resturantar i Chicago. Sigmund har hatt utstillingar mange stader i Norge, og også i Sverige, Island, Tyskland, Austerrike, Sveits, England, Spania og Amerika.

Marit Aarseth studerte norsk på Høgskulen i Volda og på Universitetet i Oslo. Ho bur i Oslo, går på Jørgen Dukans Malerskole og arbeidar med akvarell og akrylmåleri.

Gudmund Aarseth er grafisk designer med utdanning frå Asker Kunstskole og Coventry University. Han bur i Edinburgh.

Sigmund Aarseth *was born in Hjørundfjorden on the west coast of Norway in 1936, but has been living in Valdres for the last 45 years. In recent years he has focused on fine arts, but earlier projects varied from sign and banner painting to interior decoration, restoration, rosemaling and architectural drawing. Rosemaling brought him to the U.S. for the first time in 1965. Ever since, he has been visiting once or twice every year, exhibiting, teaching courses and doing interior decoration commissions in 19 states. The first projects were commissioned by the Norwegian Board of Export, and were related to trade shows in large malls. Later, there were courses run by Vesterheim Norwegian-American Museum in Decorah, Iowa, and in a number of other places from east to west. There has also been a number of interior design and decoration commissions, particularly in Chicago. Sigmund has exhibited all over Norway, as well as in Sweden, Iceland, Germany, Austria, Switzerland, England, Spain and the U.S.*

Marit Aarseth *studied Norwegian literature at Ørsta High School and at the University of Oslo. She is currently living in Oslo, where she attends Jørgen Dukan's School of Painting and works in watercolors and acrylics.*

Gudmund Aarseth *is a graphic designer educated at Asker Art School and Coventry University. He currently lives in Edinburgh, Scotland.*

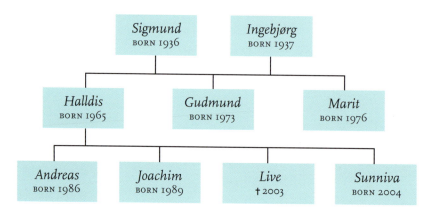

HEIME ~ At Home

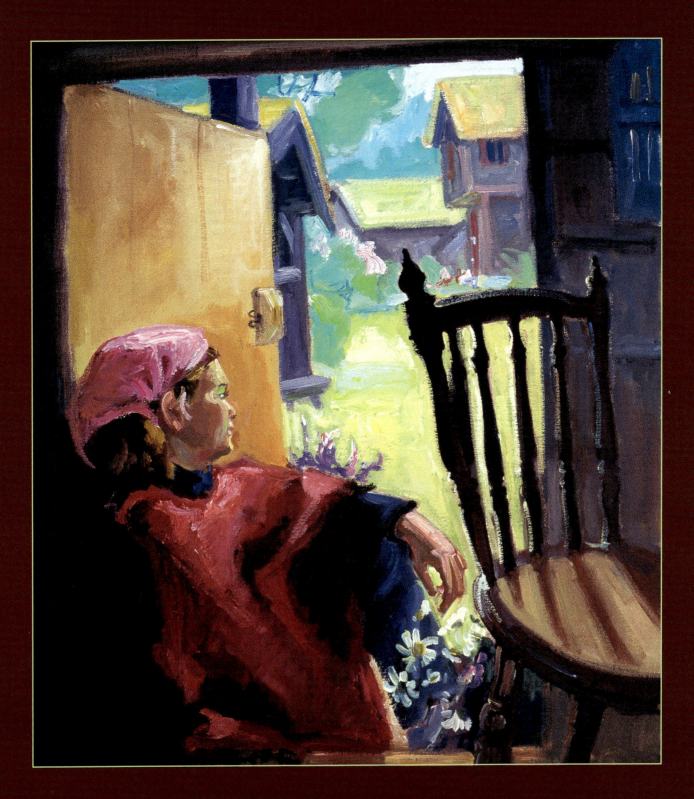

TIL VENSTRE: Marit og Magnus, måla i skarpt lys midt på dagen. Dette ser ein godt på personane, særleg Magnus. Gjennomgangsfargane er frodig raudt, raude refleksar går att i personane og vert forsterka av den grøne komplimentærfargen.

LEFT: *Marit and Magnus*, painted while they are painting the house in strong midday sun. This is clearly visible on the people, particularly on Magnus. The recurring colors are juicy reds; the reds are reflected on the figures and amplified by the green complementary colors.

NORWAY PAINTED IN LIGHT AND COLOR 17

«Modellen her, barnebarnet mitt Joachim, var av det utålmodige og urolege slaget. Kvart fem minutt spurde han kor mange minutt som var att å sitje, så her måtte det målast raskt med direkte strøk, utan å klusse. Merk dei varme refleksane på hals og hovudpartiet frå den gule vesten, det er slike refleksar som skaper sol og lys i eit bilete.»

"The model in this painting, my grandson Joachim, was rather impatient and restless. Every five minutes he was inquiring about how long he had to sit still, so it was necessary to paint quickly, with decisive brush strokes, without nitpicking. Note the warm reflections on the neck and chin from the yellow vest; it is these kinds of reflections that create a sunny and bright mood in a painting."

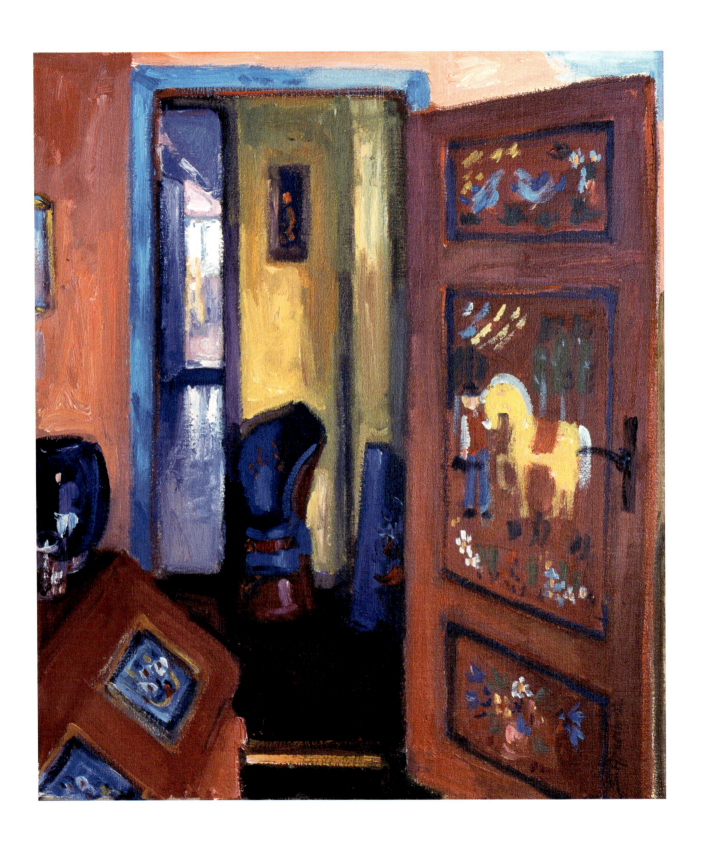

NORWAY PAINTED IN LIGHT AND COLOR 29

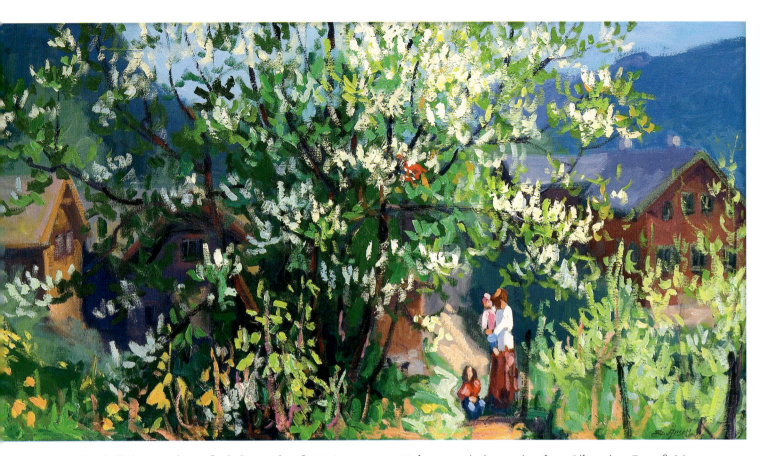

«Eit gladbilete, måla på fredsdagen den 8. Mai, som eg hugsar frå 1945. Flagget er heist og vi skimtar det gjennom lauvet. Desse modellane stod ikkje lenge i ro, men det trongst heller ikkje. Ikkje eit penselstrøk her er overmåla, så då må ein vera svært nøye når ein blandar til fargane.»

"A happy painting, painted on Liberation Day, 8 May, which I remember from 1945. The flag is hoisted, and we can just make it out through the green foliage. Every single brush stroke has been applied without overpainting it, which means you have to be particularly careful when mixing the colors."

FORRIGE SIDE: Dette biletet er måla oppe på vevrommet, eit lyst og luftig rom spesielt tileigna den gamle vevstolen som lenge låg i delar på stabburet. Rommet ligg rett over inngangsdøra, med utsyn til tunet i alle retningar gjennom dei mange småruta vindaugo.

«Vevrommet er, ganske utypisk, måla rosa og blått, og desse fargane står i sterk kontrast til den påskegule genseren Marit har på seg, og den vårgrøne tonen som lyser inn gjennom vindauget. Skjørtet er eigentleg nøytralt naturbeige, men det tek refleksar frå omgjevnadane, og desse er noko overdrivne for å skape kontrast og liv. Fokuset er på Marit sitt uttrykk, ho sit nokså konsentrert og målar sjølv. Resten er røft og lett måla, 'summarisk', som eg gjerne kallar det.»

PREVIOUS PAGE: This painting was painted in the weaving room, a light and airy room especially dedicated to the old weaving loom that for a long time had lain in pieces in the storehouse. The room is right above the main entrance to the house, with a view to the yard in all directions through the many small window panes.

"The weaving room is rather unusually painted in rose and blue. These colors are in strong contrast to the Easter-yellow sweater Marit is wearing, and the spring-green tone illuminating the room through the window. The skirt is actually a neutral color with natural beige, but it reflects the surroundings; this is somewhat exaggerated to create contrast and add life. The focus is on Marit and her expression. She is sitting in full concentration, doing her own painting. The rest of the painting is done in a rough and light manner; 'summarily,' as I would describe it."

Dette interiøret er frå gjesterommet vårt, der ho mor har mange av plantene sine. Rommet er i andre høgda, det har utsikt til urtehagen, og kveldsola kjem inn vindauga. Dette er truleg det mest tradisjonelle rommet i huset. Golv, veggar og tak er umåla, men med si eiga polering etter mange års bruk, og vask med grønsåpe. Dei breie golvborda er umåla, men mange føter har gjort dei blankpolerte gjennom meir enn to hundreår.

Gamle foto i svart-kvitt heng på veggen til høgre for døra. Dei er både frå mor og far sin familie. Her er alvorlege menn i ein fiskarbåt med segl, to jenter med lange fletter på ski, meir alvorlege menn, eit bilete av den vesle bygda der Sigmund voks opp, og bestemor Margit sitt brurebilete. Det var ho eg fekk namnet mitt etter, med litt endring. Ho var og Bestemor med stor B, for meg. Ikkje berre var ho den einaste av besteforeldra mine som levde etter eg var fødd, men ho budde også rett over tunet frå oss. Ho var snill og varm. Ho hadde eit måla treskrin full av knappar, som eg kunne tre på ei snor og laga halsband av, og ho hadde snop i skåpet.

Om rommet var umåla med bilete berre i svartkvitt, så var det slett ikkje fargelaust. To innbygde senger med eit skåp i mellom dominerer den sydlege veggen. Sengene er vakkert utskorne i tradisjonell norsk stil, og måla i preussisk blått, oker, og ein djup raudfarge. Skåpet i mellom er rosemåla i tradisjonell Telemarksstil. Linjene er sterke og kraftige, men også lyriske og leikande. Skåpdøra fører forresten ikkje berre til eit skåp. Bak nokre vinterkåper er det ei anna dør. Det vart slik etter ei ombygging av trappa. Det fører ikkje til noko meir spennande enn eit gammalt loftsrom med forelda koffertar og vesker, men det er likevel interessant å ha eit hemmeleg rom i huset.

This interior is from our guest room, where Mother is tending to some of her many plants. The room is upstairs, with a view of the herb garden, and the evening sun is peaking through the window. This is probably the most traditional room in the house. Floor, walls, and ceiling are unpainted, but with their own patina of age after old-fashioned "green soap" washing. The wooden floorboards are wide and also unvarnished, except where many feet have polished them smooth over more than two centuries.

Old black-and-white photos hang on the wall out of view to the right of the door. They are from both my mother's and father's sides of the family. There are serious men in a small fishing boat with a sail; two girls with long braids, on skis; more serious men; a photo from the little village Sigmund grew up in, and my grandmother Margit's wedding photograph. She is the one I got my name from – just slightly altered. She was a Grandmother with a capital G for me. Not only was she the only one of my grandparents still living when I was born, but she also lived in a house right across from us. She was kind and warm. She had a painted wooden box full of old buttons I could thread on a string to make necklaces, and she had candy in the cupboard.

Despite black-and-white photographs and untreated wood, the room is far from colorless. Two built-in beds with a closet in between dominate the south wall. They are decked with elaborate carvings in the traditional Norwegian style. They are also painted in deep Prussian blue, ocher, and rich red. Sigmund decorated the closet door between the beds in traditional Telemark-style rosemaling. The lines are strong and powerful, but also curvilinear and floral. The closet door not only leads to a closet. Behind some winter coats, there's another door. It leads to nothing more exciting than an attic room with old trunks and bags, plus another small room. It just ended up that way after one of the many extensions to the house was built. Still, it's interesting to have a hidden room in the house.

TIL HØGRE: To bileter frå ute-terrassa vår. På det nederste biletet er Sunniva med, fyrste sumaren på armen til bestemor. Dette er rein sumaridyll med blomane i full flor og utsikt over fjord og blånande åssider, med luftige bjørker i mellomgrunnen.

Det er vel ingen tvil om kva, eller rettare sagt kven, som er hovudmotivet her: Sunniva står tydeleg ut frå den mørke, nærast svarte, tjørebreidde husveggen der ho sit bada i sol. Det er klart at bestemor er eit viktig element også, men ho er vend vekk frå tilskodaren og ser ut over landskapet i staden. I tillegg er ho kledd i kalde fargar, og der skuggane fell går ho meir saman med bakgrunnen.

RIGHT: *Two paintings from our outdoor terrace. The lower painting shows Sunniva during her first summer, sitting on her grandmother's arm. This is the ultimate summer scene – with flowers in full bloom and a view of the fjord and ridges in the distance, with light birch trees filling the space in between.*

There's no doubt what, or rather, who, is the central element here. Sunniva clearly stands out from the dark, almost black, tar-covered wall where she sits, bathed in sunshine. Surely her grandmother is an important element also, but she is turned away from the viewer and looks out into the landscape instead. She is also dressed in cool colors, and where the shadows fall, she becomes more at one with the background.

TIL VENSTRE: Eit eksempel på at motiv kan finnast mest overalt, også der ein minst ventar det. Denne gongen det smale rommet mellom to stabbur på tunet heime. Det er nesten alltid eit spørsmål om lys, generelt legg eg vekt på at arbeidet skal ha ein direkte og spontan karakter. Det betyr slett ikkje at det er lettvint eller lettkjøpt. Det er ein intens konsentrasjon i studiet av lys og fargar. Fargane skal helst klaffe 100 prosent. Det er også heile tida ein balanse, overvegingar av kva ein ser og ikkje ser, kva ein vil fokusere på, kva ein tolkar.

Å finne, eller blande, den rette fargen, krev forsking og utprøving – det tek aldri slutt. Det er tale om livslang læring og eksperimentering. Når det gjeld utføringa, kan av og til dei penselstrøka som ser mest lettvinde ut vere dei mest krevjande og konsentrerte. Det må gjerast med rett pensel, gjerne ein som er sliten på ein spesiell måte. Undermålinga må vere passe turr, eller våt. Og målinga ein legg på må vere slik at rette karakteren kjem fram. Det dreiar seg om stofflegheit, om det er ein ullen mjuk ting, eller ei hard blank flate og så vidare.

LEFT: This painting shows that motifs can be found anywhere, even where one least expects it. This time it is the narrow space between the two storehouses in our yard at home. It is almost always a question of light. In general, Sigmund is concerned that his work should have a direct and spontaneous character.

That does not mean that it is simple and trivial. The work takes an intense focus on light and color perception. Ideally, the colors should be 100 percent right. Then there is a continual question of balance; discerning what one sees and not, what one wants to focus on, what one interprets.

To find or mix the right color requires research and experimentation; it never ends. It is a question of life-long learning, with experiments and experience. When it comes to the actual work, the brush strokes – which may seem to be the easiest – may demand the most precision. They have to be done with the right brush, perhaps one that is worn in a certain way. The undercoat must be just dry enough or wet enough. And the paint application must be such that the right character emerges. It is all about texture – whether it is a soft and fluffy object or a hard, shiny surface, etc.

«Eg trur dette er av dei beste biletene eg har måla av Marit, det er spesielt fargerefleksane på ansiktet som skaper liv i dette biletet.»

"I consider this one of the best paintings I've ever made of Marit. It is especially the color reflections on the face that create life in this painting."

«Valerie kom frå Amerika for å vera med på Jørn Hilme stemnet, og overnatta på stabbursloftet vårt. Her stemmer ho med fela på fanget på spelemannsvis. Tida var knapp, men det var kanskje ein fordel, ofte er det verste som kan skje at ein trøyttar ut eit motiv. Her er det tydeleg at fargane i bakgrunnen er valde for å framheva fargane i motivet, spesielt håret og fela.»

"Valerie came from the U.S. to participate in a local traditional music contest, and stayed overnight in the guest room in the loft of our storehouse. Here, she is tuning her Hardanger fiddle. Time was short when I did this painting, but perhaps that was an advantage; the worst that can happen is often that you 'tire out' the motif by overworking it. It is evident that the background colors were chosen to accentuate the colors of the main subject, especially Valerie's hair and the fiddle."

Stilleben med seinsumar-motiv.

Late summer still life.

TIL HØGRE: Eit bilete måla i sorg, til minne om vesle Live som ikkje fekk veksa opp. Ho døydde like før ho skulle kome til oss alle som venta og gledde oss. Det vart eit sjokk og ei sorg, men me hugsar ho gjerne som veslegjenta me gjerne skulle lært å kjenne.

RIGHT: A still life painted in grief, in memory of little Live, who was not allowed to grow up. She died just as she was about to come into the world and give joy to all who were awaiting her arrival. It was a great shock and misfortune, but we remember her as the little baby girl we would have loved to get to know.

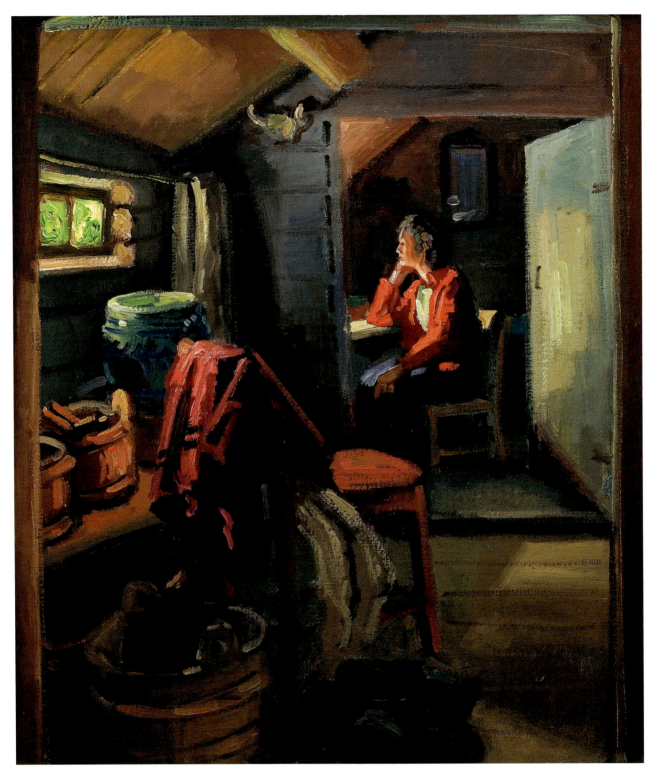

Marit på stabbursloftet. Fargemessig er det alltid ei stor utfordring å måle slike «fargelause» interiør. Ein må vera pinleg nøyaktig med fargenyansane; her har det brune treverket mange ulike fargetonar.

Marit in the loft of the stabbur (storehouse). In terms of color, it is always a significant challenge to paint such "colorless" interiors. You always have to be meticulously precise with the nuances. The brown woodwork in this painting contains a multitude of color hues.

Sunniva i hagen. *Sunniva in the garden.*

Vatn er flyktig og må målast fort og spontant. Det tidlege morgonlyset skifter også fort. Perspektivet, djupna i biletet er for ein stor del skapt med fargar.

Water is transient and has to be painted quickly and spontaneously. The early morning light also vanishes rapidly. The perspective and depth in this painting are to a great extent achieved through the use of color.

I Mjøs-området, mot Skreia berga.

Near Lake Mjøsa, toward the Skreia Hills.

Det ligg ein god del dramatikk i dette biletet, ein sumar er nesten over.

There is so much drama in this painting; another summer is almost over.

PÅ TUR MOT VEST
Traveling to the Fjords

Dei skura berga av raud granitt på Kråkerøy har former som er utfordrande å måle, ikkje minst i grått havlys.

The polished granite rocks at the island of Kråkerøy consist of shapes that are a challenge to depict, especially in flat seaside light.

Ognasanden på Jæren.

Ognasanden in Jæren, on the southwest coast of Norway.

Norskehavet frå ei sintare side. Havet er mørkt, men vert piska kvitt mot steinane. Himmelen er også enno uvêrsmørk og har ein uvanleg fiolett fargetone, men det er også ei lysrand i horisonten som ber bod om betre ver.

The Norwegian Sea, in a more aggressive light. In this painting, the sea is dark, whipped white against the rocks. The skies are still stormy with an unusual purple hue, but there is also some lighter sky in the distance, boding better weather to come.

TIL HØGRE: «Her står eg og målar mot naustrekka på Ulla på Sunnmørskysten. På Sunnmøre fiska dei lenger til havs enn noko annan stad på kysten, like ut til Storegga. Då dei fann denne fiskebanken i 1630, vart dei eldgamle nausta forlenga opp til 18 meter for å kunne gje plass til den spesielle havgåande fiskebåten med særmerkt rigg; Sunnmørsåtringen.

Dei fleste mannfolka også inne frå Hjørundfjorden, der eg kjem frå, var på slikt fiske om vinteren. Då eg voks opp under og etter krigen, utan radio, sat me ofte om kveldane og lydde til gamlekarane når dei fortalde om dette fisket ute på havet.

Naustrekka er eit monument over menn som sleit og ofra seg for å skaffe mat til seg og sine – og mange kom ikkje tilbake. Gardane på kysten har alltid vore for småe til å leve av. Desse folka og fisket la grunnlaget for det mest ekspansive området i landet når det gjeld fiske og industri. Vi har mykje å takke dei for.»

RIGHT: "Here I'm painting the boathouses at Ulla on the western coast. In the Sunnmøre region, they were fishing further out in the ocean than anywhere else along the coast. When they discovered the fishing bank of Storegga in 1630, the ancient boathouses were extended to 18 meters to accommodate the special ocean-going fishing boat with characteristic sail – the 'Sunnmørsåtring.'

Most men from the Hjørundfjord, where I'm from, participated in these fisheries in the winter. When I grew up during and after World War II, without a radio, we often sat at night listening to the old fishermen telling stories about the fishing out in the ocean.

The row of boathouses is a memorial to the men who struggled to feed themselves and their families; many did not return. The farms out at the coast have always been too small to provide livelihood on their own. These people and their fishing laid the foundations for the most prosperous area in Norway in terms of fisheries and industry – we have much to be grateful to them for."

Mølstertunet ved Voss. Dette er eit gamalt tun der husveggane har fått ein heilt eigen patina med åra. Fargene er nokså metta og mørke, i sterk kontrast til den lyse himmelen og landskapet bak. Der kan ein ane to personar som vandrar. Eg synest biletet har mykje som minner om abstrakt kunst, sjølv om ein ikkje er i tvil om kva som er avbilda.

From the Mølster farm near Voss. The exterior walls of these houses have developed a very characteristic patina over the years. The colors are saturated and dark, in stark contrast to the bright sky and the landscape in the background. You can just make out two people walking past in the background. I think this painting has many abstract qualities, although there is no doubt what is portrayed.

Årestogo på Mølstertunet. Her er paletten meir begrensa enn i biletet utanfrå; det er ingen blå himmel eller grønt gras, men eit fantastisk lys inn den opne døra. Veggane er blåsvarte av sot, og det er lyse grønlege skiferheller på golvet mot varmt treverk på dører, skåp og ulikt utstyr.

Sjølv om ein ikkje kan boltre seg i klåre primærfarger, som når ein målar ei blomstereng, er det alt anna enn einsfarga. Eg for min del synes det kan vere vel så spanande og utfordrande å leike seg med lyse og mørke valørar, varme og kalde tonar, som å ha alle regnbogens farger ferdige på tube.

From the årestogo in Mølster – an old house with simply a hatch in the roof above the fireplace rather than a chimney. The color range is more restricted than in the painting from the outside – there is no blue sky or green grass, just a stunning light in through the open door. The walls are blue-black from the soot and smoke, while the slate floor has a green hue against the warm woodwork of the doors and furniture.

Although this is no painting in which to revel in primary colors, as if you were painting a flower field, still this painting is far from monochrome. I feel that it can be just as exciting and challenging to play around with light and dark tones, and warm and cool hues, as opposed to having any color in the rainbow readily available in a tube.

Eit svært spesielt bilete, i eit miljø med få lyskjelder. Den gamle rosemåla ølbollen i tre er forma som ei stor ause, og sikkert brukt slik òg. Den er det viktigaste elementet i motivet, saman med vindauget bak. Det lyser solgult og bladgrønt inn, som ein kontrast til det mørke rommet. Det trekkjer blikket mot seg, men ein vender likevel attende til bollen med dei friske fargane. Ein ser tydeleg at lyset som fell på denne, på den tjukke bibelen og på kanten av langbordet kjem frå eit anna småruta glas.

A very characteristic painting, from an interior with few light sources. The old rose-painted beer bowl is shaped like a large ladle, and probably utilized in this manner, too. This is the most important element in the painting, combined with the window on the back wall. The luminous yellows and leafy greens contrast with the dark room and catch your eye. Your attention nevertheless returns to the bowl with its bright colors and decorations. You can also tell that the light illuminating the bowl, the old Bible and the table, comes from another window, out of view.

Eit interiør frå eit hus med historie i veggane. Atmosfæren er middelaldersk, nesten meir mot vikingtid enn notid. Her er mest ubehandla tre, men det får eit spenn av fargar og valørar der lyset fell ulikt. Det kunne nok vorte mykje beige og brunt, men eit trena auge ser det annleis, får med seg nyansar og forsterkar dei gjerne. Ein har alt frå djupsvart til solgult og blåkvitt, frå flaskegrønt til varmt raudt. Ein kan sjå korleis mest alle hovudlinjer peikar bak til høgre i rommet, mot det sumargrøne lyset som strøymer inn gjennom vindauget.

An interior from a house steeped in history. The atmosphere is more akin to medieval times than the present day. Nearly everything here is made of untreated wood, but a whole range of colors and hues is created by light hitting the different elements at different angles. It could easily have become fairly brown and beige, but a trained eye sees things differently, spots nuances and tends to accentuate them. There's everything from deep blacks to sunny yellows, bottle greens and warm reds. Nearly all the main lines in the painting point toward the bright summer light coming in through the window on the back wall.

Det er noko mektig over den høge himmelen på Jæren. Lyset endrar seg snøgt, så det er ei stor utfordring å måle der. Sol og regn skifter så fort at det ville vera mest uråd utan å ha bilen nær til å røma inn i mellom skurene.

There is something majestic about the tall skies in Jæren. The light is changing rapidly, making it a major challenge to paint there. Sun and rain alternate so quickly that it would be nearly impossible without the car within reach, to escape into between the showers.

Hjørundfjorden på Sunnmøre.   Hjørundfjorden on the west coast.

Hjørundfjorden med Slogen. Dette er eit storarta motiv som ein aldri blir lei, og som alltid syner seg frå nye sider – noko ein tydeleg ser i måleria på dei neste sidene. Dette er utsikta frå hytta vår, nær Sigmund sin barndomsheim på Sunnmøre.

Slogen (den kvasse toppen til venstre i biletet) går nær sagt rett opp frå djupet av Hjørundfjorden, og endar i ein topp med plass til berre ei handfull personar om gongen, 1600 meter over den blåe fjorden. Mot høgre ligg Stålberget, meisla ut i stein. Skiftande lys og vekslande årstider gjer dette fjellet til eit like spanande motiv kvar gong – år etter år.

This is a grand vista of which one never tires, and which always looks different – as can be seen on the following pages. It is the view from our cabin, near Sigmund's birthplace at Sunnmøre.

Slogen, the peak to the left in the painting, rises up from the depth of Hjørundfjorden, ending nearly five thousand feet above sea level in a pointed summit that can only accommodate a handful of people at a time. To the right is Stålberget, which has the distinct appearance of being chiseled out of the rock. Changing light and varying seasons make this mountain an exciting painting subject every time – year after year.

NORWAY PAINTED IN LIGHT AND COLOR 61

Stille dag i Hjørundfjorden.   *A quiet day on the Hjørund Fjord.*

Midtsumarkveld på Bondalseidet. *A midsummer night on Bondalseidet.*

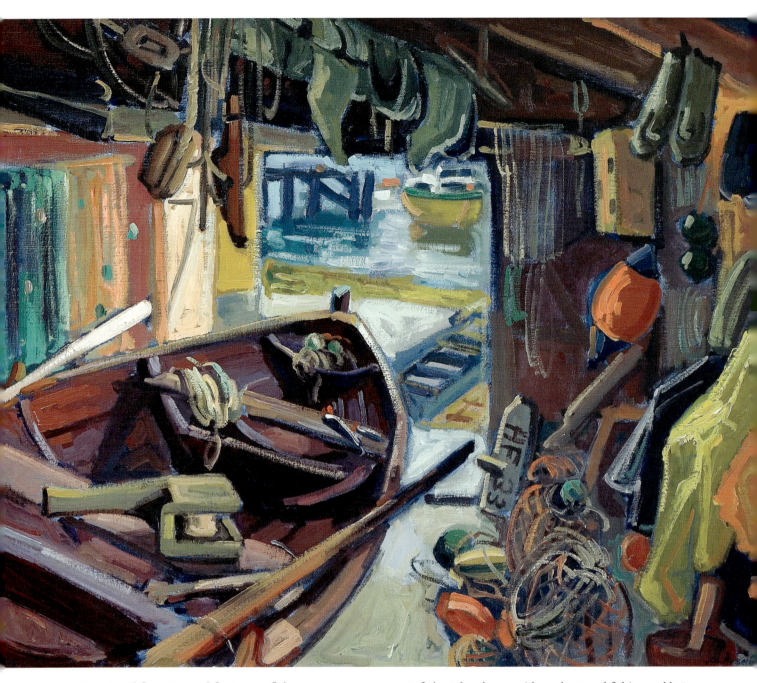

«Naustet til far min med færing og fiskevegn.» "My father's boathouse with rowboat and fishing tackle."

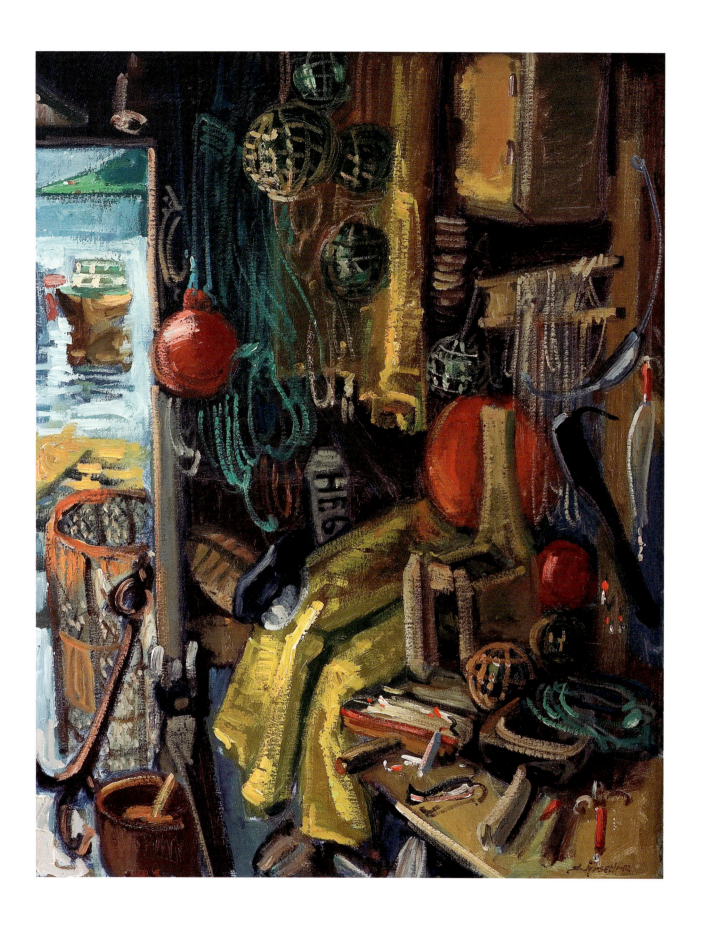

«Ingebjørg på stabburstrappa hjå Kjell-Arne, bror min.»

"Ingebjørg on the steps of the storehouse at my brother, Kjell Arne's, place."

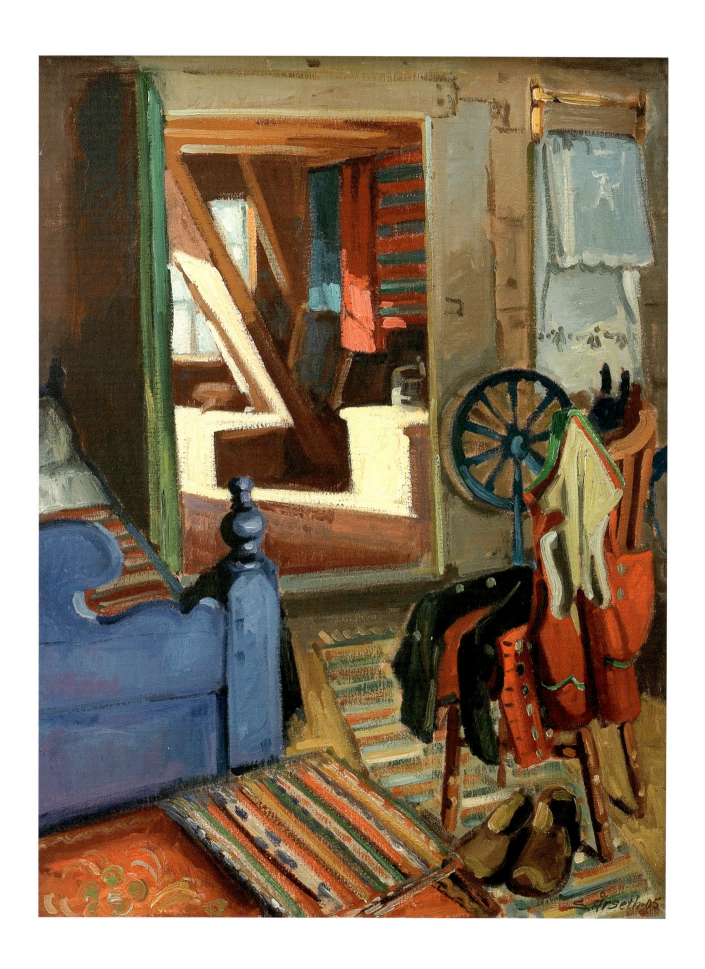

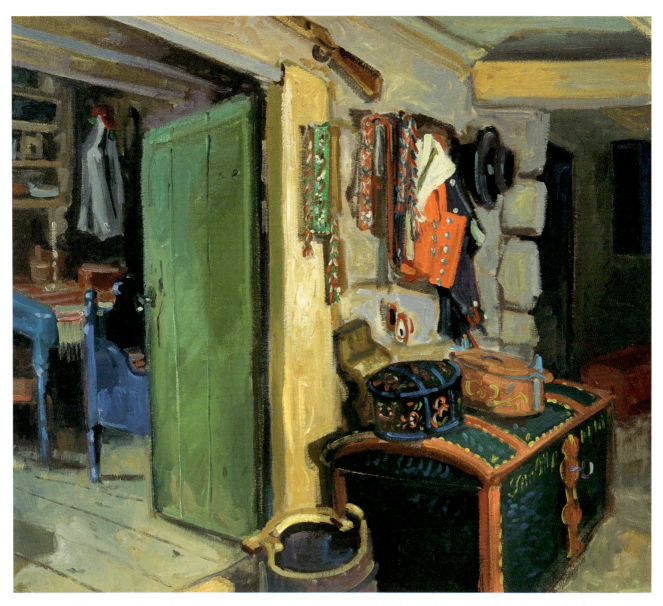

Inne på stabburet med gamle randasenger og arvestykke.   *Inside the stabbur, with old textiles and heirlooms.*

Vassliljer på Videtjørn, Bondalseidet. Det er nesten uråd å måle solsikker etter Van Gogh og vassliljer etter Monet, men det er tydeleg å sjå at dette er ein kjøligare Sunnmørsk sumar enn den franske.

Water lilies in Lake Videtjørn. It is nearly impossible to paint sunflowers convincingly after Van Gogh or water lilies after Monet. But it is quite clear that this is a chillier summer than in France.

«Dette er Rise-sætra, som var sætra for gardane der eg kjem frå. Husa er sette tett saman for å unngå snøras, men likevel har det hendt at det har gått gale. Men om sumaren er denne sætredalen ein idyll, som vert forsterka av dei taggete og mektige fjella som kransar han.

Sætringa på gamalt vis er slutt, men det knyter seg mange fine minne til slike stadar og folk likar enno å kome på sætra. Herfrå kan ein gå turar, fiske i bekkar, elver og vatn, og kose seg ved vedomnen når kvelden fell på og ein kan nyte stilla i fjelldalen, med berre bekken som brusar frå det bratte fjell.»

"This is the Rise summer farm – the summer farm for the farms where I grew up. They are placed close together to avoid avalanches in winter, but there have still been accidents. In summer, this valley is very idyllic, an impression enhanced by the jagged and majestic mountains all around.

Traditional summer farming no longer takes place here, but there are many happy memories attached to such places, and people still enjoy traveling up here in summer. From here you can go hiking or go fishing in streams, rivers and lakes. When night falls, you can sit inside by the fire, enjoying the peace and quiet of the mountain valley, with only the rushing streams breaking the silence."

Både fjella og lyset er dramatisk her vestpå.

The mountains as well as the light are dramatic in the west.

Sjølv på varme sumardagar ligg isen på vatnet i Tverradalen, for her slepp sola lite til.

Even during the warm summer days, ice still remains on the lake in Tverradalen. The mountains are too high to let much sun in.

NORWAY PAINTED IN LIGHT AND COLOR

Eit saftig vestlandsk landskap med våte berg, irrgrøn mose og rislande bekkar. Ei lokal ettermiddagsbyge fèr forbi. Bakom, inne i botnen av Tverradalen, ligg vatnet som er med på dei to forrige sidene.

A lush west-coast landscape with wet cliffs, bright green moss and trickling streams. An afternoon rain shower is just passing by. At the back of the valley is the lake that is depicted on the previous two pages.

Skår i Hjørundfjorden. Dei to einbølte og veglause gardane som ein anar nede ved fjorden til venstre, der dei enno driv med geitehald, ligg på den einaste vesle bota som kan kallast trygg for snøskred, sjølv om den «trygge» sona stoggar ved låveveggen. Her ligg gardane i glitrande sumarsol over fjell, snøbredar og fjord, med kvasse tindar som bakteppe.

The two isolated farms of Skår, where goats still provide a livelihood, are just discernible down by the fjord to the left in this painting. They are located on the only small patch of land that can be described as safe from avalanches in this area, although the "safe zone" ends just meters away from the barn. In this painting the fjord, farms, mountains and glaciers are bathed in summer sun, with jagged peaks as a backdrop.

LOFOTEN

Den taggete fjellryggen i Lofoten i Nord-Norge er no oppdelt i dusinvis med øyar som strekkjer seg utover i Norskehavet. Der er bratte og høge fjell, kraftige vinterstormar og trugande straumar.

Likevel har folk vore busette her i fleire årtusen. Grunnen er at det reine og kalde vatnet gjev gode vilkår for fiske. Små samfunn finn ein mange stadar langs foten av bratte fjell. Her har dei funne vern i små strender og lune viker. Sume stadar, der det er mogleg, dyrkar dei jorda. I fjellsidene er det berre sauer og geiter som kan tilpassa seg det bratte lendet.

På dei ytre øyane er det stort sett fiske som er leveveg for folket. Hit har det kome fiskarar og sjømenn frå heile kysten, ja, frå utlandet også. Små rorbuer har vore til overnatting, og fabrikkar har teke imot fisken og produsert ulike fiskeprodukt. Annan industri har det òg ført med seg. Det er ikkje så mykje fisk her no lenger, og mange har funne annan leveveg. Likevel er fiske ein viktig del av livet her. Den store sesongen er på seinvinteren; det er då Atlanterhavstorsken kjem inn for å gyta.

Før ein fekk frysarar, var det andre måtar å ta vare på fisken. Det mest vanlege var salting og tørking. Resultatet av den prosessen har vore ei stor eksportvare, og er det framleis. Tonnevis av tørrfisk vert seld kvart år. Svært mykje går til Spania og Portugal, ettersom det er den sentrale ingrediensen i hovudretten deira, som er Bacalao. Difor finn ein over heile Lofoten endå dei karakteristiske hjellane til å hengja torsk til tørk i den friske og salte vinden.

TIL VENSTRE: Frå Nusfjord i Lofoten. «Vi kom dit i mars og leigde ei rorbu for eit par dagar, så måtte vi finne ein annan stad, for fiskarane skulle bruka ho sjølve. Her har eg klive opp på ein fjellknaus for å fange dette spesielle mars-sollyset som strauk over fjella og vågen. Men kaldt var det.»

LOFOTEN

The jagged mountain ridge of Lofoten, in the north of Norway, now consists of dozens of islands stretching west, out into the Norwegian Sea. There are steep, rugged mountains, fierce winter storms, and strong, dangerous currents.

In spite of the inhospitable climate, people have lived in this area for thousands of years. The main reason is that the clean, cold water provides for excellent fishing. Small communities were built by the foot of the steep mountains, sheltered among the islands and by the shallow white beaches in the bays. In some places, where possible, crops are grown. On the hillsides, only goats and sheep used to the steep terrain will find their home.

The outer islands are entirely dominated by fishing. Fishermen and sailors once came here from the entire coast, and even from abroad. Small cottages provided a bed for the night, while factories received the fish and preserved it in different ways. Other businesses came with it. The fish stocks are not as plentiful as they used to be, and many have chosen other occupations. Nevertheless, fishing remains an important way of life in this region. The main season is in late winter, when the Atlantic cod come in to the coast to spawn.

Before deep-freezes, there were different ways of preserving the catch. The most common process was salting and drying. The resulting product was, and still is, a big export article. Stockfish is sold by the ton every year, mainly to Spain and Portugal, as it is the main ingredient in their staple dish, the Bacalao. It is also used for Lutefisk – which is well known among Norwegian-Americans. *That is why you will still find the characteristically shaped racks, used for hanging the cod to dry in the fresh, salty breezes, all over Lofoten.*

LEFT: *From Nusfjord in Lofoten. "We arrived in March and rented a fishermen's cabin for a few days, until the fishermen needed it again themselves and we had to find another place. Here I have climbed onto a cliff to capture the unique winter light across the mountains and the bay. I remember it being very, very cold."*

Mars-soloppgang i Lofoten.

Sunrise in March, in Lofoten.

Etter ei stormfull natt er havet enno i opprør.

After a stormy night, the ocean is still rebellious.

Fiskehjellar dominerer framgrunnen, som elles er eit tomt, kvitt felt, i dette biletet. For å formidla inntrykket av rein nysnø, som glitrar i lyse fargar, må komplementære, men svært bleike, fargar målast varsamt ved sida av kvarandre. Denne teknikken minner mykje om pointilisme, men i ei dempa form. I skuggen under stativa er dei blå og mørke sidene av denne paletten det viktigaste, så går dei over i rosa og gult til høgre. Likevel vil du finne litt av alle fargar og nyansar over heile feltet.

Det einaste som syner at menneske held til her, bortsett frå nokre små raude hus langt der bak, er dei mørke stativa, som apar etter fjellformene. Den skrå linja dei lagar ettersom dei blir mindre og mindre og svakare i fargane, fører auget oppover mot høgre. Linja held fram mot snøflekken bortanfor vatnet, til fjellet langt borte som vert eitt med den gylne himmelen.

Sidan dette er det einaste varme feltet, skaper det eit midtpunkt i biletet. Kanskje det er berre oss nordiske soltilbedarar som kjenner det slik, men eg veit i alle fall at eg alltid stoppar opp ved slike små bevis på endringar i årstidene, og at sola endeleg kjem att. Så langt nord er vinteren mest mørk – soloppgang går sakte over til solnedgang, og skaper ein forbløffande lyseffekt og særmerkt stemning.

Kanskje måleriet er meir einsfarga enn vanleg, men eg synest det er interessant med dei ulike blåtonane, og det gjev meg det rette inntrykket av frisk vinterluft. Det er ingen glatt fjellvegg. Du kan sjå korleis fjellsida får ulike fargar ettersom den er vend mot aust eller vest, og er meir eller mindre bratt. Det syner korleis naturen slit ned landskapet og formar det.

In this painting, drying racks for cod form the foreground, which is otherwise a blank, white space. Very pale and subtle colors are put next to each other to create the impression of pristine snow, glittering in pastel complementary colors. The technique is very much like pointillism, but in a subdued way. In the shade under the racks, the emphasis is on the blue and dark side of this palette, going into pinks and yellows on the right side.

The only evidence of any human presence, apart from a few tiny red houses in the distance, is the dark racks that mimic the mountain's shape. The diagonal line created by the racks, as they get smaller and fade a bit into distance, leads the eye up and to the right toward where a distant mountain merges into the golden sky.

As the only really warm-colored area, this creates a focal point in the painting. Maybe it's only we northerners, being very close to sun-worshipers, who feel this way, but I, at least, always end up dwelling at that small evidence of the seasons changing and the sun coming back once again. This far north, the winter is mostly dark – sunrise merges slowly into sunset, resulting in stunning light effects and a special atmosphere.

Perhaps this painting is more monochromatic than usual, but I find the different shades of blue intriguing, and it does give an authentic impression of crisp winter air. You can also see how the hillsides take on different shades as they turn east or west, or become steeper or flatter, showing the wear and tear of nature.

Fuglefjell i Lofoten.

TIL HØGRE: Vikinghus i Borg i Lofoten.

Nesting birds on the cliffs in Lofoten.

RIGHT: *Reconstructed Viking longhouse in Borg, Lofoten.*

Værøy og Røst, Lofoten.

The Værøy and Røst islands in Lofoten.

Frå ytre Sogn, mot Alden (til høgre i biletet), også kjent som «den norske hesten» – eit gamalt seglingsmerke for fiskarar og sjøfolk.

From Sogn, out toward the ocean and the Alden Island, also known as "The Norwegian Horse" – an old landmark for fishermen and seafarers.

Frå Oppstryn i Sognefjorden.

TIL HØGRE: Naustrekke i Sogn.

From Oppstryn in Sognefjorden.

RIGHT: Row of boathouses in Sogn.

VINTER I NORGE ❦ *Winter in Norway*

Her oppe i fjellbygda Valdres har vi vanlegvis god gamaldags kvit vinter. Dei skikkelege midtvinter-stemningane er spesielt spennande å måle – Sigmund har etter kvart vorten meir og meir opptaken av å prøve å fange den spesielle «tussete» stemninga som vi opplever då. Også det raude lyset som ei låg vintersol legg over eit kvitt landskap her i nord, er ei utfordring å få ned på lerretet, dei korte dagane rundt jul. Ein arbeider med ein svært avgrensa palett, og å skilje desse små nyansane i valørar krev intens observasjon og lang erfaring. Litt ut i februar forandrar dagslyset og stemninga seg fort, sol-lyset vert klårare og meir sitrongult att.

Up in the mountain valley of Valdres, we usually experience a good old-fashioned white winter. The mid-winter moods are particular exciting to an artist – Sigmund has become more and more interested in trying to capture the special "fairytale mood" that we experience at that time of year. The red light from a low winter sun that illuminates the snow-covered landscapes up here in the north is a challenge to capture on canvas during the short days around Christmas. You are dealing with a very restricted color spectrum, and separating these small nuances demands intense observation and long experience. When we get to February, the daylight and mood changes markedly; the sunlight is clearer and cooler in character again.

Ein typisk våt og grå novemberdag ved hytta vår på Sæbø (ved Hjørundfjorden.) Eit vått, tungt lag av snø dekkar restene av sumarens fargar. Dei nakne greinene dannar ei komplementær form til dei mørke sikk-sakk linjene i framgrunnen. Dei bryt òg opp den jamne, lys grå-blåe vassflata. Nakne kvistar på lauvtre får eit eige fiolett skjær, i motsetning til mørk grøn granskog. På fjella lengst borte ser ein ingen skilnad der skogen går over i snaufjell. Dei vert så duse og blå at ein knapt ser kvar som er snø og kvar det er bert. Dei teiknar seg likevel ganske skarpe, fordi det lyser litt opp baki der, som av klårare vêr.

Mot høgre, bak i biletet, forsvinn alle konturar i gråværet. Likevel ser ein at desse fjella ligg nærare, ikkje berre på grunn av storleik og form, men òg fordi fargane er varmare og mørkare. Her kan ein ane den snaue, fiolettaktige lauvskogen som strekkjer seg eit stykke oppover på fjellsida som vender mot oss.

Hustadneset til høgre og Lekneset til venstre ligg på kvar si side av fjorden. På båe er der blanda skog og litt dyrka mark rundt nokre hus. Hustadneset ligg på «vår» side av fjorden, berre tvers over vika. Her vert fiolettfarge som var dus og kjølig lengre bak, nokså varm og rik. Ein ser tydeleg snøklattene og overgangen til felt med granskog, og skimtar også nokre hus måla i friske fargar, omgitt av enger som enno er saftig grøne. Desse fargane skil seg ut i mellomgrunnen. Ein finn ikkje att dei same, berre i litt tyngre valør, før heilt i framgrunnen. Likevel, på grunn av stripa med sjø mellom som «skuvar» i kvar sin retning, vert neset heilt tydeleg mykje lenger bak. Det kan kanskje «hoppe» litt mot deg, men det er gjort bevisst. Biletet hadde vorte mykje mindre interessant utan dette som bryt opp i alt det tunge, våte, gråe. Dette feltet trengst òg for å balansere framgrunnen og binde biletet i hop.

Buska nede til venstre, alperose trur eg det er, kallar på merksemd ved at den har den skarpaste grønfargen i heile biletet, side om side med ein komplementær, djup oransje tone. Desse finn vi att i meir dempa variantar på stigen som slyngar seg nedover og elles der kvist og lauv stikk opp av snøen. Ein grå dag, men eit eksempel på at ein kan få mykje ut av slike dagar òg. Eg synest den spesielle, stille stemninga som rår her denne tida, før vinteren set inn for alvor, er svært godt formidla.

A typical wet and gray November day at our cabin in Sæbø (by the Hjørund Fjord). A heavy, wet layer of snow covers the summer's leftovers. The naked branches become a complementary form to the zigzag lines in the foreground. They also break up the even, light gray-blue water surface. Bare branches on a deciduous tree get their own violet hue, in contrast to dark green spruce forest.

On the mountains farthest away, one cannot distinguish what is above and below timberline. It all becomes so diffused in blue that one can hardly see what is snow and what is bare ground. One still imagines a line, though, because it lights up a little somewhere in the back, as if the weather there is clearer.

Toward the right in the back of the painting, all contours disappear in the gray weather. Yet we can see that these mountains are closer, not only by reason of size and form, but also because the colors are warmer and darker. Here one can imagine the bare, violet-toned forest that stretches upward on the mountainside toward us.

The Hustadneset headland to the right and Lekneset to the left are situated on either side of the fjord. Both places have mixed forest and some houses with cultivated fields around them. This is barely visible at Lekneset, as the distance is too great. But Hustadneset is on "our" side of the fjord, just across the bay. A touch of green moves it far up in front of the mountain in the back, and the violet color, which was diffused and cool farther back, is rich and warm. Patches of snow are clearly visible, as well as a few brightly colored houses surrounded by fields that are still bright green. This section of the painting may appear to "jump out" at you a little, but this is consciously done. The painting would have been much less interesting without these elements to break up all the wet, gray and monochrome. This section is also there to balance the foreground and thereby tie the painting together.

The shrub down on the left-hand side – I believe it is a Rhododendron – attracts attention, as it is the brightest green in the painting, next to a complementary, deep orange hue. The orange is repeated in more subdued hues on the path that winds its way downward, as well as in the leaves and shrubs that poke out of the snow.

This was painted on a gray day, but is a good example of how you can get a lot out of painting on days like these, too. I find that the distinctive, calm mood that prevails at this time of year, just before winter fully takes hold, has been particularly well captured.

På ein kjølig novemberdag gjev den no låge sola himmel og snø ein varm glød.

On a chilly November day, the low sun lends the sky and the snow a warm glow.

Det går mot vinter på Sæbø i Hjørundfjorden.   *Winter is approaching in Sæbø, by the Hjørund Fjord.*

Vinterstemning frå Norangdalen, porten til Hjørundfjorden. Og for ein port; dalen smyg seg trong mellom kvasse tindar, opp til 16-1700 meter høge. Ofte ser det ut som at vegen vert stengd, men så opnar det seg litt att og når ein er komen gjennom, er ein alltid overvelda av skiftande og dramatiske inntrykk.

 Så opnar det seg opp og blide bygder og ein fin fjord ligg der framføre ein, Hjørundfjorden, av mange kalla den vakraste fjorden i Norge. Ikkje å undrast at fyrst engelskmenn, men etter kvart også fjellklatrarar frå andre land, fann vegen hit. Og stadig nye finn vegen til denne perla midt i Sunnmørsalpane.

Winter mood from Norangdalen, the gateway to Hjørundfjorden (Hjørund Fjord). And it is quite some gateway – the valley winds itself along among peaks up to five thousand feet tall. Often it appears that the road will simply end, but then the valley opens up again. As you travel through, you are always overwhelmed by changing and dramatic impressions.

 Later the landscape opens up onto pleasant seaside communities along the Hjørund Fjord, considered by many to be the most beautiful fjord in Norway. English mountaineers were the first to come here; later, other nationalities followed. Increasing numbers are finding their way to this pearl among the "alps" on the Norwegian coast.

Hestar i Valdres-landskap.

Horses in a Valdres landscape.

«Lomen stavkyrkje i Vestre Slidre, ei av dei fem stavkyrkjene vi har i Valdres. Det er eineståande med så mange stavkyrkjer samla i eit så lite område.

Ei stavkyrkje kan i seg sjølv vera eit så iaugefallande (og populært) motiv at det lett kan verta banalt. Her har eg prøvd å formidle ei stemning rundt hovudmotivet, av det tidlause og augneblinken, som her er like viktig som motivet.»

"Lomen Stave Church is among the five stave churches in the Valdres region. It is unique to find so many of these rare churches remaining in such a small area.

A stave church is so eye-catching and popular in itself that a painting of it can easily become banal. Here, I have tried to capture an atmosphere around the building that is timeless, yet of the moment. This atmosphere is just as important as the main subject in this painting."

NORWAY PAINTED IN LIGHT AND COLOR 105

«Den lange rekkja med hestar i eit historisk vinterlandskap var eit uimotståeleg motiv», seier Sigmund om dette biletet med Lomen stavkyrkje i bakgrunnen. Å måle dyr er vanskeleg på mange måtar. Det innlysande ligg i at modellane er uvanleg eigenrådige, og ein kan neppe håpe på at dei står stille særleg lenge. No er Sigmund ein særs rask målar, men ein heil flokk hestar i kaldt vêr må ha vore ei utfordring.

Eg mistenker at polaroidkameraet har vore til hjelp her for å fange lyset som forsvinn så raskt om vinteren, og for å «fryse» rørslene til dyra, men samstundes unngå det same med måling, penslar, fingrar og føter. Eit polaroidfoto gjev ikkje att fargar på ein god måte, særskilt i kaldt vêr og under dårlege lysforhold. Likevel, formene er der, så midtvinters kan det vera eit særs godt hjelpemiddel. No har det seg også slik at vår gode ven og målarkollega, Gro, bur i eit gamalt hus rett ved kyrkja, der har det nok vore råd å koma inn og varme seg framføre peisen. Huset kan skimtast mellom snøtunge tre, til høgre for kyrkja.

På denne årstida er alt vanlegvis dekt av snø og rim. Dagslyset er sparsamt, og dette gjer fargeskalaen særs avgrensa – det går frå eit nærast svart-kvitt landskap på dagen, og så meir og meir mot blått til heile landskapet nærast lyser i mørkt, tindrande ultramarin. Det er kanskje sjølvmotseiande å prate om lys og mørke, kulde og glød i same slengen, men eg trur dei som har vore ute ein vinterkveld veit kva eg meiner. Det har med refleksar og snøkrystallar å gjera, sikkert er det at den intense blåfargen ein vinterkveld, kan ingen fargefabrikk i verda kopiere!

At fargeskalaen er avgrensa, gjer det på ingen måte enklare. Ein må vera veldig vâr på dei små nyansane og valørane, noko som kjem av års trening i å sjå ørsmå forskjellar i fargetonar. Det er og avgjerande med kunnskap om fargeperspektiv for å laga djupne der det er lite hjelp å hente frå naturen sjølv. Alt vert nokså utviska i snø og mørke, så ein må bruka dei nyansane og linjene som finst for det dei er verde. Det kan vera fjellformer, tre, bygningar eller som her, alle tre, men også med klar fokus på hestane som hovudmotiv. Sjølv om det er snakk om mjuke, organiske former, har hestane ei eiga stramheit i haldninga, og ikkje minst; kontrasten til alt det kvite gjer dei til levande, men markant utmeisla skulpturar. Her er både storleiken og valøren på hestane avgjerande for å skape djupn i biletet, dei vert mindre, sjølvsagt, men også dusare på farge der dei forsvinn oppover og bakover på jordet.

"The long row of horses in a historic winter landscape was an irresistible subject," says Sigmund about this painting with Lomen Stave Church in the background. *To paint animals is difficult in many ways. The problem is that the models are unusually strong-willed, and one can hardly hope that they will stand still very long. Sigmund is a very fast painter, but a whole herd of horses in cold weather must have been a challenge.*

I suspect the Polaroid camera has been a great help here, in order to catch the light, which disappears so quickly in the winter, and to "freeze" the motion of the animals, and to avoid the same happening to paint, brushes, fingers and feet! A Polaroid photo does not usually capture colors very accurately, particularly in dim lighting. Yet, it shows the shapes, so in the middle of winter it can be a great help. Our good friend and painting colleague, Gro, happens to live in an old house right by the church, so no doubt it was possible to come into the warmth by the fireplace there afterward. We can glimpse the house to the right of the church.

During winter everything is usually covered by snow. Daylight is scarce, which particularly restricts the color scale. The landscape ranges from nearly monochrome during the day, moving increasingly toward the blue range of the spectrum, until the whole landscape virtually glows in a dark ultramarine hue. It may be contradictory to speak of light and dark, coldness and glow, all at the same time, but I think anyone who has been outdoors on a snowy winter night will know what I am trying to say. It has something to do with the reflections from the snow crystals. One thing is certain; no paint factory in the world can replicate the intense blue hues of a winter evening!

Painting with a limited color palette does not make the work easier. It requires a keen awareness of nuances and values – something that comes from years of experience analyzing minute differences in color and values. Knowledge of color perspective and temperature to create depth is also vital when nature is of little assistance. When everything fades into snow and darkness, one has to take full advantage of the nuances and lines that are there. Some firm and solid shapes have to be present – this can be the shapes of mountains, trees, buildings, or, in this case, all of those – but with a clear focus on the horses as a main subject.

Despite their soft, organic shapes, the horses have a certain firmness in their posture. The contrast to the white surroundings makes them come alive as distinct, chiseled forms. Both the size and the hues of the horses are vital to create depth in the painting. They become smaller, of course, but also paler, as they vanish into the distance of the field.

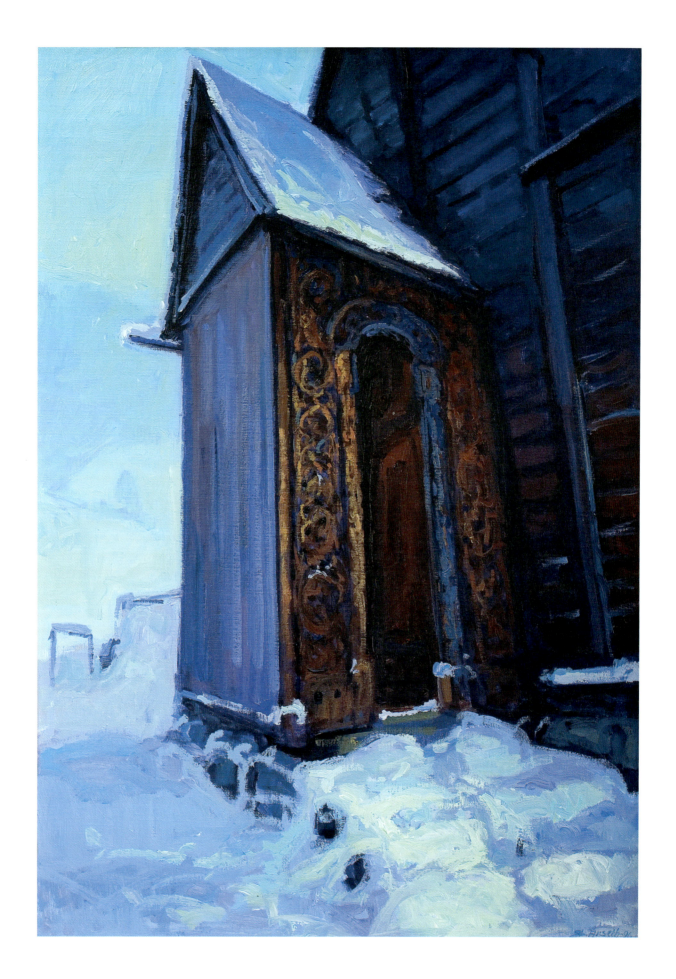

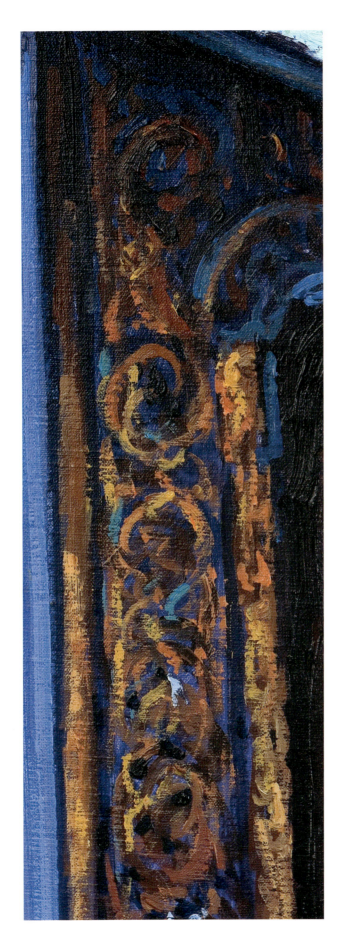

Portalen til Lomen Stavkyrkje, rikt dekorert med utskorne ornament i dragestil. Det er ikkje tilfeldig at dette motivet vart måla om vinteren med snø som eit nøytralt element som framhevar form og fargar. Det svake midtvinterlyset får fram ein glød i den solbrende overflata slik at den lyser mot deg. Dette i kontrast til det kalde lyset som fell på vestveggen av våpenhuset og den tunge gavlveggen på sjølve kyrkja. Bak anar ein eit snødekt landskap som ligg der i kjølig stille ro.

Desse middelalder treskjeringane ber bod frå ei fjern fortid med tru og tenkjemåtar vi knapt kan tenkja oss i dag. Vind og vêr har tært og slite dei ned og denne patinaen forsterkar preget av det mystiske. På detaljutsnittet ser ein at Sigmund har prøvd å få fram dette ved å måla i ein velkjend målemåte frå impresjonismen – som vår ven Jørgen Dukan beskriv det: «Her har du måla ornament utan å måle dei.»

The entrance to Lomen Stave Church, elaborately decorated with carved, early medieval "dragon-style" ornaments. It is no coincidence that this subject was painted in the middle of winter, with snow as a neutral element to accentuate forms and colors. The muted mid-winter light brings out a glow in the old sunburnt surfaces. This contrasts with the cold light falling on the west wall of the entrance and the heavy wall of the church itself. In the background we sense a snow-covered landscape frozen in calm.

These medieval woodcarvings reflect a distant past of beliefs and world-views that we can barely imagine nowadays. The weathered appearance emphasizes the mystical mood. The detail shows that Sigmund has tried to express this through a technique well known by the impressionists. Our friend Jørgen Dukan put it this way: "In this painting, you've painted ornaments without actually painting them."

NESTE SIDE: Den gamle og tradisjonsrike Ringestadgarden i Lomen, Vestre Slidre i låg vintersol. Som ein ser er ikkje to slike vinterdagar alltid like heller.

NEXT PAGE: *The old Ringestad farm in Lomen, Vestre Slidre, is steeped in history. These two paintings clearly express that two winter days can also be very different.*

NORWAY PAINTED IN LIGHT AND COLOR 111

Dette er eit typisk desemberbilete. Ved denne stigen i skogen går Sigmund mest kvar dag. Sola er låg, som den er på den tida. Sjølv om den ikkje varmar stort då, vert fargeeffektane heilt spesielle. Dette er eit ypperleg eksempel på at snø ikkje treng å vere kvit. Her finn ein alle nyansar av blått, og nokre rosa og gylne òg, alle haldne i ein lys valør.

Skogen er nærast som ein mørk masse. Den vert broten opp av lyse og mørke trestammer. Lyse og varme på den sida som vender mot sola, i eit elles kaldt bilete. Grantoppane mot den lyse himmelen bak er med på å syne kva slags skog det er, men opninga mot himmelen her er vel så viktig. Den trengst for å balansere den lyse snøen framme, og gjer at ikkje motivet vert dystert.

Lyset kjem nærast flatt etter bakken i staden for ovanfrå. Det ser ein tydeleg på korleis snøhaugane vert bada i rosa vintersol på sidene som vender mot høgre, medan dei på venstre sida er isblå. Dette byr på mange spanande lys-skugge spel, men gjer òg at ein har særs dårleg tid. Her må det arbeidast raskt og kontant, men det gjeld for så mange av motiva Sigmund målar. Likevel vert det nok aldri heilt rutine. Å fange akkurat augneblinken før sola reiser, vil alltid vere ei utfordring.

Merk dei lyse, blåe greinene som kjem stikkande inn frå sidene her og der. Dei gjer kanskje ikkje så mykje av seg ved fyrste augekast, men er særs viktige for komposisjonen. Dei er med å skape djupn i biletet, ved at dei bryt med dei mørke granene, og heller tek opp att himmelfargen som lyser mot deg. Viktigast er kanskje at dei bryt med alle dei loddrette linjene og skaper liv og dynamikk.

Dette er eit motiv eg òg har eit nært forhold til, sidan eg har vakse opp med å gå mykje i skogen. Kanskje er det difor eg synes det trass alt er eit varmt bilete, til vinterbilete å vere i alle fall.

This is a typical December painting, by the path in the woods where Sigmund walks almost every day. The sun is low, as it is at that time of the year. Even if there is not much warmth from the sun at that time, the color effects are quite unique. This painting clearly shows that snow does not have to be white; there are many nuances of blue, as well as some pink and golden hues.

The forest is more or less a dark mass. It is broken up by light and dark tree trunks, which are light and warm on the sides turned toward the sun in an otherwise cold painting. The tops of the spruce trees against the sky behind them reveal what kind of forest it is; but, more importantly, this provides an opening to the sky. This is required in order to balance the light-colored snow in the foreground. This effect also prevents the painting from becoming somber.

The light comes in very low to the ground instead of from above. We can see this clearly because the piles of snow are bathed in rose-colored winter sun on the right side, while those on the left are ice-blue. This provides much interesting light-and-shadow play. But since there is not much time while painting, you need to be quick and decisive. That goes for many of the subjects Sigmund paints. Yet, it never seems to become routine. To catch the exact moment before the sun sets will always be a challenge.

Notice the light blue branches coming in from the sides here and there. They may not do much at first glance, but they are very important to the composition. They help create depth in the painting by breaking up the darkness of the spruce trees and by repeating the color of the sky, bringing its light toward you. Most importantly, perhaps, the branches add life and a dynamic to all the vertical lines.

This is a scene I feel close to, as I grew up with many walks in the woods. Perhaps that is why I experience this as a warm painting after all, even though it is a winter scene.

Frå Skeie-tunet, Vang i Valdres.

From the Skeie farm, Vang in Valdres.

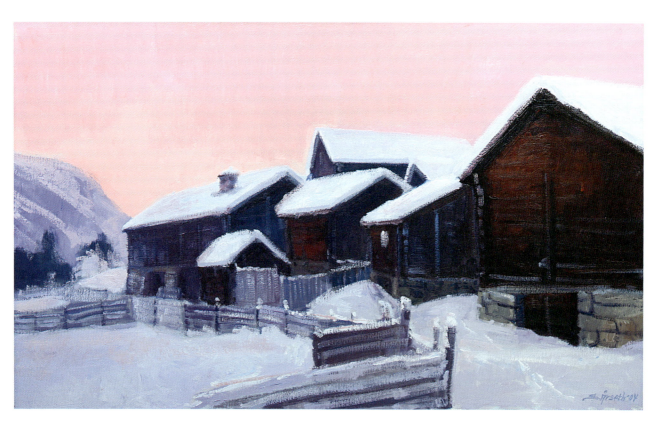

Vinterstemning frå ein gamal gard på Sogn Folkemuseum.   *Winter mood by an old farm at Sogn Folk Museum.*

Etter snøfall, frå Lomen i Vestre Slidre med Hugakollen i bakgrunnen.

TIL VENSTRE: Midtvinterkveld ved porten til Lomen stavkyrkje.

After snowfall, from Lomen in Vestre Slidre with Hugakollen in the background.

LEFT: *Evening in midwinter by the gate leading to Lomen Stave Church.*

Også nede i bygda set vinteren inn, sauene vert tekne heim, sola vert låg og dagane kortnar. Så stundar det til julehelg med fugleband på låvebrua etter gamal skikk.

Down in the valley, winter is also settling in. The sheep are taken indoors, the sun is low, and the days are getting shorter. Soon it is Christmas, with sheaves of grains for the birds above the barn doors – a widespread tradition in Norway.

NORWAY PAINTED IN LIGHT AND COLOR 121

Når eg skriv dette er det sein desember, berre dagar før sola snur. Det er på denne tida dette biletet er måla. Det er berre nokre timar med lys midt på dagen, viss himmelen er klår. Elles er det meir eller mindre mørkt heile tida. Men her i sør, det vil seie sør for polarsirkelen, kan desse klåre dagane by på litt sol, og eit heilt unikt lys.

Berre denne tida finn ein den underlege kryssinga mellom soloppgang og nedgang, der ein ikkje heilt veit kvar den eine sluttar og den andre byrjar. Dei blåe tonane av snø og skumring slepp ikkje taket. Solstrålene kjem frå så låg vinkel at dei liksom ikkje når bakken heilt. Men dei rima trea og snødekte hustaka får i kontrast eit nærast overjordisk gull-skjær. Dei tjørebreidde timberveggane har vortne gylne av sola si sakte bearbeiding, og no kjem dei ekstra fram i det spesielle lyset, og med berre den reine snøen som kontrast. Glitringa i snøkrystallene når sola treff, står i sterk kontrast mot dei dunkle områda rundt om.

Det er nok eit av dei «reinaste» lys-skugge bileta Sigmund har måla. Komposisjonen og dei rette linjene og vinklane i tre og hus gjev form og stramheit, mot den mjuke snøen og udefinerte forma på dei nakne, rima greinene. Dei er måla mest berre som lyse fargeflekkar, slik dei rett nok framstår i skarpt vinterlys. Ettersom motivet, heime på tunet, er så velkjent, trur eg nok det var dette solstreifet i ei årstid elles fylt med kulde ute og peiskos inne, som inspirerte dette måleriet.

While writing this, it is late December, when the sun is at its lowest around the winter solstice. This painting was painted on such a day. There are just a few hours of daylight – that is, if the day is clear; otherwise, it is more or less dark all the time. But here in the south – that is, south of the Arctic Circle, these clear December days may offer a little sunshine, and quite unique light.

Only at this particular time of year do we have the strange cross between sunrise and sunset, where it is hard to tell where one ends and the other begins. The blue tones of the snow and dusk will not let go. The rays of the sun are coming in at such a low angle that they don't quite reach the ground. In contrast, the frosted trees and snow-covered roofs receive an almost heavenly atmosphere of gold.

The sun's consistent touch has turned the tar-covered log walls golden. The special light at this time of year and the contrasting clean snow make this particularly apparent. Sparkling snow crystals reflect the sun and provide a strong contrast to the dark surroundings.

This may be one of the purest light-shadow paintings Sigmund has painted. The composition with the straight lines and the angles of trees and buildings give shape and solidity against the soft snow and undefined forms of the bare, frosted branches. They are painted merely as light spots of color, as they may appear in bright winter sunlight. Although Sigmund has often painted our home, I think it was this gleam of sunlight in an otherwise chilly outdoors that inspired this painting.

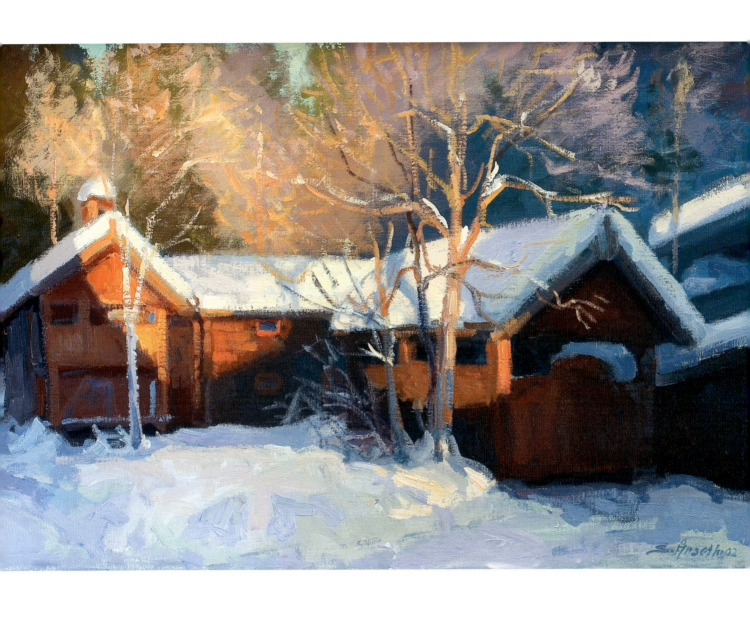

Julenatta senkar seg på tunet heime.

Christmas evening settles down over our home.

NORWAY PAINTED IN LIGHT AND COLOR 125

Utan solstreifet hadde dette biletet vorte heilt i blåtonar. Endå sola er låg og varmar lite, får ho fram dei varme, opp mot oransje, tonane i grantrea. Merk korleis snøen har ei mengde fargar og valørar, inntrykket vert likevel reint og kvitt, nett som i verkelegheita.

Without the flash of sunlight, this painting would have consisted entirely of blue hues. Although the sun is low and does not warm much, it accentuates the warm, orange hues in the spruce trees. Note how the snow consists of a multitude of colors and hues, but the overall impression is nevertheless pure white, just as in real life.

Blomster inne, men det er enno vinter ute.

Flowers at home, but it is still winter outside.

NORWAY PAINTED IN LIGHT AND COLOR 129

Her har nok ein elg eller to vandra og hjelpt målaren med stig.

A moose or two seem to have helped the artist create a path in this painting.

VÅREN KJEM Spring is Coming

Den tidlege våren i Valdres, når det enno er att litt snø som skaper former og kontrastar i landskapet, er ei spesielt interessant periode. Då kan ein finne motiv der ein minst ventar det. Så kjem det fyrste sløret av fiolett i bjørkene og isen på elvar og vatn tek til å gå opp. Det er eit privilegium å få vera ute og fylgje med på alt som foregår i naturen og skiftingane frå dag til dag, isane som går og fuglane som kjem. Når all snøen er borte og det tek til å varmast opp nede i låglandet, sjølv om det enno ligg mykje snø i Jotunheim-fjella, får vi gjerne ei grå tid og alt stagnerer. Dette er på grunn av den kalde fjellvinden som alltid kjem i ei periode då. I fjordane på Vestlandet derimot, på andre sida av fjella eit par køyretimar unna, er våren då på det aller frodigaste. Det lyse og fargesterke synet som møter ein der er like overveldande kvart år. Fossane kastar seg kvite nedover fjellsidene, og i dalane står frukttrea i blomst. I det spesielle vestlandske lyset vert grønfargane så intense at ein finn dei ikkje på paletten og det må takast i bruk alle kunster og knep for å få skildra ein avglans av det ein opplever.

Early spring in Valdres, when there is still some snow left to create patterns and contrasts in the landscape, is a particularly interesting time of year. You can find motifs where you least expect them. Soon the first hint of purple appears in the birch trees, and the ice on rivers and lakes begins to break apart. It is a privilege to be outdoors observing all the changes in nature during this time. While all the snow disappears and the temperature starts to improve down in the lowland, there's still plenty of snow left up in the Jotunheimen Mountains. This is often a gray period down in the valley, with cold winds blowing down from the mountains. Around the fjords on the west coast, on the other hand, just a couple of hours' drive away, spring reaches its lush peak at this moment. The bright and colorful vistas that await you when you arrive are equally breathtaking every year. The waterfalls cascade white down the mountainsides, and down in the valleys the fruit trees are in bloom. In the characteristic west coast light, the greens are so intense that no paints can match them, so as a painter, you have to use all kinds of tricks to convey the essence of what you experience.

Vinteren slepper taket og det går sakte mot enno ein vår.

Winter is loosening its grip, and another spring is slowly approaching.

Isløysing i elvane er flott og dramatisk å måle. Det er ikkje sikkert ein finn att same motivet berre timar seinare. Isen bryt opp og dannar skarpe interessante former og kontrastar. Her må ein hugse å sjå seg føre når ein går, om ein ikkje vil ha seg ein iskald dukkert.

The ice breaking up at the river is a dramatic motif. You can never be certain that things will remain unchanged, even if you return only hours later. As the ice breaks apart, it creates sharp and interesting shapes and contrasts. At times like this, you must also watch your step if you want to avoid an ice cold dip.

Frå garden Kvam i Vang, Valdres. Til venstre låven med den gamle høyvogna og over frå det blåe kammerset der vogga heng over senga etter gamal Valdresskikk.

On the Kvam farm in Vang, Valdres. To the left there's the barn with the old hay wagon visible through the doors. Above is the blue room where the child's cot is hanging over the bed, as was the tradition in Valdres.

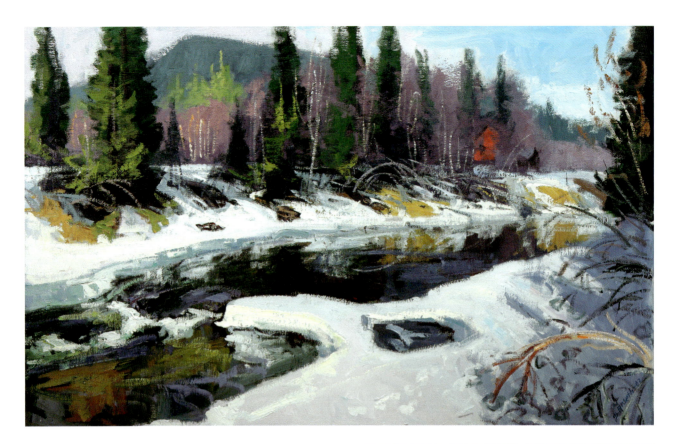

Tidleg vår ved elva. *Early spring by the river.*

Snøen brånar i Vang, mot Grindadn og Smådalen.   *The snow is melting in Vang, Valdres.*

Eit svært lyst og blidt bilete i strålande vårver frå heimbygda mi, Volbu. Eg synest eg kan høyre bekkesildring og kjenne det mildare draget i lufta som gjev forventning om ei ny årstid. Dette er det no alltid knytt ei viss spaning til i ei fjellbygd i innlandet der vinteren kan by på opptil fleire ekstranummer, om de skjønar meg. Men her byrjar det å grønskas, så ein har vel kome på «den sikre sida» no.

På nokre tre har lauvet byrja å sprette i ein skarp gulgrøn farge, andre har berre knoppa seg, noko som gjev den spesielle fiolettfargen i bjørkene ein berre ser ei kort periode på våren. Det er desse kontrastene mellom gulgrønt, fiolett og kaldt blått, i tillegg til stripene av sollys og skugge, som gjev biletet dynamikk.

Dei mørke, nærast svarte tonane i vegkanten og grantrea strammar opp og tilfører dramatikk, så det blir eit meir interessant bilete, ikkje berre «snilt.» Det kunne kanskje vorte vel uroleg òg, med skimrande flekkar av fargar, og sola som fell i striper mellom treleggane, i skarp kontrast til skuggepartia. Men stramheita i komposisjonen, den faste forma av vegen, og ikkje minst den kjølegt rolege åsen med ei stripe av jamnt blå godvershimmel, held det heile saman.

Biletet har ein særs formfast komposisjon. Vegen fylgjer ei klassisk oppadstigande linje og endar med eit vårgrønt tre, midt i «det gylne snitt.» Eit koseleg bilete, men også eit som formidlar, synest eg, den heilt eigne dirrande vårspenninga.

An exceptionally bright painting in wonderful spring weather from my home area of Volbu. I seem to hear the rushing stream and feel the mild touch in the air, which brings the anticipation of a new season. Early spring always entails a certain excitement to a mountain community; the winter may still offer a number of encores, so to speak. But here it seems the trees have begun to turn green, so one should have arrived on "the sure side" of winter now.

Some of the trees show the beginning of new, bright green leaves, while others only have buds. The birch trees exhibit that special violet color that one only sees for a brief period in the spring. These contrasts between yellow-green, violet, and cool, blue colors, in addition to the streaks of sunlight and shadow, give the painting its dynamic.

The dark, almost black roadside and the spruce trees tighten it up and add drama, making it an interesting painting, not just "nice." It could, perhaps, have become somewhat unsettled, with shimmering spots of color and the streaks of sunlight falling in between the tree trunks in sharp contrast to the shady areas. However, the tight composition, the firm line of the road, and, not least, the cool, quiet ridge with a stripe of bright blue sky, hold it all together.

The painting has a particularly form-conscious composition. The road follows an upward line, ending with a spring-green tree perfectly placed in "the golden ratio" – one of the classic principles of visual proportions. It is a quietly pleasant painting, but also one that expresses, in my opinion, that unique, simmering anticipation of spring.

Bekken sildrar og elva brusar i tidlege vårdagar.

Trickling streams and a flowing river in the early days of spring.

Vatnet fossar over alt og snøen forsvinn time for time slike solskinsdagar som her. Biletet til høgre har eit friskare, «villare» uttrykk enn det over. Dette er rolegare, med fjerne blånande åsar, teknikken er heller ikkje så røff. Det vert ein interessant kontrast mellom den fiolette knoppfargen på trea og der det byrjar å sprette i irrgrønt lauv.

Water is streaming down everywhere, and the snow is vanishing by the hour on sunny days like this. The second painting, to the right, has a fresher, wilder expression than the one above. This one is calmer, with blue hills in the distance, and is not as rough in technique. There are interesting contrasts between the purple budding trees and where bright green leaves have begun to appear.

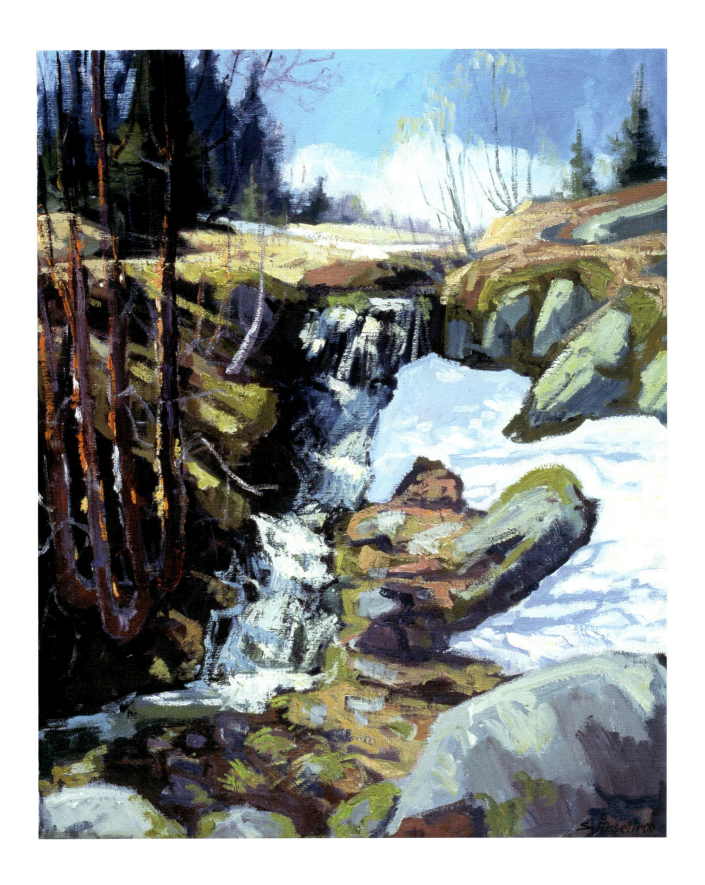

Blåveisbakke på Hedemarken.

TIL VENSTRE: Frukttre blomstring i Sogn.

Bluebells in Hedemarken.

LEFT: *Apple trees in bloom in Sogn.*

SUMAR ✤ *Summer*

Rett nok er sumaren den kortaste årstida i Valdres, men det er nok då det vert måla flest bilete likevel. Det finst eit vell av motiv då, og mange av dei rett rundt husa heime. Dagane er lange og lyse og det blømer i alle regnbogen sine fargar. Ikkje berre i bed, men overalt, på skogsenger, åkrar og langs vegkantane. Dette er den mest inspirerande årstida, men og den vanskelegaste. Sjølv når sola skin, fuglane kvitrar og det tilsynelatande er rein idyll å vera friluftsmålar, kan slikt vêr vera ei stor utfordring. Kombinasjonen steikande sol, høg temperatur og lett sommarbris er bra for klestørk, men fungerar på same måten med måling. Akrylmåling tørkar fort som det er, men no er det snakk om at ho tørkar i penselen før du får målinga på lerretet, og det er innlysande nok eit stort problem! Men stort sett er sumaren ei god tid å vere målar på, og problem med sol og varme er som kjent ikkje svært store i dette landet. Utfordringa ligg vel heller i dei endelause dagane, for ikkje å seie vekene, med overskya eller småregn der lyset er heilt flatt, og det mest spanande motivet mistar all glød.

Summer is surely the shortest season in Valdres, yet it is at this time of year that most paintings are created. It offers an abundance of motifs, much of it right around the buildings at home. The days are long and light, and there are blossoms in all colors of the rainbow. Not only is this true in the garden, but everywhere – in forest and fields, and along the roadsides. This is the most inspiring season, but also the most difficult. Even when the sun shines and birds twitter, seemingly ideal for an outdoor painter, this can be a great challenge. The combination of burning sun, high temperature, and light summer wind is great for drying the laundry, but unfortunately, it affects paint the same way. Acrylic paint dries very quickly as it is, but now it dries in the brush before you get it on the canvas, and that is obviously a serious problem. But, by and all, summer is a good time to be a painter, and sun and heat are, as we know, not really great problems in this country. The challenge may rather be the entire days and weeks with clouds and drizzling rain, when the light is entirely flat and the most exciting motif loses its glow.

Frå den frodige kunstnarheimen til Gro i Lomen, Vestre Slidre.

From the colorful artist's home of Gro in Lomen, Vestre Slidre.

Sumarmorgon på tunet heime.

Summer morning at home.

Solsikker på «solrommet» vårt.

Sunflowers in our "sunroom."

Frodig sumar på Gaalaas på Hedemarken.

Lush summer at Gaalaas in Hedemarken.

Dette er frå det opne landskapet på Furnes ved Mjøsa, mot Helgøya og Skreiaberga. Her er igjen bevisst bruk av fargeperspektiv, med dei metta, men lysande, varme fargane i forgrunnen, det mørke grøne, og over i bleike, klåre pastellar baki åsane. Merk deg korleis den mørke rekkja med tre i mellomgrunnen, nesten horisontalt midt på biletet, «skyv» den kalde, men likevel nokså irrgrøne åkeren bakover, så ei blåleg stripe med skog før den gule åkeren, som og på same måte fjernar seg bakover i biletet.

Rett nok har den grøne åkeren ein kald tone, og den gule lengre bak er synleg bleikare og kaldare enn den heilt fremst, men utan kontrastfelta imellom ville dei likevel «hoppe» for mykje mot deg, og inntrykket av avstand bli forringa. Med berre å gå frå varmt i framgrunnen til kaldare og bleikare dess lengre bak, får ein lett eit kjedeleg «fargeskala» bilete, nesten som om ein hadde brukt eit fargekart frå Jotun. Med kontrastar og komplementærfargar vert det meir spennande, det får auget til å vandre, men gjev også ro og harmoni fordi beslekta fargar går at rundt omkring i biletet.

Men likså mykje som fargane, er det linjeføringa og flatene som gjev inntrykk av luft og avstand. Dei skrå linjene som markerer grensene mellom skog, korn, gras, vatn og fjell får auget til å slynge seg oppover og bakover i biletet. Den næraste kornåkeren, delt på skrå av grøne busker og tre, dekkjer nesten halve biletet, den andre halvparten er «alt det andre», heile landskapet som vert stilisert ned til mindre, men detaljlause fargefelt. Det er denne kontrasten i storleik mellom forgrunn og bakgrunn som gjer at han her «kjem unna med» å ha dei mørke trea i mellomgrunnen slik midt i biletet; det verkar som dei ligg i det gylne snitt.

This is the open landscape at Furnes by Lake Mjøsa and the Skreia Mountains. Again we find conscious use of color perspective. There are saturated but bright and warm colors in the foreground, and dark green to pale pastel colors in the distant hills. Notice how the dark row of trees, almost horizontal in the middle of the painting, "pushes back" the cold, yet bright green, field. Then there is a bluish line of forest before the yellow field, which in the same way recedes into the painting.

The green field actually has a cold tone, and the yellow in the back appears paler and cooler than the yellow in the foreground. Without the contrasting areas between them, though, they would still "jump" too much toward you, and the impression of distance would diminish.

Simply going from warm in the foreground to colder and paler toward the back tends to create a dull "color scale" painting, almost reminiscent of a commercial color chart. Adding contrasts and complementary colors makes it all more exciting, makes the eye wander, but also provides calmness and harmony because related colors are repeated throughout the painting.

Just as significant as the choice of color, lines and expanses of color also affect the impression of space and distance. The angular lines distinguishing forest, grain, grass, water and mountains lead the eye upward and into the painting. The closest grain field, divided by an angular line of green bushes and trees, covers almost half the painting. The other half is "everything else," the whole scene stylized into smaller areas without details. The contrasts in size between the foreground and background elements are what make the perspective work. Despite the dark trees in the middle distance being right in the center, they appear to be balanced in "the golden section."

Endå eit Mjøs-bilete mot Stange kyrkje og Helgøya. Eit bilete som utstrålar ro og monumentalitet. Det er enno sumarleg og varmt, med ufargele bomullsskyer på ein klår, blå himmel, og ein kan ein førestille seg lukta av mogent korn i sola.

Her er mindre skarpe kontrastar og linjer enn i biletet frå Furnes og store, vide flater, men då kan ein tillate seg å leike meir med fargenyansar i kornåkeren utan å øydelegge den store roen. Her spenner det frå mørke rustraude og flaskegrøne fargar, til citrusfargar, bleike rosa sjatteringar og lyst solgult, nesten kvitt. Og bak kappast Mjøsa og himmelen om blåfargen.

Another painting from near Lake Mjøsa, toward Stange Church and the Helgøya Island. This is a painting that expresses peace and grandeur. The warmth of summer is still present, with cotton clouds in a clear, blue sky. One can imagine the smell of grain ready to be harvested.

There are fewer sharp contrasts and lines here than in the image above, and large, expansive fields that allow for more play with color hues without interrupting the overall peacefulness. The colors range from dark, rusty red and bottle green, to citrus and rose hues, to sunny yellow, nearly white. And in the background, the lake and the sky become a competition in blue.

Vesle Sunniva hjelper bestemor med å vatne planter i urtehagen.

Little Sunniva is helping her grandmother water the plants in the herb garden.

Marit i sving med akvarell-skrinet.

Marit in action with her watercolor set.

NORWAY PAINTED IN LIGHT AND COLOR

Eit svært spesielt, nærast abstrakt bilete. Eigentleg skulle ein ikkje tru her var noko motiv i det heile, men berre ein har augene med seg, kan ein finne motiv mest overalt. Dette er frå gamle Kvam gard i Vang i Valdres. Her bur det ikkje folk i husa lengre, i staden er tunet vorte gardsmuseum. Det er ikkje innlagt straum, og dagslyset fell inn gjennom nokre få småruta vindauge.

Takhøgda er meir enn ein vanlegvis ville tillate seg på ein fjellgard i det på den tida fattige Norge. Grunnen er nok at Kvam var lensmannsgard, med ein langt større velstand enn hjå den jamne fjellbonden. Eit av tegna på dette er at så mykje her er måla, ikkje berre skåp, kister og ting, men og veggar og dører.

Måling var status; materialane var dyre og sjeldne, og skulle ein også ha dekor, måtte ein kunne løne ein av dei omreisande dekorasjonskunstnarane. Det var heilt annleis enn ved for eksempel treskjering, der ein i prinsippet ikkje treng anna enn eit emne av tre, ein kniv og ein stor porsjon tålmod.

An unusual, nearly abstract, painting. It is hard to believe there is a motif here at all, but this actually shows that, with visual awareness, one can find a subject almost anywhere. This is from the old Kvam farm at Vang in Valdres. No one is living here anymore; instead, it has become a farm museum. There is no electricity, and the daylight comes in through a few windows, fairly large in size but divided into small window panes.

The rooms have higher ceilings than most mountain farms could allow at a time of poverty in Norway. The reason is that Kvam was the sheriff's farm, with a much greater prosperity than the average mountain farmer had. Another sign of prosperity is that so much has been decorated – not only cupboards, chests and other artifacts, but also doors and walls.

Painting had status. The materials were rare and expensive, and if one wanted painting done, one had to pay one of the itinerant artists. This was very different from woodcarving, for example, where one – in principle – only needed the wood material, a knife, and plenty of patience.

Hovudelementa i dette motivet er dei to opne dørene. Den til venstre er klart dominerande, med sollys fløymande inn i det elles dunkle rommet. Heile feltet er halde i lyse og varme tonar. Mykje gyllent, frå djup sienna, via oker til lys sitrongul, men og med innslag av friske, varme grøntonar. Det er refleksane frå det sumargrøne landskapet utanfor ein ser inne. Sjølv om ein berre ser glimt av villblomar som tittar over dørhella, representerer dei heile den solvarme

The main element in this painting is the two open doors. The one on the left is clearly dominating, with sunlight floating into the otherwise dim room. The whole area is kept in light and warm color tones. Much of it is golden, from deep sienna, via ocher, to light lemon yellow, but also with touches of refreshing, warm green tones. It is the reflection of the summer-green landscape outdoors one sees inside. Even if you merely glimpse the wildflowers peeking up along the doorstep, they represent the whole sunny, warm

og saftiggrøne sumaren ute, i kontrast til det meir livlause inne. Forutan faktisk å attgje lys og refleksar, gjer komplementærfargane raudt og grønt at det lyser ekstra mot ein. Døra er måla i grove strøk med både harmoniar og kontrastar, men alt i den varme og lyse enden av skalaen. Virkninga vert at det funklar mot deg, som når du kjem ut og augene ikkje har vant seg til det skarpe lyset.

Heile resten av biletet er nokså mørkt, men ikkje fargelaust for det. Her er mange djupe, flotte nyansar i skuggane òg. Halvt gøymt bak døra, ser ein eit høgt skåp måla i gildt bonderaudt. Sjølv om den næraste døra tek mykje merksemd, finn eg at blikket vandrar fram og attende mellom dei to. Den bakre døra vert framheva av den raude komplementærfargen på skåpet, og varme dunkle valørar i mellomgrunnen. Den blå døra får litt svakt lys, som frå eit vindauge ein ikkje ser. Ein vert mest litt nysgjerrig på kva som er bak den mørke døropninga. Og kven er det som går i desse dørene?

and flourishing summer outdoors, in contrast to the more lifeless interior. In addition to actually expressing light and reflections, the complementary colors of red and green give the light particular intensity. The door is painted with coarse strokes, containing both harmonies and contrasts, but all in the warm and light end of the spectrum. The effect is that the area twinkles toward you, like when you go outside and your eyes need to adjust to the bright light.

The rest of the painting is quite dark, but not without color. Here are also many deep and beautiful nuances in the shadows. Halfway hidden behind the door one can see a tall cupboard painted in excellent "farmer's red." Even though the nearest door commands a lot of attention, I find that my eye moves back and forth between the two. The door at the back is emphasized because of the red complementary color on the cupboard and the warm, dim colors in between. The blue door is illuminated by a somewhat faint light, as from a concealed window. One becomes a little curious as to what is there, beyond the dark opening. And who is walking through these doors?

Ved det opne glaset sit denne tyske tekstilkunstnaren på sumaropphald i Valdres ved rokken.

A German textile artist, on summer vacation in Valdres, at the spinning wheel.

Her er mykje å sjå på, men auget vert stadig leidd til personen i rommet innanfor. Kvinna vert litt mystisk der inne, slik ho snur seg vekk frå tilskodaren.

There's plenty to study in this painting, but the eye is led toward the person in the inner room. The person becomes a bit mysterious in there, turning away from the viewer.

Vår gode danske ven, Erik. Prest, forfattar, og eg er freista til å kalle han «livskunstnar», sjølv om uttrykket er noko vel slitent. Han bur i eit rikt dekorert hus, fylt med bøker og gjenstandar som vel er alt frå suvenirar frå dei mange reisene, til reine kunstskattar å rekne. På tunet har han sett opp både gildehall og si eiga vesle kyrkje, med storslagen utsikt over fjell og dalar.

Ein slik fargerik person måtte målast i sterkt lys og med spontane strøk og reine flater. Her kjem dagslyset, kaldt og klart, inn gjennom eit vindauge. Vinkelen lyset fell inn på modellen på er litt uvant, nærast bakfrå, men litt frå sida. Det gjev store kontrastar, og tydeleggjer linjer og ansiktstrekk som er med på å framheve karakteren til modellen.

Når ein skal måle hud livaktig, må ein, etter mi erfaring og meining, alltid bruke fargar langt unna det ein tenkjer på som «hudfarge», gjerne ulike grøn- og blåtonar. Dette portrettet er mellom dei meir fargesterke, med lys, nærast giftgrøn farge på kjaken vend mot oss, sterke blå reflaksar i panna og under haka, og raudtonar frå djup purpur til lys oransje.

Den røffe teknikken både harmonerer og står i kontrast til personlegdomen som vert portrettert. Sjølv med grove strøk, synest eg varmen og den underfundige humoren vert godt formidla. No er det ikkje akkurat slik at Erik går stille i dørene. Han er spontan og generøs, byr stadig på morosame og fargerike historier frå ymse himmelstrøk, eller bryt ut i sang med ei djup og kraftfull røyst. Men utan at det går på kostnad av å kunne relatere til sorg og alvor, det fekk vi erfare ved vesle Lives bortgang.

Kona Kirsten vart portrettert etterpå, og då fann Sigmund ut at han måtte bruke eit meir dempa og mjukare lys, som passa betre til hennar særs milde vesen. Då vart ein minna om at det såvisst ikkje er det same kva lys du målar ein person i!

Our good Danish friend, Erik – pastor, author, and someone who, I am tempted to say, knows "the art of living." He lives in a richly decorated house, filled with books and objects – everything from souvenirs from his extensive traveling, to what can be considered real art treasures. In his yard, he has built both a banquet hall and his own little church, with a grand view of mountains and valleys.

Such a colorful person had to be painted in a strong light, with spontaneous and pure strokes. Cool and clear daylight comes in through a window. The way the light falls on the model is somewhat unusual, as it comes almost from behind and just slightly from the side. This creates great contrasts and makes lines and facial features sharper, emphasizing the character of the model.

In order to paint lifelike skin, one must, in my estimation and experience, always use colors far from what one would consider "skin color"; perhaps even green and blue tones. This portrait is among the more color-saturated; with a light, almost venom-green, color on the cheek turning toward us, strong blue reflections on the forehead and under the chin, and red tones ranging from deep scarlet to light orange.

The rough technique used here is both in harmony with and in contrast to the personality portrayed. Even with coarse brush work, I think his warmth and cunning humor are well communicated. It is not that Erik walks around quietly. He is spontaneous and generous, constantly offering colorful and amusing stories from various continents, or breaking into song in a deep and powerful voice. But not at the cost of also being solemn and sincere, or relating to grief, which we experienced when little Live passed away.

When Erik's wife, Kirsten, had her portrait painted later on, Sigmund noticed that he had to use a more subdued and softer light, more suitable for her mild character. What a reminder that was, that it certainly makes a difference what light is used when painting a portrait!

«Liljer og den gamle trehesten min, som har si eiga historie.»

"Lilies and my old wooden play horse, which has its own stories to tell."

NORWAY PAINTED IN LIGHT AND COLOR 165

Frå heimen til kunstnaren og vår gode ven Gro.   *From the home of our good friend Gro.*

Fatskåpet med den tradisjonelle gamle Valdreslangeleiken hengande ved sidan av.

A cupboard in our living room, with an old langeleik, a traditional Valdres instrument, hanging next to it.

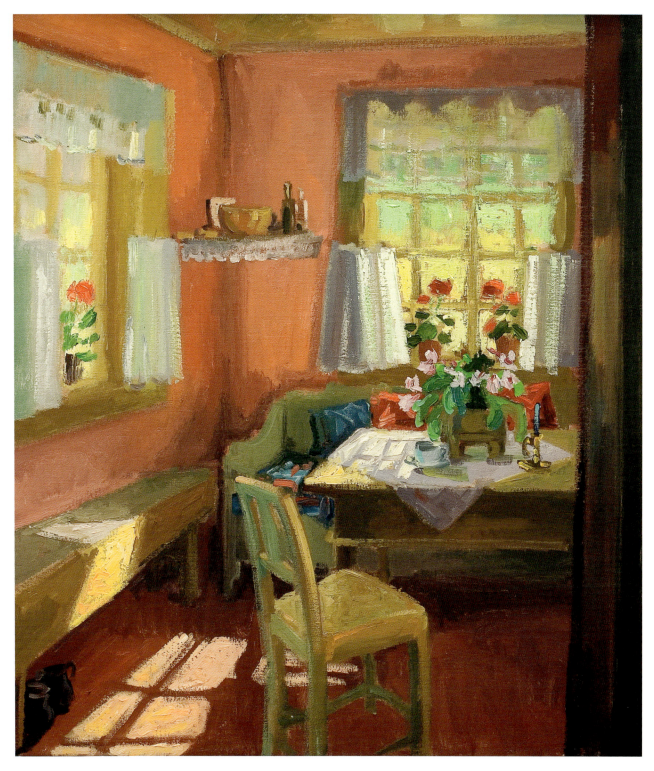

Lys inn glaset i det raude kammerset på Kvam gard.

Sunlight coming through the window in the red room at Kvam farm.

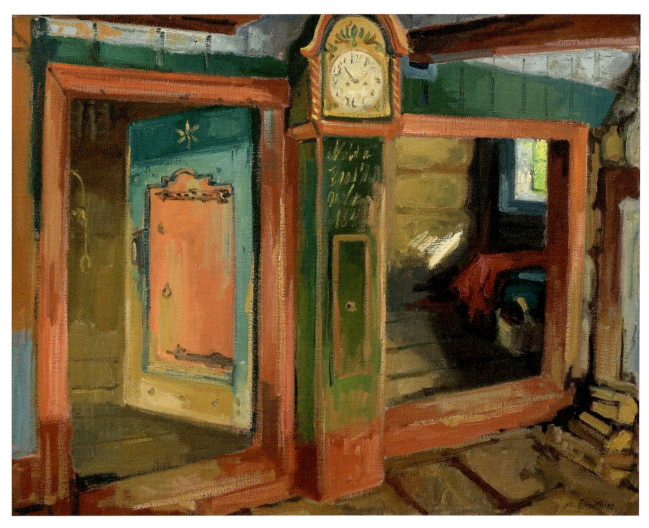

Gamal stogo frå Ål i Hallingdal. «Det var den vesle lysblenken inn glaset i klevarommet som fengde meg då eg fann dette motivet.»

Old house from Ål in Hallingdal. "It was the small beam of light from the window in the small bedroom that caught my eye when I first entered this room."

«Eg har måla denne kyrkja meir enn noko anna, ho ligg så fint til og har interessante detaljar, som kjem fram i skiftande årstider og lys. Her kom eg til å gå på baksida, der ho er så godt som svart. Til mi overrasking var dette eit originalt motiv, med glaset som spegla den grøne solbakken så det glitra som smaragd på den mørke veggen. Frå skuggesida gir kyrkja også eit monumentalt inntrykk i det opne lyse landskapet ein anar rundt.»

"I have painted this church more than any other subject; it is so ideally located and has countless interesting details that come to the fore in varying seasons and light. On this occasion, I happened to go around to the back, where the building is nearly black. To my surprise, this was an interesting subject, with the single window reflecting the green fields opposite, making it sparkle like an emerald on the dark wall. From the shadow side, the church also gives a monumental impression in the bright surrounding landscape."

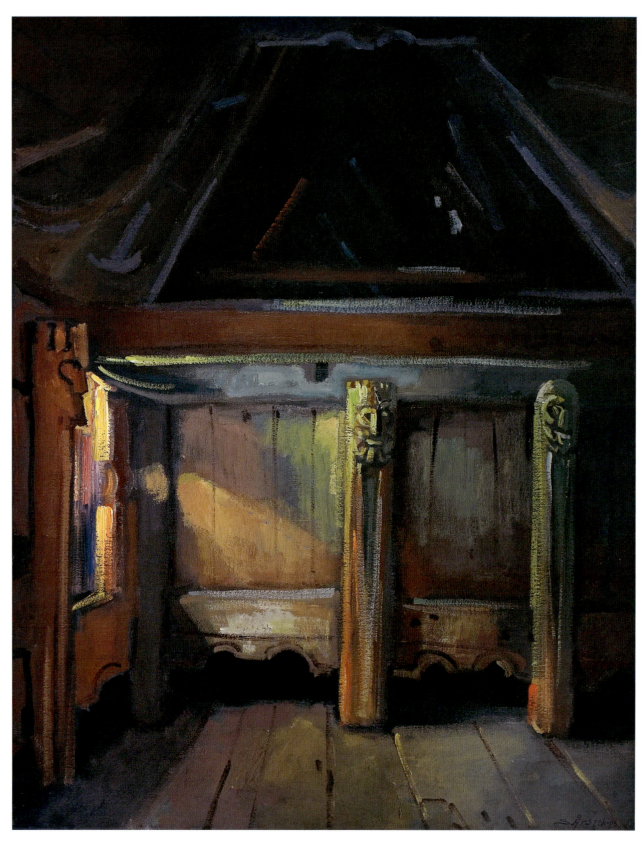

«Kallhovud» på loftsrommet i Hegge stavkyrkje. Dette rommet har ei utruleg og mystisk stemning. Kva kunne desse stolpane fortelje frå dei mange hundre år?

Carved heads on the loft of Hegge Stave Church. This room has an incredible and mysterious mood. What could these posts tell us about the centuries that have passed?

«Frå vognskjulet vårt, som også ber preg av ting som eg har fått med meg frå Amerika.»

"From our shed, which is characterized by items I have brought home from America."

Denne ballblomenga er ikkje heilt lik kvart år, men like eventyrleg. Ein må trø varsamt for ikkje å trø dei ned, sjølv om der er tusen å ta av.

This globe flower field is never quite the same two years in a row, but always equally magnificent. One has to step carefully not to tread down any of the flowers.

NORWAY PAINTED IN LIGHT AND COLOR 175

Tidleg morgon i skogen ved Stampefossen, Valdres. Dette er ei av dei små perlene som ein kan finne mange av rundt i Valdres, ofte uoppdaga av folk flest, men som målar leitar ein stadig etter nye nærmotiv. Sjølv om staden ikkje ligg så langt unna både riksveg og bensinstasjon, så har den noko opphaveleg urskogsmystisk over seg og ein dåm av gamal historie. Namnet fortel at i tidlegare tider vart noko av vasskrafta her brukt i ei «stampe», der ein «stampa» heimevove vadmålstøy for å få det meir tenleg til den tid sin bruk.

Early morning at the Stampefossen Waterfall, Valdres. This is one of the many small beauty spots to be discovered around Valdres, often unknown to most people. As a painter, you are always on the outlook for places like this in your local area. Even if the location is not far from the main road and a petrol station, there's something ancient and mystical in the mood here, as if it is a remnant of history. The name Stampefossen *tells us that the water power at some point has been used for felting home-woven woolen garments, making them stronger and more durable.*

«Her ved elvane har eg prøvd å fange to forskjellige stemningar, det fyrste i kjølig morgonlys og det andre i sein kveldsol. Dette er raskt skiftande stemningar som ein må vera kjapp for å fange.»

"Here by the river I have tried to capture two different moods, the first in cool morning light, the other in late afternoon sun. These are rapidly changing moods that you have to be quick to capture."

Dette er Sognebygda Solvorn; ei lita fredfylt og idyllisk bygd. Ho syner seg her frå si beste side ein solfylt midtsumars morgon. Merk korleis midtpartiet som er måla berre som flekkar i skimrande, lyse fargar, likevel gjev inntrykk av ei tett husklynge bada i det skarpe lyset ein tidleg morgon.

Sjølve husa har ingen detaljar, berre nokre husliknande former, slik som eit møne her og der. Det er nok til at hjernen vår oppfattar det som det er i røynda. Her er likevel dramatikk på grunn av den store mørke steinen på venstre side av vegen og trestammene, som i det skarpe motlyset er nesten svarte. Dei skaper kontrast og dynamikk i eit elles nokså lyst og lett motiv, men også stramheit og ro. Ein rusket haustdag er nok ikkje inntrykket like idyllisk, sjølv i koselege Solvorn.

This is Solvorn by the Sognefjord; a small, quaint and peaceful community, which shows itself here on a most ideal, sun-filled summer morning. Notice how the part in the middle, which is painted merely as spots in shimmering, light colors, gives the impression of houses close together, being bathed in the sharp light of the early morning.

There are no details in the group of houses, only some house-shaped elements here and there. That is still enough for the brain to imagine the rest. The big rock on the left side of the road and the tree trunks, which against the bright lights are almost black, create a certain dramatic element.

The tree trunks create a contrasting element in an otherwise bright scene, and they also hold the dynamic in a collected way. On a rough day in the fall, this impression is most likely not so charming, even in quaint little Solvorn.

Mot kveld i Jotunheimen.

Toward evening in Jotunheimen National Park.

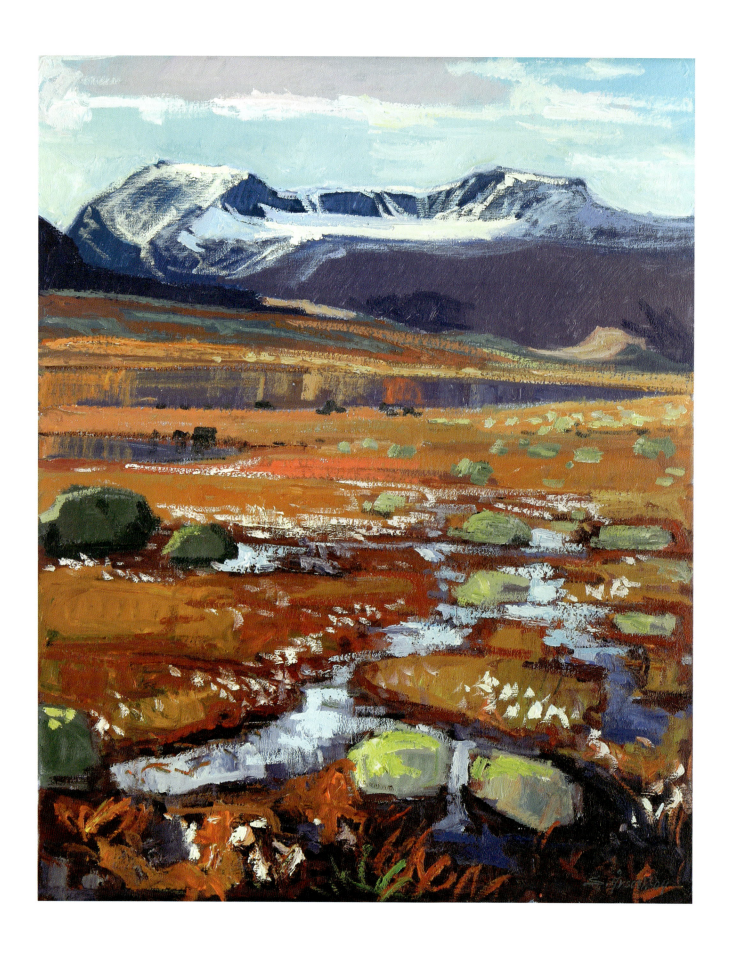

HAUSTFARGAR ❧ *Autumn Colors*

Hausten byr på gneistrande fargar, spanande motiv og ikkje minst svært varierte måletilhøve. Sjølv om vi kanskje enno kallar det fullsommar så lenge vi kan, og det slett ikkje er slutt på badesesongen nede i bygda, skal ein ikkje reise langt før ein vert minna om at det nok er kaldare tider i vente. Tek du bilen og køyrer ein snau halvtime nordover, til Beitostølen, kjenner du snart eit skarpare drag i lufta, og kanskje ein eim av nysnø inni Jotunheimen. Det er enno mange flotte motiv nede i bygda, eller i andre og varmare strøk av landet. Kornet står moge, solsikkene er gjerne på sitt høgaste og flottaste, her er knallraude rips og glinsande svartlilla solbær, ennå gror det og blømer i hagar og enger. Det er som eit siste fargesprakande klimaks før fargane forsvinn under eit kvitt teppe.

Autumn offers sparkling colors, exciting motifs, and, not least, rather varied painting conditions. Although we still consider it summer for as long as we possibly can and still go swimming in the lake, you don't have to go far to be reminded that a colder season is around the corner. Driving just a half hour up to Beitostølen, you will feel a penetrating chill in the air, and perhaps even see a dusting of snow on the Jotunheimen Mountains. There are still many splendid scenes to be painted close to home or in other, warmer, parts of Norway. The grain fields are golden and ready for harvesting, the sunflowers are at their tallest and most beautiful, there are bright red and deep-violet black currants on the bushes, and flowers are still in bloom in gardens and fields. It almost seems like the season's last climax before the colors all disappear under a white winter carpet.

Frå Slettefjell mot Kvam og Smådalen. *From Slettefjell, toward Kvam farm and Smådalen.*

NORWAY PAINTED IN LIGHT AND COLOR 185

Så er hausten her, Volbufjorden er stille, trea har sprakande gylne fargar og snart kjem det fyrste uventa snøfallet.

Autumn is here, the Volbu Fjord is still, the trees are stunningly colorful, and the first snowfall is not far away.

Så har fyrste snøen komen medan ringblomsten enno står i blomst. Her er det mykje flekkar av lauv og gras mellom den våte snøen. Den lyse einsarta bakgrunnen saman med faste husformer samlar det heile.

The first snow has come, with some flowers still in bloom. The patches of leaves and grass over a layer of snow are balanced by the monochrome background and the firm shapes of the houses.

Haustdag i skogen med våt nysnø.

An autumn day with wet snow in the forest.

Haustleg ro over Valdresflye.

Autumn peace on the Valdres high plains.

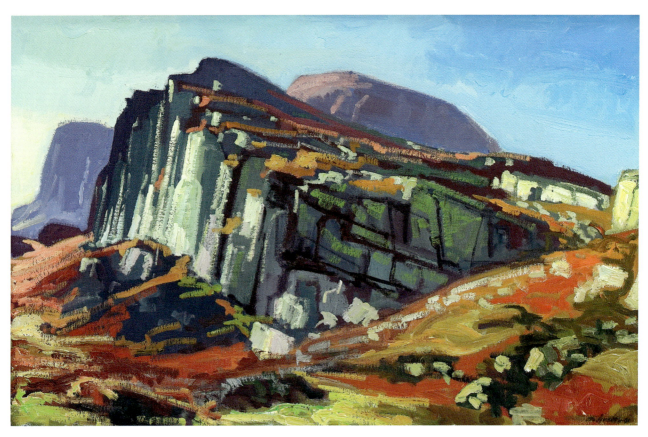

Dette er måla ein klår, fin haustdag, då fjellet eksploderer i farge. Sollyset gjer at dei ulike fasettane og dei nærast geometriske formene på knausar og stein verkeleg kjem til sin rett. Det same med fargetonane, som spenner frå fiolett-svart til det lysaste grønt.

Merk likevel at fjell-fargane vert haldne på den blå, kalde sida av skalaen. Dette verkar komplementært til dei gule, oransje og raude lyng-fargane i framgrunnen, og framhevar intensiteten i desse så dei lyser mot ein. Av fargeperspektivet ser ein at fjella bak verkeleg er langt borte.

Lufta i høgfjellet er så klår at ein ofte kan tru ting er nærare enn dei er, det har vel fleire turgåarar fått erfare. Noko dis kan det likevel vere, og om ikkje, så får målaren lage det. Det vil seie å gjera fargane lysare og kaldare til lenger unna i motivet elementa er. Lett å seie, men når ein skal gjera det, må ein vera svært nøye med valørane, og treffe eksakt den rette fargetonen.

This was painted on a nice, clear day in the autumn. The sunlight makes the different facets and geometric shapes on ridges and rocks nearest us really show their character. It does the same with the color tones, which go from violet-black to the lightest green.

Notice that the colors of the mountain, though, are kept in the blue, cool side of the scale. This works as a complement to the yellow, orange, and red heather colors in the foreground, emphasizing the intensity and causing them to radiate toward us. From the atmospheric perspective, one can tell that the mountains in the back are far away.

The air in the higher altitude is so clear that one may often think that things are closer than they are, as, undoubtedly, many mountains hikers have experienced. Some haze may still be there, and if not, the painter can create it. That means making the colors lighter, cooler and grayer the farther away the elements are. Easy to say, but while doing it, one must be extremely particular about the values and hit exactly the right color tones.

Barskt vêr og årstid krev eit barskt uttrykk. Her er kvasse, grove, raske og bestemte penselstrøk. Fjellet er ruvande og mørkt og stenger nesten for himmelen. Heile uttrykket er nokså trugande.

Det kan verke som om folk traktar etter ei opning i eit bilete, litt luft, opp og til høgre, det kan vera ur-instinktet, ikkje veit eg. Her er rett nok ei opning som framhevar nett dette partiet, med sterkt lys, til og med. Dette feltet, saman med sterke oransje-grønt-kvite kontrastar og stigande linjer i framgrunnen, byr på ein motsetnad mot ein nokså dyster og massiv bakgrunn.

Rough weather and a rough season require a rough expression. There are sharp, coarse, quick and determined brush strokes here. The mountain is overpowering and dark, almost preventing the sky from showing through. The whole expression is rather threatening.

There seems to be a longing in people to find an opening in a painting, a little air, perhaps up to the right. It can be something innate in us, although I am not the one to say. There is, in fact, an opening here that emphasizes exactly this area, even with strong light. Together with strong orange-green-white contrasts and rising lines in the foreground, this area offers a resistance to the rather dim and massive background.

«Dette var ein dag eg hadde vore høgt til fjells og måla heile dagen. Som ein ser er det haust og fyrste snøen har kome på fjelltoppane. Ein smal sigd av ein måne har allereie kome opp, sjølv om sola enno fell på toppane. Dei vert bada i eit merkeleg varmt lys, samstundes som ein ser kulda lurer. Eg var sliten og svolten og lengta heim, men denne augneblinken måtte fangast, for den varar ikkje lenge. Skuggane kryp fort oppetter høgdene. Her er dramatisk kontrast mellom lys og skugge. Stunda då heile stemninga og karakteren i landskapet er i endring frå fargesprakande, blidt og solfylt, til isande kald og svart natt.»

"This day I had been up in the mountains on the Valdres high plains, painting all day. As we can see, it is autumn, and the first snow is lying on the mountaintops. A narrow sliver of a moon has already come out, even if the final rays of sunshine are still bathing the mountains in a strange, warm light. At the same time, there is a chill mood approaching. I was weary and hungry and wanted to go home, but I had to catch this moment. It does not last long. The shadows creep quickly up the mountainsides. There are dramatic contrasts between light and shadow. This is the moment when the whole atmosphere and character of the landscape is changing from the colorful, mild and sun-filled day to an icy, chilling and dark night."

Ein still haustdag på Valdresflye.

A quiet autumn day on Valdresflye.

Ved Tyin i Vang.

At Tyin in Vang, Valdres.

Dramatisk vêr i Koldedalen.

Dramatic weather in Koldedalen, "The Cold Valley."

Det trugar med dårleg vêr i Svartdalen, Jotunheimen. I framgrunnen skimtar vi Gudmund som pakkar ned teltet i all hast.

Unsettled weather is threatening in Svartdalen, "The Black Valley," Jotunheimen National Park. In the foreground we can just make out Gudmund, dismantling the tent in a hurry.

Frå Koldedalen mot Hjelledalstind, Jotunheimen.

From Koldedalen toward the Hjelledalstind Peak, Jotunheimen.

Lange utsyn og nære ting i området ved Bitihorn.

Expansive vistas and foreground details up on the mountain plains.

Solefall ved Synshorn.

Sunset on Mount Synshorn.

«Trass i dårlege utsikter sleit eg meg inn i fjellet med utstyret mitt. Så kom uvêret med kraftige haglbyger. Det vart ein vanskeleg tørn å berge dette biletet ned att, men det gjekk så vidt det var denne gongen også.»

"Despite the poor weather forecast, I struggled into the mountains with all my painting equipment. Then the storms set in with intense hail showers. It took some effort rescuing this painting and bringing it back down from the mountains, but once again, everything ended well."

VED BITIHORN

Dette området innunder Bitihorn, på vegen opp mot Valdresflye, er ein av Sigmund sine faste plassar å måle. Det går fint an å måle bortimot same motiv eit utal gonger, berre det er interessant i utgangspunktet. Årstidene i fjellet byr på spesielt dramatiske endringar med så skiftande lystilhøve at stemninga og uttrykket aldri vert likt frå bilete til bilete. Norge er nok eit takksamt land for ein målar slik sett, med raske og store skifte, mykje vêr og storslagen, vill natur. For ein som oftast står ute på staden med lerret og staffeli, er det og noko av den største utfordringa.

I Norge generelt, og i høgfjellet spesielt, må ein rekne med bråe verskifte, slik at bardunering av staffeliet meir er regelen enn unntaket. I tillegg må ein vera budd på fire årstider, og litt til, på ein og same dag. Lang erfaring gjer at «målarbilen» er utstyrt med ekstra klede, varmedress, regntøy, vottar og lue – ein kan aldri vite. Vert det reint ille, må ein ty til å opne bakluka på bilen og krype innunder, eller heilt inn i bilen. Det er eit under at ikkje fleire bilete har blitt øydelagde av regn eller vind, men det har vel hendt at det har vorte nokså vått-i-vått...

Båtskaret, heiter det der vegen svingar inn frå ein vid, open dal mot sør, inn mellom den stupbratte sørsida av Bitihorn på den eine sida, og berg og knausar på den andre. Trass den imponerande veggen mot sør, er turen til toppen av Bitihorn lett og ufarleg om ein berre held seg unna stupet.

Det finst tallause bilete frå same område som Sigmund har måla opp gjennom åra, men heilt sikkert er det at ingen er like. På den andre sida kan ein, når motivet er såpass konstant – og det kan vel trygt seiast å vera tilfelle med Bitihorn – som kunstnar verkeleg fordjupe seg. Ein vert kjend med formene og terrenget, slik at ein ikkje treng bruke mykje tid til å finne rette plassen å stå, utsnittet, vinkelen, og til å skissere opp motivet.

Den dyrebare tida ein har til rådvelde kan nyttast til å konsentrere seg om lys og fargetonar. For oss utanfor gjev det eit blikk inn i korleis ein kunstnar utviklar seg over mange år. Ingen av bileta er like, men heller ingen av årgangane. For dei av oss som følgjer Sigmund tett, er det råd å sjå kva år eit bilete er måla. Teknikken utviklar seg frå år til år når ein er så aktiv.

AROUND BITIHORN

This area at the foot of Bitihorn Mountain, on the road toward Valdresflye, is one of Sigmund's regular places to paint. It is quite possible to paint the same vista any number of times, as long as it has an interesting starting point. The seasons in the mountains offer especially dramatic changes with such varied light conditions that the atmosphere and expression never become the same from one painting to the next. In this respect, it is a pleasant job to be a painter in Norway, with its many quick changes in weather combined with grand and unspoiled scenery. For someone who is often standing outdoors with canvas and easel, it is also part of the greatest challenge.

In Norway in general, and in the mountains especially, you have to expect sudden weather changes. Additionally, one must be prepared for four seasons and more, in one and the same day. The "painting van" is always, after years of experience, filled with equipment and extra clothing, coveralls, raincoat, mittens and a hat – you never know. Under extreme conditions, you can open the back of the car and crawl underneath, or all the way into the car. It is a miracle that more paintings have not been ruined by rain or wind, but it may have happened that the paint has had to be applied somewhat wetter than planned.

At Båtskaret, the road turns from a wide, open, southern-exposed valley toward the steep Bitihorn, with its wall on one side, and ridges and rocks on the other. In spite of the impressive southern wall, the hike to the top of the Bitihorn is easy and not dangerous, as long as one stays away from the edge.

Sigmund has painted countless paintings in this area over the years, but, certainly, there are no two alike. The advantage with a subject as constant as Bitihorn Mountain is that you, as an artist, can really immerse yourself in the motif. When you become well acquainted with the forms and the landscape, less time is required to find the right place to stand, to choose the particular view and what to include, and to do the preliminary sketching.

The valuable time one has for working can be used to focus on light and color mixing. For everyone else, this is where you can see an artist's development through the years. None of the paintings are alike, nor any of the periods in time. For those of us who follow Sigmund closely, it is possible to see which year a painting was painted. With such consistent activity, the technique develops year after year.

«Så kjem det nokre stillare dagar i området 'mitt' ved Bitihorn, men det er ein kamp slike seinhaustdagar med lyset som svinn og kulden som tek på. Eg spør meg, kor lenge kan eg orke dette? Men fjellet er praktfullt og freistande på denne tida.»

"A few days of more settled weather in 'my' area of the mountains, but painting at this time of year is still a race against the vanishing light and encroaching cold. I frequently ask myself, 'How long can I continue to manage this?' But the mountains are fabulous and luring at this time of year."

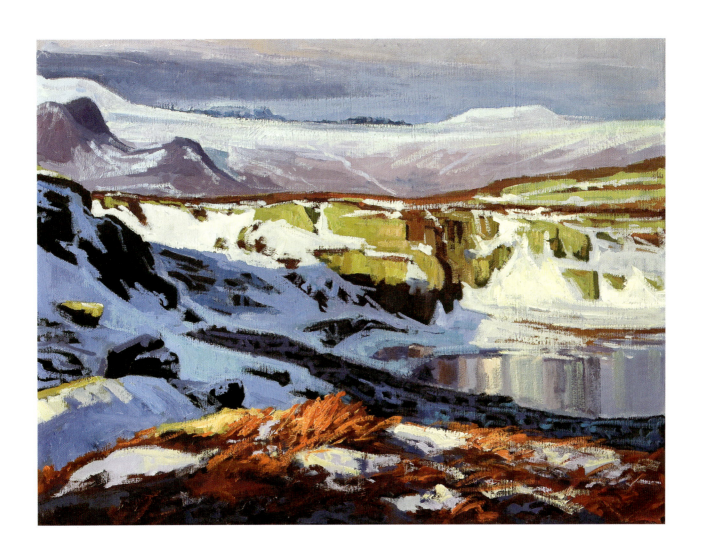

«Dette biletet vart måla under nærast umogelege tilhøve. Uroleg vêr og dramatisk lys, her må ting skje fort og spontant om motivet skal festast på lerretet.»

"This was painted under almost impossible conditions. Unsettled weather and dramatic light mean that you have to work quickly if you want to get the mood down on canvas."

Nysnøen lagar nye mønster i landskapet og skaper saman med det stadig skiftande lyset nye motiv i velkjende område.

The recent snowfall has created new patterns in the landscape. Together with the ever-changing light, this creates new motifs in a well known area.

Sein haust mot Knutshø og Valdresflye.

Late autumn toward Knutshø Mountain and the Valdres high plains.

NORWAY PAINTED IN LIGHT AND COLOR 215

«Så set vinteren inn for alvor, mollstemd og kald. Vandrarane dreg heim og eg seier farvel til fjellet som motiv for i år.»

"Winter arrives in earnest, with biting cold and melancholic moods. Mountain hikers return home, and I have to bid farewell to the mountains as a motif for this year."

Her er fullvinter på Valdresflye. Det meste er dekka av snø bortsett frå ein og annan vindutsett rabbe, eller som her, ein open bekk. Ser ein bort frå den, er mest alt heilt kvitt. Men det er for eit utrena auge. Her er nyansar, ein må vere svært nøye med fargane.

Ser ein etter, er snøen i framgrunnen i ein langt varmare fargetone enn den lenger bak, nesten rosa. Himmelen er i ein langt kaldare farge, liksom fjella bak som reflekterar himmelfargen.

Ein ser også at bekken går ifrå ein, ved at den er mørkare nære, og vert meir sløra bakover. I røynda ville du nok ikkje sjå dette på nokre meter avstand i den klåre fjellufta, men for å gje djupn må ein tenkje seg det.

Dette biletet er eit døme på at ein med hell kan lage fargeperspektiv der det mest ikkje finst. Ja, fargar – det går no mest i blåtonar, men her er det valørane som tel. Sjølv om blått er ein kald farge i seg sjølv, kjem det an på samanhengen og omgjevnaden.

Full winter on the high plains in Valdres. The plains are almost fully covered by snow, except for a few wind-blown rocks or an open creek, as seen here. Apart from the creek, this painting is basically all white. But that is just to an untrained eye. There are nuances here, with very careful use of colors.

Looking closely, one can tell that the snow in the foreground has much warmer colors than the snow farther back. It is almost rose-colored. The sky has a much colder tone, and the mountains in the background seem to reflect the color of the sky.

One can also see that the creek moves away from us, because it is darker up close and becomes more faded in the background. Generally, you would not see this in the clear mountain air. But to give depth, one has to imagine it.

This painting is an example of how one can, quite successfully, create a color perspective where color is barely present. Well, color? It seems limited to blue only, but it is the many values that count. Even if blue is in itself a cold color, it depends on the context, the surroundings. In this case, one can quite reasonably talk about cold and warm blue-tones.

Her rår avklara ro og monumentalitet. I dette biletet er ikkje spaninga knytt til vertilhøva, men meir til kontrastane og formene. Penselføringa ber preg av litt betre tid og betre vertilhøve enn på nokon av dei andre bileta. Det er ikkje like røft måla, men på den andre sida vert skiljet mellom blåsvart fjell, rein kvit snø og raudlege berre flekkar, svært sterke. Ruskeversbileta vert noko meir tåkete og utviska.

Here we have a restful scene with clarity and monumentality. The tensions are not related to the weather conditions here, but rather to contrasts and shapes. The brush strokes give the impression of more time and better conditions than in some of the other paintings. It is not as roughly painted, but on the other hand, the contrasts between blue-black mountain, pure white snow, and the rust-red bare areas, are very strong. Paintings created in rough weather tend to be more foggy and faded.

POSTKORT FRÅ UTLANDET
Postcards from Abroad

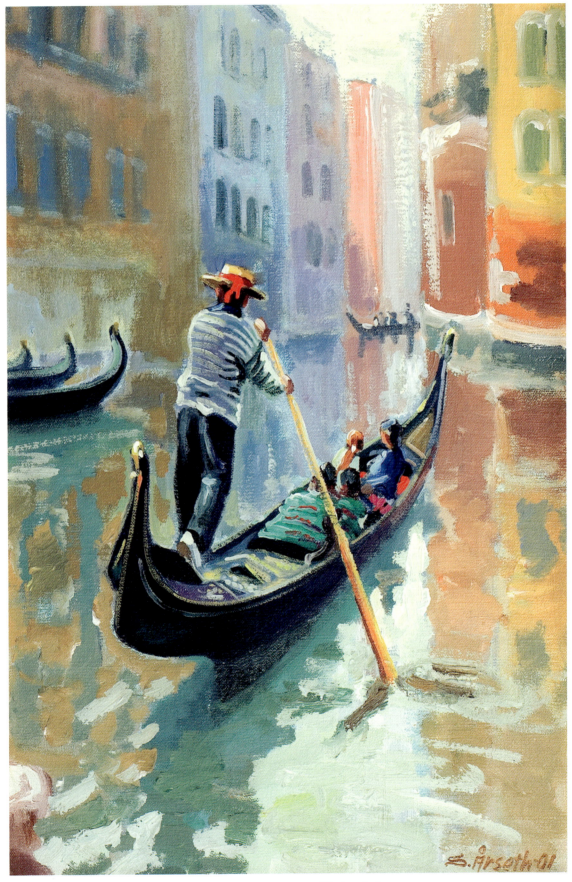

Venezia, Italia.   *Venice, Italy.*

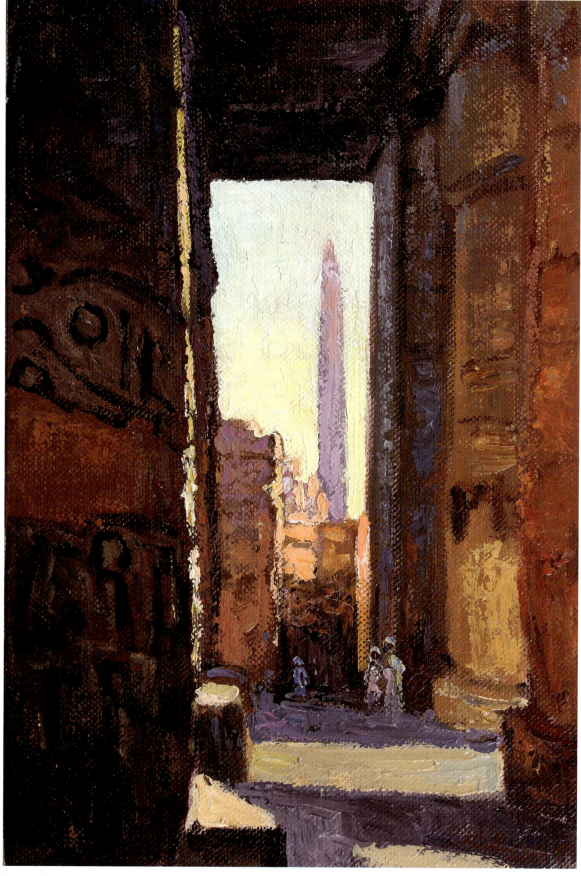

Luxor, Egypt. *Luxor, Egypt.*

TIL VENSTRE: «Intense minutt», skriv Sigmund i notata sine. Ein solnedgang i Egypt er akkurat det, berre nokre få minutt med overgang frå steikande, kvit sol til varme gule og oransje tonar, over til rosa og raudt og til slutt lilla og djup ultramarin-blå. Og nett intensiteten i det heile har vorte fanga inn på ein måte som eg synest er einestående, sjølv for ein kolorist som Sigmund.

Den skarpt avgrensa, mørke ramma rundt det skimrande, gylne lyset, og landskapet i dunkelt fiolett som vert meir og meir lilla og utviska der det fjernar seg, er ikkje typisk for han. Men så er det ikkje kvar dag ein er i Egypt, så dette er nok eit eksempel på korleis ein kan, og bør, tilpasse fargar, penselføring, komposisjon, ja – heile stilen, etter omgjevnadane for å få fram den spesielle atmosfæren på staden.

Ein sumarkveld i Valdres krev ein heilt annan og dusare palett for ikkje å gje «elg i solnedgang-effekt.» I eit fargerikt land som Egypt derimot, og med eit stramt og stilisert motiv som dette, kan ein fint tillate seg å bruke litt rosa.

LEFT: *"Minutes of intensity," Sigmund writes in his notes. A sunset in Egypt is exactly that – merely a few minutes of transition from burning, white sunshine, to warm yellow and orange tones, to rose and red, and then violet and deep ultramarine blue. And it is exactly this intensity that has been captured here – in a way, I think, that is outstanding and quite unique, even for a colorist like Sigmund.*

The sharp-edged, dark frame around the shimmering golden light, and the landscape in somber violet turning more and more pale as it fades away – this is not typical for him. But it is not every day one is in Egypt, so this is, no doubt, an example of how one can, and should, adjust colors, brush strokes, composition – actually, the whole style of expression – to the environment, in order to reveal the unique atmosphere of the place.

A summer evening in Valdres requires a totally different and more subdued palette, to avoid the so-called "moose-in-the-sunset" effect. On the other hand, in a colorful land like Egypt, and with this kind of light and motif, one can very well use a little pink.

Seglbåtar på Nilen.

Sailing boats on the Nile.

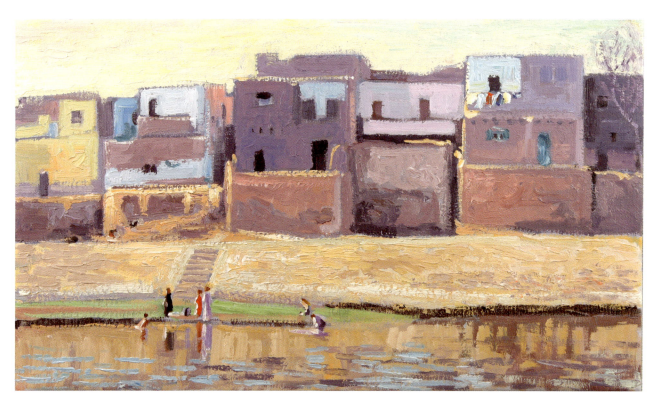

Dette biletet går i duse, delikate fargar, men det formidlar likevel det spesielle lyset som får husa til å skimre i pastell. Dette er husveggar som eigentleg går mest i gylne, brune og beige tonar om ein er der og går heilt inntil og ser. Men lys, skuggar og refleksar, saman med eit trena auge, avslører ein heil palett av ulike fargetonar. Det er òg eit bilete som lett kunne blitt uroleg. Dei mange ulike formene og fargane på husa, som ser ut til å vera bygde oppå kvarandre, står der som ein festningsmur i kontrast til folka i framgrunnen. Men den jamne, rolege stripa med sand i mellomgrunnen roar det heile ned. I tillegg verkar sanden komplementær til dei kaldare lillatonane, skyv dei frå kvarandre og skaper avstand, tilsynelatande. Dette tillet bruk av dei same fargane i framgrunnen som i bakgrunnen. Det heile har med å lure auget og hjernen til å oppfatte tre dimensjonar. Smart! Saman med ein særs stram komposisjon og gjennomtenkt linjeføring, ein harmonisk palett og bevisst bruk av reine flater, gjev heilskapen eit nærast søvnig inntrykk. Eit motiv med uvante former og fargar, meiner Sigmund sjølv.

This painting has soft and delicate colors, but still expresses that special light which makes the houses shimmer in their light tint. These walls really have mostly gold, brown and beige tones when you are there looking at them, but light, shadows and reflections, together with a trained eye, reveal a whole palette of different color tones.

This is also a painting that could easily have become disturbing to the eye, with the houses in many different forms and colors looking as if they are built on top of each other. They seem like a fortress wall in contrast to the people in the foreground, but the calm and even line of sand in the middle brings it all to rest. The sand is a complement to the cooler lilac tones, and moves these apart to create a sense of distance.

Sigmund has also used the same colors in the foreground and the background, creating the illusion for the eye, and the brain, to see three dimensions. Quite clever! Together with a very tight composition, deliberate sense of lines, a harmonious palette and conscious use of space, the total look gives an almost sleepy impression – a motif with unfamiliar forms and colors, says Sigmund himself.

Det knyter seg mykje mystikk og mange spørsmål til desse utrulege steinalder-tempela på ei solsvidd slette på Malta. Motivet innbyr til ein kubistisk, nesten abstrakt komposisjon i ein fargeskala fjernt frå alt ein kan finne her i landet. Når ein er på framande stadar er det viktig å gløyme alt om dei fargane ein brukar mest av heime, og ha augene opne for eit anna lys og andre fargar.

There are many unanswered questions and a lot of mystery attached to these amazing Stone Age temples on a sun-scorched plain on the island of Malta. The subject encourages a cubist, nearly abstract composition in a color scheme very distant from anything you would find in Norway. When painting in unfamiliar places, it is important to forget everything about the colors that you usually use, and keep your eyes open for different light and different colors.

Frå Island. Kjensla av å vera i ei mytisk, mystisk verd, vert forsterka av svovellukta som heng tung over slike vulkanske område som her.

From Iceland. The feeling of having entered a mythical, mysterious world is being emphasized by the sulfuric fumes that hang heavily in the air in this volcanic area.

Frå Island, mot Vestmannaøyer. Det islandske landskapet er ei fascinerande blanding av kontrastar: Varme – kulde, monumental ro – dramatikk. Vi nordmenn kjenner elles sterke slektskapsband med folket på Island, gjennom språk og gamal soge. Utan dei islandske skriftene ville vi ikkje kjent stort til fortida vår.

From Iceland, looking toward Vestmannaøyer. The Icelandic landscape is a fascinating mixture of contrasts: warmth – cold, monumental peace – drama. Norwegians feel a strong connection to the Icelandic people, through language and ancient history. Without the Icelandic historical sagas, we would not have known much about our own past.

Island krev ein annan palett enn Norge. Lyset er svært spesielt, vegetasjonen sparsam og vulkansk aktivitet har sett tydelege spor.

Iceland demands a different color palette from Norway. The light is very unusual, the vegetation is sparse, and volcanic activity has left clear marks.

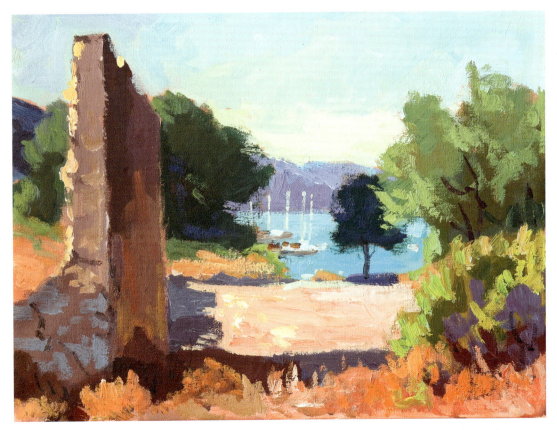

Frå ein fråflytt landsby på sørkysten av Tyrkia.

From an abandoned village on the south coast of Turkey.

Venezia med typisk havklima og lys som snøgt kan skifte frå minutt til minutt. På same måte som lyset på dette biletet, er også gondolen i rørsle og på veg.

Venice, with its typical coastal climate and light that can change from minute to minute. Just like the light, the gondola in this painting is also moving and in transit.

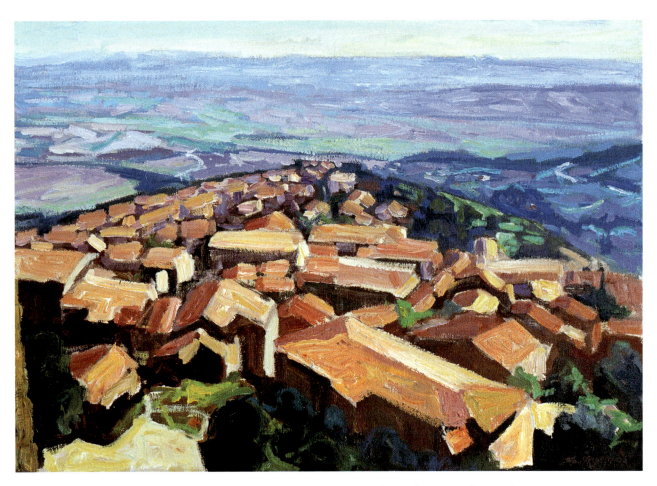

Frå borga på toppen av Montalcino i Toskana ser ein nærast ut over ein mosaikk av varme flater, bygningar og tak, mot eit luftig kulturlandskap som svinn innover mot ei disig synsrand.

From the castle on top of Montalcino in Tuscany, you can scan a virtual mosaic of warm surfaces, houses and roofs, against a cultivated landscape vanishing toward the hazy horizon.

I det vide og solfylte slettelandet i Toskana står sypressane i slanke rader – mørke vertikale kontrastar som set sit særmerkte preg på landskapet.

In the open, sunny landscape of Tuscany, the cypresses are planted in slender rows. The dark, vertical contrasts that they provide characterize this landscape.

Dette biletet frå Ranchos de Taos i New Mexico vart måla på ein tur til USA i 1987 som hele familien var med på. Eg fylte elleve år medan vi var der, og var med andre ord ikkje store jenta, men turen gjorde eit mektig inntrykk. Dette er ein liten by, men rik på historie og kultur. Eg hugsar godt lyset, den varme støvete lufta, underlege små pueblobyar med «tumbleweeds» og hundar av ukjent opphav. Og ikkje minst, den fantastiske ørken-solnedgangen som bakteppe til kyrkja fyrste kvelden vi såg henne.

    Akkurat denne kyrkja har trekt til seg mange kunstnarar, og det er lett å sjå fasinasjonen. Sjølv om ho er umåla, bygd i leire, får ho svært ulike fargar og valørar, etter som lyset fell. Jord og bygningsfargen vert her nesten rein lysegul i sola. Dei komplimentære fargane, som dei fiolette, forsterkar dei varme fargane og fortel at dette biletet er måla i eit solsvidd og varmt landskap.

This painting from Ranchos de Taos in New Mexico was done during a trip to the U.S. in 1987 when the whole family came along. I celebrated my 11th birthday while we were there, so I was still a young girl. But the trip made a powerful impression on me.

    Ranchos de Taos is a small town, but rich in history and culture. I remember clearly the light, the warm and dusty air, and small pueblo towns with tumbleweeds and dogs running loose. And, not least, the amazing desert sunset served as a backdrop for the church on the first evening we saw it.

    This particular church has attracted many artists over the years, and it is easy to see why. Even though it is unpainted and covered in clay, the colors change dramatically depending on the light and the time of day. Here, it is glowing in the sunlight, while the purple shadows emphasize the warm colors and tell us that this painting is from a warm and sun-scorched landscape.